EMPLOYER'S GUIDE TO STRIKE PLANNING AND PREVENTION

EMPLOYER'S GUIDE TO STRIKE PLANNING AND PREVENTION

Mark A. Hutcheson
Robert Sebris, Jr.
Stephen M. Rummage
Donna M. Peck-Gaines
and
Michael J. Killeen

Date of Publication: February 20, 1985

B1-1296
Practising Law Institute
New York City

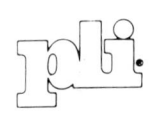

Copyright © 1985 by Practising Law Institute. All rights reserved. Printed in the United States of America. No part of this publication may be reproduced, stored in a retrieval system, or transmitted in any form by any means, electronic, mechanical photocopying, recording, or otherwise, without the prior written permission of Practising Law Institute.

Library of Congress Card Number: 84-62166

Preface

American labor relations are founded on the notion that there should be a balance of economic power between employers and unions. This fundamental premise has led to a system of resolving labor-management matters through collective bargaining, debate, and, at times, confrontation. Although adversaries usually resolve their differences amicably, employees and their unions at times resort to concerted activity to achieve their goals. Employers, sometimes protective, sometimes assertive, must be able to deal with such situations lawfully, directly, and effectively.

This book, which has emerged from years of specialized practice, offers assistance to those engaged in labor-management relations and the collective bargaining process. Its genesis is a seminar outline prepared in February 1982 by Mark Hutcheson and Bob Sebris for the American Bar Association Media Labor Law Seminar, sponsored jointly by the Labor and Employment Law Section and Forum Committee on Communications Law in Washington, D.C. Although the outline was initially limited to strike planning and mutual assistance pacts, the Practising Law Institute determined that in expanded form it could provide helpful guidance to labor lawyers and employers. We hope that this work assists the bar and labor relations practitioners in identifying and dealing with strike-related issues.

Acknowledgments

The authors are grateful to numerous individuals for their support and assistance. Those deserving special thanks include the following:

The American Bar Association for seeking initial developmental work on this project, for giving us a forum to present our views, and for its cooperation in permitting this project's expansion into a book for the Practising Law Institute.

Our partners and colleagues at Davis, Wright, Todd, Riese & Jones for their enthusiasm and support on this major undertaking, particularly Cam DeVore, Marshall Nelson, Randy Squires, and Tom Lemly.

Our colleagues, particularly Kathleen Anamosa, Jeff Belfiglio, and Carol Gown for their legal research on matters in this text.

Shirley Gorman, Joyce Dick, Debi Hobbs, Pat Nevegold, Teresa Robinson, Phyllis Stensland, and their coworkers in our word processing department, for their patience and skills in reducing garbled copy and scribbled notes to a final, legible text.

And, most important, our families for their understanding in permitting us to engage in the intellectual indulgence of writing a book, at the expense of normal family life and convenience.

Overview

Unions wield the strike threat as their most effective weapon in obtaining concessions from employers. Collective bargaining and the possibility of a strike go hand in hand in the American labor relations system. Management, however, can do much to minimize this threat by preparing for strike action. This book will assist employers and their counsel in initiating planning and in coping with strikes when they occur.

Part I: Strike Planning Considerations

An employer cannot conduct effective strike planning in the chaotic crisis atmosphere that exists once a strike has begun. Deferred planning may encourage a strike by leading the union to believe that the employer cannot respond effectively. Management must therefore devise a strategy in the calm of normal operations, well before any strike threats occur. It should develop a written strike plan that identifies as many contingencies as possible, with clear instructions for step-by-step implementation before, during, and after the strike. Part I of this book addresses the various considerations relevant to this planning.

Part II: Responding to Union Strike Activity

A comprehensive strategy helps the employer gain some control of the situation and avoid being solely defensive if its employees strike. In many respects, however, the initiative inevitably passes to the union once a strike begins. The union and its members choose the strike's form, timing, objectives, and tactics. Aside from implementing its own plan, management must be ready to react to the union's choices with the tools that the law permits. Management can enhance its ability to respond effectively to a strike by learning the ground rules that govern union action and the employer's response when the union violates them. Accordingly, Part II discusses the limitations on lawful and protected union activity.

Part III: Post-Strike Planning and Considerations

Finally, as the strike draws to a close, management must turn its attention to the resumption of normal operations. In some cases, the employer may find it appropriate to formalize this process through negotiation of a strike settlement agreement with the union. Even if it unilaterally handles post-strike issues, management must define its responsibilities to strikers who wish to return to work, as well as to any replacement workers hired during the strike. To assure coordination of each phase of its strike plan, the employer should consider the limitations on its post-strike conduct, which are discussed in Part III, well before the strike begins.

This book is not intended, nor should it be used, as a substitute for legal advice rendered after close consultation with a labor lawyer. Some aspects of labor law, such as the rules governing secondary activity, are extremely complex and difficult to understand without the assistance of experienced labor counsel. Furthermore, some highly technical legal principles that have no readily apparent connection to labor relations, such as prohibiting restraints of trade, bear upon issues that an employer may confront during a strike. When such matters arise, management should consult an attorney with specialized expertise in the relevant field.

Overview

It is not possible to identify and answer every conceivable question an employer may face during a strike. Indeed, the only limit on the variety of forms a strike can take is the creativity of minds. However, if management formulates a strike plan, tailored to its own peculiar circumstances, there should be few surprises. This book will assist the employer in reaching its goal of conducting business as usual, even if a strike occurs.

Although §13 provides, "Nothing in this Act shall be construed so as to interfere with or impede or diminish in any way the right to strike," it does not follow that an employer, guilty of no act denounced by the statute, has lost the right to protect and continue his business . . . .

NLRB v. Mackay Radio & Telegraph Co., 304 U.S. 333, 334 (1938)

Table of Chapters

Overview ix

Part I Strike Planning Considerations 1
  1. The Importance of Planning 5
  2. Pre-Strike Planning: Initial Considerations
     and Preliminaries 11
  3. The Strike Plan: "Business-As-Usual Basics" 33
  4. Strike Communications: Information, Dialogue,
     and Polling 103

Part II Responding to Union Strike Activity 143
  5. Responding to Unprotected Strikes 147
  6. Responding to Strike Misconduct and Violence 187
  7. Responding to Secondary Activity 221
  8. Responding to Jurisdictional Pressures 289

Part III Post-Strike Planning and Considerations 307
  9. Striker Reinstatement 311
  10. Strike Settlement Agreements 351
  11. Post-Strike Relationship with the Employees
      and the Union 361

Table of Contents

PREFACE	v
ACKNOWLEDGMENTS	vii
OVERVIEW	ix

Part I: Strike Planning Considerations   1

Introduction	3
Chapter One: The Importance of Planning	5
1.1 Strike Avoidance	6
1.2 Planning to Promote Prevention	7
1.3 Planning for a Balance of Power	8
1.4 Planning and Commitment	9
Chapter Two: Pre-Strike Planning: Initial Considerations and Preliminaries	11
2.1 Jurisdictional Considerations: What Law Governs?	11
2.2 Agreement Duration/Termination: Contract and Statutory Options	12
2.2.1 Evergreen Clauses	13
2.2.2 Contract Extensions	14
2.2.3 Statutory Termination Concerns	15
2.2.3.1 Section 8(d) Requirements	15
2.2.3.2 Employer Strategy Considerations	17
2.2.3.3 Health Care: Section 8(g) Requirements	18
2.3 Review of Other Union Contracts	20

Table of Contents

2.4 Nonunion Employees	20
2.5 Management Team Identification	21
2.5.1 Supervisors	22
2.5.2 Managers	23
2.5.3 Confidential Employees	23
2.6 Supervisor Problems	24
2.6.1 Supervisor—Union Member Problems	25
2.7 Union Security Agreement Problems	26
2.7.1 Dues Checkoff Considerations	27
2.7.2 Checkoff Negotiations Concerns	28
Chapter Three: The Strike Plan: "Business-As-Usual Basics"	**33**
3.1 The Strike Plan Process	33
3.1.1 Strike Committee	34
3.1.1.1 Legal Counsel	34
3.1.2 Policy Analysis and Review	35
3.1.3 Contingency Plan Development	36
3.1.4 Strike Headquarters	37
3.1.5 Management Team Communications	37
3.1.5.1 Confidentiality Requirements	38
3.1.6 Service/Production Options	38
3.1.6.1 Work Priority	39
3.1.6.2 Work Suspension	40
3.1.7 Communications System	40
3.1.8 The Media and Your Public Spokesperson	41
3.1.9 Security	42
3.1.10 Strike Insurance	44
3.1.11 Strike Reports, Log, and Evidence	44
3.1.11.1 Forms	45
3.1.11.2 Daily Reports	45

Table of Contents

3.1.11.3 Evidence Development	46
3.1.12 Special Personnel Considerations	46
3.1.12.1 Wage and Hour Requirements	47
3.1.12.2 Wages and Benefits	49
3.1.12.3 Vacations	51
3.1.12.4 Sick Leave	51
3.1.13 Striker Replacements	52
3.1.14 Subcontracting	53
3.1.15 Skills Inventory	54
3.1.16 Cross Training	54
3.1.17 Unemployment Compensation and Food Stamps	55
3.1.18 Contract Review	56
3.1.19 Union Rules	56
3.1.20 Reserve Gate Options	57
3.1.21 Transportation	57
3.1.22 Supplies/Utilities	57
3.2 Mutual Aid Pacts	58
3.3 Lockouts	61
3.3.1 When a Lockout is Permissible	62
3.3.2 Impermissible Lockouts	64
3.3.3 Pre-Impasse Versus Post-Impasse	65
3.3.4 Lockout: Use of Replacements	66
3.4 Implementing the Final Offer	68
3.4.1 Final Offer Prerequisites	68
3.4.2 Good Faith Requirement	69
3.4.3. Impasse Identification	70
3.4.4 Communicating the Final Offer	72
3.5 Health Care Employer: Special Considerations	73
3.5.1 Public Relations	74
3.5.2 Physicians' Support	74
3.5.3 Licenses/Registration	75
3.5.4 Professionals and Strikes	75

Table of Contents

3.5.5 Operations Levels	75
3.5.6 Volunteer and Family Help	76
3.5.7 Chaplain	76
3.5.8 Drug Security	76
3.5.9 Subcontracting	77
3.5.10 Dietary and Other Service Departments	77
3.5.11 Laboratory and Radiology	77
3.5.12 Patient Amenities	77
3.5.13 Visitors	78
3.6 Public Sector Employer Considerations	78
3.6.1 The Public and Politicians	78
3.6.2 Security	78
3.6.3 Essential Services	79
3.6.4 Supervisors and Unions	79
3.6.5 State Law	80
3.6.6 Illegal Actions	80
APPENDIX 3-A—Letter Re Employee Strike Planning	81
APPENDIX 3-B—Contingency Planning Manual	88
APPENDIX 3-C—Strike Plan Consideration Checklist	90
APPENDIX 3-D—Strike Headquarters Checklist	92
APPENDIX 3-E—Production/Service Priorities Matrix	94
APPENDIX 3-F—Advertisement: Employer's Wage Offer	96
APPENDIX 3-G—Advertisement: Facts About the Strike	98
APPENDIX 3-H—Strike Incident Report	100
APPENDIX 3-I—Strike Incident Report Log	101
APPENDIX 3-J—Memorandum Re Vacation Benefits	102

Table of Contents

Chapter Four: Strike Communications: Information, Dialogue, and Polling   103
  4.1 The Eve of the Strike: Pre-Strike Communications   103
    4.1.1 Anticipating the Strike Vote   103
    4.1.2 Keep Management Advised   104
  4.2 Employer Strike Communication System   104
    4.2.1 The Employer Story   106
    4.2.2 Union Membership Requirements   107
      4.2.2.1 Resignation   107
      4.2.2.2 The "Financial Core"   110
      4.2.2.3 Membership Change Procedure   113
  4.3 The Imminent Strike Situation   113
    4.3.1 The Eve of the Strike   113
    4.3.2 Strike Polling   114
    4.3.3 Union Employee Discipline and Employer Assistance   115
  4.4 Communications during the Strike   116
    4.4.1 Immediate Reactions   116
    4.4.2 Strike Communications to Employees   117
    4.4.3 Picket Line Advice   119
  Appendix 4-A.1—Memo Re Distribution of Strike Vote Information   120
  Appendix 4-A.2—Memo to Employees Regarding Strike   122
  Appendix 4-A.3—Strike Impact Chart   125
  Appendix 4-A.4—Strike Issue Analysis   127
  Appendix 4-A.5—Question/Answers Regarding Strikes   129
  Appendix 4-A.6—Strike Do's and Don't's   134
  Appendix 4-B.1—Cover Memo to Management   136

Table of Contents

    Appendix 4-B.2—Employee Poll   137
    Appendix 4-C—Union Membership Registration   139
    Appendix 4-D—Transfer to "Financial Core" Status   140
    Appendix 4-E—Crossing the Union Picket Line   141

Part II: Responding to Union Strike Activity   143

Introduction   145

Chapter Five: Responding to Unprotected Strikes   147

  5.1 Scope of the Statutory Protection of Strikes and Related Actions   148
    5.1.1 Protected Activity: Strikes and Refusals to Work for Mutual Aid or Protection   148
    5.1.2 Unprotected Activity: Partial Strikes, Slowdowns, Sit-ins, and Sickouts   149
  5.2 Contractual Waiver of the Right to Strike   151
    5.2.1 Scope of the Implied No-Strike Clause   151
    5.2.2 Scope of the Express No-Strike Clause   152
    5.2.3 Negotiating for Clear and Unmistakable Waivers of the Right to Strike   154
    5.2.4 Negotiating for Functional Independence of the No-Strike and Arbitration Clauses   156
  5.3 Responding to Union-Led Strikes in Breach of Contract   157
    5.3.1 Disciplinary Action against Employees   157

Table of Contents

5.3.2 Injunctive Relief	158
5.3.2.1 Arbitrability of the Dispute Giving Rise to the Strike	161
5.3.2.2 Scope and Enforcement of the *Boys Market* Injunction	162
5.3.2.3 Enjoining Strikes over Nonarbitrable Issues	163
5.3.3 Damage Suits	165
5.3.3.1 Suits Concerning Strikes during Bargaining	166
5.3.3.2 Persons Subject to Suit for Breach of Contract	166
5.3.3.3 Damages Recoverable	167
5.4 Responding to Wildcat Strikes	169
5.4.1 Disciplinary Action for Engaging in a Wildcat Strike	170
5.4.1.1 Discipline of Union Officers	171
5.4.2 Judicial Remedies for Wildcat Actions	172
5.4.2.1 Injunctive Relief	172
5.4.2.2 Damage Suits against Unions	173
5.4.2.3 Damage Suits against Individual Employees	175
5.4.3 Preparing for and Coping with Wildcats	176
5.5 Responding to Sympathy Strikes	176
5.5.1 Protected Status of Sympathy Strikers	177
5.5.1.1 Waiver of Sympathy Strike Rights	178
5.5.1.2 Effect of Unprotected Status of Underlying Strike	179
5.5.1.3 Lack of Concerted Activity	180
5.5.2 Replacing and Reinstating Sympathy Strikers	180

Table of Contents

    5.5.2.1 Replacement Due to Refusal to Cross Picket Lines at the Employer's Premises   180
    5.5.2.2 Replacement Due to Refusal to Cross Picket Lines at Other Employer's Premises   181
    5.5.2.3 Refusal to Cross Unfair Labor Practice Picket Lines   182
  5.5.3 Remedies For Sympathy Strikes   183
    5.5.3.1 Discipline   183
    5.5.3.2 Damages   183
    5.5.3.3 Injunctions   184
  5.5.4 Coping with Sympathy Strikes   184
APPENDIX 5-A—Telegram Re Work Stoppage in Violation of Contract   186

Chapter Six: Responding to Strike Misconduct and Violence   187
 6.1 Types of Misconduct against Which the Employer May Obtain Relief   188
 6.2 Injunctive Remedies for Strike Misconduct   191
  6.2.1 Injunctions in Federal Court   191
  6.2.2 Injunctions in State Court   191
  6.2.3 Injunctions against Trespassing by Pickets   193
  6.2.4 Procedure for Obtaining Restraining Orders and Injunctive Relief   194
  6.2.5 Scope and Effect of the Injunction   197
  6.2.6 Persons Restrained by the Injunction   198
 6.3 Damage Suits for Strike Misconduct   199
  6.3.1 Damages Recoverable   200
  6.3.2 Who May Recover Damages?   201
  6.3.3 Who is Liable for Damages?   201
 6.4 Discipline of Employees Engaged in Strike Misconduct   203

Table of Contents

6.5 Unfair Labor Practice Charges against Unions Engaging in Misconduct	205
6.5.1 Remedies for Strike Misconduct before the NLRB	206
6.5.2 Timing of the Unfair Labor Practice Charge	208
Chapter Seven: Responding to Secondary Activity	**221**
7.1 Identifying Secondary Activity	221
7.1.1 The Existence of Union Pressure against Neutral Employers	222
7.1.1.1 Threats and Coercion	222
7.1.1.2 Inducement or Encouragement of Refusals to Work	224
7.1.2 Unlawful Objectives	225
7.1.3 Pickets at Common Work Sites	227
7.1.4 Establishing a Special Schedule for the Primary Employer	229
7.1.5 Establishing Reserved Gates	231
7.1.5.1 The Industrial Plant Model	232
7.1.5.2 The Construction Site Model	233
7.1.5.3 The Ambulatory Primary Situs	234
7.1.5.4 Establishing the Gates	235
7.1.5.5 Maintaining the Gates	237
7.1.5.6 Reserved Gate Rehabilitation	239
7.1.5.7 Violation of Gates	239
7.1.6 Ally Problems	242
7.1.6.1 Performance of Struck Work	243
7.1.6.2 Common Ownership or Control	245
7.1.7 Publicity and Consumer Picketing	247
7.1.7.1 Products "Produced" by the Primary	248

Table of Contents

7.1.7.2 Products "Distributed" by the Neutral	249
7.1.7.3 Permissible Scope of Non-picketing Publicity	249
7.1.7.4 Consumer Picketing and the Integrated and Dominant Product Doctrines	250
7.1.8 Union Pressure Relating to Hot Cargo Clauses	253
7.2 Procedure upon Filing a Charge; Injunctive Relief	256
7.3 Discipline of Employees Engaging in Secondary Pressure	259
7.4 Damage Suits under Section 303	259
7.4.1 Persons Entitled to Sue	259
7.4.2 Persons Liable	260
7.4.3 Interaction between Sections 303 and 8(b)(4)	261
7.4.4 Damages in Section 303 Suits	262
7.4.5 Joinder of State Law Claims for Picket Line Misconduct	265
7.4.6 Statutes of Limitation	266
APPENDIX 7-A—Telegram Re Work Schedule of Primary Employer	267
APPENDIX 7-B—Telegram Re Work Schedule of Primary Employer	268
APPENDIX 7-C—Memo Re Strike Planning	269
APPENDIX 7-D—Reserved Gate Sign	273
APPENDIX 7-E—Neutral Gate Sign	274
APPENDIX 7-F—Telegram Re Reserved Gate	275
APPENDIX 7-G—Telegram Re Reserved Gate	276
APPENDIX 7-H—Telegram Re Reestablishment of Reserved Gate	277
APPENDIX 7-I—Telegram Re Reestablishment of Reserved Gate	278

Table of Contents

APPENDIX 7-J—Notice Re Improper Activity Related to Picketing — 279

Chapter Eight: Responding to Jurisdictional Pressures — 289

8.1 Procedure upon Filing a Charge under Section 8(b)(4)(D) — 290
8.2 Prerequisites to a Determination of the Dispute — 291
    8.2.1 Reasonable Cause to Believe that Section 8(b)(4)(D) Has Been Violated — 291
        8.2.1.1 The Objective of the Action — 291
        8.2.1.2 The Employer Subject to Pressure — 294
        8.2.1.3 The Existence of Union Pressure — 294
    8.2.2 The Existence of Competing Claims — 295
        8.2.2.1 Union Disclaimers of the Work — 296
        8.2.2.2 Determinations Despite Disclaimers — 296
    8.2.3 Absence of Agreed upon Mechanism for Settlement — 298
        8.2.3.1 Parties to the Mechanism — 298
        8.2.3.2 Differing Dispute Procedures for Some Parties — 299
        8.2.3.3 Breakdown of the Voluntary Mechanism — 300
        8.2.3.4 Procedure after NLRB Deferral to Voluntary Mechanism — 300
8.3 The NLRB's Determination of Jurisdictional Disputes — 301
    8.3.1 Standards Used to Resolve Jurisdictional Disputes — 301
    8.3.2 The Breadth of the Board's Determination — 303

Table of Contents

    8.4 Procedure after Determination of the Dispute   304
    8.5 Other Relief for Violations of Section 8(b)(4)(D)   304
        8.5.1 Injunctive Relief   304
        8.5.2 Ability to Recover Damages   306

Part III: Post-Strike Planning Considerations   307

Introduction   309

Chapter Nine: Striker Reinstatement   311

    9.1 Strikers' Status as Employees   312
    9.2 Right to Reinstatement   312
        9.2.1 Unfair Labor Practice and Economic Strikes Distinguished   314
        9.2.2 Unfair Labor Practice Strikers   316
        9.2.3 Economic Strikers   316
    9.3 Employees Entitled to Reinstatement   318
        9.3.1 Temporary Employees   319
        9.3.2 Probationary Employees   319
        9.3.3 Marginal Employees   321
        9.3.4 Employees on Leave   322
        9.3.5 Other Employees   223
    9.4 Unconditional Offers to Return to Work   323
    9.5 Unconditional Offers of Reinstatement   325
    9.6 Availability of Work   328
        9.6.1 Curtailment of Work   328
        9.6.2 Promotions, Transfers, and Rehires   329
    9.7 Reinstatement to Substantially Equivalent Positions   330
    9.8 Reinstatement Procedure   331
        9.8.1 Basis for Determining Reinstatement Priority   332

Table of Contents

9.8.2 Notice	334
9.8.3 Deadline for Return to Work	335
9.9 Employer's Liability for Back Pay	336
9.10 Termination of Reinstatement Rights	338
9.10.1 Strike Misconduct	338
9.10.2 Passage of Time	340
9.10.3 Other Employment	340
9.10.4 Failure to Return or Voluntary Resignation	341
9.10.5 Discharge	342
9.11 Status of Reinstated Strikers	343
9.11.1 Prohibition against Treatment as New Employee	343
9.11.2 Seniority	344
9.12 Status of Unreinstated Strikers	345
9.13 Status of Nonstriking Employees	346
9.14 Status of Striker Replacements	347
9.14.1 Distinguishing Temporary Replacements	347
9.14.2 Permanent Replacements	348
9.14.3 Seniority	350
Chapter Ten: Strike Settlement Agreements	351
10.1 General Considerations	352
10.2 Contractual Restrictions on Reinstatement Period and Seniority	353
10.3 Other Restrictions on Reinstatement Rights	355
10.4 Scope of the Settlement	356
10.5 Enforceability of the Agreement	356
10.6 Waiver and Leverage in Settlement Negotiations and Agreements	357
10.7 Duration of a Strike Settlement Agreement	358
10.8 Amnesty	358

Table of Contents

Chapter Eleven: Post-Strike Relationship with the Employees and the Union   361

  11.1 Administration of Employee Benefits   362
    11.1.1 Vacation Benefits   363
      11.1.1.1 Vacation Eligibility   364
      11.1.1.2 Deduction of Strike Time   366
      11.1.1.3 Rescheduling of Vacations   367
    11.1.2 Disability, Accident, and Sickness Benefits   368
    11.1.3 Insurance Benefits   370
    11.1.4 Bonuses and Other Benefits   370
  11.2 Prohibition against Discriminatory Treatment of Strikers   372
    11.2.1 Job and Shift Assignments   372
    11.2.2 Post-Strike Discipline and Other Conditions of Employment   374
  11.3 Post-Strike Treatment of Union   375
    11.3.1 Majority Status   375
    11.3.2 Withdrawal of Recognition   378

Tables   379
  Cases   379
  Statutes and Administrative Material   405
Index   409
About the Authors   419

Part I: Strike Planning Considerations

Introduction

Although most employers accept employees' right to strike and engage in other concerted activity, many do not realize employers have an equal right to confront a strike and minimize its effects. To exercise this right effectively, management must clearly define its goals and follow what are sometimes complex legal rules, just as in other areas of business planning. Management's commitment and willingness to devote substantial resources to strike planning over an extended period of time is the most important ingredient of a sound strike strategy.

A permanent strike planning committee should develop the employer's plan for coping with labor disputes. The committee should coordinate with the employer's bargaining team to assure that both are working to realize the same objectives. Once it has clearly defined the employer's goals, the strike planning committee should develop a comprehensive, written plan to govern all aspects of the employer's operations during a strike.

This plan must provide for effective communication with employees, supervisors, other unions, customers, and suppliers. It must anticipate media inquiries and establish policies for response. The committee should also explore methods of securing the employer's plant, equipment, and inventory from possible sabotage by strikers, as well as alternative means of transporting the employer's raw materials, supplies, and finished products. It must provide for the hiring and training of replacements and for the protection of those employees who cross picket lines to work during the strike. To assure continued service to customers, the committee should consider subcontracting options and mutual assistance pacts. Finally, the plan must define those circumstances in which the employer will take economic action, such as a lockout.

Clearly, the strike planning committee cannot cover these items at the last minute. It must devote considerable time, energy, and money to plan properly for a strike. Most employers will find strike planning well worth the effort because the well-prepared employer stands the best chance of avoiding the severe—and sometimes fatal—disruptive effect of a strike.

1

The Importance of Planning

The National Labor Relations Act (the Act or the NLRA) and other labor laws protect private industry employees' right to strike.[1] The Act's primary purpose is to foster economic stability by requiring that employers sit down at the bargaining table with unions to resolve differences over terms and conditions of employment.[2] Since the Act's passage in 1935, unions and employers have gone to the bargaining table countless times. More often than not the negotiations process has worked, and the parties have successfully bargained contracts. In other cases, bargaining was unsuccessful and strikes or lockouts resulted. Consequently, strike planning and prevention are essential parts of the collective bargaining process in private industry under the Act.

Like the Act, many public sector collective bargaining statutes emphasize bilateral decision-making.[3] In many jurisdictions,

---

1. 29 U.S.C. §§ 151-87. Federal labor law generally preempts state regulation of private sector labor law matters. San Diego Building Trades Council v. Garmon, 359 U.S. 236, 43 L.R.R.M 2838 (1959). However, numerous states have developed legislation providing collective bargaining for employees exempt from NLRA coverage (e.g., farm workers, public employees). Also, the Railway Labor Act regulates the railroad and airline industries. 45 U.S.C. §§ 151, *et seq.*
2. *See*, 29 U.S.C. § 151 and C. MORRIS, THE DEVELOPING LABOR LAW, 25-27 (2d Ed. 1983).
3. *See, e.g.*, the Civil Service Reform Act of 1978, 5 U.S.C. § 7101(a).

these statutes go further and outlaw public employee strikes.[4] However, public employees do not always obey the law, as the illegal 1981 strike by the Professional Air Traffic Controllers Organization (PATCO) demonstrated.[5] Therefore, preparation for public sector labor contract negotiations also requires strike planning. Regardless of the economic sector an employer serves, if management deals with a labor union, strikes and their potential impact should be part of an employer's basic planning.[6]

Although commentators on industrial relations stress the need for our labor relations system to become more cooperative,[7] collective bargaining remains an adversarial process. Strikes and strike threats are clubs to be used, or abused, to secure contract settlements on terms most favorable to a union leadership's perceived interests. This stark reality calls for management planning, resolve, and preparedness.

1.1 Strike Avoidance

A strike is industrial warfare and should not be taken lightly. Consequently, strike planning *and* avoidance should be part of

---

4. Hanslowe & Acierno, *Law and Theory of Strikes by Government Employees*, 67 CORNELL L. REV. 1055-83 (1982).
5. *See* Meltzer & Sunstein, *Public Employee Strikes, Executive Discretion, and the Air Traffic Controllers*, 50 U. CHI. L. REV. 731-99 (1983); Wohlers, *Endangered Species: the Federal Employee Strike*, 19 IDAHO L. REV. 7-30 (1983).
6. *See, e.g.*, Loomis & Mulcahy, *Strikes, Strategy and Tactics for Managers*, 8 EMPLOYEE REL. L.J. 618-47 (1983), W. MULLINS, STRIKE DEFENSE MANUAL (1980); J. BAIRD, R. CLARK, M. RYBECKI, MAINTAINING PUBLIC SERVICES (1978); H. MOORE, JR., HEALTH CARE STRIKE MANUAL (1983); C. PERRY, A. KRAMER & T. SCHNEIDER, OPERATING DURING STRIKES (1982); W. CONNOLLY, JR. & M. CONNOLLY, WORK STOPPAGES AND UNION RESPONSIBILITY (1977).
7. *See, e.g.*, remarks of John Dunlop, 113 L.R.R. 31 (1983); comments by Wayne Horowitz former FMCS Director, Daily Labor Report (BNA), p. A-10 (Dec. 8, 1983), and FMCS grant program for labor-management com-

the employer's overall labor relations program. According to one researcher, strikes occur when employees believe their needs go "unheard, unheeded, or unanswered."[8] Wages aren't the only factor. Strikes may be avoided by grievance monitoring; adherence to a reasonable disciplinary system; use of problem resolution systems; control of undesirable work shifts; and clear rules regarding equipment, procedures, overtime, and seniority.[9] Although no single practice will prevent all strikes, commitment to fair treatment and dignity in the work place is the best protection against strike votes.

Effective strike avoidance programs do not obviate the need for strike planning. Even the most generous and conscientious employer must recognize the possibility of a collective bargaining impasse or labor dispute erupting into a strike. When an employer lacks a strike plan it invariably will be on the defensive, enabling the union to gain more concessions than it should. Consequently, proper planning should be part of strike avoidance strategy. Most important, the lack of planning may actually *cause* the strike.

1.2 Planning to Promote Prevention

No one wins in a strike. Employees lose wages and benefits. The private sector employer loses business, and the public sector employer experiences a service failure. The community loses the enterprise's contribution to the local economy. Most employers therefore try to avoid a strike. Too many, however, mistakenly assume that by planning for a strike, they promote it. On the contrary, employers substantially increase the odds of a strike by ignoring its possibility. The adequately prepared employer is

---

mittees, Daily Labor Report (BNA), p. A-5 (Dec. 9, 1983). *See also Exploring Alternatives to the Strike*, MONTHLY LABOR REVIEW (Sept. 1, 1973).
8. Imberman, *Who Strikes—and Why?* 83 HARV. BUSINESS REVIEW 18 (1983).
9. *Id.*

actually less likely to incur a strike than an unprepared employer.

Good strike planning also provides a realistic picture of the employer's strengths and weaknesses. When preparing for a strike, many employers learn things about their own operational characteristics that they never knew or appreciated before. This can help develop confidence in the ability to continue operations and deal with a strike, confidence that will spill over onto the bargaining table and improve the employer's bargaining position.

Some employers believe, however, that taking the time, energy, and resources to plan for a strike diverts valuable assets from the more important bargaining process. They are wrong. Strike planning should begin long before bargaining commences and should take into account the employer's expected bargaining posture. Although development of a thorough and reliable plan requires substantial lead time, the well prepared employer will be in a better position to resolve bargaining issues without undergoing the disruption caused by a strike—and without ever finding out how well its strike plan would have worked.

The reason for this is simple. Experienced unions know that the threat of a strike is their most effective bargaining device. The strike threat loses its force if the employer, through careful planning, has convinced the union and employees that it can undergo a strike. The employer need not worry about communicating its readiness to the union directly. Unions will know if an employer is prepared to confront a strike.

1.3 Planning for a Balance of Power

Without a comprehensive strike plan, an employer is at a serious disadvantage during bargaining. Unlike the employer, a union is in the business of dealing with labor confrontations. Unions understand the advantages of strike planning and they have well established goals, procedures, and tactics for strikes. Unions affiliated with large national or international organizations, such as the AFL-CIO or the Teamsters, train their business agents, negotiators, representatives, and officers to handle strikes. Union constitutions and bylaws provide for strike benefits and discipline of members who do not cooperate in a strike.

On the other hand, most employers are inexperienced in these matters. They do not recognize the pitfalls or opportunities and the numerous issues that a strike presents. Management personnel rarely have formal strike training. Therefore, an employer must prepare methodically for the possibility of a strike, or concede a significant advantage to the union at the bargaining table.

1.4 Planning and Commitment

Effective strike planning requires management's full commitment at all levels. A strike can leave an employer in intolerable economic and political circumstances. For management, a lost strike is a union victory. More important, the atmosphere it creates for future bargaining will be unacceptable.

Not suprisingly, the planning process itself may foster the commitment necessary to make the plan work. The goal of planning is to enable the employer to conduct business as usual during a strike. If management communicates this objective to employees, supervisors, customers, media, and the community, it will project a positive attitude that will convince key personnel of its own commitment to a defined goal. The employer can earn the commitment of lower management levels by integrating them into the management team. Through its strike committee and management personnel an employer can plan for a strike and influence the outcome.

2
Prestrike Planning: Initial Considerations and Preliminaries

The goal of strike planning is to develop an efficient process that accomplishes its objectives step-by-step. Each element of a program should present a functional solution to the problems that may be encountered. Preliminary areas to study include jurisdictional requirements; contract termination, duration and extension option; contracts for other bargaining units; and the impact of a strike on other personnel, such as nonunit employees and management personnel.

2.1 Jurisdictional Considerations: What Law Governs?

Early in the planning process, an employer must determine what law governs each area of concern. The private sector employer may be covered by the National Labor Relations Act, Railway Labor Act, or even state law (e.g., agricultural workers). The public sector employer may be covered by a state omnibus statute for all employees or specific statutes dealing with different employee groups, such as uniformed personnel or teachers. Public sector statutes may also prescribe special labor relations procedures or dispute resolution techniques, such as interest arbitration, to avoid strikes.[1] While private sector case law may provide guidance, it does not control public sector labor relations.[2]

In addition to general labor law, there are separate statutes that apply to special employment problems. The employer expecting a strike should be familiar with laws relating to unemployment compensation, benefits protections, injunctive relief, wage and hour requirements, and other areas regulated by statute. Safety, health, and licensing authorities will likely be drawn into the process. Therefore, you should familiarize yourself with these regulations as well.

2.2 Agreement Duration/Termination: Contract and Statutory Options

The first step is to determine what will happen to the contract once its expected termination date arrives. Will it expire or continue in force? What statutory or contractual obligations must be satisfied?

Most labor agreements have, as the final section, a contract provision regarding continuation, amendment, or termination. Many employers neglect to study both the mechanics of such

---

1. Many labor statutes have conciliation devices to foster settlement, such as basic mediation (29 U.S.C. § 158(d)), factfinding (N.Y. CIV. SERV. L. § 209.3 *as amended*), standard "interest" arbitration (N.Y. CIV. SERV. L. § 209.4, *as amended*), or even experimental arbitration systems such as "final-offer selection" arbitration (WIS. STAT. ANNOT. § 111.77). *See Final Offer Mediation-Arbitration and the Limited Right to Strike: Wisconsin's New Municipal Employment Bargaining Law*, 1979 WIS. L. REV. 167-89.
2. Each state must be reviewed independently. *See, e.g.*, Public Employment Relations Commission v. City of Kennewick, 99 Wash. 2d 832, 664 P.2d 1240 (1983). It is questionable whether a federal statute would be constitutional, National League of Cities v. Usery, 426 U.S. 833 (1976).

clauses and the necessary interaction with statutory provisions, such as sections 8(d) and 8(g) of the National Labor Relations Act.

2.2.1 Evergreen Clauses

As a general rule, an employer may not unilaterally change terms and conditions of employment after a contract expires, except to implement its last and final offer at lawful impasse.[3] However, union security provisions, such as dues checkoff or union shop clauses, typically expire with the contract.[4] This is also true of a no-strike clause in most instances.

If the existing agreement includes a no-strike clause, it may also have an evergreen clause that keeps the contract in effect beyond its apparent termination date. An evergreen clause may operate to limit a strike for a significant period of time after the expected contract expiration date. The following example is a complex evergreen clause, that also permits either party to terminate it after substantial advance notice:

> This Agreement shall become effective at 12:01 a.m. on the first day in the first pay period after the date of execution, and shall continue in full force and effect through and including midnight, at the end of the day on _____, 19___, and shall continue in full force and effect from year to year thereafter, unless notice of desire to amend this Agreement is served by either party upon the other at least _____ calendar days prior to the date of expiration.[5] If notice to amend is given,

---

3. *See* ch. 3 for a discussion on impasse and implementing the final offer.
4. *See* Trico Products Corp., 238 N.L.R.B. 1306, 99 L.R.R.M 1473 (1978); Bethlehem Steel Co. (Shipbuilding Div.), 133 N.L.R.B. 1347, 49 L.R.R.M. 1016 (1961).
5. The length of notice required differs for health care institutions and non-health care employers under section 8(d) of the National Labor Relations Act. 29 U.S.C. § 158(d).

negotiations should commence within thirty (30) calendar days following the date of the notice, *and this Agreement shall remain in effect until the terms of a new or amended agreement are agreed upon;* provided, however, that if a notice to amend is timely given, either party may at any time thereafter notify the other in writing of its desire to terminate this Agreement as of the date stated in the notice of *termination, which date shall not be earlier than the date of expiration, and shall be at least [e.g. 30 or 60] calendar days subsequent to the giving of such notice to terminate.*

When negotiating its labor contract, an employer should consider using a broad evergreen clause with a long notice of termination period. If a union cannot legally strike without giving a fixed and expected notice, the employer has a longer period in which to prepare.

One should not, however, blindly rely on evergreen clauses. Unions sometimes violate such provisions, either by accident or design. If you are unprepared, the short-term consequences could be disastrous, regardless of available, long-run relief. Planning for strike contingencies should not be sidetracked by expectations that a union will comply with a contract or with the law.

2.2.2 Contract Extensions

If the contract makes no provision for automatic extension, it may be in your best interest to extend the contract for a limited period during bargaining. Contract extension may serve several diverse needs. First, such a special cooling off period might maintain bargaining momentum and lead to agreement. It may also create a safety margin of time to bring particular operating requirements, especially production and security needs, up to acceptable levels. Finally, an extension may give all parties an opportunity to reflect more objectively on their positions, altering the tone and tempo of the bargaining process.

Prestrike Planning

2.2.3 Statutory Termination Concerns

2.2.3.1 Section 8(d) Requirements

In addition to contractual requirements, statutory procedures must also be followed. Section 8(d) of the National Labor Relations Act controls contract termination and modification for the private sector employer. For the health care industry, section 8(d) requires that a notice to modify or terminate must be submitted to the other party at least ninety days prior to contract expiration. For other industries, it mandates that such notice be submitted sixty days in advance. Notice is not required for unfair labor practice strikes[6] or strikes pertaining to issues not related to the modification or termination of a collective bargaining agreement.[7] Public sector employers must review applicable state laws to determine the notice period and its effect.

In addition, section 8(d)(3) of the Act requires that notice of a dispute be submitted to the Federal Mediation and Conciliation Service (FMCS) in Washington, D.C., *and* appropriate state and local agencies, within thirty days of the date the bargaining notice is tendered.[8] A party apparently need not notify a state

---

6. Mastro Plastics Corp. v. NLRB, 214 F.2d 462, 34 L.R.R.M. 2484 (2d Cir. 1954), *aff'd*, 350 U.S. 20, 37 L.R.R.M. 2587 (1956).
7. Cheney California Lumber Co. v. NLRB, 319 F.2d 375, 53 L.R.R.M. 2598 (9th Cir. 1963) (notice need not specify every bargaining issue); Local 9735, Mineworkers v. NLRB, 258 F.2d 146, 42 L.R.R.M. 2320 (D.C. Cir. 1958) (strike in breach of no-strike clause). *See also*, NLRB v. Lion Oil Co., 352 U.S. 282, 39 L.R.R.M. 2296 (1957); NLRB v. Jacobs Manufacturing Co., 196 F.2d 680, 30 L.R.R.M. 2098 (2d Cir. 1952).
8. *See* Rules & Regulations of the FMCS, 29 C.F.R. §§ 1402, 1403 (1983). In 1984, the FMCS address was:

   Division of Case Control
   Federal Mediation and Conciliation Service
   2100 K Street NW
   Washington, D.C. 20427
   Telephone (202) 653-5280

agency that lacks the funding to provide mediation services.[9] Generally, the appropriate mediation agencies cooperate informally in verifying whether the required notices have been received. However, mere failure to serve an 8(d) notice to the mediation agencies will not extend a labor agreement.[10]

A strike called without proper notice is an unfair labor practice.[11] More important, any participating employee would be engaging in unprotected activity and can be terminated, not just replaced.[12]

The union's intent is not always apparent on the face of its bargaining notice. For example, a typical union notice may refer to "renewal and amendment" of the contract. Yet the agreement may refer only to "modification and termination." If the employer has doubt as to the notice's scope or intent, it must be cautious. Courts require strict compliance with contract notice mechanics.[13]

---

9. Locomotive Firemen (Phelps-Dodge Corp.) v. NLRB, 302 F.2d 198, 50 L.R.R.M. 2015 (9th Cir. 1962) (state agency authority). *See also*, Milk, Ice Cream Drivers & Dairy Employees Local 783 (Cream Top Creamery, Inc.), 147 N.L.R.B. 264, 56 L.R.R.M. 1194 (1964) (state agency deferral to FMCS).
10. Communications Workers, AFL-CIO v. Southwestern Bell Telephone Co., 713 F.2d 1126, 114 L.R.R.M. 2302 (5th Cir. 1983).
11. *See* Amax Coal Co. v. NLRB, 614 F.2d 872, 103 L.R.R.M. 2482 (3d Cir. 1980) (as to FMCS notice); Retail Clerks Local 219 (Carroll House) v. NLRB, 265 F.2d 814, 43 L.R.R.M. 2726 (D.C. Cir. 1959); Wilhow Corp., d/b/a Town & Country Supermarkets, 240 N.L.R.B. 1109, 100 L.R.R.M. 1384 (1979) (as to state agency); Peoria Chapter, Painting & Decorating Contractors, 204 N.L.R.B. 345, 83 L.R.R.M. 1367 (1973), *enforcement denied*, 500 F.2d 54, 86 L.R.R.M. 2914 (7th Cir. 1974). The Board and courts do not necessarily agree on liability of a party that acts in reliance on notice implied by the other party's actions. Hooker Chemical & Plastics Corp., 224 N.L.R.B. 1535, 92 L.R.R.M. 1419 (1976), *enforcement denied*, 573 F.2d 965, 97 L.R.R.M. 3194 (7th Cir. 1978). According to the NLRB, the noninitiating party can easily verify notices before acting.
12. *See* ch. 5 *infra*.
13. International Union of Operating Engineers, Local 181 v. Dahlem Constr. Co., 193 F.2d 470, 29 L.R.R.M. 2271 (6th Cir. 1951). *See also* Chatta-

Prestrike Planning

When union notice is deficient, an employer should nevertheless act lawfully. It must avoid entanglement in unfair labor practices that may create unanticipated employee protections by converting the strike to an unfair labor practice strike.[14]

2.2.3.2 Employer Strategy Considerations

To control events, an employer must first decide what environment it wishes to create. To increase management options, it may choose to send its own termination notice. For example, it may want to implement its final offer or have a union shop clause expire with the contract. On the other hand, it may desire to keep the status quo with the current contract remaining in effect.

Employers must be careful not to trap themselves procedurally by notice errors.[15] The employer cannot unilaterally modify existing employment terms and conditions by implementing the last and final offer unless the agreement has been properly terminated. This is true even if an employer has bargained in good faith and reached a lawful impasse in negotiations.[16]

The employer should study the contract clause and compute all of the section 8(d) time periods. If an employer elects to give notice, it should issue the mediation notices at the same time as the bargaining notice to the union to avoid service problems. The same letter can be sent to the union, the FMCS, and any state or local agencies. (See Appendix 2-A.) As an alternative, the employer may wish to send the union a letter, followed by a mediation notice through a letter or appropriate government form. (See Appendix 2-B, FMCS Form F-7, revised July 1982.) If a union fails to serve such notice and strikes, the strike is unpro-

---

nooga Mailers v. Chattanooga News Free Press, 524 F.2d 1305, 90 L.R.R.M. 3000 (6th Cir. 1975).
14. *See* ch. 9, *infra*, regarding unfair labor practice strikes.
15. *See* Robert A. Barnes, Inc., 268 N.L.R.B. No. 49, 114 L.R.R.M. 1276 (1983).
16. *See also* ch. 3, *infra*, regarding impasse.

tected and employees may be terminated.[17] Conversely, if the employer elects to serve notice, it may permit employees to strike lawfully. Consider this strategy carefully.

A legal strike cannot occur for sixty days (ninety days for healthcare institutions) after the section 8(d) notice is given to, or by, the employer, and for thirty days after notice is given to the federal and state mediation agencies. As a practical matter, an employer should prepare for a strike at any time and should not rely on expectations that a union will comply with notice requirements.

2.2.3.3 Health Care: Section 8(g) Requirements

In addition to the bargaining notice requirements of section 8(d), health care employers must monitor additional notice requirements. Section 8(g) of the Act requires a union to give at least ten days' notice to an effected "health care institution"[18] *and* the Federal Mediation and Conciliation Service *before* engaging in any strike, picketing, or other concerted refusal to work.[19]

---

17. NLRB v. Local 742, Elec. Workers, 519 F.2d 815, 90 L.R.R.M. 2747 (6th Cir. 1975), *enforcing*, 213 N.L.R.B. 824, 87 L.R.R.M. 1272 (1974); United Furniture Workers (Fort Smith Chair Co.) v. NLRB, 336 F.2d 738, 55 L.R.R.M. 2990 (D.C. Cir. 1964), *cert. denied*, 379 U.S. L.R.R.M.(1964).
18. A "health care institution" is defined by section 2(14) of the NLRA, 29 U.S.C. § 152(14), as

    any hospital, convalescent hospital, health maintenance organization, health clinic, nursing home, extended care facility, or other institution devoted to the care of sick, infirmed or aged person(s).
19. *See generally* Annot., *Construction and Application of Section 8(g) of National Labor Relations Act, Requiring Labor Organizations to Give Notice of Intention to Engage in Strike, Picketing, or Other Concerted Refusal to Work at Health Care Institutions*, 43 A.L.R. Fed. 449 (1979).

Prestrike Planning

Section 8(g) requires that the notice also state the date and time that such action will commence. Once the notice is given, it may be extended by written agreement of the parties.

The notice requirement is strictly interpreted. For example, nondisruptive informational picketing has been deemed improper if a union has not given its section 8(g) notice.[20] Unions must also give a health care institution strike notice before engaging in a sympathy strike.[21] However, section 8(g) does not limit picketing or strikes involving the employees of non-health care employers, such as construction companies doing new project work, when the health care institution is in effect a neutral employer in the dispute.[22] Nor is notice required for a threatened strike[23] or for a spontaneous strike not authorized by the union.[24]

---

20. Orange Belt Painters, District Council of Painters (St. Joseph Hospital), 243 N.L.R.B. 609, 101 L.R.R.M. 1456 (1979); District 1199, RWDSU (United Hospitals), 232 N.L.R.B. 443, 96 L.R.R.M. 1404 (1977); District 1199, RWDSU (Greater Pennsylvania Avenue Nursing, Inc.), 227 N.L.R.B. 132, 94 L.R.R.M. 1083 (1976).
21. Operating Engineers Local 39 (Kaiser Foundation Hospitals), 268 N.L.R.B. No. 8, 114 L.R.R.M. 1244 (1983).
22. The courts and the NLRB now agree on this point. *See* Laborers Local 1057 (Mercy Hospital of Laredo) v. NLRB, 567 F.2d 1006, 96 L.R.R.M. 3160 (D.C. Cir. 1977); NLRB v. Electrical Workers Local No. 388 (IBEW) (Hoffman Co.), 548 F.2d 704, 94 L.R.R.M. 2536 (7th Cir. 1977), *cert. denied*, 434 U.S. 837, 96 L.R.R.M. 2514 (1977); Beck Co., 246 N.L.R.B. 970, 103 L.R.R.M. 1002 (1979).
23. District 1199-E, RWDSU, note 25 *infra*. *See also* District 1199-E RWDSU, NLRB Advice Memo Case No. 5-CG-17 (1978).
24. East Chicago Rehabilitation Center v. NLRB, 710 F.2d 397, 113 L.R.R.M. 3211 (7th Cir. 1983), *cert. denied* 83-867 (1984); Montefiore Hospital & Medical Center v. NLRB, 621 F.2d 510, 104 L.R.R.M. 2160 (2d Cir. 1980); NLRB v. Long Beach Youth Center, Inc., 591 F.2d 1276, 101 L.R.R.M. 2501 (9th Cir. 1979); NLRB v. Rock Hill Convalescent Center, 585 F.2d 700, 99 L.R.R.M. 3157 (4th Cir. 1978); Villa Care, Inc., 249 N.L.R.B. 705, 104 L.R.R.M. 1274 (1980); Walker Methodist Residence, 227 N.L.R.B. 1630, 94 L.R.R.M. 1516 (1977); Leisure Lodge Nursing Home, 250 N.L.R.B. 912, 105 L.R.R.M. 1115 (1980).

Once the union serves notice under section 8(g), the strike must occur within a "reasonable time" of the notice time and date or the union must issue a subsequent notice.[25] Whether an employer can bring a damage suit against a union for failure to strike pursuant to an expected notice is still unresolved.[26]

2.3 Review of Other Union Contracts

If an employer has more than one bargaining unit, sympathy strikes can multiply its economic problems. If the employees will not cross other unions' picket lines, the employer may suffer production and customer service difficulties. The contracts governing bargaining units other than the one affected by current negotiations, must be studied to determine what protections each provides against sympathy strikes. The strike plan should also include strategies to counter work stoppages in sympathy with strikes by another employer's employees.[27]

2.4 Nonunion Employees

Strike planning considerations must also cover possible actions by employees not represented by unions. For example, many

---

25. Legislative history indicates that a strike should occur within seventy-two hours of its expected notice time and date. Then, at least twelve hours notice should be given of any new expected date and time. Orange Belt Painters, *supra*, n.20; District 1199-E, RWDSU (Federal Hill Nursing Center), 243 N.L.R.B. 23, 101 L.R.R.M. 1346 (1979); Bricklayers, Local 40 (Lake Shore Hospital), 252 N.L.R.B. 252, 105 L.R.R.M. 1317 (1980). Picketing commencing one hour before notice time is not a violation, if employer fails to prove adverse impact. Local 44, Service Employees International Union, N.L.R.B. Advice Memo. Case No. 3-CG-13 (1979).
26. *See* American Health Enterprises, Inc. (Colonial Manor Nursing Home), 8 CA 17271, *pending decision*, NLRB Office of the General Counsel, Division of Advice (1984).
27. *See* ch. 5, *infra*, regarding sympathy strikes.

Prestrike Planning

white collar employees are traditionally not represented. If, however, they strike in sympathy or refuse to cross the union employees' picket line, section 7's protection of concerted action applies to them. Confidential employees, traditionally excluded from representation, are still employees under the NLRA and may be protected as well.[28] Nonunion action may involve large groups of employees or individuals acting with the sanction of employee group action.[29] Be certain to anticipate and prepare for a work stoppage by all employees.

2.5 Management Team Identification

Top executive and personnel management executives are easily identified. Although their dedication and loyalty to the organization is usually clear, this is not always the case with first line management, such as supervisors, foremen, and leads. All supervisors must be identified and clearly informed about the employer's bargaining position and expected actions. However, the management team should not include borderline individuals who might have statutory employee status. This could be improper coercion under section 8(a)(1) of the Act and would likely cause leaks of key information to the union.

The problem is acute in craft industries where lower level supervisors such as foremen or leadmen are often covered by the union contract. If first-level management is in the bargaining

---

28. NLRB v. Southern Greyhound Lines, 169 N.L.R.B. 627, 67 L.R.R.M. 1368 (1968), *enforced*, 426 F.2d 1299, 74 L.R.R.M. 2080 (5th Cir. 1970). With the narrow definition of *Hendricks County* now applicable for confidential employees, this protection may not apply. See note 33 *infra*. However, such employees are not protected from discipline for misconduct. *See*, Lucky Stores, Inc., 269 N.L.R.B. No. 167, ____L.R.R.M. ____ (1984).
29. *See* Meyers Industries, Inc., 268 N.L.R.B. No. 73, 115 L.R.R.M. 1025 (1984).

unit, an employer will have security and operations problems during a strike. During bargaining or through well-planned unit clarification petitions, the management team should be identified and strengthened, so that an employer knows whom it can rely on during a strike.

2.5.1 Supervisors

Supervisors must be identified by close review of their duties. Unlike managers or confidential employees, the Act specifically excludes this group from its coverage. Section 2(11) of the Act defines a supervisor as:

> Any individual having authority, in the interest of the employer, to hire, transfer, suspend, layoff, recall, promote, discharge, assign, reward, *or* discipline other employees *or* responsibly to direct them, *or* to adjust their grievances, *or effectively* to *recommend* such action, if in the connection with the foregoing the exercise of such authority is not of a merely routine or clerical nature, but requires the use of *independent judgment.* (Emphasis added.)

The circuit courts have often required the NLRB to use a disjunctive definition,[30] observing that a supervisor's authority to exercise some, although not all, of the specified powers excludes that individual from employee status. Recently the NLRB has also placed great weight on the disjunctive nature of the definition, while still requiring careful review of an individual's duties.[31]

---

30. NLRB v. Metropolitan Life Insurance Co., 405 F.2d 1169, 70 L.R.R.M. 2029 (2d Cir. 1968), *denying enforcement of* 163 N.L.R.B. 579, 64 L.R.R.M. 1416 (1967); NLRB v. Brown & Sharp Mfg. Co., 169 F.2d 331, 22 L.R.R.M. 2363 (1st Cir. 1948), *denying enforcement of* 74 N.L.R.B. 801, 20 L.R.R.M. 1215.
31. *Compare* NLRB v. American Medical Services, 705 F.2d 1472, 113 L.R.R.M. 2343 (7th Cir. 1983); Cobra Ltd., 267 N.L.R.B. No. 52, 114

Prestrike Planning

Mere use of supervisory job titles will not be sufficient to obtain excluded status. It is the authority that a person exercises that matters. An employer should review the trend of recent NLRB decisions and carefully analyze the actual duties performed by each supervisor. In most cases, the inquiry will be most fruitful if it focuses on the individual's power to "effectively recommend" *and* exercise independent judgment.

2.5.2 Managers

Unless a manager is also a supervisor, a manager is not automatically excluded by the text of the Act. However, the Supreme Court acknowledged the existence of a managerial exclusion in the *Bell Aerospace* decision.[32] To be excluded from a bargaining unit, managers must be in a position to formulate, determine, and effectuate management policies. They need not deal in labor-management relations.

2.5.3 Confidential Employees

Employees are excluded from a bargaining unit if they serve in a confidential capacity to a manager with labor relations responsibilities.[33] An individual acting in a confidential capacity to a manager who does *not* deal in labor relations matters is not excluded. Although this case law exclusion exempts confidential employees from bargaining units, they remain employees under

---

L.R.R.M. 1027 (1983); Beverly Enterprises, d/b/a Beverly Manor Convalescent Centers, 264 N.L.R.B. 138, 111 L.R.R.M. 1336 (1982); Norwood Manor, Inc., 260 N.L.R.B. 854, 109 L.R.R.M. 1226 (1982).

32. NLRB v. Bell Aerospace Co., 219 N.L.R.B. 384, 89 L.R.R.M. 1664 (1975), *on remand from* 416 U.S. 267, 85 L.R.R.M. 2945 (1974).
33. Hendricks County Rural Electric Membership Corp. v. NLRB, 454 U.S. 170, 108 L.R.R.M. 3105 (1981).

Strike Planning

the NLRA technically and enjoy the same basic protections of the NLRA.[34]

2.6 Supervisor Problems

There must be open and careful coordination within management ranks. Special attention should be directed to first-level supervisors, whose support is vital. Although an employer can force supervisors to work during a strike,[35] their personal commitment to the employer is far superior motivation. They must believe that they are a part of the management program and be committed to maintaining operations. The employer should reinforce this attitude early. They must have a firm understanding of employer priorities, as they will be called on to work long and hard in the event of a strike.

Also, supervisor compensation packages should be carefully reviewed to assure that they meet legal requirements with respect to such matters as overtime pay. Management members should know they will be taken care of by the employer.[36]

---

34. *See* NLRB v. Poultrymen's Service Corp., 138 F.2d 204, 13 L.R.R.M. 543 (3d Cir. 1943); Pullman Standard Division, 214 N.L.R.B. 762, 87 L.R.R.M. 1370 (1974); Southern Greyhound Lines, *supra* note 28; Star Brush Mfg. Co., 100 N.L.R.B. 111, 30 L.R.R.M. 1335 (1952); American Book-Stratford Press, Inc., 80 N.L.R.B. 914, 23 L.R.R.M. 1171 (1948); Coopersville Cooperative Electric, 77 N.L.R.B. 1083, 22 L.R.R.M. 1122 (1948).
35. Discharge of a supervisor is unlawful only if it directly interferes with section 7 rights of an employee. Parker-Robb Chevrolet, 262 N.L.R.B. 384, 110 L.R.R.M. 1289 (1982), *aff'd*, 712 F.2d 1268, 113 L.R.R.M. 3175 (D.C. Cir. 1983). *See* Texas Co. v. NLRB, 198 F.2d 540, 30 L.R.R.M. 2513, (9th Cir. 1952). *See generally* NLRB v. Edward G. Budd Mfg. Co., 169 F.2d 571, 22 L.R.R.M. 2414 (6th Cir. 1948), *cert. denied*, 335 U.S. 908, 23 L.R.R.M. 2228 (1949).
36. *See* ch. 3 *infra*.

2.6.1 Supervisor-Union Member Problems

At a minimum, an employer must consider the impact of a strike on its management ranks. Foremen and first-level supervisors may also be union members. This is particularly true in traditional craft industries, such as publishing, maritime, and construction. Though an individual is technically exempt from employee status pursuant to section 2(11) of the NLRA, an employer may have bargained this exclusion away over the years and included supervisors under contract coverage. Aside from strategies to correct this through bargaining or administrative channels, such as unit clarification proceedings,[37] planning should be designed to alert these supervisors to their rights.

Unions are restricted in policing supervisor members. A union cannot discipline supervisor members for performing supervisory duties during a strike. On the other hand, the Supreme Court has held that unions can fine or discipline supervisors who are union members and who perform only "rank and file work" during a legal strike.[38] In addition, the NLRB has ruled that a union cannot discipline supervisor members who perform mostly supervisory duties with a nominal amount of bargaining unit employee work.[39] The NLRB has taken a contrary position when

---

37. *See* Rules & Regulations of the NLRB, 29 C.F.R. §§ 102.60(b), 102.61(d) (1983).
38. American Broadcasting Co., Inc. v. Writers Guild, 437 U.S. 411, 98 L.R.R.M. 2705 (1978); Florida Power & Light Co. v. International Bhd. of Electrical Workers, 417 U.S. 790, 86 L.R.R.M. 2689 (1074).
39. Bricklayers, Local 28, 265 N.L.R.B. 108, 112 L.R.R.M. 1083 (1982); New York Newspaper Printing Pressmen's Union, No. 2, 249 N.L.R.B. 1284, 104 L.R.R.M. 1332 (1980); Columbia, ITU, Union 101 (Washington Post Co.), 242 N.L.R.B. 1079, 101 L.R.R.M. 1312 (1979). *See also* American Broadcasting Co., Inc. v. Writers Guild, *supra* note 38; Meatcutters Union, Local 81, 185 N.L.R.B. 884, 75 L.R.R.M. 1247, *enforced*, 489 F.2d 794, 79 L.R.R.M. 2309 (D.C. Cir. 1972); Machinists Lodge 297 (Tacoma Boat Bldg. Co.), 270 N.L.R.B. No. 160, ___ L.R.R.M. ___ (1984).

supervisors perform more than a minimal amount of bargaining unit work.[40]

Accordingly, the management ranks must be analyzed to identify problems in union discipline of management workers who work during a strike. Along with other topics, supervisors who are union members should be advised to consider "financial core" status[41] and be kept informed of the employer's position on compensation for working supervisors.[42] Steps that convince the management team that the employer is in control must be taken.

2.7 Union Security Agreement Problems

One confusing issue that arises during a strike is the effect of union security provisions. Although the employer cannot unilaterally change basic terms and conditions of employment (absent implementation of an employer's final offer or after a contract expires with union loss of majority status), mandatory union membership and agency shop provisions do not continue after a contract terminates.[43]

---

40. IAM Local 565, N.L.R.B. Advice Memo Case No. 32-C.B.-642 (1980). Typographical Union Local 16 (Hammond Publishers, Inc.), 216 N.L.R.B. 903, 88 L.R.R.M. 1378 (1975). *See also*, Electrical Workers (IBEW) and Its Local 1 (Bergelectric Corp.), 271 N.L.R.B. No. 2, _____ L.R.R.M. _____ (1984), regarding picketing requirements of supervisor union members.
41. *See* ch. 4 *infra*.
42. *See* ch. 3 *infra*.
43. *See* Colonie Fibre Co. v. NLRB, 63 F.2d 65, 20 L.R.R.M. 2399 (2d Cir. 1947); Trico Products Corp., *supra* note 4; Bethlehem Steel Co. (Shipbuilding Div.), *supra* note 4; Chemical Workers Local 112 (American Cyanamid Co.), 237 N.L.R.B. 864, 99 L.R.R.M. 1152 (1978); Railway Clerks Local 1937 (NCR Corp.), 235 N.L.R.B. 666, 98 L.R.R.M. 1064 (1978); Typographical Union Local 53 (Plain Dealer Publishing Co.), 225 N.L.R.B. 1281, 93 L.R.R.M. 1151 (1976); Teamsters Local 25 (Tech Weld Corp.), 220 N.L.R.B. 76, 90 L.R.R.M. 1193 (1975); General Motors Corp., 134 N.L.R.B. 1107, 49 L.R.R.M. 1283 (1961).

Prestrike Planning

In a strike, employees inevitably ask questions about union membership and dues requirements. An employer should be prepared to advise employees about any obligations to the union when a contract expires. Unless employees elect to resign, they are still union members, even though the union shop clause expired. Strategy decisions should be made as to how to inform employees about their rights.[44]

2.7.1 Dues Checkoff Considerations

Employees who have signed dues deduction authorization forms, which permit automatic payroll deductions of union dues, may face a dilemma in the event of a strike. An employer may, through poor drafting, cede control of this to the union. Even if employees wish to discontinue dues deduction after contract termination, they may be unable to do so, for the specific language of the checkoff form may preclude revocation at the employee's discretion. For example, even if a union shop provision has expired and even if an employee resigns from the union, the checkoff form may still require the employee to pay dues to the union.[45] This form can constitute an independent contract between an employer, a union, and the signing employee.[46]

---

44. See also ch. 4 infra.
45. See Anheuser-Busch v. Teamsters Local 822, 584 F.2d 41, 99 L.R.R.M. 2539 (4th Cir. 1979); Steelworkers, Local 7450 (Asarco, Inc.), 246 N.L.R.B. 878, 103 L.R.R.M. 1020 (1979); Carpenter's Council (Campbell Industries), 243 N.L.R.B. 147, 101 L.R.R.M. 1394 (1979); Frito Lay v. Meatcutters, Local 540, 243 N.L.R.B. 16, 101 L.R.R.M. 1390 (1979); Trico Products Corp., supra note 4; Murtha v. Pet Dairy Products Co., 314 S.W.2d 185, 42 L.R.R.M. 285 (Tenn. App. Ct. 1957).
46. Cameron Iron Works Inc., 235 N.L.R.B. 47, 97 L.R.R.M. 1516 (1978), Atlanta Printing Specialties & Paper Product Union, Local 527, AFL-CIO (The Mead Corp.), 215 N.L.R.B. 237, 87 L.R.R.M. 1744 (1974), en-

Strike Planning

Unauthorized dues deductions are illegal under section 302 of the Labor Management Relations Act and many state statutes.[47] Therefore, employers should carefully plan a checkoff position prior to contract termination.

2.7.2 Checkoff Negotiations Concerns

When negotiating a new contract, consider whether dues checkoff provisions are terminable at will, expire during a window period during a contract, or terminate with the contract. The checkoff procedure for a labor contract is fully negotiable.[48] Generally such contract terms call for voluntary employee authorization, although the statute requires only a "written assignment" of wages.[49]

Unless the checkoff form is clearly terminable at will by the employees, it can trap unwitting employees into longstanding dues obligations. The employer should identify this hazard in planning prior to commencing negotiations. The employer may develop a new form during bargaining or propose a contract

---

forced, 523 F.2d 783, 90 L.R.R.M. 3121 (5th Cir. 1975); Distillery Workers Local 80 (Capital Hustings Co.), 235 N.L.R.B. 1264, 98 L.R.R.M. 1123 (1978).

47. 29 U.S.C. § 186.
48. U.S. Gypsum Co., 94 N.L.R.B. 112, 28 L.R.R.M. 1015 (1951), *amended*, 97 N.L.R.B. 889, 29 L.R.R.M. 1171 (1951), *modified* 206 F.2d 410, 32 L.R.R.M. 2553 (5th Cir. 1953), *cert. denied*, 347 U.S. 912, 33 L.R.R.M. 2456 (1954). *See also* H.K. Porter, 153 N.L.R.B. 1370, 59 L.R.R.M. 1462 (1965), *enforced*, 363 F.2d 272, 62 L.R.R.M. 2204 (D.C. Cir. 1966), *cert. denied*, 385 U.S. 851, 63 L.R.R.M. 2236 (1966), *on reconsideration*, 389 F.2d 295, 66 L.R.R.M. 2761 (1967), *rev'd and remanded*, 397 U.S. 99, 73 L.R.R.M. 2561 (1970).
49. *See* § 302 of the Labor-Management Relations Act, 29 U.S.C. § 186(c). However, forced dues checkoffs have been found to violate the NLRA. *See* Luke Construction Co., 211 N.L.R.B. 602, 87 L.R.R.M. 1087 (1974); American Screw Co., 122 N.L.R.B. 485, 43 L.R.R.M. 1153 (1958).

clause that includes instructions about checkoff form revocability. Unions sometimes bluster and argue that this is a nonnegotiable subject, that it is between them and the employee. This is not true, as an employer has every right to insist on the type of contractual relationship that will exist between the employee, the employer, and the union through dues checkoff.[50]

Unions take for granted many traditional contract items, such as union shops, agency shops, and dues checkoff that ensure them stability and financial security. Employers permit unions to assume that once union security provisions are agreed upon they become inalienable rights. A determined employer may use continued contract coverage of these items as leverage to obtain other desirable management protections. While care must be taken to bargain in good faith, hard bargaining is a legitimate practice.[51] These prenegotiation strategy considerations should be part of your overall preparation for a strike. When combined with a thorough strike plan, the employer will be in an optimal position.

---

50. *See* U.S. Gypsum Co., *supra,* note 48.
51. Seattle-First National Bank, 267 N.L.R.B. No. 142, 114 L.R.R.M. 1072 (1983), *supplementing,* 241 N.L.R.B. 753, 100 L.R.R.M. 1624 (1979), *on remand from,* 638 F.2d 1221, 106 L.R.R.M. 2621 (9th Cir. 1981).

Appendix 2-A

Certified Mail / Return Receipt Requested

To: [Union]
   President

   [Address]
Re: Collective Bargaining for [Employer]

Dear _____:

   This letter serves as notice to your union that [Employer] wishes to terminate [or modify] the labor agreement between the parties on [date: sixty (60) or ninety (90) days later depending on industry].*

   This letter serves as our offer to meet and confer for the purpose of negotiating an appropriate agreement.

[OPTIONAL METHOD]:This letter is being served this same day upon the Federal Mediation and Conciliation Service and our state agency [name of state agency], advising them of the existence of a dispute between us.

   Please call with any questions or comments. We look forward to resolving this dispute in the near future.

                        Sincerely,

                        _____

                        [Employer]

cc: FMCS
   State Agency

---

* The time period must comply with applicable labor contract and section 8(d) notice requirements.

Appendix 2-B

FMCS FORM F-7
REVISED JULY 82

FORM APPROVED
OMB NO. D23-R00 10

NOTICE TO MEDIATION AGENCIES

APPROPRIATE STATE OR TERRITORIAL AGENCY

TO: DIVISION OF CASE CONTROL
FEDERAL MEDIATION AND CONCILIATION SERVICE   AND
2100 K STREET, N.W.
WASHINGTON, D.C. 20427

You are hereby notified that written notice of the proposed termination or modification of the existing collective bargaining contract was served upon the other party to this contract and that no agreement has been reached.

NAME OF EMPLOYER ①	CONTRACT EXPIRATION OR REOPENING DATE ②
NAME OF UNION AND LOCAL NO. ③	CITY, STATE AND ZIP CODE OF EFFECTED ESTABLISHMENT
STREET ADDRESS OF EMPLOYER ⑤	CITY ④ STATE ZIP
STREET ADDRESS OF UNION ⑥	CITY STATE ZIP
EMPLOYER OFFICIAL TO CONTACT ⑦	A.C. PHONE ⑧	TOTAL NUMBER EMPLOYED AT EFFECTED LOCATION(S) ⑨
UNION OFFICIAL TO CONTACT ⑩	A.C. PHONE ⑪	NUMBER OF EMPLOYEES COVERED BY CONTRACT ⑫
INDUSTRY ⑬	PRINCIPAL PRODUCT OR SERVICE ⑭	THIS NOTICE IS FILED ON BEHALF OF (X) ⑮ ☐ UNION ☐ EMPLOYER
NAME AND TITLE OF OFFICIAL FILING THIS NOTICE ⑯	SIGNATURE AND DATE ⑰
STREET ⑱	CITY ⑲ STATE ZIP

Receipt of this notice does not constitute a request for mediation nor does it commit the agencies to offer their facilitites. This particular form of notice is not legally required. Receipt of notice will not be acknowledged in writing by the Federal Mediation and Conciliation Service.

NO. 1 ORIGINAL - To F.M.C.S.

FMCS Notice to Mediation Agencies

3
The Strike Plan: "Business-As-Usual Basics"

At the same time that an employer is gathering information, reviewing labor contract experience, developing negotiation priorities, and establishing strategies for collective bargaining, it should also review strike contingencies from an operations viewpoint. The employer and its labor-management advisers should consider both the legal and practical questions a strike presents. A strike planning letter from counsel to the employer can help initiate the planning process and focus this analysis. (See Appendix 3-A.) Alternatively, management can develop an internal memorandum to outline these strike planning considerations.

3.1 The Strike Plan Process

Strike planning should begin months before negotiations start. This allows an employer to take advantage of the relative tranquility of regular operations to plan for the strike that may occur if bargaining deteriorates. Thorough contingency planning is essential. Management should take care to identify direct and indirect production and service concerns. (See Appendix 3-B for a possible contingency plan outline.) The basic strike plan should cover, at a minimum, the general areas discussed in this chapter. A checklist is helpful in assigning responsibilities and preliminary target dates. (See Appendix 3-C.)

3.1.1 Strike Committee

As its first step, the employer should establish a strike committee *at least* six to nine months *before* the contract is scheduled to expire. The strike committee's members should be respected management representatives from different departments or groups. Individuals with several years of experience with the organization usually provide the best planning assistance.

This committee should be a permanent group which is functioning long before a collective bargaining impasse is reached. The committee should be responsible for working with the executive hierarchy over an extended period of time to ensure that acceptable alternatives are developed to meet all contingencies. Once a contract is agreed upon, the committee should continue to meet regularly (at least semiannually) to deal with mid-contract problems and to prepare for the next round of contract negotiations.

To the degree possible, avoid overlap of the strike committee's membership with that of the collective bargaining committee. The strike committee's role includes initial policy development, planning, workload and production/service targets, actual operations during a strike, and followup to the strike. Its functions do not include negotiating with the union. However, at least one strike committee member should be part of the negotiating committee, to assure close coordination.

3.1.1.1. Legal Counsel

Legal counsel should be part of the committee. An effective and experienced attorney can assist in several facets of committee operation. Counsel should analyze the different legal problems that could arise and provide assistance regarding each type, such as injunctive relief, corporate planning, and basic labor law advice. Arrange for counsel to be available on short notice when needed. However, remember that such counsel will need lead

The Strike Plan

time to research the legal issues presented by a strike and to prepare for necessary actions.

Counsel should pay special attention to circumstances in which injunctive relief might be obtained.[1] Whether dealing with disruptive situations or no-strike clause problems, the value of such relief depends in large measure on the speed with which it can be obtained. Counsel should therefore develop form pleadings before the strike. The pleadings should include a summons, complaint, supporting memoranda on legal issues, proposed orders, and tentative affidavit outlines, which can easily be modified during a strike situation. Presiding court officials and necessary procedures should be identified to ensure prompt processing of the papers.

Counsel should carefully study state labor injunction laws, paying particular attention to details peculiar to the jurisdiction. Many states require a bond, so early coordination with an insurance broker or bondsmen will streamline processing when needed. Do as much in advance as can be done.

3.1.2 Policy Analysis and Review

Any effective management system must have policies, goals, and procedures. Before bargaining begins, top management should work with its strike committee to establish policy. This is a particularly sensitive area for government entities and public service employers, such as media, health care, and transportation employers. Long-term and short-term "political" considerations must be balanced against day-to-day operational needs and collective bargaining goals. Remember that your strike manual may be discoverable in the event of litigation and could become public information.

The future labor relations climate desired must also be assessed. Management must decide what kind of labor relations it

---

1. See ch. 5 *infra*.

wants five and ten years from now, not just what it wants to achieve in the immediate collective bargaining experience. The scope and aggressiveness of the strike planning will have a strong impact on later labor union relationships.

Be certain to utilize the board of directors in this decision-making process. Keep them appropriately informed of significant actions and be sure they are comfortable with your position.

3.1.3 Contingency Plan Development

The strike plan should not be a short notice response to a union's strike authorization. The pressure and strain of planning around last-minute ultimatums may lead to strike-related problems and foster premature or unwise capitulation to unreasonable union demands. Instead, deliberate and systematic management planning in the form of a written, structured program should be undertaken.

The strike committee should draft a thorough and detailed contingency plan well in advance of a strike date. (See Appendix 3-B for a possible outline.) Initially this may seem like a costly and time consuming task, but since it is directed towards effective labor relations over many years, it is time and money well spent. Once a detailed plan is established, it is easily updated in future years. Also, a thorough contingency manual is often applicable to other situations, such as strike problems arising in the middle of a contract term. Furthermore, experienced legal counsel may have much of the basic material available and will be able to assist in efficiently adapting it to the program.

To be effective, a contingency manual must be comprehensive, easily understood, and concise. It also must be kept current. For obvious reasons, its contents must be kept highly confidential; only key management people should have access.

The Strike Plan

3.1.4 Strike Headquarters

Unions invariably establish strike headquarters for continuous twenty-four hour operation. Management has the same need for round-the-clock monitoring of the strike. The strike headquarters must be in a well-secured area, but should also be readily accessible to the primary workplace. The strike plan should designate a location for headquarters and address the need for special security precautions.

Ensure that necessary supplies, materials, and amenities for key personnel are available and easily obtained if necessary. This should include such basic items as food and beverages, sanitation facilities, and bedding. (See Appendix 3-D for a possible strike headquarters checklist.) Reliable communications are essential. Consider installing unlisted telephone numbers for the headquarters prior to a strike. This is especially important if a volatile situation is expected, as the union may seek to paralyze communications by making nuisance or threatening calls.

Review all zoning and licensing requirements that may bear upon the location and functioning of the headquarters. The size, complexity, and sophistication of strike headquarters vary with each employer's needs. Some employers rent trailers and other strike equipment. Others can get by with a small office or conference room. Much depends upon the individual circumstances.

3.1.5 Management Team Communications

All members of the management team, from foremen up, must realize that they are an essential part of the employer's program and they must be dedicated to its success.[2] They must be con-

---

2. Early in the process an employer must carefully identify its management team. *See* ch. 2 *supra*.

vinced of a vested interest in the employer's position. The supervisors or managers should understand that they are responsible for successfully operating their units during a strike. Implementing appropriate portions of the contingency plan on a decentralized basis increases accountability and strengthens commitment.

First-line supervisors, as well as top managers, must be regularly briefed on strike issues. Supervisors should have a solid grasp of bargaining issues and be committed to management goals so that when they are approached by employees with questions they can present the employer's views convincingly. Effective use of line supervisors also provides the best chance of learning what a union is telling employees about such important matters as tentative dates for union meetings, strike issues, strike deadlines, strategies, and strike votes. This information will be helpful to the planning process.

3.1.5.1 Confidentiality Requirements

Security of the contingency manual and other strike planning documents before and during a strike is essential. Confidentiality and management responsibilities must be well defined at all levels. Management must determine who will have access to various documents and with what authority. The most sensitive aspects of the strike plan, such as production and service priorities, should be disclosed only on a need-to-know basis.

3.1.6 Service/Production Options

Planning for continuing operations must begin early in the strike planning process. Although much of an employer's strike planning can best be implemented through the strike committee, service and production options are usually coordinated most effectively when decentralized. The existing organizational network should develop priorities and work plans for each area of

The Strike Plan

responsibility. These plans should be included as subchapters in the strike manual.[3]

If force majeure clauses excuse performance of any of the contracts, their scope should be studied. Some include labor disputes as events justifying a failure to perform. Then determine what levels of performance can be met and which are to be satisfied. Remember that long-term relationships may be jeopardized if service is terminated, even for the best of reasons.

3.1.6.1 Work Priority

The strike committee should assign priorities to work requirements in a systematic manner many weeks before a strike occurs. Again, particular groups or departments may accomplish this most effectively on a decentralized basis.

Identify minimally acceptable levels of service or production for each component of the organization. Pay particular attention to schedule changes regarding the work day, shift, or hours. To the degree appropriate, build up product and supply inventories well in advance. Designate safe storage facilities at all locations.

Assign priorities to the various production and service components, classifying each according to its relative importance. A simple system could classify each component as essential, desired, or expendable. How complex this planning should become will depend on each employer's program. Remember to satisfy licensing and regulatory requirements that may restrict alternatives.

Determine how long each priority area can be maintained at each level. A coded grid system or matrix may be helpful for such planning. (See Appendix 3-E.) This system can be made as detailed or complicated as necessary for your operation. Data processing systems can be used to establish specific schedules.

---

3. See section 3.1.3 *supra*.

Strike Planning

3.1.6.2 Work Suspension

Along with setting priorities on work product or service, make a special effort to identify work that can be reduced, such as basic maintenance, routine housekeeping, or minor recordkeeping or filing. Find out whether employees or supervisors already handling these duties can be switched to other functioning areas. Pay particular attention to the areas where work may be suspended, permanently or temporarily. Many employers find that they have greater latitude in this regard than they originally expected.

Much depends on federal, state, or local licensing and safety requirements. Study this area to avoid *hidden regulatory traps*, such as staffing or skill requirements. You should expect unions or anonymous citizens to file complaints with licensing and safety authorities in an effort to disrupt operations. Remember the right to demand that a safety inspector have a warrant before granting access to facilities.[4] However, asserting this right may have an adverse impact on long-term relations with the enforcement agency. It may also lead to unfavorable publicity, especially if an accident occurs after the inspector is turned away.

3.1.7 Communications System

The employer should develop a detailed communications network for employees and management. Communications to employees should cover strike issues, strike rights, personnel policies and procedures, and the possible polling of projected strike participants.[5] These materials should be drafted carefully and reviewed by counsel well in advance of the time they are needed. A

---

4. *See* Marshall v. Barlow's Inc., 436 U.S. 307 (1978) (Occupational Safety and Health Act inspection warrants). *See also* Donovan v. Lone Star Motel, 52 U.S.L.W. 4087 (U.S. Jan. 17, 1984) (No.82-1684) (warrants and subpoenas for Fair Labor Standards Act investigations).
5. *See* ch. 4 *infra*.

regular briefing memo or newsletter to employees working during a strike may help boost morale and keep employees informed.

Management must also have a confidential communication network that can disseminate information quickly and securely. For verbal communications, a simple "telephone tree," based on your organization chart, in which one person contacts two or three others (who then make further contacts) may be appropriate, so long as backup callers are available if the primary caller cannot be reached. Draft in advance a preprinted roster or brochure with necessary communications information as part of the contingency plan. Provide guides and ready references for contacting top executives, counsel, key staff, security, and government agencies, such as mediation, fire, police, and judicial services.

3.1.8 The Media and the Public Spokesperson

One person should be designated for all contacts with the press, radio, or television. Select an articulate person in advance. Consider training the representative to respond effectively and appropriately to media inquiries, as special skills are involved. Be certain that everyone understands this person's role, to avoid unauthorized and unfortunate media contact.

Although legal counsel may be the spokesperson, in many communities a lawyer may not be the most effective liaison with the public. You may wish instead to use someone from the local community who is knowledgeable about your organization. This is especially true for public sector employers.

An employer should remember that the media often looks for sensational news stories. Public statements should therefore be concise. Employers are rarely served well by flamboyant press conferences because public statements may be used as evidence in other proceedings. For example, a poorly thought out statement about "firing" strikers, rather than "replacing" them, could be quite harmful. Deliberate and cautious press releases are usually far more prudent. All public statements should be coordinated

Strike Planning

with top management and legal counsel. Spontaneous comments might be not only a strategic error, but slanderous, inflammatory, or coercive as well.

Reporters are often union members and may on occasion editorialize in their stories by using inflammatory words, such as "scabs" or "union busters." Because of timing concerns with live reporting, local television and radio news media are often most susceptible to this problem. You may want to address this problem by issuing press releases, which will make it more likely that reporters will use your exact words rather than their own. Newspaper advertisements explaining the employer's position may also be effective in delivering your message, particularly when the general public's support or understanding is important. (See Appendixes 3-F and 3-G.)

3.1.9 Security

Security and the appearance of preparedness during a strike are critical. The public appearance of successful preparation and readiness are usually helpful. Employee enthusiasm and participation of employees may be influenced by expectations of success.[6]

Detailed building plans and property maps should be part of an overall security plan. Analyze existing security for the different circumstances that a strike will create. Plans should be developed for people, buildings, and personal property. If you have tenants on leased property, they should be advised of possible problems and any secondary boycott remedies.

Focus on special vulnerabilities. Consider vandalism and damage to signs, buildings, equipment, and vehicles, which are particular problems for distant or isolated sites. Plan to use various special delivery or courier systems for freight and funds. Consider developing new identification badges, passes, keys, and

---

6. *See* ch. 4 *infra*, regarding permissible communications.

The Strike Plan

other entrance systems. Finally, review security needs of company property located at *all* sites. Do *not* limit review to regular business hours. Consider twenty-four hour security requirements.

Steps taken to secure people and property should be well publicized to build morale and provide a deterrent. If you use striker replacements, take open action to establish protection for them. Unfortunately, union ideals and rhetoric often turn into base language and violence during a strike, and strikers may threaten replacements. New employees should understand this. If they become fearful and apprehensive, they will be reluctant to work.

Review in detail physical security at all locations. Don't overlook the obvious. Review *all* entrances and exits, including windows, doors, fences, vents, and gates. Recheck locks. In appropriate circumstances, consider new locks, combinations, or cipher codes.

All supply schedules and routes to and from facilities must be verified and coordinated. Study the feasibility of remote site and late hour deliveries to avoid confrontations and disruption. Consider using special parking entrance privileges, such as a special pass or decal. Determine exactly how you want your employees to enter and exit. In certain cases a parking lot shuttle may be desirable. You may also use staggered starting and quitting schedules to avoid congestion. This will reduce the likelihood of confrontations with pickets.

At least one month in advance of bargaining, coordinate plans with the local police or sheriff's department and alert them to the possible need for regular patrols if a strike occurs. If a remote site labor force problem arises, contact state troopers or other state authorities as well. A *regular police presence* is especially important at the *start* of a strike at picketed locations. Some local governments have police units with special expertise in labor dispute situations.

Police involvement may cause political problems, as unions will attempt to create public pressure to limit police security. Management should endeavor to coordinate this protection early, as this assists the police department in planning and builds rapport, thus minimizing the effect of the union's political pressure. If any violence is anticipated, the authorities must be informed of the expected scope and degree.

Always consider contracting with a special private security force for the duration of the strike. Your own security force may not be familiar with the special needs and pressures of a strike. Some companies specialize in security protection during labor disputes. Many serve dual functions, such as security and personnel recruiting. Such a company may be well equipped to conduct investigations, provide physical security, and assist in court proceedings by testifying or providing affidavits. Be certain to get a detailed explanation of services, bonding, credit, and billing procedures. Demand *recent references* and check them thoroughly.

3.1.10 Strike Insurance

Insurance policies are available to protect against economic loss incurred by a strike. Employers often are not aware of or neglect to consider purchasing strike insurance. Although premiums are an extra business expense, policy protection may outweigh the costs.

An accounting department can provide a detailed cost analysis of strike insurance options, which must be based upon realistic projections of the strike's expected duration. If you already have such insurance, review the policy and consider increasing the limits or making other modifications. Counsel should review policy terms and conditions. Plan carefully to meet any notice requirements specified in the policy. Public employers must also consider any legal restrictions and public relations impact.

3.1.11 Strike Reports, Log, and Evidence

Many employers understand the need to establish thorough documentation for strike incidents. However, few provide a system that efficiently develops such information.

The Strike Plan

The incident report system could also become part of a regular documentation system for other problems after the strike situation is over.

3.1.11.1 Forms

Create a formal documentation system for incidents that may occur during a strike. A strike log system should be a formal part of the contingency plan. Utilize self-duplicating forms that ask key questions to gather essential data. (See Appendix 3-H.) This will help lower-level management gather necessary information. Detailed strike log systems will also assist security and management personnel in documenting problems, if security force employees understand the system.

In advance of the strike, establish procedures for delivering, collecting, routing, and analyzing information generated by this system. All management staff should have copies of incident report forms before a strike occurs and should be familiar with their use. Require all working personnel to document situations as they occur and telephone information to strike headquarters. Forms must be submitted *immediately* to a central source for inclusion in the strike log. (See Appendix 3-I.) These reports are essential for updating operation plans regularly, assessing strike impact, and taking necessary legal actions. They are especially important as standard procedure for remote work locations because of their vulnerability to vandalism and sabotage.

3.1.11.2 Daily Reports

In addition to the system for incident reporting, the plan should establish a daily reporting system. Even when no trouble is occurring, work locations should check in on a predetermined schedule. Sometimes local supervisors do not grasp the significance of an event that top management and counsel may deem important. This will provide a complete understanding of the current security situation.

3.1.11.3 Evidence Development

Be certain that all locations have access to automatic cameras to record property damage, striker misconduct, or secondary activity. Also, consider using videotape equipment where you anticipate trouble. Do not be conservative in estimates, as employee and property safety are involved, and convincing evidence of misconduct may be needed on short notice.

The strike incident report (Appendix 3-H) and the guidance to management on gathering information should initially be established on advice of counsel. By developing material at the request of counsel, it may fall under the attorney-client privilege and not be vulnerable to discovery in the event of litigation.[7] Consider whether this possible protection is desired. If so, establish necessary procedures to secure this right. At a minimum, this requires that the information be developed at counsel's request for use in providing legal advice and that the information gathered not be widely disseminated.

3.1.12 Special Personnel Considerations

Identify special personnel management procedures for a strike. This should include *detailed* personnel policies and requirements for recordkeeping, hiring, payroll, salary increases, overtime, termination, sick leave and vacation, employee benefits, and expense reimbursements. Review each component of the existing personnel system. For each area, determine how each item will be handled if a strike occurs.

---

7. *See generally* Upjohn Co. v. United States, 449 U.S. 383 (1981) (confidential management work-product developed at direction of counsel through company management).

The Strike Plan

3.1.12.1 Wage and Hour Requirements

Pay special attention to state and federal wage and hour laws. Determinations must be made regarding salaries, bonus payments, and overtime for personnel working during a strike. This presents a particular concern for management staff. Carefully review the compensation options and obligations prior to a strike.

The Fair Labor Standards Act (FLSA) requires that employees be compensated at time and one-half for all time worked in excess of forty hours in any one work week.[8] Section 213 of the FLSA provides an exemption from this overtime requirement for "any employee employed in a bona fide executive, administrative, or professional capacity."[9]

Regulations promulgated by the Secretary of Labor define these terms.[10] An employee may qualify for a managerial exemption under either a "long test" or a "short test." An individual satisfies the "long test" for an executive employee if all of the following criteria are satisfied:

(a) primary duty consists of management;
(b) customarily and regularly directs the work of two or more employees;
(c) has substantial hiring, firing and promoting responsibilities;
(d) customarily and regularly exercises discretionary powers;
(e) does not devote more than 20% (or as much as 40% in retail or service establishment) . . . of his hours of work in the work week to activities which are not directly and closely related to the performance of the work described in paragraphs (a) through (d) of this section;

---

8. 29 U.S.C. § 207 (1983).
9. 29 U.S.C. § 213 (1983).
10. 29 C.F.R. §§ 541.0-541.602 (1983).

(f) salary is not less than $155 per week in Continental U.S.[11]

A short-test executive is defined in a proviso to those regulations.[12] Under this proviso an employee who is compensated on a salary basis of not less than $250 per week, whose primary duty consists of management, and whose job includes the customary and regular direction of the work of two or more other employees is considered an exempt executive employee.[13] A supervisor or manager who performs unit work during a strike does not automatically lose exempt status. The regulations provide that

> a bona fide executive who performs work of a normally nonexempt nature on rare occasions because of the existence of a real emergency will not, because of the performance of such emergency work, lose the exemption.[14]

In the key case series in this area, an issue emerged as to whether managerial employees lost exempt status if they performed nonexempt work during a strike.[15] The "emergency exemption" was initially raised, but subsequently withdrawn as a defense by the employer involved. In *Brennan v. Western Union Telegraph Company* (*Western Union I*), the Court of Appeals for the Third Circuit held that "managerial personnel who perform

---

11. 29 C.F.R. § 541.1 (1983). A similar long test exists for administrative managerial employees, 29 C.F.R. § 541.2, and for professional employees (29 C.F.R. § 541.3).
12. *See* 29 C.F.R. § 541.1(f) (1983), *to be revised by*, 46 Fed. Reg. 3013, *effective date indefinitely postponed*, 46 Fed Reg. 11,972 (1981).
13. Similar short-test provisions apply to administrative employees (29 C.F.R. § 541.2(e)) and to professional employees (29 C.F.R. § 541.2(e)).
14. 29 C.F.R. § 541.109(a) (1983).
15. Brennan v. Western Union Telegraph Co., 561 F.2d 477, 484 (3d Cir. 1977), *cert. denied*, 434 U.S. 1063 (1978).

The Strike Plan

strike duty are not necessarily exempt."[16] Focusing on the short test exemption, *Western Union I* did not, however, prescribe the proper period for determining the employee's status, and that issue was remanded to the District Court.

On subsequent review, the court addressed the question in *Marshall v. Western Union Telegraph Company (Western Union II)*,[17] holding that use of a particular time period to determine the primary duty of short-test managerial employees could be accomplished only by administrative rulemaking. As the court in *Western Union II* recognized, "[I]t will be impossible, until a rule is promulgated, to determine *when* exempt status is lost under the short tests."[18]

3.1.12.2 Wages and Benefits

Consider the wage rates that will prevail during a strike. Aside from questions regarding wage and hour exemptions for managerial employees, pay special attention to the basic wage rate and benefits for employees.

If the contract remains in effect, as when a sympathy strike occurs, contract compensation must be paid to unit employees.[19] However, if an economic strike occurs after expiration of the contract, nonstriking unit employees generally must be treated in a manner consistent with the employer's impasse position.[20] But

---

16. Brennan v. Western Union Telegraph Co., *supra* note 15, at 483.
17. Marshall v. Western Union Telegraph Co., 621 F.2d 1246, 1250 (3d Cir. 1980).
18. Marshall v. Western Union Telegraph Co., *supra* note 17, at 1255 (emphasis in original). No relevant rules have since been promulgated.
19. *See* B.N. Beard Co., 248 N.L.R.B. 198, 213, 103 L.R.R.M. 1560 (1980); Hi-Grade Materials Co., 239 N.L.R.B. 947, 955, 100 L.R.R.M. 1113 (1978).
20. Carpenter Sprinkler Corp. v. NLRB, 605 F.2d 60, 69, 102 L.R.R.M. 2199 (2d Cir. 1979).

an employer is not bound to pay temporary striker replacements the same wage rates or benefits it paid under the expired agreement.[21] Also, when necessity calls for higher compensation to nonstriking employees and the employer has a lawful motive, it may be paid during the strike.[22]

Whether the employer has the obligation to pay other fringe benefits is an intricate question.[23] Generally, wage, health and welfare, and pension contribution payments need not be continued for striking workers.[24] However, contributions to such fringe benefit programs must be carefully reviewed before discontinuance, because state statutes often regulate employee rights and employer obligations in this area. You should carefully analyze appropriate local law to determine whether the state permits employees to continue coverage under an employer plan at their own expense for any period of time.[25] Also, examine the provisions of your insurance policy and consult your insurance broker. You must comply strictly with the procedural requirements of any applicable statute. The law may regulate time periods for

---

21. Leveld Wholesale, Inc., 218 N.L.R.B. 1344, 1350, 89 L.R.R.M. 1889, (1975); Imperial Outdoor Advertising, 192 N.L.R.B. 1248, 1249, 78 L.R.R.M. 1208 (1971), *enforced*, 470 F.2d 484, 81 L.R.R.M. 2908 (8th Cir. 1972). This area is complicated by the *Belknap* decision regarding the rights of permanent striker replacements, which suggests that an employer must distinguish between temporary and permanent replacement status. See ch. 9, *infra*.
22. *See* Huck Mfg. Co. v. NLRB, 693 F.2d 1176, 112 L.R.R.M. 2245 (5th Cir. 1983); Soule Glass & Glazing Co. v. NLRB, 652 F.2d 1055, 1082, 107 L.R.R.M. 2781 (1st Cir. 1981).
23. NLRB v. Great Dane Trailer, 388 U.S. 26, 65 L.R.R.M. 2465 (1967). *See generally* NLRB v. Erie Resistor Corp., 373 U.S. 221, 53 L.R.R.M. 2121 (1963). *Compare* Crown Zellerbach Corp., 266 NLRB No. 207, 113 L.R.R.M. 1121 (1983).
24. *See* Simplex Wire & Cable Co., 245 N.L.R.B. 555, 102 L.R.R.M. 1452 (1979); Trading Port, Inc., 219 N.L.R.B. 298, 89 L.R.R.M. 1565 (1975); Ace Tank & Heater Co., 167 N.L.R.B. 663, 66 L.R.R.M. 1129 (1967); General Electric Co., 80 N.L.R.B. 510, 23 L.R.R.M. 1094 (1948).
25. For example, in Washington State, *see* WASH. REV. CODE §§ 48.21.075, 48.24.025, 48.44.250

The Strike Plan

coverage. It may also require the employer to inform state agencies of the strike and advise employees in writing of their rights to continued coverage.

3.1.12.3 Vacations

Review all employee work schedules several weeks before a strike. Eliminate any planned absences if possible. Inform supervisors of the need to scrutinize carefully vacations scheduled around contract expiration time.

Establish a policy to deal with strikers' claims for vacation pay. The rules governing vacation payments for striking workers in the private sector are complicated and generally derive from federal law. Basically, accrued vacation pay policy must be equal for striking and nonstriking employees, but vacation time may be denied for strikers if there are legitimate business reasons. (See Appendix 3-J for a possible guide.)[26] Public employers, on the other hand, must carefully review state and local law.

3.1.12.4 Sick Leave

An equally perplexing problem is the abusive claim for sick leave after a strike has occurred. An employer must be careful in screening such requests. Nonstriking employees are entitled to use accrued sick leave during a strike for legitimate illness. However, whether striking employees are precluded from use of sick leave is not entirely clear.

Absent contractual language to the contrary, employees receiving accrued sickness and accident benefits at the time a strike begins may be entitled to continue to receive those benefits during the dispute. Generally, as long as the employees are disabled and do not affirmatively show support for the strike, they are

---

26. See ch. 11 *infra*, for more detailed discussion on vacation rights.

Strike Planning

eligible.[27] To terminate disability benefits, the employer must show that an employee unable to work when a strike commenced later affirmatively acted in support of the strike.[28]

In giving advice to employees, an employer likely would not want to encourage improper use of sick leave in advance of the strike. Therefore, a general notice to employees about strike benefits that will likely satisfy the NLRB might include the following:

> Nonstriking employees will be entitled to use accrued sick leave in accordance with company policies during a strike for legitimate reasons of sickness. Striking employees will not be entitled to use their sick leave if they become incapacitated during the strike.

3.1.13 Striker Replacements

Absent misconduct or other disqualifying action, economic strikers cannot be discharged. They may, however, be replaced. If you continue operations, you should consider the desirability and feasibility of hiring replacements for strikers. Be certain that you determine whether replacements will be permanent or temporary, as these designations have important consequences for the reinstatment rights of strikers.[29]

---

27. Texaco, Inc. v. NLRB, 700 F.2d 1039, 1042, 114 L.R.R.M. 3677 (5th Cir. 1983); E.L. Wiegand Division, Emerson Electric Co., 246 N.L.R.B. 1143, 103 L.R.R.M. 1073 (1979), *enforced as modified sub nom.*, E. L. Wiegand Division, Emerson Electric Co. v. NLRB, 650 F.2d 463, 107 L.R.R.M. 2112 (3rd Cir. 1981), *cert. denied*, 455 U.S. 939, 109 L.R.R.M. 2778 (1982); *contra* NLRB v. Sherwin-Williams, 714 F. 2d 1249, 114 L.R.R.M. 2506 (11th Cir. 1983), *denying enforcement of* 260 N.L.R.B. No. 1321, 109 L.R.R.M. 1338 (1982) (where employer had clear past practice of such denial during strike and followed disability plan terms).
28. Conoco, Inc., 265 N.L.R.B. No.116, 112 L.R.R.M. 1001 (1983).
29. *See* ch. 9 *infra,* for a detailed discussion on striker replacements and reinstatement rights.

The Strike Plan

Develop efficient and easily understood recruiting, orientation, and training programs for immediate staffing needs. Licensing and certification requirements must be studied and adhered to. Consider bringing in pretrained employees. If you use employment services or recruiters, check the recruiters' references thoroughly, as well as those of prospective employees.

Be careful not to violate statutes governing the use of strike breakers. State laws often prohibit the importation of strike replacements from other states under certain circumstances, usually by third-party recruiters.[30] Further, a little known federal law, the Byrnes Act, limits importation of individuals who will be used to interfere with employee rights.[31] Passed in 1936, it was designed to prohibit the transportation of violent strike breakers.

Government agencies will probably be unable to provide staffing help because of limitations regarding manpower assistance when there are labor disputes. However, verify current law for job placement programs offered by the U.S. Department of Labor Employment Service Administration and similar state agencies.[32]

3.1.14 Subcontracting

If you cannot meet all your production needs, review your subcontracting options. However, be certain that you and your subcontractors understand the impact of the "ally doctrine," which will allow the union to apply economic pressure against

---

30. *See, e.g.*, WASH. REV. CODE § 49.44.100. However, this area may be preempted by federal law. *See* Michigan State Chamber of Commerce v. State, No. 83-250399-CZ (Mich. Cir. Ct. Jan 25, 1984) 1984 DLR 34:A-1, and Teamsters Local 20 v. Morton, 377 U.S. 252, 56 L.R.R.M. 2225 (1964).
31. 18 U.S.C. § 1231.
32. For an account of AFL-CIO concern with U.S. Department of Labor's Employment Training Administration's proposed (and withdrawn) regulations, 48 Fed. Reg. 50668 (1983), *to amend* 20 C.F.R. 652.9; *see*, 114 L.R.R.M. 5 (1983).

employers who perform your subcontracted work during the strike.[33]

Also, consider any obligation you might have to bargain with the union before you commence permanent subcontracting. This is especially important in sympathy strikes, as a union may file unfair labor practice charges for refusal to bargain over "relocation" of unit work while a contract is in effect.[34] If permanent subcontracting is contemplated, you must meet appropriate contractual notice and discussion requirements.

3.1.15 Skills Inventory

Review minimum work qualifications of all employees, including management and other nonunit employees. Determine which employees, supervisors, and managers have the capability, experience, and skills to perform struck work. When planning and making projections of skills needed, identify employees who can be expected to cross a picket line and determine if they can be trusted to be transferred to other jobs. Also find out which persons have essential skills, licenses, and certificates.

This process should be initiated at least four to six months prior to the strike. Large organizations should consider developing a data processing system to log and track such data so the information can be updated easily and applied to other problems, such as internal recruiting needs.

3.1.16 Cross Training

Because special circumstances may require staff assignment revisions, some nonunit personnel must be minimally trained in

---

33. See ch. 7 *infra*.
34. *See* First National Maintenance Corp. v. NLRB, 452 U.S. 666, 107 L.R.R.M. 2705 (1981); Fibreboard Paper Products Corp. v. NLRB, 379 U.S. 203, 57 L.R.R.M. 2609 (1964); Milwaukee Spring, Division of Illinois Coil Spring Co., 268 N.L.R.B. No. 87 (1984).

The Strike Plan

all areas of operations. This creates greater management flexibility. Decide how much training will be necessary for each nonunit employee and review necessary license and certification requirements. Develop training programs and material in advance. Prepare to hold classes a few months before a strike. Also prepare special orientations for new workers. Conduct such training off-site, or if it must be on site, outside of work hours and well in advance of the perceived need.[35]

3.1.17 Unemployment Compensation and Food Stamps

The availability of unemployment compensation benefits during a strike is governed by state law.[36] It is generally a complex and intricate area. In many states strikers are not entitled to unemployment compensation if specific circumstances exist, such as the employer's continued operation at reduced levels. Through coordination with counsel, strategies and recordkeeping systems can be developed in advance to enhance management's position with respect to unemployment compensation proceedings.

Also, review *current* federal law and regulation regarding food stamps eligibility. Under present law, employees not already receiving such assistance prior to a strike may not sign up as a result of a strike.[37]

A strike plan should include a summary of state and federal law on the availability of unemployment compensation and food

---

35. Unions are not entitled to information about such programs. *See* NLRB v. A.S. Abell Co., 624 F.2d 506, 104 L.R.R.M. 2761 (4th Cir 1980), *denying enforcement of* 230 N.L.R.B. 1112, 95 L.R.R.M. 1493 (1977); San Diego Newspaper Guild, Local 95 (Union Tribune) v. NLRB, 548 F.2d 863, 94 L.R.R.M. 2923 (9th Cir. 1977), *enforcing*, 220 N.L.R.B. 1226, 90 L.R.R.M. 1619 (1975).
36. *See* N.Y. Telephone Co. v. N.Y. State Dept. of Labor, 440 U.S. 519, 100 L.R.R.M. 2896 (1979); Hawaiian Telephone Co. v. Hawaii Department of Labor, 614 F.2d 1197, 103 L.R.R.M. 3042 (9th Cir. 1980), *cert. denied*, 446 U.S. 984, 104 L.R.R.M. 2431 (1980).
37. 7 U.S.C. § 2015(d) (3) (1983).

stamps. You may wish to send a letter to your employees summarizing the availability of these benefits during a strike.[38]

3.1.18 Contract Review

Study labor contracts for your other bargaining units. Be sure that you have a good understanding of the force and effect of their no-strike, picket line, and struck work clauses. If your contracts clearly prohibit actions in sympathy with another unit's strike, employee dismissals and suits for damages may be appropriate. You should also consider seeking injunctive relief.[39]

3.1.19 Union Rules

Obtain copies of current union constitutions and bylaws well in advance of the strike. The Labor-Management Services Administration of the United States Department of Labor can provide such material from its Regional Office. Also, Department of Labor union reports, such as Report LM-2, can provide you with internal union financial information to help in assessing the strike's impact on the union. This will assist in predicting just how long a strike the union can undertake.

Carefully review international and local union rules for language that purports to restrict employees in the exercise of their rights. In particular, look for advice on employee rights pertaining to crossing of picket lines, resignation from the union, or change of membership status to "financial core."[40] Study *current* information and review it well before a strike.

---

38. *See* Appendix 4-A.5 *infra.*
39. *See* ch. 5 *infra.*
40. *See* ch. 4 *infra.*

The Strike Plan

3.1.20 Reserve Gate Options

The reserve gate is an option that you may wish to employ to minimize strike disruption. You may use this device to permit "neutral" employers free access to a picketed jobsite or facility. Use of the reserve gate requires adherence to strict guidelines.[41]

If you intend to designate a reserve gate, you may wish to reach agreement with the union on some basic ground rules. This could avoid unnecessary aggravation and legal expenses. If you expect difficulties, alert the NLRB Regional Office to the situation in advance, as this will likely expedite case handling. Even when you cannot establish legally effective reserve gates, you may be able to make an agreement with the union to set up entrances that the parties mutually agree will be treated as reserved. A union may cooperate in order to gain public and employee support.

3.1.21 Transportation

Review all traffic patterns of employees and suppliers. Study departure and arrival times. Identify the shortest and safest entry and departure routes. Consider special hours and parking privileges. Determine whether shuttle services are needed to get employees into a struck facility. Identify cost and security concerns for any new systems.

3.1.22 Supplies/Utilities

You should study all supply, utility, and maintenance needs to determine what you will require during the strike. Go over your records for the same season in past years. Identify how you will handle potential problems, such as supply or utility interruptions once a strike occurs.

---

41. *See* ch. 7 *infra*.

Strike Planning

Contact suppliers and ascertain their willingness and ability to make deliveries during a strike. Seek written verification from them on their commitment to continue doing business with you in the event of a strike. Look for force majeure or other escape clauses that may excuse performance of their contracts.

If suppliers are unwilling to approach the premises, consider a safe and secure drop location at another site and arrange to pick up materials at other locations. Develop a transportation plan to allow such a system to operate smoothly. Stockpile supplies to the degree feasible. Make sure stored resources are adequately secured.

3.2 Mutual Aid Pacts

In preparing for a strike, management should consider entering into a mutual aid or assistance pact (MAP) as an alternative method of continuing production and maintaining operations.[42] A MAP is an alliance with other employers, usually within the same industry, through which centralized decisions and coordinated actions can be developed to plan for and deal with a strike. A MAP may be developed with a multiemployer bargaining group.[43] However, if a multi-employer unit is established, and employers are not just participating in closely coordinated bargaining, the involved union will have some control on an employer's attempts at withdrawal. On the other hand, the existence of a binding mutual aid pact between two or more employers can have a significant impact on the effectiveness of any strike. Joint action by employers can effectively pressure unions in the same way that concerted action by unions is used to pressure employers.

---

42. *See, e.g.*, Braniff Master Executive Council v. CAB, 693 F.2d 220, 111 L.R.R.M. 3041 (D.C. Cir. 1982).
43. Airline Pilots Ass'n v. CAB, 502 F.2d 453, 456 n.12, 87 L.R.R.M. 2140, 2141 n.12 (D.C. Cir. 1974).

The Strike Plan

A MAP agreement should contain a statement of purpose, which should be limited to labor relations issues. It should set out some system for the exchange of information among its members. Most important, a MAP should describe the assistance and support responsibilities of each member employer. If a multiemployer bargaining association is involved, a MAP might also provide for joint development of bargaining strategy and proposals over common union contracts or shared labor concerns.

The parties to a MAP should strive to maintain a united front in all proposals and positions. The agreement may permit parties to change positions or reach a separate agreement on any matter before a strike occurs. It should, however, provide that if the parties are in agreement on positions when a strike does occur, such agreement constitutes an "association position." There should be a timetable during which the MAP is expected to run and a point at which it may also be suspended. The plan should also provide for termination by agreement of the MAP members.

The plan should specify the situations when the MAP will not apply. For example, will it apply if the parties are not in agreement at the beginning of a strike? Will it apply if a strike or work stoppage occurs at a time other than during negotiations for a new contract with a common union?

Some MAPs provide for nonstruck employers to assume production responsibilities of other members and address the handling of production and distribution costs. Others provide for coordinated lockouts if a multiemployer bargaining association is involved.[44] Obviously, careful advanced planning is necessary to

---

44. *See* text accompanying notes 50 & 51 *infra;* Evening News Ass'n, 166 N.L.R.B. 219, 65 L.R.R.M. 1425 (1967), *aff'd sub nom.* Teamsters Local 372 v. NLRB, 404 F.2d 1159, 70 L.R.R.M. 2061 (6th Cir. 1968), *cert. denied,* 395 U.S. 923, 71 L.R.R.M. 2294 (1969). A lockout, even in the absence of a formal multiemployer bargaining association, is also permissible. *See, e.g.,* Weyerhauser Co., 166 N.L.R.B. 229, 65 L.R.R.M. 1428 (1967), *enforced sub nom.* Western States Regional Council No.3 v. NLRB, 398 F.2d 770, 68 L.R.R.M. 2506 (D.C. Cir. 1968).

Strike Planning

provide for all considerations during a lockout. Further, after a reasonable period of time, such as sixty to ninety days after all operations have been shut down, it may be desirable for the parties to reach agreements with striking unions independently. Therefore, the MAP agreement should be flexible so that members can terminate some or all of their mutual assistance obligations under such circumstances.

The MAP should provide for the assessment of financial penalties against a nonstruck MAP member who does not fulfill its obligations under the mutual assistance pact. Daily liquidated damages should be agreed upon in advance with the amount of the damages correlated to the severity of the failure to comply with the MAP. For example, a greater fine should be charged for a failure to lock out and shut down than for lesser infractions, such as failure to provide temporary replacements.[45] An escalator clause may be attached to a liquidated damages provision that will vary according to a price index such as that published by the U.S. Bureau of Labor Statistics.

One concern is that a mutual assistance pact may be arguably an antitrust violation. Generally, antitrust laws do not regulate labor relations matters.[46] The United States Supreme Court held that a union lacks standing to claim that an employers' association violates the Sherman Act because the union was "neither a consumer nor a competitor in the market in which trade was restrained."[47]

Thus far, antitrust challenges to MAPs have been unsuccessful.[48] One court held that a multiemployer association agreement

---

45. *See also* text accompanying note 68, *infra*.
46. Apex Hosiery Co. v. Leader, 310 U.S. 469, 6 L.R.R.M. 647 (1940); W.P. Kennedy v. Long Island R.R., 319 F.2d 366, 53 L.R.R.M. 2545 (2d Cir.), *cert. denied*, 375 U.S. 830, L.R.R.M. 2313 (1963).
47. Associated General Contractors of California, Inc. v. California State Council of Carpenters, 103 S.Ct. 897, 112 L.R.R.M. 2753 (1983).
48. *See* Airline Pilots Ass'n. v. Civil Aeronautics Board, 502 F.2d 453, 87 L.R.R.M. 2140 (D.C. Cir. 1974), *cert. denied*, 420 U.S. 972, 88 L.R.R.M. 3014 (1975); Railroad Trainmen v. Long Island R.R., 319

The Strike Plan

that permitted selected employers to continue operation with payments to an escrow fund did not violate antitrust laws.[49] Another court held that an agreement between a retail food supplier and a wholesale supplier, whereby the wholesaler lent employees to the retailer on a temporary basis to perform retail meat cutting during an economics strike by the retailer's employees, does not constitute a violation of the antitrust laws.[50] The court reasoned that the continued operation of a business by replacement of economic strikers, that is sanctioned by federal labor law, furthers competition and therefore does not violate antitrust law.[51] To minimize the likelihood of antitrust allegations, however, there must not be any price-fixing, allocation of sales territories or product distribution, or prohibition of competition.

A pitfall of mutual aid pacts is that the employers in the pact may be classified as the allies of one another, and the union will be entitled to take strike action against all of the employers, not just the primary employer. Employers in a MAP must anticipate and plan for such union reactions and should warn subcontractors so that they are not caught unaware.[52]

3.3. Lockouts

A lockout is the withholding of employment by an employer by completely or partially shutting down its business to get con-

---

F.2d 366, 53 L.R.R.M. 2545 (2d Cir.), *cert. denied*, 375 U.S. 830, 54 L.R.R.M. 2313 (1963); Clune v. Publishers Ass'n., 214 F. Supp. 520, 52 L.R.R.M. 2437 (S.D.N.Y.), *aff'd*, 314 F.2d 343, 52 L.R.R.M. 2575 (2d Cir. 1963); Six-Carrier Mutual Aid Pacts, 29 C.A.B. 168 (1959).

49. Mid-America Regional Bargaining Ass'n. v. Will County Carpenters District Council, 106 L.R.R.M. 2489 (N.D. Ill. 1981), *aff'd*, 675 F.2d 881, 110 L.R.R.M. 2143 (7th Cir.), *cert. denied*, 111 L.R.R.M. 2528 (1982).
50. Meat Cutters, Local 576 v. Wetterau Foods, 597 F.2d 133, 101 L.R.R.M. 2171 (8th Cir. 1979).
51. *Id.*, 597 F.2d at 135, 136, 101 L.R.R.M. at 2172, 2173.
52. *See* ch. 7 *infra*.

Strike Planning

cessions or resist demands from its employees.[53] Generally speaking, however, the term lockout applies to a temporary layoff of employees during a strike rather than a total severance of the employment relationship.[54]

The employer's right to lock out may be viewed as the counterpart to the employee's right to strike.[55] Just as employees may go out on strike, the employer may cease furnishing work to employees in an effort to get more desirable contract terms for the employer.[56] But unlike a strike, in a lockout the employer cannot automatically hire permanent replacements for continuing its operation. It must in most instances rely instead on its own supervisors and non-union personnel as temporary replacements.[57]

3.3.1 When a Lockout Is Permissible

To be legal, a lockout must be motivated by a legitimate business reason and not by anti-union animus (a hostile motive) or a desire to avoid altogether the obligation to bargain with the union.[58] In general, it makes no difference whether an employer uses a lockout as an offensive or a defensive weapon.[59]

---

53. C. MORRIS, THE DEVELOPING LABOR LAW 1034 (2d ed. 1983).
54. Associated General Contractors, 138 N.L.R.B. 1432, 51 L.R.R.M. 1215 (1962).
55. Morand Bros. Beverage Co. v. NLRB, 190 F.2d 576, 582, 28 L.R.R.M. 2364, 2368 (7th Cir. 1951); Iron Molder's Local 125 v. Allis-Chalmers Co., 166 Fed. 45, 50 (7th Cir. 1908).
56. Ottawa Silica Co., 197 N.L.R.B. 449, 80 L.R.R.M. 1404 (1972), *enforced*, 482 F.2d 945, 84 L.R.R.M. 2300 (6th Cir. 1973), *cert. denied*, 415 U.S. 916, 85 L.R.R.M. 2465 (1974).
57. Iron Molders Local 125 v. Allis-Chalmers Co., 166 Fed. 45, 52 (7th Cir. 1908); Jeffery-DeWitt Insulator Co. v. NLRB, 91 F.2d 134, 137, 1 L.R.R.M. 634 (4th Cir.), *cert. denied*, 302 U.S. 731, 2 L.R.R.M. 623 (1937).
58. 29 U.S.C. § 158(a) (1), (a) (3); Bedford Cut Stone Co., 235 N.L.R.B. 629, 98 L.R.R.M. 1003 (1978). *Compare* American Ship Building Co. v. NLRB, 380 U.S. 300, 58 L.R.R.M. 2672 (1965) *and* NLRB v. Wire

The Strike Plan

Before instituting a lockout, an employer should ask two questions: (1) What is the business reason for this lockout?[60] (2) Can the union show that this lockout is an attempt to avoid bargaining or is motivated by a desire to destroy the union? It should not impose a lockout if it cannot justify it with a legitimate business reason or if the answer to the second question is "yes."

Lockouts have been found justified by a variety of economic motivations. For example, an employer may lock out employees to protect its property from strike violence.[61] An employer is also permitted to lock out employees to counteract picket lines that prevent deliveries of raw materials to its facility.[62] A lockout is permissible when intermittent work stoppages prevent continuous operation of the employer's facility.[63] An employer who reasonably anticipates a strike may be permitted to lock out its employees to ensure continued operation using supervisors and nonunit employees.[64] Finally, and most important, an employer may lock out employees for the sole purpose of bringing economic pressure to bear on the union and enhance the employer's bargaining position.[65] However, an employer commits an unfair

---

Products Mfg. Corp., 484 F.2d 760, 84 L.R.R.M. 2038 (7th Cir. 1973) *with* NLRB v. Brown Food Store, 380 U.S. 278, 58 L.R.R.M. 2663 (1965).

59. Delhi-Taylor Refining Div., Hess Oil & Chemical Corp., 167 N.L.R.B. 115, 65 L.R.R.M. 1744 (1967), *enforced sub nom.* Hess Oil & Chemical Co. v. NLRB, 415 F.2d 440, 72 L.R.R.M. 2132 (5th Cir. 1969) *cert. denied,* 397 U.S. 916, 73 L.R.R.M. 2537 (1970). Even a partial lockout has met with Board approval provided all other tests are met. Laclede Gas Co.,187 N.L.R.B. 243, 75 L.R.R.M. 1483 (1970).
60. *See, e.g.,* Shelly & Anderson Furniture Mfg. Co. v. NLRB, 497 F.2d 1200, 1203, 86 L.R.R.M. 2619, 2622 (9th Cir. 1974) (lockout violated 8(a) (3) and (1) of NLRA because it was punitive and was not caused by economic or production necessities).
61. Link-Belt Co., 26 N.L.R.B. 227, 6 L.R.R.M. 565 (1940).
62. Hobbs, Wall & Co., 30 N.L.R.B. 1027, 8 L.R.R.M. 107 (1941).
63. International Shoe Co., 93 N.L.R.B. 907, 27 L.R.R.M. 1504 (1951).
64. WGN of Colorado, Inc., 199 N.L.R.B. 1053, 81 L.R.R.M. 1369 (1972).
65. American Ship Building Co. v. NLRB, 380 U.S. 300, 58 L.R.R.M. 2672 (1965).

Strike Planning

labor practice by threatening a lock out to pressure a union into bargaining with a multiemployer association with whom the union had not agreed to bargain.[66]

In the context of multiemployer associations, the employers may protect the integrity of the association by locking out all of their employees in response to a selective or whipsaw strike against one of the association's members.[67] A court will compel a member of an employer association, to whom it has assigned its bargaining rights, to comply with a lockout ordered by the association in aid of negotiations for a new collective bargaining agreement.[68] This same rule applies to employers who have established a common interest through the use of a MAP.[69]

3.3.2 Impermissible Lockouts

If an employer locks out employees to avoid bargaining on mandatory subjects, the lockout is illegal.[70] Also, an employer cannot lock out employees in support of bad faith bargaining positions.[71] Finally, the employer must be able to show signifi-

---

66. Siebler Heating & Air Conditioning, Inc., 219 N.L.R.B. 1124, 90 L.R.R.M. 1239 (1975).
67. NLRB v. Truck Drivers Local 449 (Buffalo Linen Supply Co.), 353 U.S. 87, 39 L.R.R.M. 2603 (1957); Duluth Bottling Ass'n, 48 N.L.R.B. 1335, 12 L.R.R.M. 151 (1943).
68. Construction Industry Contractors v. Donald M. Drake Co., 93 L.R.R.M. 2924 (W.D. Wash. 1976).
69. Evening News Ass'n, 166 N.L.R.B. 219, 65 L.R.R.M. 1425 (1967), *aff'd sub nom.* Teamsters Local 372 v. NLRB, 404 F.2d 1159, 70 L.R.R.M. 2061 (6th Cir. 1968), *cert. denied*, 395 U.S. 923, 71 L.R.R.M. 2294 (1969).
70. NLRB v. Rapid Bindery, 293 F.2d 170, 48 L.R.R.M. 2658 (2d Cir. 1961); Scott Mfg. Co., 133 N.L.R.B. 1012, 48 L.R.R.M. 1784 (1961), *enforced sub nom.* NLRB v. U.S. Air Conditioning Corp., 302 F.2d 280, 50 L.R.R.M. 2151 (1st Cir. 1962).
71. Schmutz Foundry and Machine Co., 251 N.L.R.B. 1494, 105 L.R.R.M. 1491 (1980), *enforced*, 678 F.2d 657, 110 L.R.R.M. 2425 (6th Cir. 1982); Vore Cinema Corp., 254 N.L.R.B. 1195, 106 L.R.R.M. 1349 (1981).

The Strike Plan

cant business reason, such as economic justification, before locking out. For example, an employer that locked out union employees when their union had struck other employers that were members of a multiemployer bargaining association commits an unfair labor practice when it is not a member of the multiemployer bargaining association[72] and the labor dispute only had an indirect impact on the employer's bargaining position.

3.3.3 Pre-impasse Versus Post-impasse

If the parties are at impasse, a lockout is permissible if the tests set forth above are met.[73] The same rule appears to apply in the case of a pre-impasse lockout, although the employer must be aware that its business justification will be scrutinized closely.[74] In one case, the NLRB found a lockout justified when the union had engaged in work stoppages in the past and was threatening to engage in a strike during the employer's busy season.[75] Acceptable justification may not be so easily demonstrated in other cases. For example, a lockout after only two negotiation sessions and a failure to respond to a union's counteroffer was held to be evidence of bad-faith bargaining.[76]

---

72. David Friedland Painting Co., 158 N.L.R.B. 571, 62 L.R.R.M. 1085 (1966), *enforced*, 377 F.2d 983, 65 L.R.R.M. 2119 (3d Cir. 1967).
73. American Ship Building v. NLRB, 380 U.S. 300, 58 L.R.R.M. 2672 (1965).
74. Lane v. NLRB, 418 F.2d 1208, 72 L.R.R.M. 2439 (D.C. Cir. 1969) (use of pre-impasse lockout); NLRB v. Dalton Brick & Tile Corp., 301 F.2d 886, 49 L.R.R.M. 3099 (5th Cir. 1962).
75. Darling & Co., 171 N.L.R.B. 801, 68 L.R.R.M. 1133 (1968), *enforced sub nom.*, Lane v. NLRB, 418 F.2d 1208, 72 L.R.R.M. 2439 (D.C. Cir. 1969). The NLRB has not indicated that it draws any analytical distinctions between an impasse during negotiation of a first contract and an impasse following negotiation of subsequent contracts. Tomco Communications, Inc., 220 N.L.R.B. 636, 90 L.R.R.M. 1321 (1975), *enforcement denied sub nom.*, NLRB v. Tomco Communications Inc., 567 F.2d 871, 97 L.R.R.M. 2660 (9th Cir. 1978).
76. Edward J. Alexander, d/b/a Strand Theatre, 235 N.L.R.B. 1500, 98 L.R.R.M. 1225 (1978), *enforced sub nom.*, NLRB v. Alexander, 595 F.2d

Strike Planning

In deciding upon a pre- or post-impasse lockout, the employer must not forget to give proper notices under section 8(d) of the National Labor Relations Act[77] if the collective bargaining agreement has not expired.[78] The notice requirements under section 8(d) are the same requirements that a union must comply with before calling a strike.[79] Under section 8(d) a party desiring termination or modification of an existing collective bargaining agreement must send out appropriate written notices, continue the contract in full force during this cooling off period, and offer to meet and confer with the other party for the purpose of negotiating a new contract or a contract containing proposed modifications. During the sixty-day notice period (ninety days for health care institutions) there can be no lockout.

3.3.4 Lockout: Use of Replacements

It is not yet clear to what extent the employer can continue operations using replacements following a lockout. An employer that is part of a multiemployer association engaged in an association-wide lockout can hire temporary replacements.[80] The employer is permitted to respond to the inquiries of locked-out employees by informing them: (1) that they cannot return to their jobs as members of the striking union against whose whipsaw strike the lockout was invoked; (2) that the employer can only use temporary nonunion employees as replacements during the lockout; and (3) that if the locked-out union employees be-

---

454, 101 L.R.R.M. 2115 (8th Cir.), *cert. denied,* 444 U.S. 899, 102 L.R.R.M. 2441(1979).
77. 29 U.S.C. § 158 (d).
78. Edward J. Alexander, d/b/a Strand Theatre, 235 N.L.R.B. 1500, 98 L.R.R.M. 1225 (1978), *enforced sub nom.* NLRB v. Alexander, 595 F.2d 454, 101 L.R.R.M. 2115 (8th Cir.) *cert. denied,* 444 U.S. 899, 102 L.R.R.M. 2441 (1979).
79. *See* ch. 2 *supra.*
80. NLRB v. Brown Food Store, 380 U.S. 278, 58 L.R.R.M. 2663 (1965).

The Strike Plan

came nonunion members of the labor market, it might be possible for them to be hired temporarily for the duration of the lockout.[81] These statements are permitted so long as they recite "existing facts in the light of applicable law."[82] The employer may not, however, promise the union member a job if he resigns from the union during a lockout nor may he induce the employee to do so.[83] It is uncertain whether the employer can hire permanent replacements in such circumstances.[84]

The single employer apparently may hire temporary replacements for locked-out employees if the lockout occurs after impasse.[85] However, some courts draw distinctions as to whether the lockout was offensive or defensive and will not permit hiring replacements in offensive lockouts.[86] Moreover, neither the Board nor the courts have approved the use of permanent replacements by single employers for locked-out employees under any conditions.[87]

---

81. NLRB v. Martin A. Gleason, Inc., 534 F.2d 466, 472-73, 91 L.R.R.M. 2682, 2690-91 (2d Cir. 1976).
82. *Id.*
83. *Id.* at 2692.
84. NLRB v. Brown Food Store, 380 U.S. 278, 293, 58 L.R.R.M. 2663 (1965).
85. Inter-Collegiate Press v. NLRB, 486 F.2d 837, 84 L.R.R.M. 2562 (8th Cir. 1973), *cert. denied sub nom.*, Bookbinders Local 60 v. NLRB, 416 U.S. 938, 85 L.R.R.M. 2924 (1974); Johns-Manville Products Corp., 223 N.L.R.B. 1317, 92 L.R.R.M. 1103 (1976), *enforcement denied*, 557 F.2d 1126, 96 L.R.R.M. 2010 (5th Cir. 1977), *cert. denied sub nom.*, Oil Chemical & Atomic Workers v. Johns-Manville Products Corp., 436 U.S. 956, 98 L.R.R.M. 2617 (1978); WGN of Colorado, Inc., 199 N.L.R.B. 1053, 81 L.R.R.M. 1369 (1972); NLRB General Counsel Advice Memo No. 5-CA-11747, 104 L.R.R.M. 1167 (1980).
86. Inland Trucking Co. v. NLRB, 440 F.2d 562, 76 L.R.R.M. 2929 (7th Cir., 1971) *cert. denied*, 404 U.S. 858, 78 L.R.R.M. 2465 (1971).
87. Kelly-Goodwin Hardware Co., 269 N.L.R.B. No.10, 115 L.R.R.M. 1240 (1984); Loomis Courier Service Inc., 235 N.L.R.B. 534, 98 L.R.R.M. 1083 (1978), *enforcement denied*, 595 F.2d 491, 101 L.R.R.M. 2450 (9th Cir. 1979).

3.4 Implementing the Final Offer

When strike momentum seems to be building, an employer has two strategic options regarding terms and conditions of employment. It can maintain the status quo or it can announce its intentions to implement management's final offer. If done properly, this announcement can prevent a strike, or diminish its size and strength, by educating employees as to what the employer's bargaining position is (something that may not have been made clear by the union) and by assisting employees in weighing the pros and cons of striking.

Implementing a final offer is not something that should be done casually. A determination must be made as to whether the employer has the legal basis for implementing the final offer. The employer should also carefully prepare a communications plan for announcing the final offer. Timing is critical.

3.4.1 Final Offer Prerequisites

There are stringent legal requirements that must be satisfied before an employer can implement a final offer. Failure to comply with these requirements can result in unfair labor practice charges which, in turn, would convert an economic strike into an unfair labor practice strike.[88]

The prerequisites to implementing a final offer are: (1) expiration of the prior union contract, (2) good faith bargaining, and (3) a bargaining impasse on mandatory subjects of bargaining.[89] The most difficult prerequisites to define are (2) and (3) because decisions are made on a case-by-case basis. A discussion of when a contract expires, including automatic renewals and extension agreements, is contained elsewhere in this book.[90]

---

88. See ch. 9 *infra*.
89. Carpenter Sprinkler Corp. v. NLRB, 605 F.2d 60, 64, 102 L.R.R.M. 2199 (2d Cir. 1979); Seattle-First National Bank, 267 N.L.R.B. No. 142, 114 L.R.R.M. 1072 (1983).
90. See ch. 2 *supra*.

3.4.2 Good Faith Requirement

The inquiry into whether good faith bargaining has occurred consists of a determination whether there was a sincere effort to reach agreement.[91] Good faith bargaining requires that the employer "participate actively in the deliberations so as to indicate a present intention to find a basis for agreement."[92] This implies both an open mind and a sincere desire to reach an agreement, based on the total conduct of the parties.[93]

The NLRB will not find impasse, but instead a refusal to bargain in good faith, if it concludes that the employer is merely going through the motions of bargaining. Known as "surface bargaining," this practice may include: predetermined and inflexible positions towards such subjects as union security and merit increases; dilatory tactics in scheduling bargaining meetings; arbitrary withdrawal of previously agreed-upon provisions; and submission of significant new proposals in an advanced stage in the negotiations.[94] However, tendering a counterproposal that is claimed to be predictably unacceptable is not alone enough to justify a finding of lack of good faith if the proposal does not foreclose future discussion.[95]

---

91. Chicago & Northwest Railroad v. United Transportation Union, 402 U.S. 570, 77 L.R.R.M. 2337 (1971); NLRB v. American National Ins. Co., 343 U.S. 395, 30 L.R.R.M. 2147 (1952).
92. NLRB v. Montgomery Ward & Co., 133 F.2d 676, 686, 12 L.R.R.M. 508 (9th Cir. 1943); Benson Produce Co., 71 N.L.R.B. 888, 19 L.R.R.M. 1060 (1946).
93. NLRB v. Virginia Electric & Power Co., 314 U.S. 469, 9 L.R.R.M. 405 (1941).
94. Yearbook House, 223 N.L.R.B. 1456, 92 L.R.R.M. 1191 (1976); Valley Oil Co., 210 N.L.R.B. 370, 86 L.R.R.M. 1351 (1974); Wheeling Pacific Co., 151 N.L.R.B. 1192, 58 L.R.R.M. 1580 (1965); Moore Drop Forging Co., 144 N.L.R.B. 165, 54 L.R.R.M. 1024 (1963); Duro Fittings Co., 121 N.L.R.B. 377, 42 L.R.R.M. 1368 (1958).
95. *See, e.g.*, NLRB v. Tomco Communications, Inc., 567 F.2d 871, 883, 97 L.R.R.M. 2660 (9th Cir. 1978), *denying enforcement to* 220 N.L.R.B. 636, 90 L.R.R.M. 1321 (1975).

3.4.3 Impasse Identification

Impasse is a difficult status to identify. Impasse is generally considered to have occurred when collective bargaining reaches a stalemate and the parties, despite their good faith, have exhausted the prospects of reaching an agreement.[96] Generally, at this point both parties must be unwilling to compromise,[97] although the mere expression of intransigence is not in and of itself controlling.

The courts and the Board review, on a case-by-case basis, whether a legal impasse exists. Cases are brought to the Board when the union files a bad faith bargaining charge under the Act. If the employer disagrees with the Board's decision, it appeals the decision to the courts.

To determine whether an impasse has been reached, the Board considers the parties' bargaining history, their good faith, the length and frequency of the negotiations, the importance of the issues, and the parties' contemporaneous understanding of the state of the negotiations.[98] Simply meeting once or twice is not sufficient to assert impasse, especially if the employer and the union have a history of lengthy, difficult negotiations.[99]

There is no impasse if the employer insists that the union agree to items that are not mandatory subjects of bargaining.[100] Al-

---

96. Saunders House v. N.L.R.B., 719 F.2d 683, 114 L.R.R.M. 2977, 2979 (3d Cir. 1983); Taft Broadcasting Co., 163 N.L.R.B. 475, 64 L.R.R.M. 1386 (1967), *enforced sub nom.*, American Federation of Television & Radio Artists v. NLRB, 395 F.2d 622, 67 L.R.R.M. 3032 (D.C. Cir. 1968).
97. Huck Mfg. Co. v. NLRB, 693 F.2d 1176, 1186, 112 L.R.R.M. 2245 (5th Cir. 1982).
98. Saunders House v. NLRB, 719 F.2d 683, 114 N.L.R.B. 2977, 2979 (3d Cir. 1983); Seattle-First National Bank, 267 N.L.R.B. No. 142, 106 L.R.R.M. 2621 (1983).
99. Carpenter Sprinkler Corp. v. NLRB, 605 F.2d 60, 102 L.R.R.M. 2199 (2d Cir. 1979); Seattle-First National Bank, 267 N.L.R.B. No. 142, 106 LRRM 2621 (1983).
100. NLRB v. Wooster Div. of Borg-Warner Corp., 356 U.S. 342, 42 L.R.R.M. 2034 (1958). *See also* National Fresh Fruit & Vegetable Company v. NLRB, 565 F.2d 1331, 97 L.R.R.M. 2427 (5th Cir. 1978).

The Strike Plan

though an employer may have pursued a nonmandatory bargaining subject in negotiations, it cannot *insist* upon it to impasse.[101] Consequently, the employer should delete all nonmandatory subjects of bargaining from its final offer, if it wants to declare an impasse should the union refuse the offer.[102] Examples of nonmandatory subjects of bargaining include: selection of a bargaining representative,[103] indemnification agreements or bonds,[104] internal union affairs,[105] and settlement of unfair labor practice charges.[106] By contrast, mandatory subjects of bargaining include basic rates of pay,[107] pensions,[108] group health insurance,[109] and work hours.[110]

---

101. NLRB v. Wooster Div. of Borg-Warner Corp., 356 U.S. 342, 42 L.R.R.M. 2034 (1958).
102. If the employer fails to do this, a lawful impasse does not occur and the employer's implementation of the final offer would be an unfair labor practice. Huck Mfg. Co. v. NLRB, 693 F.2d 1176, 112 L.R.R.M. 2245 (5th Cir. 1982). If employees then strike, the strike would be an unfair labor practice strike. Carpenter Sprinkler Corp. v. NLRB, 605 F.2d 60, 102 L.R.R.M. 2199 (2d Cir. 1979).
103. NLRB v. American Compress Warehouse, 350 F.2d 365, 59 L.R.R.M. 2739 (5th Cir. 1965), *cert. denied*, 382 U.S. 982, 61 L.R.R.M. 2147 (1966); Racine Die Casting Company, 192 N.L.R.B. 529, 77 L.R.R.M. 1818 (1971).
104. Scripto Manufacturing Company, 136 N.L.R.B. 411, 9 L.R.R.M. 156 (1941); Arlington Asphalt Company, 136 N.L.R.B. 742, 49 L.R.R.M. 1831 (1962), *enforced sub nom.*, NLRB v. Davison, 318 F.2d 550, 53 L.R.R.M. 2462 (4th Cir. 1963).
105. NLRB v. Darlington Veneer Company, 236 F.2d 85, 38 L.R.R.M. 2574 (4th Cir. 1956); N.L.R.B. v. Corsicana Cotton Mills, 178 F.2d 344, 24 L.R.R.M. 2494 (5th Cir. 1949).
106. Stackpole Components Company, 232 N.L.R.B. 723, 96 L.R.R.M. 1324 (1977); Griffin Inns, 229 N.L.R.B. 199, 95 L.R.R.M. 1072 (1977).
107. 29 U.S.C. § 158(d); Gray Line Inc., 209 N.L.R.B. 88, 85 L.R.R.M. 1328 (1974), *enforced in part and reversed in part*, 512 F.2d 992, 89 L.R.R.M. 2192 (D.C. Cir. 1975); Braswell Motor Freight Lines Inc., 141 N.L.R.B. 1154, 52 L.R.R.M. 1467 (1963) (overtime), *supplemental opinion*, 154 N.L.R.B. 101, 59 L.R.R.M. 1711 (1965), *enforced sub nom.* Teamsters Local Unions v. NLRB, 370 F.2d 226, 63 L.R.R.M. 2288 (D.C. Cir. 1966).
108. Inland Steel Company, 77 N.L.R.B. 1, 21 L.R.R.M. 1310, *enforced*, 170 F.2d 247, 22 L.R.R.M. 2506 (7th Cir. 1948), *cert. denied*, 336 U.S. 960, 24 L.R.R.M. 2019 (1949).

3.4.4 Communicating the Final Offer

Once the employer suspects a bargaining impasse exists and does not wish to continue the status quo, it should consider publicizing its intentions to implement its final offer. This can be most effective if a strike has not yet occurred.

First the employer must review its intended last offer to make sure that it does not contain any nonmandatory subjects of bargaining. Second, the employer should identify the offer by number or by date, e.g., "management's eighth offer" or "management's October 24, 1984 offer." This will avoid any confusion as to what offer is being discussed. Finally, the employer should consider sending a cover letter to the union that recites, in a factual manner, the following details:

1. collective bargaining history, including frequency and length of meetings;
2. number of proposals put forward by management;
3. significant compromises agreed upon by the parties;
4. correction of any untrue statements made by the union;
5. highlights of the latest offer and how well it compares with other labor agreements in the industry;
6. warnings about the disadvantages of a strike, such as lost income;
7. statement that the offer is management's final offer;
8. statement that the offer be accepted by a certain date or management will assume the parties are still at impasse, the offer is revoked, and that it cannot be subsequently automatically accepted by the union without reoffer; and
9. notice that management has discretion to implement the final offer after the deadline date.

Of the above items for such a letter, items 7, 8, and 9 are most important.

---

109. W. W. Cross & Company v. NLRB, 174 F.2d 875, 24 L.R.R.M. 2068 (1st Cir. 1949).
110. Meatcutters v. Jewel Tea Company, 381 U.S. 676, 59 L.R.R.M. 2376 (1965); Timken Roller Bearing Company, 70 N.L.R.B. 500, 18 L.R.R.M.

The Strike Plan

Copies of the cover letter or a summary memorandum should be sent to all employees so that they understand what the employer's bargaining position is and what is likely to happen if the union does not respond to the final offer. The letter must be factually accurate and complete. It should not contain promises of rewards or threats of punishment that amount to an effort to bargain directly with employees rather than the union.[111]

If employees have an opportunity to consider what has taken place during collective bargaining and what is contained in management's final offer, they may be less inclined to want to strike, or, if the union declares a strike, to support the strike. Moreover, if the employer can implement its final offer prior to strike action, employees may decide that they are better off without a strike. Remember, however, that in implementing a final offer the employer may change only those terms and conditions of employment that were the subject of collective bargaining and were part of its final offer.[112] For example, the employer cannot increase wages more than it provided in its last offer, nor can it add or subtract other benefits.[113]

3.5 Health Care Employer: Special Considerations

Although a health care employer will have advance notice of a strike under section 8(g) of the Act,[114] it should not have a false

---

1370 (1946), *enforcement denied on other grounds*, 161 F.2d 949, 20 L.R.R.M. 2204 (6th Cir. 1947).
111. J.I. Case Co. v. NLRB, 321 U.S. 332, 14 L.R.R.M. 501 (1944); K-D Mfg. Co., 169 N.L.R.B. 57, 67 L.R.R.M. 1140 (1968), *enforced*, 419 F.2d 467, 73 L.R.R.M. 2013 (5th Cir. 1969); Flowers Baking Co., 161 N.L.R.B. 1429, 63 L.R.R.M. 1462 (1966).
112. NLRB v. Katz, 369 U.S. 736, 50 L.R.R.M. 2177 (1962).
113. NLRB v. Katz, 369 U.S. 736 (1962); Huck Mfg. Co. v. NLRB, 693 F.2d 1176, 112 L.R.R.M. 2245 (5th Cir. 1982).
114. *See* ch. 2 *supra*.

sense of security or rely on last minute planning. A hospital or nursing home's medical responsibilities require the highest standards of care and treatment, which must be met at all times. If this is not possible, consider eliminating unnecessary services and reducing the patient census.

3.5.1 Public Relations

Public relations and community image may be most vital to the health care employer. Perceived health care hazards may cause irreparable damage to its reputation. If members of the public believe that a facility is unable to operate safely, they will not seek admission or stay at the facility. The patient census may be cut dramatically.

Be sure that patients and their families are fully aware of your position upon the advent of a strike. They should understand what you are trying to accomplish, that you are *being struck*, and that you are not creating a strike. You should be positive and cooperative with all concerned.

3.5.2 Physicians' Support

Physicians have a special place in a health care organization. However, they may feel that they can best contribute to the facility by direct intervention with employees. Despite their abilities, they must be counselled about their proper role. The facility's management must speak with one voice and control all transactions so that the strike's length is minimized and unfair labor practices are avoided.

Internal public relations with physicians is critical. Keep them on your side. Doctors should be assured that you will provide adequate levels of care. You should advise them of the controls that management has implemented.

The Strike Plan

3.5.3 Licenses/Registration

Licensing requirements must be met at all times. You must be sure to provide proper levels of care and make every effort to ensure that staff members qualified to provide such care are performing appropriate services. However, merely satisfying minimum levels is not sufficient for effective patient relations. Care consistent with your established standards must be maintained. If this proves impossible, patients should be transferred to other facilities or admissions should be restricted.

3.5.4 Professionals and Strikes

Do not delude yourself that because you have white collar workers operating in a health care facility, there will not be a strike or trouble will not arise. A strike is an economic war. Tempers can flare and bring out the worst in individuals. When hiding in the anonymity of the union picket line, employees can do surprising things. Be ready for problems and do not expect timid employee reactions.

3.5.5 Operations Levels

Setting work priorities is vital in health care. Tiered planning with specified levels of program operation should be maintained and established on departmental levels. A matrix planning system may be an acceptable way to accomplish this requirement. (See Appendix 3-E.) Decide what level of strike participation will permit a specific level of services. As a strike draws near, carefully monitor the number and types of patients being admitted, so that you can deal with the patient load adequately if a strike occurs. Remember that medical staff can, if necessary, perform some nursing functions, such as drawing blood, administering intravenous injections, or giving medication.

Be certain that your plan accounts for all organizational units at each operational level (full service, elective surgery only, or full shutdown). Develop staff reorganization plans for administrative, personnel, accounting, nursing, dietary, housekeeping, laboratory, radiology, laundry, maintenance, and engineering departments. Pay particular attention to vital services, such as the emergency room or intensive care. If you use an outside ambulance service, verify whether there will be any picket line problems. Arrange back-up service as needed.

3.5.6 Volunteer and Family Help

Carefully review licensing requirements and determine areas where volunteers may assist. Be certain that you comply with wage and hour requirements. Pay special attention to family circumstances. If relatives are willing to help with minor needs, check for regulatory problems. Training may be required for some areas, so be sure basic orientation is readily available.

3.5.7 Chaplain

Be certain the chaplain understands the management position. Although the chaplain should not be forced to support the employer program, be certain that negative sentiments regarding your position are not fostered in the community.

3.5.8 Drug Security

Immediately before a strike occurs, and again when it commences, re-verify pharmaceutical controls and inventories. This is a high priority item to protect against licensing problems and theft.

3.5.9 Subcontracting

With the exception of nursing care, most services can be easily subcontracted. This is especially true for laundry, dietary, maintenance, and other routine functions. Furthermore, there may be nursing pools in your vicinity that can supply trained and experienced staff. The options available regarding this resource may be surprising.

3.5.10 Dietary and Other Service Departments

Pay special attention to cleanliness and dietary requirements. Patients' food must remain nourishing and appealing. You may want to request that ambulatory patients take meals in the hospital cafeteria. Also, consider offering free meals to employees who work odd hours during the strike.

Basic service, courtesy, and cleanliness must be stressed. Housekeeping, laundry, and maintenance functions must be maintained at high levels. These departments are usually the easiest to subcontract.

3.5.11 Laboratory and Radiology

Protection of the extraordinarily expensive laboratory and radiology equipment is vital to maintain service and avoid exorbitant repair or replacement costs. To avoid apprehension about the security of extremely sensitive patient records, the system should be reviewed.

3.5.12 Patient Amenities

Do not ignore the need to keep patients comfortable. For example, you can improve patient comfort with television service in each room at nominal cost. Minimum survival is not an acceptable standard. Treat this as a priority. Seek family help with entertainment options, such as videotapes, games, routing of periodical literature, and snacks.

3.5.13 Visitors

Unlike a factory, a health facility's daily routine includes numerous outside visitors. Guests are part of patient convalescence. You cannot permit a strike to interfere with visitors' convenient access to the facility. However, be sure that thorough, but not confusing or imposing, security precautions and visitation regulations are strictly followed.

3.6 Public Sector Employer Considerations

Government employers face a wide range of problems unique to the public sector. A strike will raise strategic, regulatory, and constitutional issues. Consultation with special counsel experienced in public sector labor relations is usually helpful.

3.6.1 The Public and Politicians

For the public employer, the community members are the shareholders *and* clients. Politicians will want action that pleases the public. An absolute premium is to be placed on satisfying the public that it is being taken care of and that the government is not acting improperly.

3.6.2 Security

Safety and security present special problems for the public sector employer. Because uniformed personnel are often union

The Strike Plan

members, they must be carefully monitored to be sure that they uphold the law regarding striking employees.

As political winds are fickle, be cautious on how much of the details of your strike plan is presented to elected officials. Although elected officials must be kept informed and made a part of the broad policy decision making process, you should carefully weigh the consequences before making them part of policy implementation. Unions have considerable political influence and may try to obtain information from such sources.

3.6.3 Essential Services

In designating service priorities, certain areas are obviously essential. The public employer must pay special attention to police, fire, sanitation, and some health care services. These areas are usually budget "footballs" as well.

The relative priorities of other services may be seasonal. Trash removal is more important in the summer. Highway department work may be more significant in winter months, because of snow removal. Parks department services are needed more in the summer. Pay special attention to such variations.

3.6.4 Supervisors and Unions

Public sector labor relations is a conglomeration of diverse systems. Some states by statute [115] or case law [116] permit supervisors to be represented by unions. This dramatically increases the problem of dual loyalty beyond that experienced by private sector employers. If supervisors are in bargaining units, strike planning is extremely complicated. Consider advising them of their resignation or "financial core" membership options.[117]

---

115. *See, e.g.*, Wis. Stat. § 111.70(3)(d) (1974 and Supp. 1983), *as amended*.
116. *See, e.g.*, Municipality of Metropolitan Seattle v. Department of Labor & Industries, 88 Wash. 2d 925, 568 P.2d 775 (1977).
117. *See* ch. 4 *infra*.

3.6.5 State Law

Federal law regulates public employers in only a few matters, such as equal employment requirements. You must therefore carefully review your state and local employment law requirements. Study the wage and hour statute and collective bargaining statute. Special state statutory or constitutional employment protections may exist for public employees. You must scrutinize such provisions.

3.6.6 Illegal Actions

Public employee strikes are illegal in many jurisdictions.[118] Yet strikes may still occur, and you may still need to seek injunctive relief immediately. Absent misconduct, however, picketing is usually not proscribed by strike prohibitions, as it is viewed as a first amendment free speech right.

Injunctive relief should be sought only after careful analysis. Local judges may be highly political on labor matters and may tend to inject themselves in local disputes. Carefully verify what your law prohibits and permits. For example, not all state law injunction constraints, such as a "Little Norris-LaGuardia Act," apply to public employment labor disputes. Your strike plan should be prepared for such contingencies.

---

118. *See, e.g.*, Mo. Ann. Stat. § 105.530 (Vernon 1967 and Supp. 1983); Alaska Stat. § 23.40200(b) (1972); Ala. Code 37 § 450(3) (1971 Supp.); Nev. Rev. Stat. § 288.230(2) (1969).

Appendix 3-A

(Date)
[Employer]   Personal and Confidential

_____
_____

    Re: [Employer] Strike Planning

Dear _____:

    To respond to our recent discussion on [date], I have drafted this letter to provide some initial considerations for strike planning. Hopefully, your labor relations situation with the [International Union], Local Union [No.____] will not culminate in a strike. However, despite your best efforts at the bargaining table, impasse may be inevitable. Therefore, it is important to start properly preparing for a strike situation. Being ready for a strike may also help you achieve your bargaining goals with the union.

    I suggest that you immediately review basic strike planning guidelines. I recommend that you consider at least the following areas:

    1. <u>Lockout.</u> Consider a lockout. This weapon can be most effective. It is, however, a serious course of action that must be cautiously weighed as an option. Also, special rules apply and must be carefully studied.

    2. <u>Service/Production.</u> Immediately verify all long term and short term <u>(service or production)</u>

Strike Planning

requirements. Talk to contracting parties and establish whether there are any penalties or contract forfeiture possibilities for late production. Do your agreements have a force majeure clause to excuse performance level changes? Also, advise such parties of potential problems that may arise if a strike occurs.

3. <u>Subcontracting.</u> Identify all acceptable subcontracting sources. Brief subcontractors on the possibility of a strike and the possibility of short notice work assignments. Beware of "ally" problems (i.e., extending the strike to other employers). Verify any potential union problems (e.g., picket line loyalty) with subcontractors.

4. <u>Management Team.</u> Identify key managers and supervisors for briefing purposes. Conduct a preliminary briefing in the near future to advise them of the collective bargaining situation and your position. This will also assist key personnel in developing a management team perspective.

5. <u>Internal Communications.</u> Develop a communication system and network for employees regarding strike issues, strike rights, and polling of expected strike participants. (<u>See</u> enclosed documents.)

6. <u>Strike Planning Committee.</u> Establish a permanent Strike Planning Committee for management. Because of the size of your organization, it may be necessary to overlap it with the bargaining committee. You should, however, avoid this if possible. The Strike Planning Committee should be responsible for maintaining operations and not for collective bargaining.

7. <u>Strike Headquarters.</u> Identify a central and safe location for strike headquarters. It must be well secured but readily accessible to the primary work place. Ensure

The Strike Plan

that necessary facilities for key personnel (food, sanitation, bedding, etc.) are available. Consider installing unlisted telephone numbers prior to a strike situation.

8. Security. Review security at all work locations immediately and begin coordination with local police regarding the need for regular patrols if a strike occurs. This should not be done formally until a strike is imminent. At this point be sure you talk informally with your local police officials so they know that collective bargaining is starting to deteriorate. Let them know about a concern for vandalism. If you establish a good rapport prior to the strike, it will be helpful later.

Also, be sure to speak to a local security company regarding strike protection. Like any other "insurance policy," such protection adds more cost. But if a situation develops that calls for it, you will be glad you have it. Typically, such companies not only provide physical security, but will assist in developing evidence and furnish support in damage actions and criminal prosecutions.

Finally, develop a strike incident report system. Do this in advance. Have cameras (videotapes are quite helpful) ready. Evidence may be needed in damage actions or in seeking injunctive relief.

9. Strike Insurance. Do you have strike insurance? Have you considered this option? Policies are available and may help offset financial losses during a strike.

10. Public Spokesperson/Publicity. Designate a single spokesperson for communications with the media. One spokesperson should be used for all purposes. The individual should be articulate and generally experienced in responding to media inquiries. You may wish to use your attorney. Remember, the media is

Strike Planning

looking for a sensational story, so be deliberate and reticent in public communications without appearing evasive.

11. Employee Schedules. Immediately review all employee work schedules. Be sure you have an exact understanding on expected employee attendance during the potential strike. Please note that you are not allowed to cancel accrued and scheduled vacation once a strike occurs.

12. Temporary Replacements. Begin looking into possible sources of temporary employees in the area. Be sure that you and your personnel director have streamlined all training and hiring procedures for new employees without sacrificing essential quality and production requirements. Be careful to establish proper wage rates. You probably should alert possible personnel sources now. Hiring notices must clearly indicate temporary employment status unless you have made a considered determination to hire permanent replacements.

13. Permanent Replacements. Determine early whether you will use permanent or temporary replacements. The rights and responsibilities vary greatly.

14. Work Priorities. Assign priorities to your work requirements. Identify what you need to stockpile and do so now. This requires inventory review of supplies and products. Also, for planning purposes, identify minimally acceptable levels of necessary production for each of your contracts. Be sure that your department heads help you in this planning and that they are frank and truthful about workload requirements.

15. Work Suspension. Identify any work that can be suspended for the short term with minimal cost

The Strike Plan

consequences (e.g., basic maintenance of certain work areas, routine cleanliness, marginal or long-term contract needs, keeping current on minor recordkeeping or filing, etc.). However, be certain no regulatory requirements are ignored.

16. <u>Skills Inventory.</u> Review the work qualifications of all employees (management or other nonunit employees) and determine which employees out of your total work pool have the capabilities (and any necessary certifications) to perform struck work. Also, identify how much training will be needed for which employees. If they are union members, consider union discipline if they work during the strike.

17. <u>Nonunit Workforce Reassignment.</u> In assessing work priorities of nonunit employees, identify any work that can be delayed or reduced. Also, identify how these employees may be reassigned to handle work needs. Further, do not limit subcontracting considerations to struck work, but also consider nonunit work and the ability to move nonunit employees to struck work if necessary. Determine wage and compensation systems (e.g., bonus and overtime options or requirements).

18. <u>Supplies.</u> Study all supply and maintenance needs to determine requirements and stockpiling potential and logistics. Determine how deliveries and pick-ups will be handled in the event of a strike. Make informal and confidential contacts with all suppliers and transporters to ascertain their willingness and ability to make deliveries during a strike. Remember that you will likely have picket lines established and this could present problems. Keep accurate notes on your conversations with other companies and consider following up with a confirmation letter. Also, identify whether you have the ability to pick up materials at other locations and establish a centralized "drop point" or staging area

Strike Planning

away from the facility. If suppliers refuse to cross picket lines, this could alleviate problems.

19. Strike Log. Establish a formal documentation system in case a strike occurs. Such a "strike log" will be essential in documenting occurrences as they arise, provide for immediate submission of log entries to a central source for review and maintenance. This will provide essential information in any future litigation.

20. Management and Communications. Be sure that you consult with your managers and supervisors to ensure that they are part of the planning process. On the one hand, you do not wish to take unnecessary chances regarding leaks of confidential positions. But these individuals must be convinced that they are part of the management team. They may be called upon to work hard hours under difficult circumstances. They must be persuaded they have a stake in the outcome. Establish an appropriate method to inform your Board of Directors.

21. Union Rules. Review the union constitution and bylaws regarding strikes, picketing, strike funds, picket pay, fines, etc. Employees will need clear and certain answers regarding their rights. I can easily obtain a copy of such material and will begin this review.

22. Unemployment Benefits. State laws are often very confusing regarding strikers' rights to unemployment compensation. In many cases strikers are not entitled to benefits, but this can be a complex determination. I will be glad to discuss this in detail at a later date. It is clear, however, that under current federal law strikers cannot sign up for food stamps.

23. Personnel Policies and Procedures. Special rules for personnel practices apply in strikes. You should identify exactly how you will compensate workers

The Strike Plan

(wages and benefits) and develop checklists and forms to handle this.

24. <u>Contingency Manual.</u> You may wish to formally establish a Contingency Manual (a specific, step-by-step procedural strike plan). Such a manual is typically quite helpful in a strike because it calls for less on-the-spot thinking when an emotional situation arises. If you would like me to help you in this regard, I will be glad to do so. We have such materials to assist in your planning. I have enclosed a draft table of contents from a manual that we typically use.[119]

25. <u>Preparedness.</u> After reading this letter you may be slightly troubled with the extent of preparation for a strike. Certainly, all of the considerations I have raised may seem overwhelming. However, by advance planning and step-by-step action, the situation is usually manageable. While a strike must be taken very seriously, particularly in your [business/service], it is a situation that can be adjusted to well. Frankly, it has been my experience that when a company is prepared and willing to consider taking a strike, and also shows its union employees this, it is then in its best bargaining position.

We certainly hope that a strike will not occur, but if you are ready for it, you may get the most effective results in the long run. Should you have any questions or comments, please do not hesitate to call upon me at work or at home. My home telephone number is _____. I look forward to working with you and other management staff of [Employer].

       Very truly yours,

Enclosures

---

119. *See* Appendix 2-B.

Appendix 3-B

[EMPLOYER]
Contingency Planning Manual
(Date)

CONTENTS

Page

Section 1.	Introduction and Purpose	....
1.1	Contingency Planning: Basic Purpose	....
1.2	Overview of Contingency Planning Manual Content	....
1.3	Preliminary Contingency Planning Checklist	....
Section 2.	Management Program	....
2.1	Employer Policy	....
2.2	Strike Committee	....
2.2.1	Legal Counsel	....
2.3	Strike Headquarters	....
2.4	Management Team	....
Section 3.	Internal Communications Planning	....
3.1	Employer Communications Center	....
3.2	Confidential Management Communications Chain	....

The Strike Plan

Page

3.3	Daily Reports	
3.4	Management Communications ...	
3.5	Employee Rights Information	
Section 4.	External Communications Plan ..	
4.1	General Approach	
4.2	Customer External Communication Plan: General	
4.3	Customer External Communication Plan: Specific Responsibilities ..	
4.4	Media Contact	
4.5	Government Contact	
Section 5.	Employer Security Plan	
5.1	General	
5.2	Guard Coverage and Procedures ..	
5.3	Security of Physical Properties ...	
5.4	Special Areas of Vulnerability	
5.5	Strike Insurance	
Section 6.	Personnel Policies, Procedures, and Records	
6.1	Recordkeeping and Related Items .	
6.2	Special Hiring Procedures	
6.3	Payroll Procedures	
6.4	Salary Increase Procedures	
6.5	Special Termination Procedures ..	
6.6	Sick Leave and Vacations	
6.7	Employee Benefits	
6.8	Expense Reimbursement	
6.9	Miscellaneous	
Section 7.	Basic Procedures	
7.1	Key Support and Service Levels Defined	
7.2	Production/Service Priorities	
7.3	Component Operations Plans	

Appendix 3-C

Strike Plan Consideration Checklist

	Staff Assigned	Draft Date	Final Date
1. Strike Committee			
A. Legal Counsel			
2. Policy Development and Review			
3. Strike Plan Development			
4. Strike Headquarters			
5. Management Team Review			
6. Service/Production Options			
A. Work Priority			
B. Work Suspension			
7. Communications System			
8. Public Spokesperson			
9. Security			
A. Internal Security			
B. External Security			
10. Strike Insurance			
11. Strike Log			
12. Employee Work Schedules			
13. Strike Replacements			
14. Subcontracting			
15. Skills Inventory			

The Strike Plan

	Staff Assigned	Draft Date	Final Date
16. Cross Training			
17. Personnel Policies and Procedures			
18. Employment Statute Review			
19. Contract Review			
A. Labor			
B. Nonlabor			
20. Union Constitution and Bylaws			
21. Reserve Gate Options			
22. Transportation			
23. Supplies/Utilities			

Appendix 3-D

<u>Strike Headquarters Checklist</u> *

1. <u>Basic Supplies/Services.</u>

    A. Food/beverage services (canned goods, catering capabilities, cafeteria options, licensing requirements, etc.).
    B. Laundry service.
    C. Bedding (on site or offsite).
    D. Paperwork supplies and equipment (paper, envelopes, pens, pencils, staplers, typewriters, and related supplies).
    E. Sanitation (showers, restrooms, soap, etc.).
    F. Reference materials (manuals, laws, regulations, etc.).

2. <u>Comfort Items.</u>

    A. Television/radios.
    B. Videotape equipment/movies.
    C. Magazines/newspapers.
    D. Provide non-smoking and smoking areas.
    E. Adequate tables and chairs.
    F. Games (video, ping pong, pool, etc.).
    G. Personal Storage (clothes, gear, etc.).

---

* Verify local zoning and safety requirements for each option if strike situation may create different use.

The Strike Plan

3. <u>Safety/Security.</u>

    A.   First Aid kit (bandages, aspirin, etc.).
    B.   Flashlights/candles.
    C.   Fire extinguishers.
    D.   Unlisted telephone numbers (basic and hotline).
    E.   Citizen band and police radio.
    F.   Telephones and paging systems.
    G.   Internal and external security systems.

4. <u>Miscellaneous Equipment/Supplies.</u>

[Develop as needed.]

Appendix 3-E

PRODUCTION/SERVICE PRIORITIES MATRIX*

		Short Term	Medium Term	Long Term	Indefinite
	Months:	(0-1)	(1-3)	(3-6)	(6+)
I.	**Production/Service**				
A.	Subproduct/Service	1	1	1	1
B.	Subproduct/Service	1	1	1	1
C.	Subproduct/Service	3	3	2	1
D.	Subproduct/Service	3	2	2	1
E.	Subproduct/Service	2	2	2	2
F.	Subproduct/Service	3	3	3	2
G.	Subproduct/Service	3	2	2	1
II.	**Support Components/Requirements**				
A.	Security	1	1	1	1
B.	Emergency Services	1	1	1	1
C.	Receiving (Storage)	2	2	1	1
D.	Shipping/Delivery	2	1	1	1
E.	Equipment Maintenance	3	2	2	1
F.	Building Maintenance	3	3	3	1
G.	Licensing Review	1	1	1	1
H.	Personnel Program	1	2	1	1
I.	Accounting/Purchasing	3	2	1	1
J.	Advertising	1	1	1	1

* Note: This chart presents hypothetical values and examples.

The Strike Plan

K.	Design/Engineering	2	2	1	1
L.	Testing	2	2	1	1

Key:

Essential/Critical (Maintain) = 1
Desired/Helpful (Reduction) = 2
Expendable (Suspend/Terminate) = 3

Appendix 3-F

Is the Greyhound Wage Package fair?

Average Salaries Plus Benefits:*

Greyhound Drivers	$32,238
Greyhound Terminal Personnel (baggage handlers, ticket clerks, and janitors)	$24,382
• Policemen	$20,299
• Head nurses	$21,757
• Firefighters	$19,313
• High school teachers	$20,463
• Public accountants	$31,697

*Source: Statistical Abstract of the U.S. 1982-83, U.S. Dept. of Labor 1982-83.

Why Greyhound must have parity.

Greyhound Lines is struggling to regain its historic position as the low-cost transporter of people in America. We are doing this against formidable odds in a new competitive environment of cut-rate airline and bus fares.

Greyhound Lines has the highest labor costs of any carrier in the intercity bus industry.

Our labor costs are 30% to 50% higher than other major bus companies in America. Our principal competitor, for example, has contracts with the ATU which are more than 30% lower than our pre-strike labor costs. That fact makes it impossible for us to effectively compete against both the new regional airlines and against other bus companies, both of whom can cut their fares and still prosper.

Consider these comparisons of Greyhound Lines' fares with the fares of the new regional airlines (pre-strike fares):

You be the judge.

The proposed wage and benefits package offered to Greyhound Lines employees would leave these employees *the best paid in the entire intercity bus industry.* And well paid by *any* standard. Yet many officials of the Amalgamated Transit Union recommended to their rank and file that the company's latest offer be rejected.

Many responsible voices have counseled otherwise, including the editorial pages of leading newspapers from around the nation:

"We get the impression that Greyhound is playing for keeps. Strikers should be careful not to underestimate the management's determination...."

"The company's demand for a pay cut obviously is an affront to the union, but Greyhound can claim considerable justification. It is not just that the firm's labor costs are higher than those of other bus lines; Greyhound is now encountering price competition from the cut-rate airlines." (*The Milwaukee Journal,* November 15, 1983)

"If any company is to survive in the new world of competition, it must be willing to compete." (*Tulsa World,* November 15, 1983)

"Greyhound Lines is in precarious economic straits. Deregulation ended the days when the Interstate Commerce Commission protected inefficiency, high costs and unprofitable routes through regulations that guaranteed monopoly service. The arrival of competition that is more fierce apparently has not caught up with strikers, who still think this must be 1970." (*The Arizona Republic,* November 6, 1983)

"In salary alone, Greyhound drivers average $27,437. Now check that figure of people with limited training and responsibility with the salary schedule for Palm Beach County teachers. At the top of the teacher scale are teachers with a doctor's degree and 19 years of experience — at $25,803." (*West Palm Beach* (Fla.) *Evening Times,* November 3, 1983)

Newark to Norfolk	**Buffalo to Portland, Maine**
Greyhound Lines fare: $56.15	Greyhound Lines fare: $79.00
People Express fare: $23.00	People Express fare: $45.00
San Francisco to Phoenix	**Buffalo to New York City**
Greyhound Lines fare: $79.00	Greyhound Lines fare: $41.35
Southwest fare: $60.00	People Express fare: $23.00

Despite the best equipment and facilities, convenient schedules, and dedicated, professional employees, we cannot offer similar low fares because of our higher labor costs.

This is what the union rejected.

Proposed Greyhound Wages and Benefits Versus Other Class I Carriers, most of whom also are represented by the Amalgamated Transit Union.
(November 18, 1983 offer):

	Greyhound Lines Average	Other Class I Carriers Average
Drivers	$32,238	$27,352
Mechanics and Service Personnel	25,144	20,190
Terminal Personnel	24,382	17,746
Office Personnel	19,481	14,660

Employees' right to know.

The bus line is up and running, and shortly we will double our present level of service. As we bring the bus line back to full service, we have no choice but to hire permanent replacements for those employees who refuse to return to work. We have tried through this gradual start-up to protect existing employees' jobs as long as possible. Each day the strike continues, however, and each permanent replacement who is hired mean the disappearance of the jobs once held by current employees. No one should underestimate the company's resolve to operate!

PARITY IS VITAL TO OUR SURVIVAL!

Greyhound Lines, Inc.

Advertisement: Employer's Wage Offer

Appendix 3-G

PAID AD

TO THE COMMUNITY
AND
EMPLOYEES OF TACOMA BOATBUILDING CO.

FACTS ABOUT THE STRIKE

* We have missed hundreds of millions of dollars worth of ship orders due solely to having the world's highest shipyard labor rates.

* Our largest customer, the U.S. Navy, publicly announced, "No more West Coast Contracts at such disparate rates."

* If we are to survive, we must compete <u>NOW</u>. This position is the same as steel, autos, and other industries competing abroad.

* Nine shipyards of the Pacific Coast Shipbuilders' Association are paying the highest composite shipbuilding rates in the nation. They are:

    $7.00 per hour above Gulf Coast
    $4.00 per hour above East Coast
    $7.00-$12.00 per hour above Korea and Japan

- We asked for a 10 percent ($1.35/hour) reduction in wages to narrow the gap. It was rejected.

- The union asked for a 16 percent ($3.00/hour) increase plus unlimited cost of living adjustment.

- We counterproposed a "no increase" settlement in wages with negotiated monies for fringe benefits. The union negotiators rejected the counteroffer.

- The union called a strike, refusing to take our improved offer back to the members. This reflects a total lack of consideration to the employer, the customers, and their members.

- In December 1982 our administrative employees took a 10 percent and our officers a 20 percent reduction in pay.

- Our union employees have had 10 years of quarterly increases, but still can't see the real world economics changing with regard to competing in autos, steel, shipbuilding and all industries that compete abroad.

- Many of our employees tell us they would accept "zero increase," but the union refused to put the offer to a vote. Why?

- We will not and cannot permit irresponsible unionism to put us out of business.

- Our gates are open to employees desiring to work, and we do intend to continue to work.

- We have established a toll-free Hot Line. The number is **1-800-633-7515**.

TACOMA BOATBUILDING CO.

Advertisement: Facts about the Strike

Appendix 3-H

No. _____*

STRIKE INCIDENT REPORT

This information is gathered at the direction of legal counsel. Access and use is restricted. Treat it as <u>confidential</u> and forward to: _____ by courier.

Date This Report Was Filled Out	Time This Report Was Filled Out
Name of Person Filling Out Report	Date of Incident
Time of Incident	Location of Incident

Describe Incident _____
_____
_____
_____

Names of Union Officials Present at Incident	List of **Witnesses to** Incident (Name, **Address,** Phone)

_____
_____
_____
_____
_____

---

* Prenumbered system. Forms are to be self-duplicating.

Appendix 3-I

STRIKE INCIDENT REPORT LOG*

This information is gathered at the direction of legal counsel. Access and use is restricted. Treat it as <u>confidential</u>.

Incident Number	Person (and Title) Making Report	Description (Date, time and Brief Statement)
_____	_____	_____
_____	_____	_____
_____	_____	_____
_____	_____	_____
_____	_____	_____
_____	_____	_____
_____	_____	_____

* Maintain log at strike headquarters.

Appendix 3-J

MEMORANDUM

TO: Supervisors
FROM: Personnel Department
RE: Vacation Benefits

For production requirements, the following policies apply regarding vacation during a strike:

1. Employees who remain on the job and have not scheduled vacation in advance will be <u>required</u> to delay it until after strike settlement.

2. Nonstriking employees on vacation when a strike occurs will be <u>asked</u> to return to work (if bargaining unit employees), or <u>required</u> to return (if managerial/supervisory).

3. Nonstriking employees who have scheduled vacation when a strike occurs or is in progress will be <u>asked</u> to defer the vacation and continue working (if bargaining unit employees), or be <u>required</u> to do so (if managerial/supervisory).

4. Eligible striking employees will be paid for <u>accrued</u> vacation time as <u>scheduled</u> or upon <u>request</u>.*

---

* Verify current law in your part of the country. *See also* section 11.1 *infra*.

4
Strike Communications: Information, Dialogue, and Polling

4.1 The Eve of the Strike: Prestrike Communications

As bargaining progresses, an employer should gradually implement its contingency plan. Well before the expiration of the current contract, the strike committee should begin to meet regularly, at least every two weeks, to discuss strike preparation and anticipated problems.

4.1.1 Anticipating the Strike Vote

When a strike is likely or drawing near, consider disseminating carefully drafted information to the employees. Exercise caution so that the union cannot legitimately argue that you are seeking to bargain around the union, derogating its status, or engaging in unlawful direct dealing with employees. Further, such communication should not take the form of disparaging propaganda. Such material can backfire and strengthen employee-union solidarity. Carefully written and planned communications to employees and supervisors, if used judiciously, may strengthen your position.

A union may mislead or keep employees uninformed of key issues in an imminent strike situation. On the eve of a strike, you can expect the union to slant issues dramatically in an effort to

Strike Planning

obtain strike votes. It may make promises to manipulate the vote. In some cases, it may grossly distort, fabricate, or totally avoid key issues. An employer should anticipate such practices. With good strategy, an employer may be most effective by beating the union to the punch on the issues. Or it can choose to counter union communications with thorough, accurate, and timely information on bargaining specifics and employee rights.

4.1.2 Keep Management Advised

To maximize effective use of its plan, management should periodically brief supervisors and managers on strike issues and expectations. Make an effort to be positive and determined; apprehension of a strike should not be communicated. Rather, foster an attitude of business-as-usual planning. The message that management presents to its supervisors will inevitably be transmitted to employees and to the union.

As a strike becomes more probable, supervisors become even more important to successful strike planning. They will channel employee questions to you and can provide information on union developments. This is a sensitive period and they should be kept well informed and comfortable with your position. They should also have a good understanding of basic procedures about what they can and cannot do. (See Appendix 4-A.)

4.2 Employer Strike Communication System

Once a strike-vote meeting is expected, management should have a strike communication system ready to provide employees with an accurate summary of the status of collective bargaining, the issues at impasse, and employee rights. While this may not be desirable or effective in all cases, it should be considered as a way to respond to the union by developing support for the management position. An employer should also cautiously determine whether to implement its final offer.[1]

The main purpose of a pre-strike vote communication system is to advise employees truthfully of strike issues, options, and problems. Depending upon circumstances, you may want to release information only when a strike is imminent, or you may wish to gradually discuss your position as bargaining progresses. Your information releases may be detailed or brief. If you elect a comprehensive program, it should inform employees of their legal and contractual rights and obligations in the event of a strike. It should address issues on which employees will have significant questions, such as health insurance, vacation, sick leave, credit union privileges, unemployment benefits, food stamps, replacement, union membership, and union discipline. It should let employees know that the employer is prepared and dedicated, and it should inform them how a strike could affect each of them personally.

The format for pre-strike communications should be tailored to fit your needs. The extent and complexity of materials should be adapted to the timing of your situation and the employees' level of sophistication. Particular care must be taken to *update* legal materials with recent case law developments. Public sector employers must analyze the constraints of state statutes that are unique to them.

To the degree possible, line supervisors should distribute the information to employees. Using the supervisor to convey information generally strengthens their support and commitment to the employer, as it makes them part of the strike planning process. It also improves opportunities for employee-management dialogue and acquisition of information on key issues. However, supervisors must be schooled and monitored to avoid ad libs that could lead to inadvertent misstatements and unfair labor practices. Communication materials should be strictly controlled and used within set guidelines.

---

1. *See* ch. 3 *supra*.

Strike Planning

4.2.1 The Employer Story

An employer strike communication system is an expression of the employer's free speech, permissible under section 8(c) of the NLRA.[2] So long as communications do not threaten, improperly interfere with, coerce, disparage, or bargain around the union or offer improper inducement, management is free to tell its side of the story.[3] Basic materials covering a strike's impact on employees, the strike issues, and possible questions and answers could be distributed. (See Appendix 4-A.) You should include clear assurances to employees of noncoercion and noninterference.

In communicating with employees regarding an imminent strike vote, an employer should try to convince them of the merits of its position, the sincerity and strength of its convictions, and the problems that could arise from a strike. Persuasive materials given to employees may avert a "pro-strike" result at a union strike vote meeting, or they may reduce the election margin. Even if employees overwhelmingly endorse a strike, the employer's information still provides important feedback. It tells the employer of expected employee loyalty to the union. The employer can then act accordingly.

At the pre-strike vote stage, your supervisors should also be periodically asked for predictions on the likely effect of a strike. They should give their projections on how many bargaining unit employees they expect would engage in a strike or respect picket lines. *Polling* of employees by the employer should *not* be under-

---

2. 29 U.S.C. § 158(c). *See generally* NLRB v. Gissell Packing Co., 395 U.S. 575, 71 L.R.R.M. 2481 (1969) (election case).
3. *See, e.g.*, Huck Mfg. Co. v. NLRB, 693 F.2d 1176, 112 L.R.R.M. 2245 (5th Cir. 1982) (strike); NLRB v. Tex-Tan, Inc., 318 F.2d 472, 53 L.R.R.M. 2298 (5th Cir. 1963) (nonstrike); Swarco, Inc. v. NLRB, 303 F.2d 668, 50 L.R.R.M. 2262 (6th Cir. 1962), *cert. denied*, 373 U.S. 931 (1961) (first amendment); NLRB v. Superior Fire Proof Door & Sash Co., 289 F.2d 713, 47 L.R.R.M. 2816 (2d Cir. 1961) (nonimpasse); Wantagh Auto Sales Co., Inc., 177 N.L.R.B. 150, 72 L.R.R.M. 1541 (1969) (lockout).

taken at an early point in the bargaining process. However, it is permissible later when a strike is imminent.[4]

4.2.2 Union Membership Requirements

As part of an employer's strike planning, and in directing communications to employees, management should advise employees about their rights to choose freely whether to engage or *not to* engage in a strike. All too often employees only hear about their obligation to strike and the threat of union discipline if they do not.

Other choices are available. For obvious reasons, unions do not alert their membership to these options. There are steps that employees who wish to work during a strike can take to protect themselves from union discipline. At the appropriate time, management should make employees aware of those alternatives. Two employee options are full union resignation *or* transfer to "financial core" status, which limits the employee's union obligation to payment of dues and fees. Both are controversial and likely to be challenged by the union.

4.2.2.1 Resignation

There is currently a controversy as to whether, and to what extent, a union member employee may resign or change membership status when a strike is imminent. The dispute involves the employees' dilemma regarding the exercise of their section 7 rights to engage in or refrain from participating in "concerted activity" when they are also required to be a union member through a union shop clause. The conflict arises from the tension between an employee's freedom and the union's claimed institutional need for solidarity through membership control. Recent developments in the law have greatly complicated this area, so

---

4. *See* section 4.3.2 *infra*.

Strike Planning

→ special attention must be directed towards review of emerging case law when giving guidance or advice.

Employees should be advised to be extremely careful in resignation decisions. A union has a right to discipline employee members who cross a lawful picket line while maintaining *full* union membership.[5] In essence, a contract exists between a full union member and the union through the union's constitution. This membership contract controls the conduct of the member vis-à-vis the strike. However, the Supreme Court has made it equally clear that an employee must be free to escape the hold of the union membership contract.[6] Once the employee does so, post-resignation conduct cannot be restricted.[7] According to the Supreme Court a union has "no more control over the former member than it has over the man in the street."[8]

With post-resignation conduct regulation foreclosed, unions attempted to limit resignation during strikes through vague procedural hurdles in union constitutions and bylaw clauses. These were uniformly rejected.[9] At a minimum, the union must give employees clear notice of resignation limits, cannot impose sub-

---

5. NLRB v. Allis-Chalmers Manufacturing Co., 388 U.S. 175, 65 L.R.R.M. 2449 (1967) (union can fine members and fines are court enforceable).
6. Scofield (Wisconsin Motor Corp.) v. NLRB, 394 U.S. 423, 70 L.R.R.M. 3105 (1969). *See also* Booster Lodge No. 405, International Ass'n of Machinists (Boeing Co.) v. NLRB, 412 U.S. 84, 83 L.R.R.M. 2189 (1973). These early cases were not confronted with membership resignation restrictions.
7. *See* NLRB v. Granite State Joint Board, Textile Workers Union of America, Local 1029, 409 U.S. 213, 81 L.R.R.M. 2853 (1972). *See also* Machinists, Local 1994 (O.K. Tool Co., Inc.), 215 N.L.R.B. 651, 88 L.R.R.M. 1120 (1974).
8. *Granite State, Id.* at 217, 2854.
9. *See* National Association of Broadcast Employees & Technicians, Local 531 (Skateboard Productions, Inc.), 245 N.L.R.B. 638, 102 L.R.R.M. 1250 (1979). However, by memorandum opinion the Ninth Circuit held that the instant rule was not ambiguous and remanded for review of the sixty-day waiting period. NABET v. NLRB, No. 79-7548, 108 L.R.R.M.

Strike Communications

jective standards for membership resignation, and must prove employee awareness and consent to any such limitations.[10]

One court laid out clear guidelines when it ruled that a union's internal authority should not supersede the individual's statutory right to refrain from union activity.[11] That court also noted that the mere filing of charges by a union against its members for resigning and going to work was an unfair labor practice. It held that proposed fines or disciplinary measures were inherently coercive and that they did not need to be implemented to violate the NLRA.[12]

This area was greatly complicated by the NLRB's 1982 decision in *Dalmo Victor II*.[13] In the *Dalmo Victor* case series, the union had refused to let employees resign during or within fourteen days of a strike. In *Dalmo Victor II* the Board held in a plurality opinion that such resignation restrictions tied to a

---

2104. *See also* TKB International Corp., 240 N.L.R.B. 1082, 100 L.R.R.M. 1426 (1979); Coast Valleys Typographical Union Local 650 (The Daily Breeze, Division of Copley Press, Inc.), 221 N.L.R.B. 1048, 91 L.R.R.M. 1078 (1975) (ambiguity, lack of notice to employees, and no objective standards.)

10. *See* Local Lodge 758, Int'l Ass'n of Machinists, AFL-CIO (Menasco, Inc.), 267 N.L.R.B. No. 73, 114 L.R.R.M. 1187 (1983); Teamsters Local 36 (Strong Bldg. Materials), 255 N.L.R.B. No. 187, 113 L.R.R.M. 1095 (1983); Teamsters Local 439 (Loomis Courier Service, Inc.), 237 N.L.R.B. 220, 99 L.R.R.M. 1026 (1978); Local 1384, UAW (Ex-Cell-O Corp.), 227 N.L.R.B. 1045, 94 L.R.R.M. 1145 (1977).

11. NLRB v. Oil, Chemical & Atomic Workers Int'l Union, Local 6-578, AFL-CIO, 619 F.2d 708, 713, 103 L.R.R.M. 2895 (8th Cir. 1980)

12. *Id. See also* Engineers and Scientists Guild (Lockheed), 268 N.L.R.B No. 42, 115 L.R.R.M. 1004 (1983) (maintenance of union constitution provision precluding resignation during strike coercive on its face); International Typographical Union and Its Local 47 (Register Publishing Co.) 270 NLRB No. 213, 116 L.R.R.M. 1333 (1984).

13. Machinists Local 1327, Int'l Ass'n of Machinists, AFL-CIO, (Dalmo Victor II), 263 N.L.R.B. 984, 111 L.R.R.M. 1115 (1982), *on remand from*, 608 F.2d 1219, 102 L.R.R.M. 2583 (9th Cir. 1979), *den. enf. of*, 231 N.L.R.B. 719, 96 L.R.R.M. 1160 (1979) *(Dalmo Victor I).*

Strike Planning

strike's occurrence were not permissible. Two members of the Board asserted that *any* restriction on membership resignation was unlawful. However, two other members indicated that up to a thirty-day waiting period before a resignation became effective (not necessarily tied to the occurrence of a strike) would be acceptable. Only one member supported the union rule at issue.[14] Under the NLRB's *Dalmo Victor II* rule, all that could be clearly said was that a waiting period of more than thirty days for a resignation was illegal.

The Ninth Circuit Court of Appeals, denied enforcement of the Board's decision in *Dalmo Victor II*, throwing the area into further controversy.[15] The controversy is on the way to being resolved however, by the Board's decision in *Neufeld Porsche-Audi*.[16] The NLRB responded to the Ninth Circuit's rejection of its *Dalmo Victor II* rule, and held that there could be *no* restraints upon an employee's right to resign from a union. Unions will obviously challenge this new rule, and the Board and Court decisions in this volatile area must be carefully monitored.

4.2.2.2 The Financial Core

Employees have another alternative that is short of complete resignation. This option is the "financial core" membership status. It is a long-standing, but rarely discussed, middle-ground right. Union speakers avoid it, perhaps because it is the safest option for nonstriking employees to consider. It is especially

---

14. However, it was suggested that in extraordinary circumstances a longer waiting period may be reasonable. *Id.* 263 N.L.R.B. at 987, n.21.
15. Machinists Local 1327 v. NLRB, 792 F.2d 1212, 115 L.R.R.M. 2972 (9th Cir. 1984). The Seventh Circuit, has ruled that there can be *no* resignation restrictions. Pattern Makers League of North America, 265 N.L.R.B. No. 170, 112 LRRM 1030 (1982), *enforced*, _____ F.2d _____, 115 L.R.R.M. 2264 (7th Cir. 1984), *cert. granted sub. nom.* Pattern Makers League v. N.L.R.B. No. 83-1894, 1984 D.L.R. No. 191: A-9 (Oct. 2, 1984).
16. Machinists Local Lodge 1414 (Neufeld Porsche-Audi), 270 N.L.R.B. No. 209, 116 L.R.R.M. 1225 (1984).

useful where, because a union shop clause may find its way into future contracts, employees are hesitant to resign from the union before a strike.

Sections 8(a)(3) and 8(b)(2) of the Act authorize unions and employers to agree upon a union shop clause that requires an employee to "tender dues and initiation fees" to the union or be discharged. The Supreme Court has long recognized the conflict between forced union membership under a union shop clause and an employee's personal freedom under section 7 to refrain from union membership.[17] To minimize employees' dilemma, the Court ruled that required union membership under a lawful union shop clause can be "whittled down to its financial core."[18] In essence, employees can be forced to pay union dues, but cannot be forced to be full union members.[19] Nor can they be held liable for fines, assessments, or other monetary penalties. They are generally not aware of this right, however, and they consequently neglect to exercise it. When employees try it they may be met with union resistance and noncooperation.[20]

The significance of the flexibility that the financial core option provides cannot be overstressed. From a practical standpoint, if

---

17. General Motors Corp. v. NLRB, 373 U.S. 734, 742, 53 L.R.R.M. 2313 (1963).
18. *Id. See also* United Food and Commercial Workers Local 506 (Alpha Beta Co.), 265 N.L.R.B. 1290, 112 L.R.R.M. 1127 (1983); SEIU Local 680 (Leland Stanford Jr. University) v. NLRB, 601 F.2d 980, 101 L.R.R.M. 2212 (9th Cir. 1979), *aff'g*, 232 N.L.R.B. 97 L.R.R.M. 1186 (1978); Hershey Foods Corp., 207 N.L.R.B. 897, 85 L.R.R.M. 1004 (1974), *enforced*, 513 F.2d 1083, 89 L.R.R.M. 2129 (9th Cir. 1975).
19. Union Starch & Refining Co., 87 N.L.R.B. 779, 25 L.R.R.M. 1176 (1949), *enforced*, 186 F.2d 1008, 27 L.R.R.M. 2342 (7th Cir. 1951), *cert. denied*, 342 U.S. 815, 28 L.R.R.M. 2625 (1951). As to the union's duty to properly explain membership options, *see* Teamsters Local 302 v. Vevoda, 116 L.R.R.M. 3191 (N.D. Cal. 1984).
20. *See, e.g.*, United Food & Commercial Workers, Local 506, (Alpha Beta Co.), 265 N.L.R.B. 162, 112 L.R.R.M. 1127 (1982).

Strike Planning

an employer is operating in a traditional craft industry, with high probability of continued unionization (and a union shop clause), the employee will have no real ability to sever a relationship with the union. Once a contract is settled and employees return to work, an employee who resigned completely may need to seek readmission to the union and will probably be charged new initiation fees. There will probably be some gamesmanship regarding membership reapplication or threatened discipline as well. Thus, full resignation may not be desirable. However, under the financial core option, employees satisfy their financial obligations without jeopardizing future employment, and thus reduce the likelihood of union harassment.

Union supporters may argue that the Ninth Circuit's reversal of *Dalmo Victor II* destroys the financial core option. This, however, ignores the NLRB's subsequent decision in *Neufeld Porsche-Audi*. Also, to even make such claims, a union must have a valid rule relating to financial core membership, and it must be communicated to members. Because they seldom willingly admit that financial core status exists, unions generally have no such rule in their constitutions or bylaws.

An employer should feel free to explain to employees the rights and options under the financial core theory. It should also consider whether to advise employees that it will pay any fines the union may lawfully levy because an employee has followed this advice.[21] In this way employees would know that they will not be left completely vulnerable to union pressure once a strike is over.

---

21. *See* Dean Foods Company, 266 N.L.R.B. No. 192, 113 L.R.R.M. 1097 (1983) Menasco Inc., note 10 *supra*; Rochester Musicians Ass'n, 207 N.L.R.B. 647, 85 L.R.R.M. 1345, *enforcement denied on other grounds*, 514 F.2d 988, 89 L.R.R.M. 2193 (2d Cir. 1975) (immaterial that employer paid fine being challenged). *Contra*, Baney Wilkerson Constr. Co., 145 N.L.R.B. 704, 55 L.R.R.M. 1030 (1964) (promise to pay fine linked with threat to fire employee for failure to cross picket line). *See also* section 4.3.3 *infra*. Special review should be made of provisions of the Labor Management Relations Act, 29 U.S.C. § 186, which limit employer payments to unions.

Strike Communications

4.2.2.3 Membership Change Procedure

For the employer whose contract has a union shop clause requiring union membership, the timing of a union member's decision to resign or shift into financial core status is critical. A union will not voluntarily tell employees about resignation rights.

If employees choose to exercise either option (resignation or financial core status), they must affirmatively communicate their decision to the union.[22] To avoid union discipline, a letter or notice must be received by the union *before* the employee crosses a picket line.[23] (See Appendixes 4-C and 4-D, for possible sample letters.) Employees should send such letters certified or registered mail, return receipt requested. A copy should be sent to the employer and one should be kept for the employee's own records.

4.3 The Imminent Strike Situation

4.3.1 The Eve of the Strike

The union view may carry the day and employees may vote to engage in a strike. Strike authorization is often sought and given primarily so that the union committee will have more leverage at the bargaining table. Employees may vote for a strike under this rationale, only to be dragged into participation when bargaining breaks down.

---

22. Distillery Workers Local 80 (Capitol Husting Co.), 235 N.L.R.B. 1264, 98 L.R.R.M. 1123 (1978) (membership resignation in feasible manner sufficient, no special form required); Local 340, Potters (Macomb Pottery Co.), 175 N.L.R.B. 756, 71 L.R.R.M. 1174 (1969).
23. *See* TKB International, note 9 *supra;* Local 1012, United Electrical, Radio & Machine Workers (General Electric Co.), 187 N.L.R.B. 375, 76 L.R.R.M. 1038 (1970).

Strike Planning

Once a strike is clearly imminent, based on objective grounds such as union strike authorization and notice to the employer, an employer has additional rights in preparing for a strike. It may escalate its communications with individual employees. If prestrike vote communications were not issued, the same general type of material can be released immediately prior to the strike to inform employees of their options. (See Appendix 4-A.) Employees should again be reminded about their financial core and membership resignation rights, as well as management's preparedness.

4.3.2 Strike Polling

If a strike appears imminent, management may, with certain restrictions, poll its employees about their intentions to actually participate in a strike. (See Appendix 4-B.) Such a poll may be helpful in preparing to operate during the strike.

Strike polling must be conducted carefully and certain specific protective guarantees must be made to employees. Such polling has been tested before the NLRB and in the courts. Polling has been deemed lawful when a strike is imminent, employees are advised of the purpose of the poll, participation in the poll is absolutely voluntary, employees are guaranteed protection against reprisal, and direct or implied threats of discharge, promise of benefits, or perceived efforts to have the union decertified are avoided.[24] Polling has been held to be improper when it

---

24. *See* Montefiore Hospital v. NLRB, 621 F.2d 510, 104 L.R.R.M. 2160 (2d Cir. 1980); Mosher Steel Co., 90 L.R.R.M. 1459, 220 N.L.R.B. 336 (1975); Great Atlantic & Pacific Tea Co., Inc., Birmingham Division, 210 N.L.R.B. 593, 86 L.R.R.M. 1444 (1974); W.A. Schaffer Pen Co., 199 N.L.R.B. 242, 81 L.R.R.M. 1209 (1972); Industrial Towel & Uniform Service Co., 172 N.L.R.B. 2254, 69 L.R.R.M. 1201 (1968); Road Home Construction Corp., 170 N.L.R.B. 688, 68 L.R.R.M. 1191 (1968). *See generally* Gulf-Wandes Corp. v. NLRB, 595 F.2d 1074, 101 L.R.R.M.

Strike Communications

has been coupled with other unlawful conduct such as mass discharges, threats of discipline, or offers of bribes.[25]

Strike polling can help identify the strength of a potential strike and the union's ability to accomplish its goals. Management's position at the bargaining table will be greatly enhanced if a union calls a strike when a clear majority of employees will continue to work. At a minimum, a poll provides a valuable opportunity to have employees face the issue directly before the strike deadline.

An employer's candid judgment of its work force is of paramount importance and may be more valuable than a poll. If an employer elects to conduct a poll, management should not blindly rely on the results. Following union advice, employees may purposely mislead management by falsely stating their intentions, or they may subsequently change their minds. A poll should be prepared confidentially and conducted quickly to minimize the possibility of union sabotage.

4.3.3 Union Employee Discipline and Employer Assistance

In anticipation of a strike, employees may ask management for legal assistance. Management should be careful not to encourage employees to sue the union and challenge it about their rights. While an employer cannot provide funding to initiate such

---

2373 (5th Cir. 1979) (interrogation); Struksnes Construction Co., 165 N.L.R.B. 1062, 65 L.R.R.M. 1385 (1967) (polls).
25. *See, e.g.*, Smith's Complete Market, Inc., 237 N.L.R.B. 1424, 99 L.R.R.M. 1247 (1978); Cagle's Inc., 234 N.L.R.B. 170, 98 L.R.R.M. 1117 (1978); Commercial Management, Inc. d/b/a/ Continental Manor & Nursing Home, 232 N.L.R.B. 1066, 97 L.R.R.M. 1247 (1977); Television Wisconsin, Inc., 224 N.L.R.B. 722, 93 L.R.R.M. 1494 (1976); Farmers Cooperative Compress, 169 N.L.R.B. 290, 67 L.R.R.M. 1266 (1968); Cooks Market, Inc., 159 N.L.R.B. 1182, 62 L.R.R.M. 1436 (1966).

Strike Planning

suits,[26] it may provide legal assistance to employees in defending themselves against union discipline.[27]

Further, under appropriate conditions prior to a strike an employer may offer to pay employee fines. When a union has already indicated that it could not fine employees for failure to respect a sympathy picket line, and the employer advised the employees that they could either recognize or refrain from supporting the picket line, the NLRB has upheld an employer guarantee to pay union fines.[28]

4.4 Communications during the Strike

4.4.1 Immediate Reactions

When a strike is called, a union will try to catch an employer unprepared and in as vulnerable a position as possible. Management, therefore, should be ready to gradually implement its strike plan in a businesslike way. Your strike committee should

---

26. *See* Harris v. Plasterers & Cement Masons, Local 406, 619 F.2d 1164, 103 L.R.R.M. 2884 (7th Cir. 1980) (regarding "interested" employer under 29 U.S.C. § 411 (a)(4)); International Union United Automobile, Aerospace and Agr. Imp. Workers v. National Right to Work Legal Defense and Ed. Foundation Inc., 590 F.2d 1139, 99 L.R.R.M. 318 (D.C. Cir. 1978) (legitimate legal aid group not an "interested employer"); Adamaczewski v. Local 1487, Int'l Ass'n of Machinists, AFL-CIO, 496 F.2d 777, 86 L.R.R.M. 2592 (7th Cir. 1974), *cert. denied*, 419 U.S. 997 (1974).
27. *See* International Bhd. of Electrical Workers, Local 336 v. Illinois Bell Telephone Co., 496 F.2d 1, 86 L.R.R.M. 2590 (7th Cir. 1974), *cert. denied*, 419 U.S. 897 (1974) (regarding 29 U.S.C. § 411(a)(4)); Leeds & Northrup Co., 155 N.L.R.B. 1292, 60 L.R.R.M. 1482 (1965) (regarding 29 U.S.C. § 158(a)(1)). *Compare*, Standard Plumbing & Heating Co., 185 N.L.R.B. 444, 75 L.R.R.M. 1065 (1970) (employer statement legal); *compare* Smith's Complete Market, 237 N.L.R.B. 1429, 99 L.R.R.M. 1247 (1978) (improper conduct overall).
28. Dean Foods, note 21 *supra*.

convene at once. Managers and supervisors should be advised of program responsibilities. Your board of directors should be alerted to the situation. If your contingency plan is ready to be implemented, there should be very few surprises. It will provide a ready and easily followed script.

Immediate notice to the security force and verification of all security systems and protection should be a top priority. You may consider calling major clients or customers to advise them of your intentions, even if you have given some preliminary assurances. Good customer relations are vital to long- and short-term success. Make all contact according to the contingency manual. You will have to adapt to special circumstances. If there is media or community interest in the strike, be prepared to issue appropriate press releases on short notice.

4.4.2 Strike Communications to Employees

In most cases, an employer should communicate with its employees during a strike. Under section 8(c) of the NLRA, employers have broad communication rights, including the right to communicate directly with employees about collective bargaining and strike issues, provided the employer communications are not intended to undermine or bypass the union as the employees' exclusive collective bargaining representative.[29] This prohibition extends to threats or promises intended to erode support for the union among employees.[30]

Despite the recognized general rules, it is difficult to define precisely what is lawful communication. Each communication, and the factual circumstances surrounding it, must be carefully

---

29. NLRB v. General Electric Co., 418 F.2d 736 (2d Cir. 1969), *cert. denied*, 397 U.S. 965 (1970).
30. *See* 29 U.S.C. § 158(c); Swarco, Inc. v. NLRB, 303 F.2d 668 (6th Cir. 1962), *cert. denied*, 373 U.S. 931 (1963); Youngstown Sheet & Tube Co., 238 N.L.R.B. 1082, 99 L.R.R.M. 1380 (1978).

analyzed. Furthermore, before a communication is released, all supervisors and management personnel should be advised of its content to enable them to respond to any employee reactions to the communication.

An employer may inform employees of the status of negotiations and the employer's position[31] so long as the information is accurate and does not misrepresent the union's position or make direct appeals to employees.[32] An employer can send out written communications outlining its bargaining position and request that employees return to work if there are no threats and no coercion involved.[33] Similarly, the employer may tell striking employees that jobs are available to them, that striking employees will be replaced if necessary, and that their best interests are served by abandoning the strike.[34] However, the employer cannot attempt to induce employees to return to work or discourage them from joining the strike by offering increased benefits if they abandon the strike or threaten loss of benefits if they continue to strike.[35]

---

31. See Peat Mfg. Co., 251 N.L.R.B. 1117, 1137, 105 L.R.R.M. 1476 (1980); Wantagh Auto Sales Inc., 177 N.L.R.B. 150, 72 L.R.R.M. 1541 (1969).
32. See Buffalo Bituminous, Inc. v. NLRB, 564 F.2d 267, 96 L.R.R.M. 2884 (8th Cir. 1977); Colony Furniture Co., 144 N.L.R.B. 1582, 54 L.R.R.M. 1308 (1963).
33. See Kansas Milling Co. v. NLRB, 185 F.2d 413, 27 L.R.R.M. 2048 (10th Cir. 1950); Pilot Freight Carriers, 223 N.L.R.B. 286, 92 L.R.R.M. 1246 (1976). As to employer ads to employees, see Celanese Corp., 95 N.L.R.B. 664, 28 L.R.R.M. 1362 (1951).
34. See American Welding & Industrial Sales, Inc., 214 N.L.R.B. 1086, 88 L.R.R.M. 1415 (1974); American Steel & Pump Corp., 121 N.L.R.B. 1410, 42 L.R.R.M. 1564 (1958).
35. See Lockwoven Co., 245 N.L.R.B. 1362, 102 L.R.R.M. 1533 (1979), enforced, 622 F.2d 296, 104 L.R.R.M. 2652 (8th Cir. 1980); Harris-Teeter Super Markets, Inc., 242 N.L.R.B. 132, 101 L.R.R.M. 1130 (1979), enforced, Nos. 79-1612 and 79-1792. 106 L.R.R.M. 3076 (D.C. Cir. 1981); Rawleigh Co., 90 N.L.R.B. 1924, 26 L.R.R.M. 1421 (1950).

4.4.3 Picket Line Advice

Working management and employees must avoid problems with picket lines. When there is violence during a strike, it usually occurs as workers cross the picket line while arriving at or leaving the workplace. You should be sure that security and police are present, especially at the beginning of a strike.

In advance of a strike, you should advise employees as to the safest route or means of coming to work. (See Appendix 4-E for a possible memorandum.) When crossing a picket line, workers should not stop and engage in debate. Arguments should be avoided. Threats, curses, gestures, and name-calling should not be condoned and, if the picketers engaged in such conduct, should not be reciprocated. If there is any trouble, employees should be directed to call a special telephone number at once.

Appendix 4-A.1

Cover Memo to Supervisors with Memo and Attachments

TO: All (<u>Employer</u>) Supervisors and Managers
FROM: _____
RE: Distribution of Strike Vote Information

As you know, there is a strike vote planned by (<u>Union</u>). Because of the potential impact on each of us, the enclosed materials provide pertinent information for all (<u>Employer</u>) employees. Four steps are suggested to deal properly with this crucial subject.

1. Please see that copies of each of the four (4) documents (this includes the Memo to Employees, Strike Impact Chart, Strike Issues Analysis, and Questions and Answers Regarding Strikes) are distributed to all employees immediately.

2. You should hold a staff meeting today to cover information contained in the four (4) documents. Your meeting should be held before your employees actually vote on the strike.

3. Please provide immediate feedback on the results of your meeting to your direct superiors.

4. Also, by the end of the week, advise your immediate superior as to your best "guestimate" of how many employees would likely support whatever strike action might subsequently occur. This should be

Strike Communications

accomplished on your own, without directly contacting your employees to ascertain their intentions at this time.

Any question you may have can be answered by contacting either the Personnel Office ([phone number]) or me ([phone number]).

Thank you for your continuing support.

Appendix 4-A.2

Memo to Employees Regarding Strike

TO: All Employees of (Employer)
FROM: _____
RE: Potential Strike Activity

No doubt, most of you are aware of the imminent strike situation involving (Employer) and (Union).

Despite the many bargaining sessions between the parties, we have been unable to reach final agreement on our contract. As a result, it appears that (Union) will be calling a work stoppage. We want you to understand fully the impact and significance of joining in or supporting such activity. Not only does a strike affect (Employer), it can have a dramatic effect on you and your family. Should (Union) actually call a strike, you should carefully consider the serious consequences that it could have on you as well as on (Employer).

First of all, if you participate in strike activity, you will receive no pay or compensation from (Employer). Not all unions provide strike benefits, and if they do, they are often partial payments only, not your full wages.

You will not be entitled to unemployment compensation if you go out on strike.[1] Neither will you be eligible for food stamps.[2]

---

1. Verify state law.
2. Check current federal law.

Strike Communications

You will receive no fringe benefits from (employer). All benefits, such as hospital, medical, dental and life insurance coverage will be discontinued upon your participation in a strike, unless maintained by you at your expense.[3] You will not accrue benefits such as seniority, vacation, or sick leave.

It will take you an extremely long time to regain wages lost during a strike. For your review, I have attached a chart that helps you calculate the financial impact you may incur in a strike.

You should understand that (Employer) intends to continue operations in the event of a strike. Replacements will be hired if necessary.

[Optional paragraph . . . One final note: if a strike is called and you do not join the union in strike activity, the union may be able to lawfully discipline you, if you are a full member. You have protected rights that you may exercise to avoid such action. A union member must resign or reduce membership status to "financial core" membership (payment of union dues only) before crossing a picket line to avoid those fines. The union must have received notice of the resignation or change in status before the employee crosses the picket line. If you elect to do this, send your letter by registered or certified mail, return receipt requested to the union and keep a copy. Because we expect to remain a "union shop," employees must maintain at least "financial core" status (i.e., tender union dues) to avoid possible discharge under union security provisions and to avoid union discipline.][4]

---

3. Verify state law and policy requirements.
4. Edit according to existing union security provisions and your strategy decision.

Strike Planning

Whether to participate in a strike is a serious decision you will very likely be faced with in the next few days. Certainly, the major impact this will have on the lives of your friends, neighbors, and others in the community who depend on (Employer) should also be considered. It is imperative that you understand all the ramifications of such a decision.

We are certainly hoping that a strike will not occur and we intend to do what we can to avoid a strike. However, we must all understand the consequences of such a possibility and be prepared. For your information, we have attached three (3) items. The first, as discussed above, is the strike impact chart. The second is what we feel is an accurate representation of the strike issues. The third provides questions and answers regarding strikes. We hope that those of you who have the important decision to make will seek the answers to any other questions you may have from your supervisor.

Appendix 4-A.3

Strike Impact Chart

[EMPLOYER]

Everyone Loses in a Strike

Employees sacrifice paychecks, and it takes a long time to recover the loss.

(Employer) loses revenue and often (customers). The community is harmed. Money that might otherwise be available for more jobs and expansion is lost.

Unions claim a strike is their strongest economic weapon, but some union leaders use strike threats and strikes with complete disregard for how it will affect employees.

Union leaders lose no paychecks during a strike.

Those same union leaders generally "call the shots" on when to strike and for how long.

Remember a strike hurts you and your family. It also threatens and inconveniences your friends, neighbors and others in the community.

Strike Planning

ASSUMING AVERAGE WAGE OF $7.00*

DAYS TO MAKE UP STRIKE LOSSES ASSUMING THE FOLLOWING IMPROVEMENT IN ECONOMICS AS A RESULT OF THE STRIKE

Working Days of Strike	Earnings Lost (Based on 8-Hour Day)	0 Improvement	5 Cents Improvement	10 Cents Improvement	20 Cents Improvement
5 days	$ 280.00	Never	140 weeks	70 weeks	35 weeks
10 days	560.00	Never	280 weeks	140 weeks	70 weeks
15 days	840.00	Never	420 weeks	210 weeks	105 weeks
20 days	1,120.00	Never	560 weeks	280 weeks	140 weeks
30 days	1,680.00	Never	840 weeks	420 weeks	120 weeks
60 days	3,360.00	Never	1,680 weeks	840 weeks	420 weeks
90 days	5,040.00	Never	2,520 weeks	1,260 weeks	630 weeks

DON'T FORGET TO SUBTRACT AT LEAST $_____ PER WEEK FOR UNION DUES FROM THE POSSIBLE INCREASE. THIS WILL EXTEND THE RECOVERY PERIOD.

* *NOTE*: Use realistic average wage for your employees and recompute tables.

Appendix 4-A.4

Strike Issues Analysis

<u>   (Employer)   </u>
<u>STRIKE ISSUES</u>

As you may know, union officials have sent a notice announcing a strike vote, which will be taken by union members during the week of _____. Therefore, many of our employees who are eligible to vote have an important decision to make. This matter will affect all of us, our families, and the community, in some way, and we should all be aware of the issues and their impact. Those eligible to vote should vote, and <u>(Employer)</u> recognizes that each member has the right to make this decision as he or she sees fit. We only want to be sure that those voting have all the facts at their disposal.

<u>STRIKE ISSUES:</u>

Union officials have published ____ issues in their strike referendum notice to the union's membership. Our bargaining unit employees must decide, first, whether the issues as stated by the union are accurate and, second, whether any of the issues are meaningful enough to cause them to leave their jobs. The issues are:

_____
_____
_____
_____.

Strike Planning

(EMPLOYER'S) RESPONSE TO THE STRIKE ISSUES:

_____
_____
_____
_____
_____
_____

FOR YOUR INFORMATION:

Also attached for the review of all (Employer) employees are some questions and answers which will no doubt occur to you regarding the potential strike situation. If we are to avoid the situation, it is important for all of us to work together with free-flowing communications. We hope those of you who have the important decision to make will seek the answers to any other questions you may have from your supervisors and will elect not to strike. In the meantime, bargaining unit employees can be assured that the (Employer) will continue its efforts to meet and negotiate with the (Union) a mutually satisfactory agreement.

Appendix 4-A.5

Question/Answers Regarding Strikes

(EMPLOYER)

QUESTIONS AND ANSWERS REGARDING STRIKES[1]

The following questions and answers have been prepared for the information of all employees in the event some form of strike action is actually called by the (Union). If employees have additional questions, they should feel free to ask their supervisors for answers. If any supervisor is unable to answer an employee's question, call either the Personnel Office (_____) or the office of the _____ (_____) immediately for an answer.

Q. Will there be a strike against the (Employer)?
  A. The (Employer) hopes not, but does not know whether or not there will, in fact, be a strike. That is up to the union officials.

Q. Do members of the bargaining unit have to strike?
  A. No. All bargaining unit employees, including dues paying members of the union as well as nonmembers, will have full opportunity to to continue working. The (Employer) hopes they choose to do so.

---

1. It is imperative that you verify current legal developments in this volatile area.

Strike Planning

Q. Can the union stop (Employer) employees from working?

    A. Absolutely not. All employees can work if they want.

Q. If there is a strike, when will it take place and for how long?

    A. This, too, is up to the union. The (Employer) has no control over these decisions. Union officials are apparently seeking authority to call a strike for up to ____ working days.

Q. Does the (Employer) plan to keep operating if there is a strike?

    A. Yes, the (Employer) plans to keep its doors open and to continue operations to meet its obligations to the community.

Q. What about union fines or penalties against members who refuse to strike?

    A. Unions often fine members for working behind the picket lines. We understand that this is possible under the union's constitution.

Q. Can a union member avoid paying fines for working instead of striking?[2]

    A. Yes. A union member can withdraw from union "membership" prior to crossing the picket line. This can done by simply sending a letter to the union notifying it of the employee's withdrawal from membership. It must be received by the

---

2. A decision must be made to advise employees about the "financial core" option. An employer must also consider whether a union shop will likely be in the next contract.

Strike Communications

union before you cross the line. This does not mean, however, that an employee can merely cease paying dues to the union. Rather, a member may reduce his or her status to that of a dues paying member only ("financial core" member) by sending a letter to the union stating such intention.

Q. Can strikers be replaced?
A. Yes, and they will be, if necessary, either temporarily or permanently as the situation requires. We have decided to _____.

Q. If there is a strike, will striking employees receive pay while on strike?
A. No. They will not receive pay from (Employer) while on strike.

Q. What about fringe benefits for strikers?[3]
A. If there is a strike, employees who choose to participate in the strike will be allowed to continue group life, medical, and dental insurance. However, these employees will be required to pay full premiums for this coverage beginning immediately. No other benefits will be available to strikers.

Q. Can an employee take sick leave during a strike?[4]
A. Only nonstriking employees will be entitled to use sick leave during a strike for legitimate reasons of sickness. Striking employees will not be permitted to use their sick leave.

---

3. Check you state law and insurance policies.
4. Update recent case developments.

Strike Planning

Q. <u>Can an employee use vacation time during a strike?</u>[5]
A. Striking employees will not be able to take vacation time to strike. Nonstriking employees will also not be able to take vacation time during the strike, unless the presence of the nonstriking employee on the job is not critical to the continuation of (<u>Employer</u>) operations. Employees on vacation when the strike commences will receive their regular vacation benefits.

Q. <u>Are striking employees eligible to receive unemployment compensation benefits during a strike?</u>[6]
A. The law disqualifies those who are unemployed due to a stoppage of work because of their participation in a strike or other labor dispute.

Q. <u>What about food stamps?</u>[7]
A. Under federal legislation you cannot sign up for food stamps as a result of a strike.

Q. <u>What about picket lines?</u>
A. (<u>Employer</u>) anticipates that any picketing will be conducted peacefully as required by law. We have no indication and no reason to believe that any illegal picketing or violence will occur. Recognizing that such acts are possible, however, (<u>Employer</u>) asks that any unusual circumstances be reported through organizational channels.

---

5. Update recent case developments.
6. Verify your state law.
7. Verify current federal law.

Strike Communications

Q. Should an employee cross a picket line?
A. Each employee must decide this individually. However, failure to report to work will result in loss of pay and benefits. (Employer) intends to continue operation during any strike. If an employee is prevented from gaining safe access to work, the employee should call the supervisor and/or the Personnel Office for assistance. Under no circumstances should any employee exchange comments with picketers.

Q. What can union members do to prevent a strike?
A. Union members can vote against a strike authorization. The (Employer) encourages members to do so.

Q. If union officials call a strike, how can an employee be protected against the possibility of permanent replacement?
A. By refusing to participate in the strike and continuing to work.

The (Employer) remains hopeful that there will not be a strike and that employee relations continue to be normal without disruption. Your patience and understanding, and your support for the (Employer) and your community are appreciated.

Appendix 4-A.6

[EMPLOYER]

STRIKE DO's & DON'T's

It appears that the [Union] will soon call a strike against the [Employer]. As a supervisor, you need to be aware that the employees are allowed to strike under Section 7 of the National Labor Relations Act. If there is a strike, it is imperative that we take the proper action. Failure to adhere to these "do's and don'ts" could result in serious consequences for the company.

DO's

1. We can keep our eyes and ears open—observe events carefully.
2. We can answer employees' questions about the strike and the company's plan—but make sure information is accurate.
3. We can tell employees that they can be permanently replaced if they strike.
4. We can hire either temporary or permanent replacements for the strikers. Tell these new employees whether they are permanent or temporary.
5. We can remind employees they do not accrue service time and benefits during the strike.[1]
6. We can photograph—unobtrusively—activities on the picket line.

---

1. Check contract language and past practice.

DON'T's

1. We cannot threaten employees with discharge or discipline because of their participation in a legal strike.
2. We cannot spy on union meetings or engage in improper surveillance.
3. We cannot openly photograph or take notes concerning who is on the picket line, as this tends to intimidate the employees.
4. We cannot interrogate employees about their intention to participate in the strike, or their opinions about it.
5. We cannot tell employees they cannot continue their group insurance—they can if *they* pay the premium (for up to six months).[2]
6. Because of the uncertainty of facts at this time, we cannot tell employees they *are* *not* eligible for unemployment benefits—say you *don't* *believe* they will be under the statute.[3]

MUSTS

1. We must keep our eyes and ears open.
2. We must document occurrences by completing an incident report.
3. We must report any incidents immediately.
4. We must use our communication system for supervisors and management so everyone knows what is going on!
5. We must keep matters confidential and check if we have any questions.
6. We must prepare for security problems—contact the local police to alert them to possible vandalism.
7. We must prepare for violence, including having a camera available for documentation, blank incident reports and a first aid kit.

---

2. Check policy language and state law.
3. Check state law.

Appendix 4-B.1

Cover Memo to Management

TO: All (Employer) Supervisors and Managers
FROM: _____
RE: Polling Employees on Strike Intentions

Despite the best efforts of the (Employer), we have reason to believe that a strike by the (Union), is imminent. In order to maximize service to our (Customers), the (Employer) must determine which employees of the (Employer) will be refusing to perform their regular functions during the strike.

Accordingly, we have prepared the enclosed questionnaire to be distributed to all employees of the (Employer) whether or not these employees are in one of the bargaining units, and whether or not they are members of the (Union). Employees are to be permitted to complete these on work time. Be sure you do not direct or order employees to answer or refrain from striking, however. Retain the originals of the questionnaire at your work location, but report compilations immediately to me (_____).

Appendix 4-B.2

Employee Poll

TO: All Employees of (Employer)
FROM: _____
SUBJECT: Determination of Whether Employees Intend to Work or Strike

The (Employer) has received notice of intent to strike from (Union), which represents some of our employees for purposes of collective bargaining. The union has indicated that a strike will occur. It is the (Employer's) intention to continue service for our community during any strike.

In order for the (Employer) to meet its responsibilities to customers and out community, it is necessary to ascertain the intent of individual employees as to whether they intend to work during this strike. We make this inquiry for no other purpose. As the bottom of this memorandum is a separate detachable form upon which each employee is asked to state his or her intentions with respect to the strike which the (Union) has called.

(Employer) can assure you that there will be no reprisals taken against any employee who expresses a desire to strike rather than work. So that an individual employee's decision can be made in private and so that the result of the employees' expressed wish to either

Strike Planning

the result of the employees' expressed wish to either work or strike remain somewhat confidential, this "poll" is being conducted in writing. It should again be emphasized that the results of this poll will be used only to consider the question of staffing and the number of replacement personnel that may be required.

Please complete the questionnaire below and return it to your supervisor as soon as possible.

_____

1. Name: _____ Date: _____
2. Work Location: _____
3. Job Classification: _____
4. Shift: _____
5. Supervisor's Name: _____
6. ☐ I will work during any strike. ☐ I will not work.

Appendix 4-C

CERTIFIED OR REGISTERED MAIL,
RETURN RECEIPT REQUESTED

TO: _____
       Secretary-Treasurer
       [Local Union] No. _____

_____

SUBJECT: Union Membership Resignation

Dear _____:

    Effective immediately I completely resign from the union. As such, I will make no payments to the union and I am no longer bound by any union constitutions, bylaws, or rules of any kind.

                               Sincerely,

                               Employee

[Employee should also keep copy for personal records.]

Appendix 4-D

<u>CERTIFIED OR REGISTERED MAIL, RETURN RECEIPT REQUESTED</u>

TO: _____
      Secretary-Treasurer
      [Local Union] No. ____
      _____
      _____

SUBJECT: Transfer to "Financial Core" Status

Dear _____:

    Effective immediately I change my membership from that of full member to that of a financial core member. As such I will only pay appropriate union dues and fees, and I am no longer bound by any union constitutions, bylaws, or rules of any kind.

                                    Sincerely,

                                    Employee

[Employee should also keep copy for personal records.]

Appendix 4-E

TO: All Employees
FROM: _____
RE: Crossing the Union Picket Line

(<u>Employer</u>) appreciates your support of our position in the strike called by the union. We will do the best we can to protect you. You can help in this regard by avoiding controversial situations.

Some helpful points to remember are:

1. Do not participate in threats, gestures, curses, or name calling.

2. Do not stop and get involved in arguments or debates. You do not have to defend your action to anyone.

3. Move deliberately, but at a safe speed, through a picket line. Absent a hazardous situation, do not stop.

4. If trouble is expected or actually occurs, contact _____ at _____ immediately.

5. If you are physically blocked, do not try to enter. Leave the scene and call _____ at _____ at once.

6. As soon as anything unusual occurs give information at once to _____ at _____. Take detailed notes at once.

Part II: Responding to Union Strike Activity

Introduction

Sound contingency planning must take into account what unions may and may not do to disrupt operations and exert economic pressure in support of their demands. Although the law permits unions to use economic weapons, such as strikes, it lays ground rules designed to ensure that unions and employees do not gain economic advantage by violating their agreements, breaching the public peace, or involving innocent parties in disputes. These rules limit both the type and the timing of permissible strike activities. A general familiarity with the legal principles underlying these limitations enhances an employer's ability to use them to advantage.

The planning process should, then, include consideration of the myriad legal problems that may accompany a strike. This requires close consultation with legal counsel to assure that a coordinated legal strategy is in place before a strike begins. During the strike, counsel should be kept advised of developments rather than consulted only as problems arise. Because it eliminates the necessity for extensive background briefing, continuous consultation will permit legal action to be taken promptly when necessary. It will also afford counsel the opportunity to decide which facts are pertinent to an evaluation of the legal situation.

Advance consultation with counsel may not be feasible when strike action occurs without warning, as often happens with strikes in violation of the union contract, sympathy strikes, and so-called jurisdictional disputes. Employers and employer's counsel should still plan for these occurrences, especially if the industry is prone to such work stoppages. Indeed, the best way to assure that such activities do not occur is to demonstrate readiness to mount a well thought out and immediate response to events. The starting point, of course, is to determine what the law permits in any situation.

5
Responding to Unprotected Strikes

The right of unions and employees to participate in strikes and similar acts of economic coercion lies at the heart of the American labor relations system. Federal statutes and laws in many states, for example, preclude courts from issuing injunctions against strikes and picketing except in extraordinary circumstances.[1] Perhaps more significant, the National Labor Relations Act generally prohibits employers from disciplining employees who strike over terms and conditions of employment.

However, not all strikes and work stoppages are protected. When employee activity is *unprotected*, management may discipline participating employees. The union may test the legality of discipline in proceedings before the NLRB, which has the primary responsibility for determining the scope of the Act's protections. When employee activity is *unlawful*, as when it violates a collective bargaining agreement, the employer may also be able to obtain an injunction or, in some cases, recover damages from the union. Effective strike planning requires that an employer know what employee activity the law protects, as well as what options management has in any situation.

---

1. *See* 29 U.S.C. §§ 104, 107; *see also, e.g.*, N.Y. LABOR L. §§ 807, 808; MASS. GEN. L., ch. 214, § 6; IND. CODE §§ 22-6-1-4, *et seq.*; UTAH CODE §§ 34-19-1, *et seq.*

Responding to Strikes

5.1 Scope of the Statutory Protection of Strikes and Related Actions

5.1.1 Protected Activity: Strikes and Refusals to Work for Mutual Aid or Protection

Section 7 of the Act gives private sector employees the right to undertake "concerted activities for the purpose of collective bargaining or other mutual aid or protection." This protects employees who strike or refuse to work because of disputes over terms and conditions of employment.[2] It may also protect a lone employee's actions if the employee is invoking a right grounded in an existing labor agreement, even without an express reference to the contract,[3] or if the employee acts "on the authority of other employees."[4] Because they are not for mutual aid or protection, strikes over management philosophy or individual grievances are not protected by section 7 of the Act.[5] Nor does the Act protect

---

2. NLRB v. Washington Aluminum Co., 370 U.S. 9, 50 L.R.R.M. 2235 (1962); *see* Daniels Constr. Co., 267 N.L.R.B. No. 194, 114 L.R.R.M. 1159 (1983).
3. NLRB v. City Disposal Systems, Inc., 52 U.S.L.W. 4360, 115 L.R.R.M. 3193 (1984); Interboro Contractors, Inc., 157 N.L.R.B. 1295, 61 L.R.R.M. 1537 (1966), *enforced*, 388 F.2d 495, 67 L.R.R.M. 2083 (2d Cir. 1967).
4. Meyers Industries, Inc., 268 N.L.R.B. No. 73, 115 L.R.R.M. 1025, 1029 (1984). For the nine years prior to *Meyers*, the NLRB had applied a more liberal test, finding a lone employee's actions "concerted" if they addressed matters of concern to other employees, such as safety. *See* Alleluia Cushion Co., 221 N.L.R.B. 999, 91 L.R.R.M. 1131 (1975). The courts, however, were less receptive to a single employee's claims of concerted activity with respect to actions not taken to enforce a collective bargaining agreement. Scooba Mfg. v. NLRB, 694 F.2d 82, 84, 112 L.R.R.M. 2113 (5th Cir. 1982); Krispy Kreme Doughnut Corp. v. NLRB, 635 F.2d 304, 105 L.R.R.M. 3407 (4th Cir. 1980).
5. Keyway, a Division of Phase, Inc., 263 N.L.R.B. 1168, 1170, 111 L.R.R.M. 1196, 1198 (1982).

concerted activity that seeks to usurp or undermine the Union's role as employee representative.[6]

Section 8(a)(1) of the Act prohibits employers from interfering with, restraining, or coercing employees because of their exercise of section 7 rights. This effectively precludes the discipline or discharge of employees who strike or refuse to work because of disputes over terms and conditions of employment.[7] Section 8(a)(1) does not, however, insulate employees from discipline for engaging in certain types of economic coercion, even if their goal is mutual aid and protection.

5.1.2 Unprotected Activity: Partial Strikes, Slowdowns, Sit-ins, and Sickouts

Section 7 does not protect slowdowns and partial refusals to work. An early case established the principle that an employee who reports and is paid must put in a full day's work.[8] Employees who engage in work slowdowns therefore may be severely disciplined.[9] Similarly, the Act does not protect employees who refuse to perform only a portion of their normal activities; an employer may discipline employees engaging in such a "partial strike."[10]

"Sit-ins" or "sit-down" strikes, in which employees refuse to leave the employer's premises, have traditionally been regarded

---

6. Emporium Capwell Co. v. Western Addition Community Organization, 420 U.S. 50, 88 L.R.R.M. 2660 (1975).
7. See NLRB v. Washington Aluminum Co., 370 U.S. 9, 50 L.R.R.M. 2235 (1962).
8. Elk Lumber Co., 91 N.L.R.B. 333, 26 L.R.R.M. 1493 (1950); see also Classic Products Corp., 226 N.L.R.B. 170, 177, 93 L.R.R.M. 1279 (1976).
9. See Clarklift of St. Louis, Inc., 259 N.L.R.B. 12, 15, 108 L.R.R.M. 1261 (1981) (discharge of union steward for advocating slowdown).
10. Audobon Health Care Center, 268 N.L.R.B. No. 14, 114 L.R.R.M. 1242 (1983).

as unprotected activity.[11] In the past, employers were ordinarily within their rights in discharging or disciplining workers who protested by refusing to leave at the conclusion of their shift. This principle has eroded somewhat over the past decade, as the NLRB and the courts have displayed an inclination to consider a sit-in protected activity, so long as it is a brief protest that does not interfere with other workers' production.[12] When a sit-in impedes work, however, the employer may discipline the employees responsible.

Sickouts, which involve employee abuse of sick leave provisions, are more troublesome. Because sickouts are complete refusals to work, they are generally protected activity.[13] However, overruling the NLRB, one court has held that an employer could lawfully discipline employees for falsely calling in sick, even though they would have been protected had they simply walked out.[14] To justify such discipline, the employer must show that the unprotected activity (i.e., misuse of sick leave and untruthful claims of illness) prompted the discipline, which would have been imposed even in the absence of the protected action (i.e., the refusal to work).[15] An employer will be in a better position to meet this burden if he has a clearly established practice of disciplining employees who abuse sick leave.

---

11. NLRB v. Fansteel Metallurgical Corp., 306 U.S. 240, 4 L.R.R.M. 515 (1939); Peck, Inc., 226 N.L.R.B. 1174, 93 L.R.R.M. 1434 (1976).
12. United Merchants & Mfrs., Inc. v. NLRB, 554 F.2d 1276, 95 L.R.R.M. 2369 (4th Cir. 1977); Overhead Door, 220 N.L.R.B. 431, 90 L.R.R.M. 1257 (1975), *enforced in part*, 540 F.2d 878, 93 L.R.R.M. 2147 (7th Cir. 1976).
13. *See, e.g.* A.J. Librera Disposal Service, Inc., 247 N.L.R.B. 829, 833, 103 L.R.R.M. 1286 (1980).
14. Charge Card Association v. NLRB, 653 F.2d 272, 109 L.R.R.M. 2725 (6th Cir. 1981), *denying enforcement of* 247 N.L.R.B. 835, 103 L.R.R.M. 1298 (1980).
15. *See* American Steel Works, 263 N.L.R.B. 826, 111 L.R.R.M. 1136 (1982) (discharge for participating in wildcat unlawful when it would not have occurred but for employee's protected activity).

5.2 Contractual Waiver of the Right to Strike

A union may waive employees' right to strike by entering into contracts in which the union and the employees it represents pledge to refrain from striking during the term of the agreement. Once these promises have been made, traditional legal principles favoring the integrity of voluntary agreements prevail over the statutory protection of the right to strike. An employer confronted with a strike in breach of an agreement therefore has a range of remedies. Their effectiveness, however, depends largely upon the scope of the no-strike clause in the agreement with the union.

5.2.1 Scope of the Implied No-strike Clause

Even if a contract does not expressly prohibit employees from striking, a no-strike obligation will be inferred if the parties have agreed upon binding arbitration for disputes arising under the contract.[16] A surprising number of employers still rely exclusively on such implied no-strike obligations, failing to spell out what may be the employer's most important protection under its union agreement. However, the scope of the union's implied obligation may be far narrower than the employer needs.

A union's implied duty to refrain from striking extends only to strikes over disputes covered by the contractual arbitration clause. Under this principle, known as the "coterminous doctrine," the issue underlying a particular strike must be arbitrable under the agreement for the strike to be prohibited.[17] One court has also held that an implied no-strike clause protects only

---

16. Teamsters, Local 174 v. Lucas Flour, 369 U.S. 95, 49 L.R.R.M. 2717 (1962).
17. *See* Gateway Coal v. Mine Workers, 414 U.S. 368, 382, 85 L.R.R.M. 2049, 2055 (1974).

against strikes and not against union-led slowdowns.[18] Although this peculiar view has been rejected,[19] it underlines the risks an employer runs when the contract fails to specify the union's duties.

5.2.2 Scope of the Express No-strike Clause

An explicit no-strike clause may offer only slightly more protection than that implied from the existence of a binding arbitration provision. Many contracts contain vaguely worded no-strike clauses, in which unions agree generally to refrain from work stoppages during the term of the agreement. Even if not specifically phrased, such clauses are usually deemed to prohibit slowdowns, sickouts, concerted refusals to work overtime, and similar subterfuges.[20] Absent bargaining history clearly showing that the parties intended otherwise, however, the scope of a nonspecific clause will be deemed coterminous with the grievance and arbitration procedure,[21] just as an implied no-strike obligation would be. Under this principle, a general no-strike clause will not pro-

---

18. Jessop Steel Co. v. United Steelworkers, 428 F. Supp. 172, 175-76, 94 L.R.R.M. 3089, 3091 (W.D. Pa. 1977).
19. The Seattle Times Co. v. Mailers Union, Local 32, 664 F.2d 1366, 1368, 109 L.R.R.M. 2353, 2354 (9th Cir. 1982).
20. Elevator Manufacturers Assn. v. Elevator Constructors, Local 1, 689 F.2d 382, 386, 111 L.R.R.M. 2631, 2633 (2d Cir. 1982). Tenneco Chemicals, Inc. v. Teamsters Local 401, 520 F.2d 945, 947-48, 90 L.R.R.M. 2147, 2149 (3d Cir. 1975); California Trucking Association v. Teamsters, Local 70, 94 L.R.R.M. 2981, 2989 (N.D. Cal. 1977) (implied no-strike obligation), *aff'd in part, rev'd in part*, 679 F.2d 1275, 108 L.R.R.M. 2955 (1981), *cert. denied*, 111 L.R.R.M. 2744 (1982).
21. NLRB v. Southern California Edison Co., 646 F.2d 1352, 1367, 107 L.R.R.M. 2667, 2676 (9th Cir. 1981). An employer's obligation to arbitrate may extend beyond the contract's expiration for disputes arising out of the expired agreement. Under the coterminous doctrine, the union's obligation not to strike over arbitrable grievances may also survive the contract's expiration. Goya Foods, Inc., 238 N.L.R.B. 1465, 99 L.R.R.M. 1282 (1978).

hibit sympathy strikes,[22] nor will a nonspecific no-strike provision bar work stoppages precipitated by an employer's serious unfair labor practices.[23] Finally, in a decision that the Third Circuit Court of Appeals refused to enforce, the NLRB held that a broad no-strike clause would not prohibit a strike over a dispute with a health and welfare fund.[24]

A union *may* waive the right to strike over issues not subject to grievance arbitration.[25] Such a waiver must, however, be clear

---

22. *See, e.g.*, Gary-Hobart Water Corp. v. NLRB, 511 F.2d 284, 88 L.R.R.M. 2830 (7th Cir.), *cert. denied*, 423 U.S. 925 (1975).
23. Mastro Plastics v. NLRB, 350 U.S. 270, 281-83, 37 L.R.R.M. 2587 (1956); Arlan's Department Store, Inc., 133 N.L.R.B. 802, 48 L.R.R.M. 1731 (1961); *cf.* Dow Chemical Co. v. NLRB, 636 F.2d 1352, 105 L.R.R.M. 3327 (3d Cir. 1980), *cert. denied*, 454 U.S. 818 (1981) (holding unfair labor practice strike violated no-strike clause when strike arose from dispute over interpretation of contract rather than anti-union actions). An unfair labor practice may be deemed serious for these purposes if it is "destructive of the foundation on which collective bargaining must rest." Mastro Plastics, 350 U.S. at 281; *see also* Caterpillar Tractor Co. v. NLRB, 658 F.2d 1242, 1244, 108 L.R.R.M. 2460, 2463 (7th Cir. 1981).
24. Pacemaker Yacht Co., 253 N.L.R.B. 828, 106 L.R.R.M.. 1017 (1980), *enforcement denied*, 663 F.2d 455, 108 L.R.R.M. 2817 (1981).
25. The union cannot, however, waive employees' rights to stop work because of "abnormally dangerous" working conditions, at least when there is "ascertainable objective evidence" of a safety hazard. Gateway Coal Co. v. Mine Workers, 414 U.S. 368, 85 L.R.R.M. 2049 (1974); *see also* Whirlpool Corp. v. Marshall, 445 U.S. 1 (1980) (under OSHA regulation, employee may refuse a task if employee has reasonable apprehension of serious injury and reasonably believes no less drastic alternative is available). If conditions are not abnormally dangerous, contracts that require arbitration of safety disputes may be construed to ban work stoppages over allegedly inadequate safety. Irvin H. Whitehouse & Sons v. NLRB, 659 F.2d 830, 108 L.R.R.M. 2578 (7th Cir. 1981), *denying enforcement of* 252 N.L.R.B. 997, 105 L.R.R.M. 1412 (1980); NLRB v. Maryland Shipbuilding & Drydock Co., 683 F.2d 109, 110 L.R.R.M. 3272 (4th Cir. 1982), *denying enforcement of* 256 N.L.R.B. 410, 107 L.R.R.M. 1283 (1981); *see also* American Freight System v. NLRB, 114 L.R.R.M. 3513 (D.C. Cir. 1983).

and unmistakable from "express contractual language or . . . unequivocal extrinsic evidence bearing upon ambiguous contractual language."[26] Traditionally, the NLRB has gone to great lengths to avoid finding such a clear and unmistakable waiver when the contract contains only a general no-strike clause, even if bargaining history suggests that the parties intended the clause to encompass strikes over nonarbitrable issues.[27] Some courts have been more willing than the NLRB to find such a waiver based upon a general no-strike clause in combination with extrinsic evidence of the parties' intent.[28] Others have adhered to the NLRB's strong presumption against finding a waiver in such circumstances.[29]

5.2.3 Negotiating for Clear and Unmistakable Waivers of the Right to Strike

An employer cannot assume that a general no-strike clause will protect against anything more than strikes over issues subject to

---

26. Operating Engineers, Local 18 (Davis-McKee, Inc.), 238 N.L.R.B. 652, 99 L.R.R.M. 1307 (1978); Gary-Hobart Water Corp., 210 N.L.R.B. 742, 86 L.R.R.M. 1210 (1974), *enforced* 511 F.2d 284, 88 L.R.R.M. 2830 (7th Cir.), *cert. denied*, 423 U.S. 925, 90 L.R.R.M. 2921 (1975).
27. *See, e.g.*, W-1 Canteen Service, Inc., 238 N.L.R.B. 609, 99 L.R.R.M. 1571 (1978), *enforcement denied*, 606 F.2d 738, 102 L.R.R.M. 2447 (7th Cir. 1979). *But see* St. Regis Paper Co., 253 N.L.R.B. 1224, 1229, 106 L.R.R.M. 1207 (1981) (examining bargaining history).
28. *See, e.g.* W-1 Canteen Service, Inc. v. NLRB, 606 F.2d 738, 743, 102 L.R.R.M. 2447, 2448 (7th Cir. 1979); ACF Industries, Inc. v. NLRB, 641 F.2d 561, 106 L.R.R.M. 2518 (8th Cir. 1981); Pacemaker Yacht Co. v. NLRB, 663 F.2d 455, 108 L.R.R.M. 2817 (3d Cir. 1981); Ryder Truck Lines v. Teamsters, Local 480, 727 F.2d 594, 115 L.R.R.M. 2912 (6th Cir. 1984).
29. NLRB v. Southern California Edison, 646 F.2d 1352, 107 L.R.R.M. 2667 (9th Cir. 1981); Delaware Coca-Cola Bottling Co. v. Teamsters, Local 326, 624 F.2d 1182, 104 L.R.R.M. 2776 (3d Cir. 1980); NLRB v. Gould, Inc., 638 F.2d 159, 105 L.R.R.M. 2788 (10th Cir. 1980), *cert. denied*, 452 U.S. 930 (1981).

the contractual grievance arbitration machinery. Consequently, it may be prudent negotiation strategy to seek the most detailed no-strike clause possible, prohibiting every conceivable type of work stoppage for every conceivable reason.[30] For such a clause to be effective, it must be *specific* and not contain any language limiting its scope. The following is one example of such a clause:

> Neither the union nor its members, agents, representatives, or employees, or persons acting in concert with them, shall directly or indirectly incite, encourage, authorize, or participate in any strike, walkout, slowdown, sickout, or other work stoppage of any nature or for any reason whatsoever during the life of this agreement, whether or not the work stoppage or its cause relates to an issue that is subject to or covered by the grievance procedure contained herein. Activities prohibited by the preceding sentence shall include, but not be limited to, sympathy strikes, political strikes, picketing, handbilling, wildcats, walkouts, unfair labor practice strikes of any kind, strikes relating to any third parties (such as, but not limited to, health and welfare, pension or trust funds), slowdowns, boycotts, or any other interference with the operations of the employer, including any refusal to cross any other labor organization's or group's picket line.

---

30. This strategy is not without its hazards. If the employer seeks, but fails to obtain, a specific waiver of rights, the resulting contract is unlikely to be viewed as waiving such rights. *See* Gary-Hobart Water Corp., 210 N.L.R.B. 742, 86 L.R.R.M. 1210 (1974), *enforced*, 511 F.2d 284, 88 L.R.R.M. 2830 (7th Cir. 1975), *cert. denied*, 423 U.S. 925 (1976). By the same token, rejection of a *union* proposal for specific preservation of such rights is also significant. ACF Industries v. NLRB, 641 F.2d 561, 567, 106 L.R.R.M. 2518 (8th Cir. 1981). *But see* NLRB v. Southern California Edison Co., 646 F.2d 1352, 107 L.R.R.M. 2667 (9th Cir. 1981) (union's failure to obtain proposed clause preserving sympathy strike right not determinative).

Any employee who directly or indirectly authorizes, engages in, encourages, sanctions, recognizes, or assists in any work stoppage or action described in the preceding paragraph, or who refuses to perform services duly assigned to him, shall be subject to immediate discharge.

The uncertainty and flux of the law in this area precludes uncritical reliance on such a clause. Counsel should be consulted during labor negotiations to determine the current state of the law with respect to waivers of employees' strike rights.[31] Because detailed waivers offer an employer greater flexibility in disciplining employees, obtaining injunctive relief against work stoppages, and pursuing damage remedies against the union, they should be sought at the bargaining table.

Unions are apt to balk at proposals for the inclusion of such language. The hesitant union should be reminded that the absence of industrial strife, for whatever reason, is a key consideration for the employer's acceptance of a collective bargaining agreement containing provisions of importance to the union.

5.2.4 Negotiating for Functional Independence of the No-strike and Arbitration Clauses

When a detailed waiver of the right to strike cannot be negotiated, the employer should take steps to assure that the grievance arbitration procedure is not tied to the no-strike clause. A close relationship between the two provisions makes it more likely that

---

31. For example, although the NLRB has never ruled on the issue, there have been hints that an employer's insistence to the point of impasse on a clause waiving the right to strike over unfair labor practices could itself be an unfair labor practice. *See* NLRB, REPORT OF THE GENERAL COUNSEL ON CASEHANDLING DEVELOPMENTS (2d Quarter, 1977). One court has also expressed doubts that such a clause would be an effective or legal provision. Dow Chemical Co. v. NLRB, 636 F.2d 1352, 1361, 105 L.R.R.M. 3327 (3d Cir. 1980), *cert. denied*, 454 U.S. 818 (1981).

Unprotected Strikes

the union will not be held to breach the contract if it strikes over nonarbitrable issues.[32] When the arbitration and no-strike clauses appear in different sections of the agreement and do not depend upon one another, the union will find it more difficult to argue that their scope is coextensive. One court has read a general no-strike clause having no functional relationship to the grievance arbitration procedure as waiving the right to strike over nonarbitrable issues.[33]

5.3 Responding to Union-led Strikes in Breach of Contract

5.3.1 Disciplinary Action against Employees

By entering into an agreement containing a no-strike clause, a union waives employees' statutory right to strike. Consequently, employees who strike in violation of a no-strike clause are engaging in unprotected conduct. An employer does not violate the law if it disciplines or discharges participating employees.[34] The Act

---

32. *See* Ryder Truck Lines v. Teamsters, Local 480, 705 F.2d 851, 857, 113 L.R.R.M. 2193, 2195 (6th Cir.), *vacated pending rehearing en banc*, 710 F.2d 233, 113 L.R.R.M. 3226 (6th Cir. 1983), *on rehearing*, 727 F.2d 594, 115 L.R.R.M. 2912 (6th Cir. 1984). Although the employer ultimately prevailed in *Ryder*, the Sixth Circuit's initial opinion illustrates the difficulty caused by an apparent relationship between the no-strike and grievance arbitration provisions.
33. United States Steel Corp. v. NLRB, 711 F.2d 772, 778, 113 L.R.R.M. 3227, 3231 (7th Cir. 1983); Inland Steel Co. v. NLRB, 719 F.2d 205, 114 L.R.R.M. 3414 (7th Cir. 1983); *see* W-1 Canteen Service, Inc. v. NLRB, 606 F.2d 738, 744, 102 L.R.R.M. 2447 (7th Cir. 1979).
34. NLRB v. Sands Manufacturing Co., 306 U.S. 332, 4 L.R.R.M. 530 (1939); Fisher Foods, Inc., 245 N.L.R.B. 685, 698, 102 L.R.R.M. 1513 (1979).

Responding to Strikes

permits disciplinary action even if the union, rather than the affected employees, leads the work stoppage.[35] The touchstone for discipline should be the contract itself, which may make specific provision for the discipline of strikers.

An employer wishing to impose discipline for breach of the no-strike obligation should take care not to waive its right to do so by agreeing to return the employees to work. A promise to take "all employees" back to work, or a pledge to engage in "no reprisals" may show forgiveness or condonation of the employees' unprotected action.[36] Any discipline imposed after the employer has condoned the conduct will violate section 8(a)(1) of the Act.

5.3.2 Injunctive Relief

The Norris-LaGuardia Act[37] generally prohibits federal courts from issuing injunctive relief in labor disputes. Many states have little Norris-LaGuardia Acts imposing similar limitations on their courts.[38] The Supreme Court has, however, recognized a narrow exception to these limitations, permitting injunctions against

---

35. *See* Dow Chemical Co. v. NLRB, 636 F.2d 1352, 1362, 105 L.R.R.M. 3327 (3d Cir. 1980), *cert. denied*, 454 U.S. 818 (1981); Electrical, Radio and Machine Workers, Local 1113 v. NLRB, 223 F.2d 338, 343, 36 L.R.R.M. 2175 (D.C. Cir. 1955); *see also* Atkinson v. Sinclair Refining Co., 370 U.S. 238, 246, 50 L.R.R.M. 2433 (1962). A union may even breach its duty to fairly represent its members if it knowingly exposes members to discipline by leading a contractually prohibited work stoppage. Teamsters, Local 299 (McLean Trucking Co.), 270 NLRB No. 188, 116 LRRM 1287 (1984).
36. Richardson Paint Co. v. NLRB, 574 F.2d 1195, 1203, 98 L.R.R.M. 2951 (5th Cir. 1978); Jones & McKnight, Inc. v. NLRB, 445 F.2d 97, 102, 77 L.R.R.M. 2705 (7th Cir. 1971). *But see* Virginia Electric & Power Co., 262 N.L.R.B. 1119, 1126, 111 L.R.R.M. 1054 (1982) (finding no condonation).
37. 29 U.S.C. §§ 101, *et seq.*
38. *See, e.g.*, N.Y. LABOR L. §§ 807, 808; MASS. GEN. L., ch. 214, § 6; IND. CODE §§ 22-6-1-4, *et seq.*; UTAH CODE §§ 34-19-1, *et seq.*

Unprotected Strikes

work stoppages in derogation of grievance arbitration mechanisms found in the contract. In *Boys Markets, Inc. v. Retail Clerks Union, Local 770*,[39] the Court held that a strike may be enjoined if it is over a dispute that the parties are bound to arbitrate and is in violation of a no-strike obligation in the collective bargaining agreement. To allow strikes to continue in such circumstances, the Court reasoned, would violate federal labor law's fundamental preference for arbitration as a means of resolving disputes.

An employer's request for injunctive relief under authority of *Boys Markets* is ordinarily joined with a claim for damages arising from the strike. Both causes of action arise under section 301 of the Labor-Management Relations Act,[40] which provides that federal courts have jurisdiction over suits alleging violations of collective bargaining agreements. State courts also have authority to issue injunctions against breaches of a no-strike clause.[41] Indeed, although state courts hearing suits alleging breaches of labor contracts are generally bound to follow federal substantive law,[42] some restrictions on federal injunctive relief may not apply in state actions. A few state courts have indicated a willingness to enjoin strikes that a federal court would likely leave untouched.[43] As a practical matter, however, federal law governs this field, as unions generally remove state actions for injunctive relief to federal court before the state court acts.[44]

---

39. 398 U.S. 235, 74 L.R.R.M. 2257 (1970).
40. 29 U.S.C. § 185.
41. William E. Arnold Co. v. Carpenters, 417 U.S. 12, 86 L.R.R.M. 2212 (1974).
42. Teamsters, Local 174 v. Lucas Flour, 369 U.S. 95, 49 L.R.R.M. 2717 (1962).
43. For example, in Textile Workers, Local 1127 v. Blackburn's Manufacturing Co., 349 So. 2d 46, 96 L.R.R.M. 2977 (Ala. 1977), Alabama's high court affirmed entry of injunctive relief even though the strike in question was not over an arbitrable dispute. In such circumstances, a federal court probably would not have entered such relief. *Compare* Purex Corp. v. Teamsters, Local 618, 705 F.2d 274, 112 L.R.R.M. 3433 (8th Cir. 1983).
44. *See* Granny Goose Foods v. Teamsters, Local 70, 415 U.S. 423, 85 L.R.R.M. 2481 (1974).

Before issuing an injunctive under authority of *Boys Markets*, a federal district court must find that an employer has met the traditional equitable tests for injunctive relief. This requires the employer to demonstrate that: (1) there is a substantial likelihood that it will ultimately prevail at trial; (2) it will suffer irreparable injury if the injunction is not entered; (3) the threatened injury to the employer outweighs the damage the union will suffer if the injunction is entered; and (4) the injunction would not be adverse to the public interest.[45] Some federal courts have held that the employer must also meet at least some of the procedural requirements of the federal Norris-LaGuardia Act before a *Boys Markets* injunction may issue.[46] Although the provisions of this Act in large measure duplicate traditional equitable standards, it also requires efforts at voluntary resolution of the dispute, testimony in open court, and entry of certain findings of fact.[47] Before seeking an injunction, then, employer's counsel should consider the attitude of the relevant court of appeals with respect to the application of Norris-LaGuardia. Otherwise, a well-founded petition for injunctive relief could fail because it does not comply with the Act's provisions.

Because *Boys Markets* focused upon arbitration as a means of settling labor disputes, unions have long argued that an employer

---

45. Jacksonville Maritime Assn. v. Longshoreman, ILA, 571 F.2d 319, 322-23, 98 L.R.R.M. 2184 (5th Cir. 1978). A few courts have held that an employer will satisfy the requirement that it demonstrate the likelihood of prevailing on the merits if it shows that there is a genuine dispute over an arbitrable issue. *See* Aluminum Workers, Local 215 v. Consolidated Aluminum Corp., 696 F.2d 437, 442, n.2, 112 L.R.R.M. 2299 (6th Cir. 1982).
46. United Parcel Service, Inc. v. Teamsters, Local 804, 698 F.2d 100, 105, 112 L.R.R.M. 2648, 2649 (2d Cir. 1983); Celotex Corp. v. OCAW, 516 F.2d 242, 246, 89 L.R.R.M. 2372, 2376 (3d Cir. 1975). Other courts have been more hesitant to apply Norris-LaGuardia's restrictions. *See, e.g.,* United States v. Cunningham, 599 F.2d 120, 126, n.12, 101 L.R.R.M. 2508 (6th Cir. 1979).
47. 29 U.S.C. §§ 107-09.

Unprotected Strikes

must prove its willingness to arbitrate before the strike can be enjoined. This argument has generally been rejected.[48] As a condition to granting a *Boys Markets* injunction, however, the federal district court will compel the employer to arbitrate the dispute, thus providing the union a means of resolving whatever issues caused the strike.[49] The court will also require the employer to post a bond for damages, payable to the union, in case it is ultimately decided that the injunction was wrongfully issued.[50]

5.3.2.1 Arbitrability of the Dispute Giving Rise to the Strike

In *Buffalo Forge Co. v. Steelworkers*,[51] the Supreme Court held that pre-arbitration injunctions against strikes could issue only when the dispute precipitating the work stoppage could be resolved by arbitration between the employer and the union it sought to enjoin. The employer in *Buffalo Forge* was thus unable to obtain a *Boys Markets* injunction to halt a *sympathy strike* by Steelworkers Union members because the underlying dispute involved the employer and a union other than the Steelworkers. Arbitration between the employer and the Steelworkers, whose strike it wanted to enjoin, could not resolve the underlying issues, rendering injunctive relief inappropriate.

---

48. United Parcel Service, Inc., v. Teamsters, Local 804, 698 F.2d 100, 105, 112 L.R.R.M. 2648 (2d Cir. 1983); Jacksonville Maritime Assn. v. Longshoreman, ILA, 571 F.2d 319, 325, 98 L.R.R.M. 2184, 2190 (5th Cir. 1978).
49. United Parcel Service, Inc., v. Teamsters, Local 804, 698 F.2d at 105; United States Steel Corp. v. Mine Workers, 534 F.2d 1063, 1078, 91 L.R.R.M. 3031 (3d Cir. 1976).
50. *See* 29 U.S.C. § 107. In one unusual case the court held that the union could recover damages for a wrongfully issued injunction in amounts in excess of the required bond. United States Steel Corp. v. United Mine Workers, 456 F.2d 483, 79 L.R.R.M. 2518 (3d Cir.), *cert. denied*, 408 U.S. 923 (1972).
51. 428 U.S. 397, 92 L.R.R.M. 3032 (1976).

Responding to Strikes

Buffalo Forge also prevents an employer from obtaining *Boys Markets* pre-arbitration injunctive relief against strikes over political issues.[52] More important, the requirement that the underlying dispute be arbitrable will generally prevent an employer from obtaining a *Boys Markets* injunction against strikes in support of bargaining demands. Even if the work stoppage clearly violates an evergreen clause or a contract extension agreement, few collective bargaining contracts provide for the arbitration of collective bargaining issues (generally known as "interest arbitration").[53] This does not mean that the employer cannot recover damages in such cases.[54]

When faced with a suit for an injunction, a union may go to great lengths to claim that the dispute underlying the strike is not arbitrable. As a result, the employer should take care to characterize the underlying issues so there is no doubt as to arbitrability. Earlier union descriptions of the dispute that favored the employer's position should be carefully documented to prevent the union from reframing the issues after the employer files an injunction action.

5.3.2.2 Scope and Enforcement of the *Boys Markets* Injunction

Most *Boys Markets* injunctions order cessation of the strike that prompted the employer to seek relief, requiring striking employees to return to work. Because of the necessity for detailed factual findings each time a strike is enjoined, the injunction usually will not expressly prohibit future violations of the no-strike clause.

---

52. Jacksonville Bulk Terminals v. Longshoremen, ILA, 457 U.S. 702, 110 L.R.R.M. 2665 (1982). Strikes over political issues might, however, be unlawful secondary activity. *See* Longshoremen, ILA, v. Allied International, Inc., 456 U.S. 212, 110 L.R.R.M. 2001 (1982). Chapter 7 discusses the availability of injunctions against secondary strikes.
53. Purex Corp. v. Teamsters, Local 618, 705 F.2d 274, 276, 112 L.R.R.M. 3433 (8th Cir. 1983).
54. Section 5.3.3.1, *infra*, discusses the ability to recover damages in these circumstances.

Unprotected Strikes

The court may enter an injunction against future strike activity only when it identifies a recurring pattern of union no-strike clause violations.[55] Although such prospective relief is unusual, an employer should seek it whenever the union's past conduct shows a lack of respect for its no-strike obligation.

Regardless of its breadth, the injunction will probably require the union and its officers to undertake specific actions to halt the strike, including disseminating the back-to-work order, disavowing the strike, and encouraging employees to return to work. After receiving notice of a *Boys Markets* injunction, unions,[56] their officers,[57] and individual employees[58] may be held in civil or criminal contempt of court if they fail to comply. In some cases, courts will order the union to pay contempt fines to the employer to compensate for losses occasioned by disregard of the injunction.[59]

5.3.2.3 Enjoining Strikes over Nonarbitrable Issues

The nonarbitrability of the underlying strike issue will not necessarily preclude injunctive relief. If the union has clearly waived the right to strike over nonarbitrable issues,[60] the employer may file a grievance under the contract, asking the arbitrator to find that the union has violated its no-strike obligation.

---

55. United Parcel Service, Inc. v. Teamsters, Local 804, 698 F.2d 100, 110, 112 L.R.R.M. 2648 (2d Cir. 1983); United States Steel Corp. v. Mine Workers, 534 F.2d 1063, 1077, 91 L.R.R.M. 3031 (3d Cir. 1976).
56. Jim Walter Resources, Inc. v. Mine Workers, 609 F.2d 165, 169, 103 L.R.R.M. 2225 (5th Cir. 1980).
57. Consolidation Coal Co. v. Mine Workers, Local 1702, 683 F.2d 827, 829, 110 L.R.R.M. 2911 (4th Cir. 1982).
58. United States v. Cunningham, 599 F.2d 120, 101 L.R.R.M. 2508 (6th Cir. 1979).
59. Consolidation Coal Co. v. Mine Workers, Local 1702, 683 F.2d 827, 830, 110 L.R.R.M. 2911 (4th Cir. 1982); Jim Walter Resources, Inc. v. Mine Workers, 609 F.2d 165, 169, 103 L.R.R.M. 2225 (5th Cir. 1980).
60. *See* sections 5.2.2, 5.2.3, 5.2.4, *supra*.

If the arbitrator agrees, the employer may *then* obtain an injunction enforcing the arbitrator's decision *even though* the underlying dispute is not arbitrable.[61]

This type of injunction differs from relief under *Boys Markets* in that it cannot be issued until *after* arbitration. Because its effectiveness depends upon the speed with which the employer and the arbitrator act, the employer may wish to negotiate a special expedited arbitration clause for grievances over no-strike clause violations. The clause might provide for a permanently designated arbitrator, for arbitration of the dispute within twenty-four hours after notice is given to the union, and for issuance of an award within twelve hours after arbitration.[62]

Such a procedure may be used only if the contract gives the employer the right to file grievances. Many collective bargaining agreements permit only employees or unions to file grievances and initiate arbitration proceedings. Such a one-way grievance procedure makes sense for most employers most of the time. It gives the employer the right to take whatever action it deems appropriate, subject to the union's right to file a grievance if it disagrees. If, on the other hand, the employer has access to the grievance procedure, the union may argue that the contract requires an arbitrator's approval before implementation of certain management proposals. The union may also claim that submission to the arbitrator is a prerequisite to an employer's lawsuit seeking injunctive relief or damages.[63]

---

61. United Parcel Service, Inc. v. Teamsters, Local 804, 698 F.2d 100, 106-07, 112 L.R.R.M. 2648, 2651 (2d Cir. 1983); New Orleans Steamship Ass'n. v. Longshoremen, ILA, Local 1418, 626 F.2d 455, 468, 105 L.R.R.M. 2539 (5th Cir. 1980), *aff'd sub nom.* Jacksonville Bulk Terminals, Inc. v. ILA, 457 U.S. 702, 110 L.R.R.M. 2665 (1982).
62. An expedited arbitration clause containing similar time limitations appeared in the contract considered in United Parcel Service, Inc. v. Teamsters, Local 804, 698 F.2d at 106-07, 112 L.R.R.M. 2648, at 2651.
63. *See* Drake Bakeries, Inc. v. American Bakery & Confection Workers, Local 50, 370 U.S. 254, 50 L.R.R.M. 2440 (1962); *see also* United Parcel Service, Inc. v. Teamsters, Local 804, 689 F.2d at 106-07, 112 L.R.R.M. 2648, at 2650.

Unprotected Strikes

An employer should carefully weigh these considerations before seeking access to the grievance procedure. He might also consider the possibility of securing limited access to the procedure solely for purposes of resolving alleged no-strike clause violations. Even such a carefully circumscribed clause may require an arbitrator's decision before management may request judicial relief for an unlawful strike. The consequences of this restriction should be balanced against the likelihood that the employer will need injunctive relief against a strike over a nonarbitrable issue.

5.3.3 Damage Suits

To remedy injuries suffered before a restraining order is obtained, or because of an inability to obtain a restraining order, the employer should consider filing a suit against the union for damages. Section 301 of the Labor-Management Relations Act gives federal courts the power to hear "[s]uits for violation of contracts between an employer and a labor organization representing employees."[64] Although state courts also have jurisdiction over such suits, they must apply federal law to assure that national labor policy is uniformly respected.[65] Actions filed initially in state court are frequently removed to federal court at the union's request.[66] Thus, as a practical matter, most suits alleging breaches of collective bargaining agreements are resolved in federal district courts.

---

64. 29 U.S.C. § 185(a).
65. Teamsters, Local 959 v. King, 572 P.2d 1168, 97 L.R.R.M. 2123 (Alaska 1977). The statute of limitations for an action under section 301, however, is governed by state law. UAW v. Hoosier-Cardinal Corp., 383 U.S. 696, 61 L.R.R.M. 2545 (1966). Generally, the state statute of limitations for written contracts governs a suit for breach of a collective bargaining agreement. See Kaufman & Broad Home Systems v. Firemen, 607 F.2d 1104, 102 L.R.R.M. 3033, 3035 (5th Cir. 1979).
66. Under 28 U.S.C. § 1441(a), a defendant may remove to federal court "any civil action brought in a state court of which the district courts of the United States have original jurisdiction . . . ."

5.3.3.1 Suits Concerning Strikes during Bargaining

The no-strike obligation ordinarily expires at the same time as the contract. However, many contracts contain evergreen clauses providing that the contract is to remain in effect after its stated expiration date, so long as neither party gives notice of termination.[67] Such clauses will continue the union's no-strike obligation into the negotiating period. If a union strikes in violation of the evergreen no-strike clause, it may be liable for damages just as if it struck in the middle of the contract term.[68] Employers and unions may also agree upon contract extensions to provide stability during negotiations. Strikes in violation of a contract so extended may subject the union to liability.[69]

5.3.3.2 Persons Subject to Suit for Breach of Contract

The employer cannot sue individual employees for their violation of the contractual no-strike obligation.[70] Instead, section 301 contemplates suits against unions. Traditional principles of agency law will apply in determining whether the union is responsible for employees' breach of the no-strike clause.[71] The

---

67. See ch. 2, *supra*, discussing the advisability of evergreen clauses.
68. California Trucking Ass'n v. Teamsters, Local 70, 94 L.R.R.M. 2981, 2983 (N.D. Cal. 1977), *aff'd in part, remanded in part*, 679 F.2d 1275, 108 L.R.R.M. 2955 (9th Cir. 1981), *cert. denied*, 111 L.R.R.M. 2744 (1982).
69. Certified Corp. v. Teamsters, Local 996, 597 F.2d 1269, 101 L.R.R.M. 2584 (9th Cir. 1979).
70. Complete Auto Transit v. Reis, 451 U.S. 401, 107 L.R.R.M. 2145 (1981); Atkinson v. Sinclair Refining Co., 370 U.S. 238, 50 L.R.R.M. 2433 (1962).
71. *See* Labor Management Relations (Taft-Hartley) Act § 301 (e), 29 U.S.C. § 185 (e)(1976). A union is liable under this standard if its agents, acting within the general scope of their agency, authorize, participate in, or ratify the activity. Carbon Fuel Co. v. Mine Workers, 444 U.S. 212, 216-17, 102 L.R.R.M. 3017, 3019 (1979); *see also* North River Energy Corp. v. Mine Workers, 664 F.2d 1184, 1190, 109 L.R.R.M. 2335, 2340 (11th

Unprotected Strikes

employer must establish the union's liability by a preponderance of evidence.[72]

5.3.3.3 Damages Recoverable

A union's breach of its no-strike obligation entitles the employer to recover its

> actual loss sustained . . . as a direct result of the breach and which may reasonably be supposed to have been in the contemplation of the parties as the probable result of such a breach at the time the agreement was made.[73]

As a general rule, this includes damages for sympathy strikes induced by a strike in breach of the contract.[74]

Courts have awarded a wide variety of damages under these general principles. Employers whose operations have been halted by a strike, for example, have recovered lost profits for the strike's duration, lost profits on future contracts cancelled because of the strike, fixed overhead for the period of the shutdown, and salaries paid to idled production workers.[75] Fixed overhead may include health insurance payments for idled em-

---

Cir. 1981). This contrasts with the federal Norris-LaGuardia Act, which requires "clear proof" of a union's "*actual* participation in, or *actual* authorization of [the wrongful] acts, or of ratification of such acts after *actual* knowledge thereof" as a predicate to union liability for misconduct. 29 U.S.C. § 106; *see* ch. 6, *infra*.

72. *See* Mine Workers v. Gibbs, 383 U.S. 715, 736, 61 L.R.R.M. 2561 (1966) (discussing §§ 301 and 303 of Labor-Management Relations Act).
73. Eazor Express, Inc. v. Teamsters, 520 F.2d 951, 967, 89 L.R.R.M. 3177 (3d Cir. 1975), *cert. denied*, 424 U.S. 935 (1976).
74. California Trucking Ass'n v. Teamsters, Local 70, 679 F.2d 1275, 108 L.R.R.M. 2955, 2965 (9th Cir. 1981), *cert. denied*, 111 L.R.R.M. 2744 (1982).
75. Trap Rock Co. v. Teamsters, Local 470, 91 L.R.R.M. 3022, 3030-31 (E.D. Pa. 1976).

ployees, as well as a proportion of property taxes on idled property[76] and straight-line depreciation or rental costs on idled equipment.[77] When an employer attempts to continue operating during the unlawful strike, it may recover the compensation paid to replacements (less the compensation savings by reason of the strike), profits lost due to inefficiency of replacements, and the added cost of purchasing necessary material that the employer would have produced had the strike not occurred.[78] A percentage of fixed overhead equal to the percentage of lost production may also be recoverable if the employer continues operating.[79]

Most courts will allow the employer to collect prejudgment interest on damages from the date of the strike's termination.[80] The interest rate is generally set by state statute. An employer may also recover "extraordinary expenses necessitated by strike activity,"[81] such as security costs and excess freight or demurrage

---

76. Tenneco Chemicals, Inc. v. Teamsters, Local 401, 520 F.2d 945, 90 L.R.R.M. 2147 (3d Cir. 1975); Airco Speer Carbon-Graphite v. Electrical Workers, IUE, Local 502, 479 F. Supp. 246, 252-53, 108 L.R.R.M. 2770 (W.D. Pa. 1979), *vacated and remanded*, _____ F.2d _____ (3d Cir. 1980), *on remand*, 494 F. Supp. 872, 108 L.R.R.M. 2779 (W.D. Pa. 1980), *aff'd*, 649 F.2d 858, 108 L.R.R.M. 2816 (3d Cir. 1981).
77. California Trucking Ass'n v. Teamsters, Local 70, 679 F.2d 1275, 1291, 108 L.R.R.M. 2955, 2967 (9th Cir. 1981) (straight-line depreciation), *cert. denied*, 111 L.R.R.M. 2744 (1982).
78. Delaware Coca-Cola Bottling Co. v. Teamsters, Local 326, 474 F. Supp. 777, 789, 102 L.R.R.M. 2727, 2732-35 (D. Del. 1979), *rev'd on other grounds*, 624 F.2d 1182, 104 L.R.R.M. 2776 (3d Cir. 1980).
79. *See* Tenneco Chemicals, Inc. v. Teamsters, Local 401, 520 F.2d 945, 950, 90 L.R.R.M. 2147, 2151 (3d Cir. 1975).
80. The Seattle Times Co. v. Mailers Union, Local 32, 644 F.2d 1366, 1368, 109 L.R.R.M. 2353 (9th Cir. 1982); Eazor Express, Inc. v. Teamsters, 520 F.2d 951, 973, 89 L.R.R.M. 3177 (3d Cir. 1975).
81. California Trucking Ass'n v. Teamsters, Local 70, 94 L.R.R.M. 2981, 3000 (N.D. Cal. 1977), *aff'd in part, rev'd in part*, 679 F.2d 1275, 108 L.R.R.M. 2955 (9th Cir. 1981), *cert. denied*, 111 L.R.R.M. 2744 (1982).

charges.[82] As a general rule neither punitive damages[83] nor attorneys' fees[84] may be recovered under section 301.

5.4 Responding to Wildcat Strikes

An employer sometimes faces work stoppages instigated by renegade employees who are not controlled by either the local or the international labor organization. These activities often will be protected by section 7.[85] When unauthorized employee-led work stoppages occur despite a valid contractual waiver of the right to strike, however they are not protected. A no-strike clause makes it more likely that any work stoppages the employer experiences will not be expressly authorized by the union, for most union leaders know better than to call openly for a strike in breach of contract.

The term wildcat strike is generally used to describe work stoppages that both violate the contract and lack explicit union authorization. Wildcat strikes present unique problems for the

---

82. Airco Speer Carbon-Graphite v. Electrical Workers, IUE, Local 502, 479 F. Supp. 246, 253, 108 L.R.R.M. 2770 (W.D. Pa. 1979), *vacated and remanded*, ___ F.2d ___ (3d Cir. 1980), *on remand*, 494 F. Supp. 872, 108 L.R.R.M. 2779 (W.D. Pa. 1980), *aff'd* 649 F.2d 858, 108 L.R.R.M. 2816 (3d Cir. 1981).
83. Delaware Coca-Cola Bottling Co. v. Teamsters, Local 326, 474 F. Supp. 777, 102 L.R.R.M. 27 (D. Del. 1979), *rev'd on other grounds*, 624 F.2d 1182, 104 L.R.R.M. 2776 (3d Cir. 1980); Teamsters, Local 959 v. King, 572 P.2d 1168, 1177, 97 L.R.R.M. 2123, 2129 (Alaska 1977).
84. The Seattle Times Co. v. Mailers Union, Local 32, 664 F.2d 1366, 1370, 109 L.R.R.M. 2353, 2355 (9th Cir. 1982). Presumably, attorneys' fees would be recoverable if the contract provided that the prevailing party was entitled to them in the event of suit alleging breach of the agreement.
85. Strikes not authorized by the union will generally be considered protected unless they undermine the union's status as exclusive bargaining representative. *See* East Chicago Rehabilitation Center v. NLRB, 710 F.2d 397, 113 L.R.R.M. 3241, 3244 (7th Cir. 1983), *cert. denied*, 115 L.R.R.M. 2904 (1984); Hoffman Beverage Co., 163 N.L.R.B. 981, 65 L.R.R.M. 1011 (1967). *But see* Lee A. Consaul Co. v. NLRB, 469 F.2d 84, 81 L.R.R.M. 2580 (9th Cir. 1972).

employer. They often result as much from deteriorating relationships between the union and the employees as from any employer-related cause, which makes it more difficult to anticipate and prevent spontaneous employee action. In addition, it is harder to defuse a wildcat strike because the employer may not be able to identify the leaders of the stoppage. Nevertheless, many strike planning principles discussed in the preceding chapters will assist employers confronted by wildcat activity.

5.4.1 Disciplinary Action for Engaging in a Wildcat Strike

By definition, the true wildcat strike violates a contractual no-strike clause. It is thus unprotected activity for which participating employees may be disciplined.[86] The employer need not discipline every employee involved in the stoppage. The NLRB has held that the Act permits an employer to discharge or otherwise discipline only a few of the participating workers as examples to the rest.[87]

Unions often file grievances protesting the use of selective discipline after a wildcat strike. Arbitrators have been inclined to reverse the employer's action when the amount of discipline imposed bears no apparent relationship to the degree of the affected employees' participation. Discipline is most likely to be upheld if it is limited to those employees exercising leadership roles in the stoppage.

---

86. NLRB v. Sands Mfg., 306 U.S. 332, 4 L.R.R.M. 530 (1939).
87. *See, e.g.*, Virginia Electric & Power Co., 262 N.L.R.B. 1119, 1125, 111 L.R.R.M. 1054 (1982); McLean Trucking Co., 175 N.L.R.B. 440, 450-51, 71 L.R.R.M. 1051, 1056-57 (1969); California Cotton Coop. Ass'n, 110 N.L.R.B. 1494, 1496-97, 35 L.R.R.M. 1390, 1391-92 (1954).

5.4.1.1 Discipline of Union Officers

An employer may not single out union officers for special discipline in the wake of a wildcat unless they have exercised leadership roles in the work stoppage or violated a contractual provision "clearly imposing contractual duties on [union] officials to insure the integrity of no-strike clauses."[88] A union officer who instigates or leads a wildcat strike may be more severely disciplined than other workers. However, a general no-strike provision in a union contract will not justify disproportionate discipline of union officers who merely participate in wildcat action.[89] Authority for such special discipline may, in the absence of a leadership role, be derived solely from a clear and unmistakable contractual provision imposing a duty on union officers to prevent or halt wildcat strikes.

Neither the NLRB nor any court has yet explained what type of clause meets this standard. A provision specifically providing for discipline of union officers in the event of their inaction, such as the following, may prove sufficient:

> Officers and agents of the union, including shop stewards, shall not cause, sanction, approve, or participate in any strikes (including sitdowns, stayins, slowdowns, sickouts, or any other stoppages of work). Such officers and agents will cooperate with the Employer in every way possible and use their best efforts to prevent any such stoppages of work and to terminate such stoppages that may occur as soon as possible. Any officers and agents that are employees of the Employer shall be subject to discipline, including discharge, for violation of this provision.

Because this area of the law has recently been the subject of considerable judicial attention, counsel should be consulted before relying on such a clause.

---

88. Metropolitan Edison Co. v. NLRB, 51 U.S.L.W. 4350, 112 L.R.R.M. 3265 (U.S. 1983).
89. Brunswick Corp., 267 N.L.R.B. No. 68, 114 L.R.R.M. 1043 (1983).

5.4.2 Judicial Remedies for Wildcat Actions

5.4.2.1 Injunctive Relief

Pre-arbitration injunctions against wildcat activity may be obtained only when the underlying dispute is subject to contractual arbitration.[90] But many wildcat strikes do not involve an arbitrable issue. They may involve internal union disputes or be in sympathy for another union's strike. Such strikes generally cannot be enjoined unless the employer first obtains an arbitrator's determination that the wildcat strike breaches the contract.[91]

Even if an arbitrable grievance precipitates the wildcat strike, an injunction may still be difficult to obtain. When the union has not in any way authorized the strike and has no contractual duty to end it, courts will not enjoin the union.[92] Mass action involving the local union's entire membership, when combined with the absence of union efforts to end the strike, may, on the other hand, lead a court to enjoin the union and require it to take affirmative steps to end the strike.[93]

In a true wildcat situation, an injunction against the union may do little to return the strikers to work. The employer should therefore consider seeking an injunction against particular individuals known to be leading or actively participating in the work stoppage. The logistics of getting an injunction against individuals are apt to be more complicated than in actions against a

---

90. Complete Auto Transit, Inc. v. Reis, 451 U.S. 401, 416, n.18, 107 L.R.R.M. 2145 (1981); Buffalo Forge Co. v. Steelworkers, 428 U.S. 397, 407, 92 L.R.R.M. 3032 (1976); Gateway Coal Co. v. Mine Workers, 414 U.S. 368, 380-87, 85 L.R.R.M. 2049 (1974).
91. See, e.g., Automobile Transport Inc. v. Ferdnance, 420 F. Supp. 75, 77, 92 L.R.R.M. 3610, 3612 (E.D. Mich. 1976) (refusing to enjoin wildcat caused by dispute between strikers and union). Sections 5.3.2.3 and 5.5.3.3 discuss in greater detail the availability of injunctions against strikes over nonarbitrable issues.
92. Dresser Industries v. Steel Workers, Local 4601, 110 L.R.R.M. 2661, 2663 (W.D.N.Y 1981).
93. Keebler Co. v. Bakery Workers, Local 492-A, 104 L.R.R.M. 2625, 2628 (E.D. Pa. 1980).

union. An employer must be prepared to serve named individuals personally with the petition for injunctive relief, as well as any orders issued by the court. This may be time consuming and troublesome. But when the union has lost control of striking employees, this may offer the employer its only means of returning strikers to work without acceding to their demands.

5.4.2.2 Damage Suits against Unions

Employers may recover damages from a union that has authorized, instigated, encouraged, or ratified a wildcat strike.[94] A union may be deemed to have authorized a strike if it advocates the employees' grievances in a fashion indicating that it is asserting the strike's validity.[95]

Some employers have also attempted to hold unions liable for not taking steps to end wildcat strikes. In *Carbon Fuel Co. v. Mine Workers*,[96] the Supreme Court held that an international union and one of its districts were not liable for failing to abate a pattern of wildcat activity. By agreeing merely to "maintain the integrity of [the] contract," the unions had not obligated themselves to use best efforts to halt work stoppages.[97] The Court refused to imply such an obligation. It did suggest, however, that parties could agree to impose contractual duties on unions to quell wildcat actions.[98]

---

94. California Trucking Ass'n v. Teamsters Local 70, 679 F.2d 1275, 108 L.R.R.M. 2955 (9th Cir. 1981), *cert. denied*, 111 L.R.R.M 2744 (1982).
95. North River Energy Corp. v. Mine Workers, 664 F.2d 1184, 1190, 109 L.R.R.M. 2335, 2338 (11th Cir. 1981). Union authorization will not be inferred from efforts to return employees to work by resolving the grievances underlying the wildcat action. Steelworkers v. Lorain, 616 F.2d 919, 922, 103 L.R.R.M. 2627 (6th Cir. 1980), *cert. denied*, 451 U.S. 983, 107 L.R.R.M. 2394 (1981).
96. 444 U.S. 212, 102 L.R.R.M. 3017 (1979).
97. 444 U.S. at 222.
98. 444 U.S. at 219.

Responding to Strikes

Since *Carbon Fuel*, employers have rarely succeeded in showing the existence of an affirmative union duty to prevent wildcat strikes.[99] One court has held a union liable for damages when it breached a contract clause requiring it to cooperate with the employer in halting wildcat strikes.[100] To achieve the same result, an employer may wish to bargain for a clause in which the union pledges to use best efforts to end unauthorized work stoppages:

> The Union will not cause or sanction or take part in any strikes (including, sitdowns, stayins, slowdowns, sickouts, or any other stoppages of work). The Union will cooperate with the Employer in every way possible and exert its best efforts to prevent any such stoppages of work and to terminate such stoppages that may occur as soon as possible.[101]

This clause should *not* be coupled with a provision absolving the union from damages for work stoppages that the union does not authorize, ratify, support, or encourage. The presence of such exculpatory language may make it impossible to recover damages based upon the union's inaction even when the contract also requires the union to undertake best efforts.[102]

Despite the absence of a best efforts clause, a union's inactivity may be deemed to be ratification of a wildcat strike when its attempts to stop the strike are so meager that its approval can be

---

99. *See, e.g.,* Consolidation Coal v. UMW, Local 1261, 500 F. Supp. 72, 109 L.R.R.M. 2331 (D. Utah 1980), *aff'd,* 725 F.2d 1258, 115 L.R.R.M. 2470 (10th Cir. 1984); *see also* Alabama Power Co. v. Laborers, Local 1333, 734 F.2d 1464, 116 L.R.R.M. 3209 (11th Cir. 1984) (finding that union had fulfilled contractual duty).
100. Airco Speer Carbon-Graphite v. Local 502, International Union of Elec., Radio & Mach. Workers, 494 F. Supp. 872, 875, 108 L.R.R.M. 2779, 2781 (W.D. Pa. 1980), *aff'd,* 649 F.2d 858, 108 L.R.R.M. 2816 (3d Cir. 1981).
101. Adapted from Airco Speer Carbon-Graphite, *supra* note 100, 494 F. Supp. at 875, 108 L.R.R.M. 2781.
102. Steelworkers v. Lorain, 616 F.2d 919, 922, 103 L.R.R.M. 2627, 2630 (6th Cir. 1980), *cert. denied,* 451 U.S. 983 (1981).

Unprotected Strikes

inferred.[103] And when all the union's members participate in the wildcat, a *local* union's authorization of the strike may be presumed. Such mass action by the membership indicates that striking employees are not "engaged in an adventure of their own,"[104] rendering the local liable for the breach of the no-strike clause.[105]

5.4.2.3 Damage Suits against Individual Employees

In *Complete Auto Transit, Inc. v. Reis*,[106] the Supreme Court held that section 301(a) does not authorize damage actions against individual employees for engaging in wildcat strikes. To cope with this limitation, employers might consider bargaining for contract clauses giving arbitrators the right to award damages against individual employees for participating in wildcats.[107] Unions will resist such a clause, however, and its legality and enforceability, even if obtained, are doubtful.[108]

---

103. Consolidation Coal v. Local 1702, Mine Workers, 709 F.2d 882, 886, 113 L.R.R.M. 3000, 3003 (4th Cir. 1983) (finding union ratification implied in lack of action to end strike), *cert. denied*, 114 L.R.R.M. 3392 (1983); U.S. Steel Corp. v. Mine Workers, 598 F.2d 363, 366, 101 L.R.R.M. 2830, 2832 (5th Cir. 1979); Owens-Illinois, Inc. v. Glass Bottle Blowers, Local 29, 114 L.R.R.M. 3454, 3465 (C.D. Cal. 1983).
104. North River Energy Corp. v. Mine Workers, 664 F.2d 1184, 1194, 109 L.R.R.M. 2335, 2342 (11th Cir. 1981).
105. Consolidation Coal v. Mine Workers, Local 1702, 709 F.2d 882, 885, 113 L.R.R.M. 3000, 3002 (4th Cir. 1983). *But see* Consolidation Coal v. UMW, Local 1261, 725 F.2d 1258, 115 L.R.R.M. 2470 (10th Cir. 1984).
106. 451 U.S. 401, 107 L.R.R.M. 2145 (1981).
107. Note, *An Employer's Recourse to* [sic] *Wildcat Strikes Includes Fashioning His Own Remedy*, 57 NOTRE DAME L. 598, 611-13 (February 1982); Comment, *An Employer's Remedies against Individual Union Members for Breach of a No-Strike Provision in a Collective Bargaining Agreement*, 18 TULSA L. J. 110, 130-32 (Fall 1982).
108. *Id.*

175

5.4.3 Preparing for and Coping with Wildcat Strikes

To protect against wildcats, an employer should establish and publicize a policy that employees are subject to discipline, including discharge, if they violate the contractual no-strike pledge. The employer should include this policy in any employee manual that it distributes.

As soon as wildcat action occurs, the employer should immediately notify the local union of the unlawful activity. When the union has a contractual obligation to undertake efforts to return employees to work, the notification should emphasize this duty. (See App. 5-A, Sample Notice to Union.) If the union has clearly lost control of bargaining unit employees, the employer might also try to resolve the situation by dealing with recognized employee leaders, as well as with the union.

If an employer disciplines wildcat participants or leaders, it should expect the union to file grievances, which may well be pursued through arbitration. Arbitrators commonly disapprove discipline that they see as disproportionate to the employee's responsibility. Because the employer usually bears the burden of proof in discipline cases,[109] it must carefully document the justification for its action. The employer should gather as much information as possible regarding the actual role of employees in the wildcat *before* imposing discipline. The employer's file relating to the discipline should include any notes or memoranda drafted in connection and contemporaneous with that action.

5.5 Responding to Sympathy Strikes

When a union strikes, it will usually establish a picket line in hope that workers not directly involved in the dispute will refuse

---

109. *See* F. ELKOURI & E. ELKOURI, HOW ARBITRATION WORKS 621 (3d ed. 1973).

to cross and thus increase pressure on the employer. Employees who honor another bargaining unit's picket line are sympathy strikers and are generally engaged in activity protected by the Act. An employer planning to operate during a strike must therefore be sensitive to the rights afforded nonunion employees and employees from other bargaining units who refuse to work because of the existence of a picket line. This requires particular care in planning a strategy for dealing with sympathy strikes.

Sympathy strikes generally occur in one of two situations. In the first, a strike by one union induces other employees of the same employer to strike. This situation often arises in manufacturing industries with multiple bargaining units. In the second situation, workers of a second employer who must enter the struck premises to work, such as deliverymen and subcontractors, honor the picket line. This scenario is more common in the retail and construction industries. Thus, the employer of the sympathy strikers may not be the employer in the underlying dispute. Employers should bear this distinction in mind, as their rights and remedies, especially with respect to replacement, differ in the two situations.

5.5.1 Protected Status of Sympathy Strikers

An employer cannot discharge or discriminate against sympathy strikers engaged in protected activity. However, the Act does not protect all sympathy strikes. If a sympathy striker's activity is unprotected, that striker *may* be disciplined or discharged. Accurate characterization of the sympathy strike is therefore essential in determining remedies.

Sympathy strikers honoring a lawful picket line at their employer's premises are clearly engaged in mutual aid and protection. Such sympathy strikes are thus protected concerted activity.[110] Most courts and the NLRB hold that sympathy strikers

---

110. Gary-Hobart Water Corp. v. NLRB, 511 F.2d 284, 88 L.R.R.M. 2830 (7th Cir.), *cert. denied*, 423 U.S. 925, 90 L.R.R.M. 2921 (1975); Cooper Thermometer, 154 N.L.R.B. 502, 59 L.R.R.M. 1767 (1965).

honoring picket lines at a customer's premises also are engaging in protected concerted activity, though some circuit courts have yet to resolve the issue.[111] One court, agreeing with the NLRB, has even held that an employee who crosses a picket line but refuses to perform struck work is a protected sympathy striker.[112]

5.5.1.1 Waiver of Sympathy Strike Rights

A union may waive sympathy strikers' statutory protection in a collective bargaining agreement.[113] Sympathy strikes in violation of the agreement will be unprotected. However, the NLRB has long required that a sympathy strike waiver be in "clear and unmistakable" terms.[114] It will ordinarily find a waiver only if the contract explicitly limits sympathy strike rights *or* if the parties' bargaining history leaves no doubt that the union intended to effect a waiver.[115] The NLRB has refused to infer a waiver of protection from ambiguous clauses relating to employees' right to honor picket lines.[116] It has also gone to great lengths

---

111. NLRB v. Browning-Ferris Industries, 700 F.2d 385, 112 L.R.R.M. 2882 (7th Cir. 1983), and cases cited therein; *see also* Eastex, Inc. v. NLRB, 437 U.S. 556, 565, 98 L.R.R.M. 2717 (1978) (concerted activity includes action "in support of employees of employers other than their own").
112. General Tire & Rubber, 190 N.L.R.B. 277, 77 L.R.R.M. 1215 (1971), *enforced*, 451 F.2d 257, 78 L.R.R.M. 2836 (1st Cir. 1971). The court declined to decide whether the employee's actions would have been protected if the employee had notice of the expected assignment of struck work before crossing the picket line. 451 F.2d at 258, 78 L.R.R.M. at 2837.
113. NLRB v. Rockaway News Supply Co., 345 U.S. 71, 31 L.R.R.M. 2432 (1953).
114. Local 18, Operating Engineers (Davis-McKee, Inc.), 238 N.L.R.B. 652, 99 L.R.R.M. 1307 (1978).
115. *See* St. Regis Paper Co., 253 N.L.R.B. 1224, 1229, 106 L.R.R.M. 1207 (1981) (relying on bargaining history).
116. Keller-Crescent Co., 217 N.L.R.B. 685, 89 L.R.R.M. 1201 (1975), *enforcement denied on other grounds*, 538 F.2d 1291, 92 L.R.R.M. 3591 (7th Cir. 1976).

to avoid finding a clear and unmistakable waiver in a broad no-strike clause, even when bargaining history suggests that the union understood that the contract contained a waiver.[117] Nor will the NLRB read a general no-strike clause as a waiver of the right to honor pickets protesting an employer's serious unfair labor practices.[118]

Some courts have been more willing than the NLRB to find a clear and unmistakable waiver based on a broad no-strike clause and other outside evidence, which usually takes the form of bargaining history.[119] Other courts defer to the NLRB's strong presumption against waivers.[120] An employer is thus well advised to negotiate for specific waivers of sympathy strike rights to assure maximum flexibility of response in case of a strike.[121]

5.5.1.2 Effect of Unprotected Status of Underlying Strike

A sympathy strike is not protected if the underlying strike or picket line is unprotected, regardless of whether the sympathy

---

117. Chevron U.S.A., Inc., 244 N.L.R.B. 1081, 1084, 102 L.R.R.M. 1311, 1316 (1979); W-1 Canteen Service, Inc., 238 N.L.R.B. 609, 99 L.R.R.M. 1571 (1978), *enforcement denied*, 606 F.2d 738, 102 L.R.R.M. 2447 (7th Cir. 1979).
118. Pilot Freight Carriers, 224 N.L.R.B. 341, 92 L.R.R.M. 1338 (1976); *see also* NLRB v. C.K. Smith, Inc., 569 F.d 162, 167, 97 L.R.R.M. 2460 (1st Cir. 1977), *cert denied*, 436 U.S. 957 (1978).
119. United States Steel Corp. v. NLRB, 711 F.2d 772, 113 L.R.R.M. 3227 (7th Cir. 1983); ACF Industries, Inc. v. NLRB, 641 F.2d 561, 106 L.R.R.M. 2518 (8th Cir. 1981); W-1 Canteen Service v. NLRB, 606 F.2d 738, 743, 102 L.R.R.M. 2447 (7th Cir. 1979).
120. NLRB v. Southern California Edison, 646 F.2d 1352, 107 L.R.R.M. 2667 (9th Cir. 1981); NLRB v. Gould, Inc., 638 F.2d 159, 105 L.R.R.M. 2788 (10th Cir. 1980), *cert. denied*, 452 U.S. 930 (1981); Delaware Coca-Cola Bottling v. Teamsters, Local 326, 624 F.2d 1182, 104 L.R.R.M. 2776 (3d Cir. 1980).
121. Section 5.2.3, *infra*, discusses considerations relevant to negotiating such waivers.

strikers know of this fact.[122] Further, even when an underlying *strike* is lawful, the NLRB has held that sympathy strikers are not protected if they honor an unlawful secondary picket line.[123]

5.5.1.3 Lack of Concerted Activity

A sympathy strike is protected because it is a form of concerted activity. An employee who refuses to cross a picket line out of fear acts to protect *personal* interests rather than labor solidarity. One court has therefore held that such an employee is engaged in unprotected activity.[124]

5.5.2 Replacing and Reinstating Sympathy Strikers

Although workers have the right to engage in sympathy strikes in the absence of a contractual waiver, employers have the right to operate their businesses. Therefore, while an employer may not discharge or retaliate against a lawful sympathy striker, replacement is usually permitted.

5.5.2.1 Replacement Due to Refusal to Cross Lines at the Employer's Premises

A sympathy striker who refuses to cross a picket line set up by economic strikers at the premises of the sympathy striker's employer acquires the status of an economic striker. The employer

---

122. American Tel. & Tel. Co., 231 N.L.R.B. 556, 562, 96 L.R.R.M. 1144 (1977); Pacific Tel. & Tel. Co., 80 L.A. 1151 (1983) (Alleyne, Arb.).
123. Chevron U.S.A., Inc., 244 N.L.R.B. 1081, 1086, 102 L.R.R.M. 1311 (1979).
124. G&P Trucking v. NLRB, 539 F.2d 705, 92 L.R.R.M. 3652 (4th Cir. 1976); NLRB v. Union Carbide, 440 F.2d 54, 76 L.R.R.M. 2181, 77 L.R.R.M. 2894 (4th Cir. 1971), *cert. denied*, 404 U.S. 826 (1971). The NLRB has refused to adopt this reasoning. Ashtabula Forge, Division of ABS Co., 269 N.L.R.B. No. 138, 115 L.R.R.M. 1295 (1984).

Unprotected Strikes

may replace the sympathy striker. If the replacement is temporary, the sympathy striker is entitled to reinstatement upon tendering an unconditional offer to return to work. If the replacement is permanent, the sympathy striker is not entitled to reinstatement until an opening arises, even if the striker unconditionally offers to return.[125] An employee cannot, however, be discharged for a legal sympathy strike.[126]

5.5.2.2 Replacement Due to Refusal to Cross Lines at Other Employer's Premises

As a general rule, sympathy strikers who respect an economic picket line at the premises of their employer's customer are also considered economic strikers. They may be replaced, but not discharged.[127] Here, however, the employer must show a *business need* to replace the striker with an employee who will cross the picket line.[128] Once the employer shows a business need, the burden shifts to the worker to prove that replacement was retali-

---

125. *See* Marlene Industries Corp. v. NLRB, 712 F.2d 1011, 1019, 113 L.R.R.M. 3655 (6th Cir. 1983); Butterworth-Manning-Ashmore Mortuary, 270 N.L.R.B. No. 148, 116 L.R.R.M. 1193 (1984). Chapter 9 discusses reinstatement rights in greater detail.
126. Teamsters Local 162 v. NLRB, 568 F.2d 665, 97 L.R.R.M. 2917 (9th Cir. 1978); NLRB v. Southern Greyhound Lines, 426 F.2d 1299, 74 L.R.R.M. 2080 (5th Cir. 1970); Newberry Energy, 227 N.L.R.B. 436, 94, L.R.R.M. 1307 (1976).
127. NLRB v. Browning-Ferris Industries, 700 F.2d 385, 112 L.R.R.M. 2882 (7th Cir. 1983); Torrington Constr. Co., 235 N.L.R.B. 1540, 98 L.R.R.M. 1135 (1978). As the court in *Browning-Ferris* observes, however, some courts have not decided whether a sympathy striker honoring picket lines at a customer's premises is engaged in protected activity.
128. *See* NLRB v. Southern California Edison Co., 646 F.2d 1352, 1369, 107 L.R.R.M. 2667 (9th Cir. 1981); Overnite Transportation, 212 N.L.R.B. 515, 87 L.R.R.M. 112 (1974); Redwing Carriers, 137 N.L.R.B. 1545, 50 L.R.R.M. 1440 (1962), *aff'd*, 325 F.2d 1011, 54 L.R.R.M. 2707 (D.C. Cir. 1963).

ation for protected activity.[129] The employer's burden is not heavy. One court recently held that an employer could replace (but not discharge) drivers who would be needed later to fill orders at a struck customer and who said they would not cross a picket line.[130] In another case, an employer was allowed to replace a driver who refused to handle a delivery to a struck customer located on his regular route. But the NLRB found that the same employer could not, after the struck customer's delivery had been made, replace a driver who had previously refused to switch routes to handle the delivery.[131]

Sympathy strikers replaced for refusing to cross other employers' picket lines must ordinarily be reinstated when they have unconditionally offered to return to work. If permanent replacements have been hired, the striker must await a job opening.[132]

5.5.2.3 Refusal to Cross Unfair Labor Practice Picket Lines

Sympathy strikers who refuse to cross an *unfair labor practice* picket line at their employer's premises have the same rights as unfair labor practice strikers. They may be replaced temporarily and must be reinstated when the underlying strike ends.[133] It is not clear whether sympathy strikers honoring an unfair labor practice strike at a customer's premises have the same reinstatement rights.[134]

---

129. NLRB v. William S. Carroll, Inc., 578 F.2d 1, 4, 98 L.R.R.M. 2848 (1st Cir. 1978).
130. NLRB v. Browning-Ferris Indus., 700 F.2d 385, 112 L.R.R.M. 2882 (7th Cir. 1983).
131. Thurston Motor Lines, 166 N.L.R.B. 862, 65 L.R.R.M. 1674 (1967).
132. NLRB v. Browning-Ferris Indus., 700 F.2d 385, 112 L.R.R.M. 2882 (7th Cir. 1983).
133. Hotel & Restaurant Employees, Local 19, 240 N.L.R.B. 240, 100 L.R.R.M 1354 (1979), *enforcement denied without opinion*, 628 F.2d 1357, 111 L.R.R.M. 2515 (9th Cir. 1980); C.K. Smith & Co., 227 N.L.R.B. 1061, 95 L.R.R.M. 1617 (1977), *enforced*, 569 F.2d 162, 97 L.R.R.M. 2460 (1st Cir. 1977), *cert. denied*, 436 U.S. 957 (1978).
134. The fact that the sympathy strikers' employer had committed unfair labor practices clearly helped persuade the First Circuit to approve broad

Unprotected Strikes

5.5.3 Remedies for Sympathy Strikes

5.5.3.1 Discipline

Sympathy strikers engaged in protected activity ordinarily cannot be discharged or suspended. If a sympathy strike is unprotected, however, the strikers may be disciplined or discharged.[135] Union officers normally cannot be disciplined more severely than others for failure to stop an unprotected sympathy strike.[136]

5.5.3.2 Damages

If a sympathy strike violates the union contract, the sympathy strikers' union may be held liable for damages under section 301.[137] Likewise, the union in the underlying dispute may sometimes be held liable if it causes damaging sympathy strikes by unlawfully striking or authorizing an illegal wildcat strike.[138]

---

reinstatement rights for sympathy strikers honoring unfair labor practice pickets at their employer's premises. NLRB v. C.K. Smith, Inc., 569 F.2d at 1660. This consideration will not be present when the unfair labor practices have been committed by a *customer* of the sympathy strikers' employer.

135. NLRB v. Keller-Crescent Co., 538 F.2d 1291, 92 L.R.R.M. 3591 (7th Cir. 1976) (suspension); Montana-Dakota Utilities Co. v. NLRB, 455 F.2d 1088, 79 L.R.R.M. 2854 (8th Cir. 1972) (suspension); St. Regis Paper Co., 253 N.L.R.B. 1224, 106 L.R.R.M. 1207 (1981) (discharge).

136. *See* Metropolitan Edison v. NLRB, 51 U.S.L.W. 4350, 112 L.R.R.M. 3265 (U.S. 1983). The scope of this protection is discussed in greater detail in Section 5.4.1.1, *supra*.

137. Iowa Beef Processors v. Meat Cutters, 597 F.2d 1138, 101 L.R.R.M. 2235 (8th Cir), *cert. denied,* 444 U.S. 840 (1979); Owens-Illinois, Inc. v. Glass Bottle Blowers, Local 29, 114 L.R.R.M. 3454 (C.D. Cal. 1983). The principles governing breach of contract suits against unions are considered in section 5.3.3, *supra*.

138. California Trucking Ass'n. v. Teamsters, Local 70, 679 F.2d 1275, 1288, 108 L.R.R.M. 2955, 2965 (9th Cir. 1981), *cert. denied,* 111 L.R.R.M. 2744 (1982).

5.5.3.3 Injunctions

Under *Buffalo Forge,* sympathy strikes ordinarily cannot be enjoined pending arbitration because such strikes are not called over issues that the sympathy strikers and their employer have agreed to arbitrate.[139] Rather, they concern issues involving another union, and often another employer. In most cases, sympathy strikes may be enjoined only if an arbitrator first determines that the stoppage violates the contract's no-strike clause.[140]

Sympathy strikes may also be enjoined if the sympathy strikers have joined in the underlying strike, seeking the same concessions as the other strikers. The sympathy strike will then be over these arbitrable issues. In most cases it will be difficult to prove that the sympathy strikers ratified or adopted the cause of the underlying strike.[141] The employer must at least be prepared to prove a close nexus between the two unions and their contract demands.[142]

A sympathy strike cannot be enjoined simply because the underlying strike is illegal. The employer's remedy in such circumstances is to seek injunctive relief against the illegal activity.[143]

5.5.4 Coping with Sympathy Strikes

If both the underlying and the sympathy strikes are against the same employer, the employer should coordinate its efforts re-

---

139. Section 5.3.2.1 discusses this issue in greater detail.
140. Section 5.3.2.3 discusses post-arbitration injunctions, as well as methods of securing expedited arbitration with respect to breaches of the no-strike clause.
141. *See, e.g.,* Zeigler Coal Co. v. Mine Workers, 556 F.2d 582, 96 L.R.R.M. 3360 (7th Cir. 1977), *cert. denied,* 436 U.S. 912 (1978); Southern Ohio Coal Co. v. Mine Workers, 551 F.2d 695, 94 L.R.R.M. 2609 (6th Cir.), *cert. denied,* 434 U.S.876 (1977).
142. *See, e.g.,* Cedar Coal Co. v. Mine Workers, 560 F.2d 1153, 95 L.R.R.M. 3015, 3030 (4th Cir. 1977), *cert. denied,* 434 U.S. 1047 (1978); Keebler Co. v. Bakery Workers, 104 L.R.R.M. 2426, 2427 (N.D. Ga. 1980).
143. Southern Ohio Coal v. Mine Workers, 551 F.2d 695, 704, 94 L.R.R.M. 2609 (6th Cir.), *cert. denied,* 434 U.S. 876 (1977).

Unprotected Strikes

garding the two classes of strikers. The response to a sympathy strike will be seen by other strikers as evidence of the employer's resolve. It must therefore be planned with due regard to the fundamental goals of overall strike strategy. In the short term, the clear right to replace sympathetic strikers may be a useful tool.

When the picket line is at another employer's premises, the actions taken by one employer can complement the other's approach. The employer involved in the underlying dispute should notify suppliers and customers to expect a picket line. The picket line should be monitored for signs of violence or physical obstruction. Sometimes another gate that is not being picketed can be made available, though it may not be legally immune from picketing.[144]

So that schedules can be changed if necessary, the employer of potential sympathy strikers should ask its workers to commit to either honoring or crossing an anticipated picket line.[145] Available supervisory personnel should be prepared to substitute for sympathy strikers, even though there is no requirement that the employer use supervisors rather than replacements. The employer should keep careful records of the number of employees needed on the picketed premises and the number willing to cross the picket line, so that it can justify replacement of sympathy strikers.

---

144. *See* Steelworkers (Carrier Corp.) v. NLRB, 376 U.S. 492, 55 L.R.R.M. 2698 (1964). Chapter 7 discusses the circumstances in which a reserved gate may be used to limit the location of lawful picketing.
145. Chapter 4 discusses permissible polling procedures.

Appendix 5-A

TELEGRAM

TO: (Primary Union)

FROM:_____

SUBJECT: Work Stoppage in Violation of Contract

On _____,employees represented by your union ceased work in violation of the Collective Bargaining Agreement between your union and this company, _____. We have already contacted [or tried, but were unable to contact] you by telephone regarding this problem. Under the Collective Bargaining Agreement, you are obliged to use every reasonable effort to terminate this unlawful work stoppage. We expect your union to fulfill that obligation. Should you fail to do so, the company will take all steps necessary, including legal action for breach of the Collective Bargaining Agreement, to hold your union responsible for all damages resulting from the unlawful work stoppage.

6
Responding to Strike Misconduct and Violence

Strike-related violence and misconduct are among the most troubling problems in modern labor relations, in part because the causes in any particular case may be obscure. Occasionally an employer can anticipate strike misconduct, as in those instances when strikers become visibly frustrated by the duration of the strike or the employer's ability to operate despite their efforts. More frequently, however, the unexpectedly vicious behavior sometimes provoked by labor disputes leaves the employer confused and bewildered. Because such emotions interfere with the clear thinking necessary to develop an appropriate response to misconduct, an employer must, before the strike, give careful consideration to the possibility that these problems will occur and be prepared to act swiftly to counter them.

Local labor conditions and an employer's history of employee relations provide clues as to whether strike-related misconduct is likely to occur. In addition, certain unions and industries historically have been connected with a disproportionate amount of violent strike activity,[1] suggesting that strike misconduct may have some institutional impetus. You should therefore consider the past experience of other employers in your industry, espe-

---

1. See A. THIEBLOT & T. HAGGARD, UNION VIOLENCE: THE RECORD AND THE RESPONSE BY COURTS, LEGISLATURES, AND THE NLRB 49-65 (University of Pennsylvania 1983) (tabulating violent incidents by labor union and industrial group).

cially those that deal with the same unions, as well as your own bargaining history, when evaluating the possibility of violence or other misconduct. During the strike, you should keep an eye out for mass action by pickets, for the "protective cover of the mob allows individuals to act with less fear of reprisal."[2]

If violence or misconduct seems imminent, you may take several steps to blunt its impact. At one extreme, you may cease operations until tempers cool, as violence, or the threat of violence, is frequently directed at employees who work during the strike. On the other hand, you may choose to continue operating and request assistance from law enforcement personnel. Many larger police departments have specially trained personnel to deal with labor strife. In those communities, close consultation with law enforcement officials in advance of trouble will be helpful. You should do your best to maintain amicable relations with the strikers and the community as a whole. When misconduct occurs despite these efforts, you have numerous remedies at your disposal. These must be exercised without delay to minimize the disruption that invariably accompanies misconduct.

6.1 Types of Misconduct against Which the Employer May Obtain Relief

Because the Constitution protects free speech, an employer generally has no remedy against peaceful labor picketing that does not breach a no-strike clause and advances a lawful objective.[3] The Supreme Court has held, however, that the Constitu-

---

2. *Id.* at 487.
3. *See* Thornhill v. Alabama, 310 U.S. 88, 6 L.R.R.M. 697 (1940). The National Labor Relations Act does limit the use of picketing for certain specified objectives, such as obtaining recognition of a union or exerting secondary pressure. This regulation of picketing is permitted under the Constitution. Longshoremen, ILA v. Allied International, Inc., 456 U.S. 212, 226, 110 L.R.R.M. 2001 (1982); Electrical Workers v. NLRB, 341 U.S. 694, 705, 28 L.R.R.M. 2115 (1951).

Strike Misconduct and Violence

tion does not protect mass picketing that obstructs ingress or egress from an employer's premises and threatens injury to employees desiring to work,[4] abusive language and threats designed to intimidate those crossing the picket line,[5] or picketing in the context of a "pattern of violence."[6] In these circumstances, a court's power to protect public safety by limiting picketers' activities takes precedence over constitutional guarantees of free speech. That power is frequently exercised in the following situations:

Mass Picketing. Strikers cannot, by the sheer number of pickets, either block the employer's premises or intimidate persons seeking to enter or leave.[7]

Actual Violence. Actual violence against employees or persons seeking to enter or exit the employer's premises is unlawful, just as any other assault would be.[8]

Property Damage. The courts uniformly condemn strikers who damage the employer's property.[9] Strikers may also damage per-

---

4. See Allen-Bradley Local No. 1111, United Elec. Radio and Mach. Workers v. Wisconsin Employment Relations Board, 315 U.S. 740, 10 L.R.R.M. 520 (1942).
5. Youngdahl v. Rainfair, 355 U.S. 131, 41 L.R.R.M. 2169 (1957).
6. Milk Wagon Drivers Union v. Meadowmoor Diaries, Inc., 312 U.S. 287, 7 L.R.R.M. 310 (1941).
7. People v. Spear, 32 Cal. App. 2d 164, 89 P.2d 445 (1939), *cert. denied*, 308 U.S. 555 (1939); Pedigo v. Celanese Corp., 205 Ga. 392, 54 S.E.2d 252, 24 L.R.R.M. 2163 (Ga. 1949), *cert. denied*, 338 U.S. 937 (1950); Weyerhaeuser Timber Co. v. Everett District Council of Lumber & Sawmill Workers, 11 Wash. 2d 503, 119 P.2d 643, 9 L.R.R.M. 745 (1941); Westinghouse Elec. Corp. v. United Elec. Radio & Mach. Workers, 353 Pa. 446, 46 A.2d 16, 17 L.R.R.M. 890 (1946); PTA Sales, Inc. v. Retail Clerks, Local No. 462, 96 N.M. 581, 633 P.2d 689, 113 L.R.R.M. 2833 (1981).
8. See Building and Constr. Trades Council v. Brown & Root, Inc., 417 So. 2d 564, 113 L.R.R.M. 3101, 3133 (Miss. 1982); Altemose Constr. Co. v. Building & Constr. Trades Council, 296 A.2d 504, 449 Pa. 194, 81 L.R.R.M. 2562 (1972), *cert. denied*, 411 U.S. 932 (1973); *see also* Curreri v. Teamsters, Local 251, 722 F.2d 6, 114 L.R.R.M. 3423 (1st Cir. 1983) (action for damages).
9. Bottoms v. B&M Coal Corp., 405 N.E.2d 82, 109 L.R.R.M. 3091 (Ind. App. 1980); Milano v. Hotel & Restaurant Employees, Local 164, 72

sonal property of employees who work during the strike. This too, of course, is unlawful.[10]

Abusive or Threatening Language. The Constitution does not protect abusive language or threats against those crossing the picket line.[11] Although abuse of this type is generally directed at employees choosing to work during the strike, harassment and intimidation of a struck employer's customers are also unlawful.[12]

Surveillance. Strikers may not engage in surveillance designed to intimidate customers or employees who cross picket lines.[13]

Libel or Slander. Courts tend to be lenient with respect to verbal give-and-take during a strike. They do not, however, sanction *malicious* libel or slander of the employer or its products.[14]

L.R.R.M. 2126 (N.Y. Sup. 1969); Premium Distributing Co. v. Teamsters, Local 174, 35 Wash. App. 36, 664 P.2d 1306 (1983).
10. Building and Constr. Trades Council v. Brown & Root, Inc., 417 So. 2d 564, 113 L.R.R.M. (Miss. 1982).
11. Steelworkers v. Alabaster Lime Co., 286 Ala. 489, 242 So. 2d 658, 76 L.R.R.M. 2079 (1970); *see* Boyd v. Deena Artware, Inc., 239 S.W.2d 86, 28 L.R.R.M 2024 (Ky. App. 1951).
12. United Parcel Service, Inc. v. Teamsters, Local 25, 421 F. Supp. 452, 93 L.R.R.M. 2671 (D. Mass. 1976); PTA Sales, Inc. v. Retail Clerks, Local 462, 96 N.M. 581, 633 P.2d 689, 113 L.R.R.M. 2833 (1981).
13. Nahas v. Retail Clerks, Local 905, 144 Cal. App. 2d 820, 302 P.2d 829, 38 L.R.R.M. 2740 (Cal. App. 1956) (photographing employees crossing the picket line); State *ex rel.* Girard v. Percich, 557 S.W.2d 25 (Mo. App. 1977) (following customers after departure from plant).
14. Linn v. United Plant Guard Workers, 383 U.S. 53, 61 L.R.R.M. 2345 (1966); Capital Parcel Delivery Co. v. Teamsters, Local 150, 105 L.R.R.M. 3351 (E.D. Cal. 1980); Dunn Brothers, Inc. v. Retail Clerks, 67 L.R.R.M. 2609 (Tenn. 1967), *modified,* 72 L.R.R.M. 2075 (Tenn. 1969). Calling an employee who works during a strike a "scab" is lawful. *See* Thomas v. Flavin, 397 N.Y.S.2d 286, 96 L.R.R.M. 2618 (1977).

6.2 Injunctive Remedies for Strike Misconduct

6.2.1 Injunctions in Federal Court

The most effective way to end violence or misconduct is to obtain a court order requiring pickets to stop unlawful conduct. Although injunctions against unlawful picketing may be obtained in federal court,[15] the Norris-LaGuardia Act (also known as the "Anti-Injunction Act") establishes strict procedural and substantive prerequisites to issuance of such an order.[16] In addition, employers may find it difficult to assert grounds for federal jurisdiction over strike misconduct.[17] As a consequence, employers generally turn to state courts for relief from violence and misconduct.

6.2.2 Injunctions in State Court

In many states, courts will issue injunctions against picket line misconduct if an employer meets the traditional equitable test for such an order: (1) the employer must have a certain and clearly ascertained right that needs protection; (2) it must be subject to immediate and irreparable injury if the injunction is denied; (3) there must be a probability that the employer will ultimately succeed at trial against the persons or organizations it seeks to enjoin; *and* (4) the employer's ability ultimately to recover dam-

---

15. *See, e.g.*, Westinghouse Broadcasting Co. v. Dukakis, 412 F. Supp. 580, 92 L.R.R.M. 2729 (D. Mass. 1976).
16. *See* 29 U.S.C. § 107 (requiring a showing that police are unable or unwilling to protect the employer's property, that denial of relief will harm the employer more than granting relief will harm the union, and allowing issuance of injunction only against those who actually have threatened, engaged in, or authorized violence).
17. *See, e.g.*, Florida Power & Light v. Building Trades Council, 107 L.R.R.M. 2862 (M.D. Fla. 1981); Beacon Moving & Storage v. Teamsters, Local 814, 362 F. Supp. 442, 82 L.R.R.M. 2221 (S.D.N.Y. 1972).

ages for the misconduct must be inadequate to fully protect its rights.[18] In cases of actual union violence, the employer can usually meet these requirements.

Obtaining an injunction may be more difficult in the many states that have adopted statutes analogous to the federal Norris-LaGuardia Act. Like their federal counterpart, these statutes ordinarily recognize the judiciary's power to restrain picketing that is accompanied by violence, threats, intimidation, or similar conduct.[19] The employer may need to show, however, that it has attempted to settle the labor dispute through negotiation or mediation[20] and that law enforcement agencies have been unable or unwilling to control the violence.[21] Proof of the union's actual participation in, authorization of, or ratification of the misconduct may also be required by state statute, as it is by federal law.[22] Such statutory restrictions must be carefully considered *before* injunctive relief becomes necessary. Indeed, the employer should study the requirements for an injunction in its jurisdiction well before the strike, so that the necessary proof may be efficiently collected if misconduct occurs.

Unions sometimes respond to actions for an injunction by arguing that the National Labor Relations Board has exclusive jurisdiction over labor matters. This claim is founded on the principle that state courts may not exercise jurisdiction if particu-

---

18. See Yellow Cab Co. v. Production Workers, Local 707, 416 N.E.2d 48, 1980-81 Trade Cas. (CCH) ¶ 63,839 (Ill. App. 1980); Isthmian S.S. Co. v. National Marine Eng. Ben. Assn., 41 Wash.2d 106, 247 P.2d 549, 30 L.R.R.M. 2643 (1952).
19. See, e.g., Mass. Gen. L. Ann. ch. 214, § 6; Ind. Code Annot., §§ 22-6-1-1 et seq.; Utah Code, §§ 34-19-1, et seq.; N.Y. Lab. Law § 807.
20. See, e.g., Hospital Employees, District 1199E v. Lafayette Square Nursing Center, Inc., 34 Md. App. 619, 368 A.2d 1099, 94 L.R.R.M. 2776 (Md. App. 1977).
21. See, e.g., Baton Rouge Coca Cola Bottling Co. v. General Truck Drivers, Local 5, 403 So. 2d 632, 113 L.R.R.M. 2712 (La. 1981); see also Rochester Telephone Corp. v. Communication Workers, 456 F.2d 1057, 79 L.R.R.M. 2770 (2d Cir. 1972) (construing Norris-LaGuardia Act).
22. See 29 U.S.C. § 107(a).

Strike Misconduct and Violence

lar union conduct is *either* arguably protected *or* arguably prohibited by federal labor statutes.[23] States are free to act, however, when strikers' conduct touches matters of traditionally local concern, such as the interest in protecting the public against violence, infliction of mental distress, threats of violence, or willful libel.[24] State courts thus may have the power to enjoin strikers' unlawful conduct, even if charges relating to the same picketing are pending before the NLRB.[25]

6.2.3 Injunctions against Trespassing by Pickets

State courts' ability to prohibit pickets from trespassing is more restricted. The National Labor Relations Act protects trespass in those rare circumstances where it is necessary for the effective exercise of employees' rights to engage in concerted activity.[26] When an employer demands that pickets stop trespassing, the union may therefore file an unfair labor practice charge under section 8(a)(1) of the Act, which prohibits an employer from interfering with employees' concerted activity.[27]

If the union files such a charge, state courts will decline jurisdiction over an employer's efforts to enjoin the trespass, at least

---

23. San Diego Building Trades Council v. Garmon, 359 U.S. 236, 43 L.R.R.M. 2838 (1959).
24. See Sears, Roebuck & Co. v. Carpenters, 436 U.S. 180, 195, 98 L.R.R.M. 2282 (1978); PTA Sales, Inc. v. Retail Clerks, Local 462, 96 N.M. 581, 633 P.2d 689, 113 L.R.R.M. 2833 (1981).
25. State *ex rel.* Retail Store Employees, Local 655 v. Black, 603 S.W.2d 076, 108 L.R.R.M. 2650 (Mo. App. 1980).
26. Hudgens v. NLRB, 424 U.S. 507, 91 L.R.R.M. 2489 (1976). The Supreme Court has observed that "such situations are rare and that a trespass is far more likely to be unprotected than protected." Sears, Roebuck & Co. v. Carpenters, note 24 *supra*, at 205.
27. *See* Giant Food Markets, Inc., 241 N.L.R.B. 727, 729, 100 L.R.R.M. 1598 (1979), *remanded*, 633 F.2d 18, 105 L.R.R.M. 2916 (6th Cir. 1980). Petitioning for an injunction to prevent pickets from trespassing does not, however, violate section 8(a)(1). *Id.*

in the absence of violence or mass picketing.[28] If the union does not file a charge following the employer's demand that the trespassing stop, however, the state court is free to grant the employer's request for an injunction.[29] Otherwise, the employer, who cannot initiate a proceeding before the NLRB to have the trespassing declared illegal, would be denied any means of resolving the legality of the trespass.

An employer that wants to enjoin trespassing pickets, then, must first demand that the union cease the objectionable activity. The employer may then proceed with its state court action only if the union declines both to halt the trespass and to file a charge with the NLRB. Thus, the employer's efforts to restrain the peaceable trespass may subject it to an unfair labor practice charge and yet yield no tangible results. This possibility should be considered before demanding that picketers stop trespassing.

6.2.4 Procedure for Obtaining Restraining Orders and Injunctive Relief

If an employer is prepared to respond promptly to strike misconduct, a judicial decree restraining the unlawful activity can often be obtained within twenty-four hours. Legal proceedings usually begin with a complaint or petition seeking injunctive relief against the union. The employer should also file papers asking for a temporary restraining order that will limit strikers' activities until the court can more thoroughly analyze the employer's claims. The application for the restraining order must be accompanied by detailed affidavits describing the conduct com-

---

28. Wiggins & Co. v. Retail Clerks, Local 1557, 595 S.W.2d 802, 106 L.R.R.M. 2726 (Tenn. 1980).
29. Sears, Roebuck & Co. v. Carpenters, & Co. note 24, *supra*, at 207; Shirley v. Retail Store Employees Union, Local 782, 225 Kan. 470, 592 P.2d 433, 101 L.R.R.M. 2844 (1979); *see* People v. Bush, 39 N.Y.2d 529, 349 N.E.2d 832, 92 L.R.R.M. 3268, 3272 (1976) (affirming convictions for criminal trespass).

Strike Misconduct and Violence

plained of, its participants, the affiliation of the participants (to the extent that can be determined), and the likely effect of continued misconduct on the employer. Preparation of these affidavits will be simplified if witnesses record their observations shortly after seeing the misconduct. (See Appendix 6-A, Witness Checklist for Picket Line Misconduct.) Courts will often consider a photograph or film of the misconduct[30] and such evidence can be particularly persuasive.[31] The employer must be prepared to authenticate photographic evidence by having a witness—preferably the person taking the photographs—confirm that the photographs accurately depict the strikers' activity.

Hearings on these emergency applications for relief usually must be specially scheduled with the court. After making arrangements for the hearing, the employer's counsel must contact the union or its lawyers (if they are known) to advise that the action is being filed and to indicate the scheduled time for hearing on the application for a restraining order. This step should not be overlooked, as the courts normally will not grant relief unless a genuine effort has been made to reach the union and give it an opportunity to respond.[32]

Applications for temporary restraining orders are often decided on the basis of affidavits. In federal court, and in some states, testimony is required.[33] Even if witnesses are not manda-

---

30. See, e.g., United Parcel Service, Inc. v. Teamsters, Local 25, 421 F. Supp. 452, 93 L.R.R.M. 2671, 2675 (D. Mass. 1976); Pease & Co. v. Local 1787, 59 Ohio App. 2d 238, 393 N.E.2d 504, 103 L.R.R.M. 2785 (1978).
31. The employer must avoid indiscriminate use of photography. Taking pictures of peaceful, lawful picketing may be considered an unfair labor practice, as it may imply that the employer intends to retaliate against strikers because of their protected activity. See United States Steel Corp. v. NLRB, 682 F.2d 98, 110 L.R.R.M. 2002 (3d Cir. 1982); NLRB v. Colonial Haven Nursing Home, Inc., 542 F.2d 691, 701-02, 93 L.R.R.M. 2241 (7th Cir. 1976).
32. Bettendorf-Stanford Bakery Equipment Co. v. UAW, Local 1906, 49 Ill. App. 3d 20, 363 N.E.2d 867, 95 L.R.R.M. 2890 (Ill. App. 1977). But see Steelworkers v. Alabaster Lime Co., 286 Ala. 489, 242 So. 2d 658, 76 L.R.R.M. 2079 (1970) (affirming issuance of injunction without notice).
33. See, e.g., 29 U.S.C. § 107.

Responding to Strikes

tory, an employer representative having personal knowledge of the union's activities and their impact on the employer's operations should attend the hearing and be prepared to testify. If the evidence persuades the judge that action must be taken, a short-term restraining order, usually lasting from ten days to two weeks, will be entered.[34] The order will probably prohibit the union from engaging in certain activities and require the employer to post a surety bond, payable to the union. The employer should come to the hearing prepared to file that bond, which is intended to cover damages in case a court later determines that the order was wrongfully issued.

If the court grants the restraining order, it will schedule a preliminary injunction hearing. This hearing will ordinarily be set for the day the restraining order expires. Unlike a temporary restraining order, a preliminary injunction is of indefinite duration, designed to remain effective until a final judgment is entered in the case. As a consequence, the court will expect the employer to make a more concrete showing of the union's misconduct before entering such an order. Detailed affidavits and live testimony should be carefully prepared for the preliminary injunction hearing, as with the hearing on the temporary restraining order. Although the bond filed in connection with the temporary restraining order will usually suffice, the employer should also be prepared to file a new bond promptly if the preliminary injunction is entered.

The employer's ultimate goal may be to secure a permanent injunction against strike misconduct. This can be entered only after a trial on the employer's complaint and only if the trial court finds that the unlawful activity will continue unless restrained.[35] If a union and its members have faithfully complied

---

34. The Norris-LaGuardia Act prescribes a five-day limit on temporary restraining orders. 29 U.S.C. § 107. Applicable state statutes should be reviewed to determine if analogous provisions exist.
35. *See* Washington Post Co. v. Printing & Graphic Communications Union, Local 6, 92 L.R.R.M. 2961, 2970 (D.C. Super. 1976).

Strike Misconduct and Violence

with the terms of a preliminary injunction, some courts will be hesitant to make the order permanent. If faced with such reluctance, an employer should argue that only the entry of a permanent injunction will prompt the union's continued adherence to the law.

6.2.5 Scope and Effect of the Injunction

Because courts generally may not enjoin peaceful picketing, they will restrict picketing only to the extent necessary to prevent a recurrence of misconduct. (See App. 6-B, Sample Preliminary Injunction.) Injunctions frequently limit the number of pickets, restrict their placement and behavior, and prohibit all interference with ingress to or egress from the employer's premises.[36] A union or its members who violate these restrictions after receiving notice of the injunction may be held in contempt of court.[37] The court may require the union to reimburse the employer for any damage caused by its contempt.[38]

When the strikers' misconduct is particularly egregious and the employer shows that the pattern of violence is so pervasive that no picketing can be conducted peaceably, courts have authority to order cessation of all picketing without violating the Constitution.[39] Such broad orders are rarely appropriate, and some state

---

36. See, e.g., Safeway Trails, Inc. v. United Transportation Union, Local 1699, 84 L.R.R.M. 2430 (D.D.C. 1973); Steelworkers v. Alabaster Lime Co., 286 Ala. 489, 242 So. 2d 658, 76 L.R.R.M. 2079 (Ala. 1970); Boston Buffalo Express v. Teamsters, Local 25, 114 L.R.R.M. 2767 (Mass. Super. 1982); General Electric v. Electrical Workers, Local 182, 47 N.C. App. 153, 266 S.E.2d 750, 100 L.R.R.M. 2191 (N.C. App. 1980).
37. Molders, Local 164 v. Superior Court, 138 Cal. Rptr. 794, 95 L.R.R.M. 2943 (Cal. App. 1977) (only those with notice of an injunction may be held in contempt).
38. See Premium Distr. Co. v. Teamsters, Local 174, 35 Wash. App. 36, 664 P.2d 1306 (1983).
39. Milk Wagon Drivers Union v. Meadowmoor Dairies, Inc., 312 U.S. 287, 293-95, 7 L.R.R.M. 310 (1941); Teamsters, Local 612 v. Bowman Trans-

statutes, like the federal Norris-LaGuardia Act, specifically prohibit injunctions against peaceful picketing.[40] Furthermore, regulation of peaceful picketing arguably lies within the exclusive domain of the National Labor Relations Board. The NLRB therefore may be able to obtain a federal court order prohibiting the enforcement of a state court injunction against peaceful picketing.[41]

6.2.6 Persons Restrained by the Injunction

The employer seeking the injunction must do its best to identify participants in the misconduct. The Norris-LaGuardia Act prohibits issuance of federal court injunctions except against those persons or organizations that can be shown to have actually participated in, authorized, or ratified the misconduct.[42] State "little" Norris-LaGuardia Acts may contain similar preclusions. Even in states where such statutes do not exist, most courts will require evidence that the persons or organizations to be enjoined have committed unlawful acts. When it is essential for the preservation of peace, however, some courts have been willing to enjoin misconduct by a labor organization even though the evidence fails to disclose conclusively the organization's responsibility for the unlawful acts.[43] These cases are the exception rather than the rule.

---

port, 276 Ala. 563, 165 So. 2d 113, 56 L.R.R.M. 2348 (1964); Altemose Constr. v. Building & Constr. Trades Council, 449 Pa. 194, 296 A.2d 504, 81 L.R.R.M. 2562 (1972), *cert. denied*, 411 U.S. 932 (1973) (prohibiting peaceful pickets within 200 yards of employer's jobsites); Jay Kay Metal Specialties Corp. v. Doe, 53 L.R.R.M. 2583 (N.Y. Sup. 1963); UFW Organizing Committee v. LaCasita Farms, Inc., 439 S.W.2d 398, 402, 71 L.R.R.M. 2160 (Tex. Civ. App. 1968).

40. *See, e.g.*, Yu v. Hotel Employees, Local 294, 105 L.R.R.M. 2358 (Wash. App. 1979); *see also* 29 U.S.C. § 104(e).
41. NLRB v. Nash-Finch Co., 404 U.S. 138, 78 L.R.R.M. 2967 (1971).
42. 29 U.S.C. § 107(a).
43. *See, e.g.*, Cross Co. v. Auto Workers, 371 Mich. 184, 123 N.W.2d 215, 54 L.R.R.M. 2109 (Mich. 1963). *But see* Louisiana-Pacific Corp. v. Lumber

Strike Misconduct and Violence

An employer should make sure that it appears before the court with clean hands.[44] A court will not be sympathetic to a request for an injunction from an employer that has itself breached the peace. Moreover, the injunctive remedy is a double-edged sword. If the employer has engaged in violence to retaliate against picket line misconduct, its actions may also be enjoined.[45] And even when the employer's conduct is exemplary, the court may impose some limits on its actions, as a "political" gesture to balance the injunction against the union.

6.3 Damage Suits for Strike Misconduct

An employer may be economically injured by strike misconduct even if an injunction is entered. Suits for damages are available to remedy these losses, including those suffered because of pre-injunction conduct. Because they do not rest on any federal statutory provision, such lawsuits are ordinarily prosecuted in state court.[46] When they share a common factual nucleus with actions arising under federal law (such as a lawsuit for the union's breach of a collective bargaining agreement), claims relating to violent picketing may be pursued in federal court.[47] An action may also proceed in a federal court under its diversity

---

and Sawmill Workers, Local 2949, 296 Or. 537, 679, P.2d 289, 116 L.R.R.M. 2991(1984) (requiring "clear proof" of union's involvement).

44. The mere fact that an employer has engaged in contingency strike planning does not mean that it lacks clean hands. Washington Post Co. v. Printing & Graphic Communications Union, Local 6, 92 L.R.R.M. 2961, 2975 (D.C. Super. 1976).
45. Stearns Mining Co. v. Mine Workers District 19, 96 L.R.R.M. 2545 (Ky. Cir. Ct. 1977) (limiting number of armed security guards posted by employer).
46. See Construction Workers v. Laburnum Constr. Corp., 347 U.S. 656, 34 L.R.R.M. 2229 (1954).
47. See, e.g., Flame Coal v. Mine Workers, 303 F.2d 39, 50 L.R.R.M. 2272 (6th Cir.), cert. denied, 371 U.S. 891 (1962); Virginia Electric & Power Co. v. Boilermakers, 103 L.R.R.M. 3144 (D.W. Va. 1980); see also Bonnano Linen Service v. McCarthy, 708 F.2d 1, 113 L.R.R.M. 2449 (1st

jurisdiction, when the injured party and those engaging in the misconduct are citizens of different states and the damages sought exceed $10,000.[48]

6.3.1 Damages Recoverable

An employer may recover only those damages proximately caused by the violent or abusive conduct.[49] Sales lost due to a shutdown caused by threats of violence are a typical item of damage,[50] as is the value of property destroyed during violence.[51] The cost of security services hired to protect against violence is clearly recoverable.[52] In some states, employers may also recover punitive damages.[53]

Cir.), *cert. denied*, 454 U.S. 404, 114 L.R.R.M. 2976 (1983) (federal court has jurisdiction over claim for violent picketing against union, joined with suit based on unlawful secondary activity, but not over claim against individuals).

48. *See* Curreri v. Teamsters, Local 251, 722 F.2d 6, 114 L.R.R.M. 3423 (1st Cir. 1983).
49. Stryjewski v. Teamsters, Local 830, 451 Pa. 550, 304 A.2d 463, 83 L.R.R.M., 2640 (Pa. 1973); *see* Rainbow Tours, Inc. v. Teamsters, 704 F.2d 1443, 1448, 113 L.R.R.M. 2383, 2387 (9th Cir. 1983).
50. Fibreboard Paper Prod's. Corp. v. East Bay Union of Machinists, Local 1304, 56 L.R.R.M. 2840 (Cal. App. 1964).
51. Virginia Elec. & Power Co. v. Boilermakers, 103 L.R.R.M. 3144, 3165-66 (N.D. W. Va. 1980); Premium Distr. Co. v. Teamsters, Local 174, 35 Wash. App. 36, 664 P.2d 1306 (1983) (damages for violation of injunction).
52. Bonanno Linen Service v. McCarthy, 708 F.2d 1, 113 L.R.R.M. 2449 (1st Cir.) *cert. denied*, 454 U.S. 404, 114 L.R.R.M. 2976 (1983); Virginia Elec. Power Co. v. Boilermakers, 103 L.R.R.M. 3144, 3165 (N.D. W. Va. 1980).
53. United Aircraft Corp. v. Machinists, 161 Conn. 79, 285 A.2d 330, 340, 77 L.R.R.M. 2436, 2448 (1971) *cert. denied*, 404 U.S. 1016 (1972); U.A.W. v. American Metal Products Co., 56 Tenn. App. 526, 408 S.W. 2d 682, 57 L.R.R.M. 2462 (1964); *see* Allen Trucking Co. v. Mine Workers, 319 F.2d 594, 53 L.R.R.M. 2648 (6th Cir. 1963).

Strike Misconduct and Violence

6.3.2 Who May Recover Damages?

An action for damages caused by picket line misconduct is like any lawsuit based on traditional principles of law. The employer being struck does not have to bring the lawsuit. Any victim of the misconduct who suffers reasonably foreseeable damages may sue. For example, a distributor prevented by violence from picking up goods at its supplier's premises may recover damages from the responsible union.[54] Those who are injured physically may also recover.[55]

6.3.3 Who is Liable for Damages?

An employer may seek damages from specific individuals engaged in misconduct. In most cases, however, economics dictate that the union be the principal object of the action for damages. To hold a labor organization liable for strike violence, the employer must show that the participants in the misconduct were the union's agents,[56] that the union expressly or impliedly authorized the conduct,[57] or that the union ratifed the conduct after it occurred.[58] Federal law and many state statutes specifically re-

---

54. Desire Fashions, Inc. v. Garment Workers, 47 L.R.R.M. 2764 (Pa. C.P. 1960).
55. Curreri v. Teamsters, Local 251, 722 F.2d 6, 114 L.R.R.M. 3423 (1st Cir. 1983); McDaniel v. Textile Workers Union, 36 Tenn. App. 236, 254 S.W.2d 1, 30 L.R.R.M. 2560 (1952), *cert. denied*, 31 L.R.R.M. 2193 (Tenn. 1952).
56. United Aircraft Corp. v. Machinists, 161 Conn. 79, 285 A2d 330, 77 L.R.R.M. 2436, 2444 (1971) *cert. denied*, 404 U.S. 1016 (1972); Titus v. Tacoma Smelterman's Local 25, 62 Wash 2d 461, 389 P.2d 504, 54 L.R.R.M. 2051 (1963).
57. U.A.W. v. American Metal Products Co., 56 Tenn. App. 526, 408 S.W.2d 682, 57 L.R.R.M. 2462 (1964); *see generally*, Annotation, *Liability of Labor Union or Its Membership for Torts*, 36 A.L.R.3d 405 (1971).
58. Curreri v. Teamsters, Local 251, 722 F.2d 6, 114 L.R.R.M. 3423, 3425 (1st Cir. 1983); Coats v. Construction & General Laborers Union, Local

Responding to Strikes

quire clear proof that the union authorized the unlawful activity, participated in it, or ratified it after having gained actual knowledge of it.[59]

This standard makes it difficult to hold a union liable for actions of unidentified individuals.[60] An employer may meet the clear proof requirement, however, if it shows continued union support for picketing characterized by "a pattern of violence" as well as "overt aid to accused troublemakers."[61]

Suit against the international union should be considered, especially when the local union lacks significant assets.[62] Because of its general lack of participation in local activities, an international union is unlikely to be held liable for strike misconduct.[63] Courts will, however, hold the international liable if the employer can prove its involvement.[64]

185, 15 Cal. App. 3d 908, 93 Cal. Rptr. 639 (1971) (misconduct by union's employees).

59. *See, e.g.*, 29 U.S.C. § 106; Mine Workers v. Gibbs, 383 U.S. 715, 737, 61 L.R.R.M. 2561, 2569 (1966); Kolodziej v. Electrical Workers, Local 697, 92 L.R.R.M. 3537, 3543 (N.D. Ind. 1975), *aff'd*, 535 F.2d 1257, 93 L.R.R.M. 2019 (7th Cir.), *cert. denied*, 429 U.S. 857 (1976).

60. *See, e.g.*, Ritchie v. United Mine Workers, 410 F.2d 827, 71 L.R.R.M. 2267 (6th Cir. 1969).

61. Bonanno Linen Service v. McCarthy, 708 F.2d 1, 113 L.R.R.M. 2449 (1st Cir.) (union's "knowing tolerance" of violence rendered it liable), *cert. denied*, 454 U.S. 404, 114 L.R.R.M. 2976 (1983); Curreri v. Teamsters, Local 251, 722 F.2d 6, 114 L.R.R.M. 3423, 3425 (1st Cir. 1983).

62. The local's assets are disclosed on Department of Labor Form LM-2.

63. *See* Federal Prescription Service, Inc. v. Meat Cutters, 527 F.2d 269, 91 L.R.R.M. 2091 (8th Cir. 1975); Artesia v. United Steelworkers, 87 N.M. 134, 529 P.2d 1255, 88 L.R.R.M. 2584 (1974).

64. *See, e.g.*, Kerry Coal Co. v. Mine Workers, 637 F.2d 957, 965, 106 L.R.R.M. 2225, 2230 (3d Cir.), *cert denied*, 454 U.S. 823 (1981); Mine Workers v. Meadow Creek Coal Co., 263 F.2d 52, 43 L.R.R.M. 2445 (6th Cir.), *cert. denied*, 359 U.S. 1013 (1959). Some union constitutions require strike approval at the international level. An employer might point to such a provision as justifying the international's accountability for strike misconduct.

6.4 Discipline of Employees Engaged in Strike Misconduct

Employees have no right to engage in misconduct in the course of concerted activity. As a consequence, employers may discipline employees engaging in violence or similar serious misconduct during a strike. Such employees also may forfeit their reinstatement rights.[65]

Although both unfair labor practice and economic strikers may be discharged for strike misconduct, different standards have ordinarily been applied. For economic strikers, the NLRB has looked only to the seriousness of the strikers' conduct to see if a discharge was warranted. For unfair labor practice strikers, the NLRB has balanced the seriousness of the strikers' misconduct against the gravity of the employer's unlawful conduct.[66] The continued vitality of this balancing test, however, is doubtful, as two NLRB members have recently opined that *only* the seriousness of employee misconduct is relevant in examining the legality of a discharge, even when the employer has committed unfair labor practices.[67]

The misconduct cases decided by the NLRB and the federal courts are inextricably linked to their particular fact situations. Several general conclusions, however, can be drawn. Misconduct occurring on the picket line may be viewed more leniently than the same behavior occurring far away from the picket line's emotional atmosphere.[68] Historically, the NLRB viewed a

---

65. Termination of reinstatement rights is more fully explored in ch. 9, *infra*.
66. NLRB v. Thayer Co., 213 F.2d 748, 34 L.R.R.M. 2250 (1st Cir.), *cert. denied*, 348 U.S. 883, 35 L.R.R.M. 2100 (1954); *see* Local 833, Automobile Workers v. NLRB, 300 F.2d 699, 49 L.R.R.M. 2485 (D.C. Cir.), *cert. denied sub nom.* Kohler Co. v. UAW., 370 U.S. 911, 50 L.R.R.M. 2326 (1962), Coronet Casuals, 207 N.L.R.B. 304, 84 L.R.R.M. 1441 (1973).
67. Clear Pine Mouldings, Inc., 268 N.L.R.B. No. 173, 115 L.R.R.M. 1113 (1984). The other two members of the NLRB declined to address this issue but appeared to adhere to the existing standard.
68. Associated Grocers of New England, Inc. v. NLRB, 562 F.2d 1333, 96 L.R.R.M. 2630 (1st Cir. 1977); NLRB v. W.C. McQuaide, Inc., 552 F.2d

Responding to Strikes

striker's express or implied threats as justifying a discharge only if accompanied by physical gestures or actual violence.[69] The federal appellate courts, however, often refused to enforce the NLRB's reinstatement orders in such cases.[70] In response, the NLRB has retreated from its prior decisions, now holding that verbal threats unaccompanied by physical acts will justify discharge when they reasonably tend to coerce or intimidate.[71] Abusive or threatening activity will probably continue to be viewed less seriously if the abuse or threats are directed at nonstrikers or striker replacements rather than at customers or customers' employees.[72] Finally, a series of incidents may justify discharge even if any single incident in the series would not have been serious enough to warrant discharge and termination of reinstatement rights.[73]

519, 94 L.R.R.M. 2950 (3d Cir. 1977); Tribune-Star Publishing Co., Inc., 78 L.A. 1153 (1982) (Katz, Arb.).

69. Garrett Railroad Car & Equipment, 255 N.L.R.B. 620, 107 L.R.R.M. 1103 (1980), *enforcement denied in part on other grounds*, 683 F.2d 731, 110 L.R.R.M. 2919 (3d Cir. 1982); Arrow Industries, Inc., 245 N.L.R.B. 1376, 102 L.R.R.M. 1525 (1979); MP Industries, Inc., 227 N.L.R.B. 1709, 1711, 94 L.R.R.M. 1608, 1611 (1977). *But see* Midwest Solvents, Inc., 251 N.L.R.B. 1282, 105 L.R.R.M. 1224 (1980), *enforced*, 696 F.2d 763, 112 L.R.R.M. 2276 (10th Cir. 1982) (denying that NLRB doctrine prohibits discharge where threats are not accompanied by physical violence).

70. *See, e.g.*, NLRB v. Moore Business Forms, Inc., 574 F.2d 835, 98 L.R.R.M. 2773 (5th Cir. 1978); Associated Grocers v. NLRB, 562 F.2d 1333, 96 L.R.R.M. 2630 (1st Cir. 1977); PepsiCola of Lumberton, Inc., 496 F.2d 226, 86 L.R.R.M. 2251 (4th Cir. 1974); NLRB v. Trumbull Asphalt Co., 327 F.2d 841, 55 L.R.R.M. 2435 (8th Cir. 1964).

71. Clear Pine Mouldings, Inc., 268 N.L.R.B. No. 173, 115 L.R.R.M. 1113 (1984). One circuit court has already expressed its approval of the NLRB's new standard. *See* Newport News Shipbuilding Co. v. NLRB, 116 L.R.R.M. 3042 (4th Cir. 1984).

72. Montgomery Ward & Co. v. NLRB, 374 F.2d 606, 64 L.R.R.M. 2712 (10th Cir. 1967). *But see* PBA, Inc., 270 N.L.R.B. No. 143, 116 LRRM 1162 (1984) (seriousness of threats against employees measured by same standards as threats against customers).

73. Firestone Tire & Rubber Co. v. NLRB, 449 F.2d 511, 78 L.R.R.M. 2591 (5th Cir. 1971).

Strike Misconduct and Violence

Physical property damage of any substantial nature is generally sufficient to support a discharge, provided the employer can establish that the discharged striker or strikers were responsible for the damage.[74] Displaying weapons, such as firearms, on the picket line has also been held to warrant discharge of either economic or unfair labor practice strikers.[75] Physical violence against people will likewise justify discharge.[76]

6.5 Unfair Labor Practice Charges against Unions Engaging in Misconduct

Section 7 of the National Labor Relations Act gives employees the right to *refrain* from engaging in concerted activities, including strikes. Section 8(b)(1)(A) of the Act makes it an unfair labor practice for a union to restrain or coerce employees in the exer-

---

74. Garrett Railroad Car & Equipment, 255 N.L.R.B. 620, 625, 107 L.R.R.M. 1103, 1104 (1980), *enforced in relevant part*, 683 F.2d 731, 110 L.R.R.M. 2919 (3d Cir. 1982). The Sixth Circuit has recently criticized the NLRB for its allocation of the burden of proof in such cases. According to the court, the employer need only show "a basis for an honest belief that the employees had engaged in serious misconduct." Schreiber Manufacturing, Inc. v. NLRB, 725 F.2d 413, 115 L.R.R.M. 2559 (6th Cir. 1984). The employer's action should then be upheld, the court wrote, unless the NLRB General Counsel can "establish that the employees did not participate in such conduct." *Id.*
75. Advance Industries Division-Overhead Door Corp. v. NLRB, 540 F.2d 878, 93 L.R.R.M. 2147 (7th Cir. 1976); *see also* NLRB v. A. Duie Pyle Inc., 730 F.2d 119, 115 L.R.R.M. 3428 (3d Cir. 1984) (use of knife in picket line altercation). *But see* Newport News Shipbuilding Co. v. NLRB, 116 L.R.R.M. 3042 (4th Cir. 1984) (carrying sheathed hunting knife on picket line not serious misconduct because it did not tend to coerce or intimidate).
76. AMPAC (Kane-Miller Corp.), 259 N.L.R.B. 1075, 109 L.R.R.M. 1075 (1982); Tidewater Oil Co., 145 N.L.R.B. 1547, 55 L.R.R.M. 1213 (1964).

cise of this right.[77] A union violates this section if, to assure a strike's effectiveness, it threatens an employee with physical harm or, by means of mass picketing, prevents employees from entering their employer's premises.[78] Union violence directed against non-employees also may violate section 8(b)(1)(A) when it is likely to come to employees' attention, thus warning them of the consequences of resisting the union.[79] Threats or violence against managers or supervisors may be seen as unlawfully coercing *strikers* by implicitly suggesting the consequences if they fail to continue supporting the strike.[80]

6.5.1 Remedies for Strike Misconduct before the NLRB

If an employer intends to seek prompt monetary or injunctive relief in state court, there may be nothing gained from filing a section 8(b)(1)(A) charge against the union. The NLRB will not award damages to either employers or employees injured by picket line misconduct.[81] The NLRB's reluctance is consistent

---

77. It is generally lawful, however, for a union to promulgate internal rules calling for union discipline of members who refuse to honor a sanctioned, legal strike. As a voluntary association, the union may prescribe rules for its members' conduct.
78. See, e.g., Operating Engineers, Local 542 v. NLRB, 328 F.2d 850, 55 L.R.R.M. 2669 (3d Cir.), cert. denied, 379 U.S. 826 (1964), 57 L.R.R.M. 2239; Machinists, Local 758 (Menasco, Inc.), 267 N.L.R.B. No. 73, 114 L.R.R.M. 1187 (1983); see also NLRB v. Teamsters, Local 639, 362 U.S. 274, 45 L.R.R.M. 2975 (1960).
79. See, e.g., NLRB v. Union Nacional de Trabajadores, 540 F.2d 1, 6, 92 L.R.R.M. 3425 (1st Cir. 1976), cert. denied, 429 U.S. 1039 (1977); United Furniture Workers, Local 140 (Brooklyn Spring Corp.), 113 N.L.R.B. 815, 822, 36 L.R.R.M. 1372 (1955), enforced, 233 F.2d 539, 38 L.R.R.M. 2134 (2d Cir. 1956).
80. Machinists (General Electric Co.), 183 N.L.R.B. 1225, 1231, 75 L.R.R.M. 1094 (1970).
81. Roofers, Local 30 (Associated Builders & Contractors, Inc.), 227 N.L.R.B. 1444, 94 L.R.R.M. 1624 (1977).

with the legislative history of the Act, which indicates that Congress did not intend the NLRB's authority to extend to the award of compensatory damages in such circumstances.[82] For somewhat inexplicable reasons, the NLRB has also refused to award back pay to employees kept from work because of a union's violation of section 8(b)(1)(A).[83]

The NLRB's Regional Director has the power to seek an injunction against activity that violates section 8(b)(1)(A).[84] The Regional Director will request injunctive relief only after conducting a thorough investigation, thus acting less rapidly than the employer could by filing its own action for a restraining order. However, the employer may benefit from a public relations standpoint if the NLRB, rather than the employer, seeks the injunction. In such circumstances, the employer is more likely to be perceived as a victim rather than an aggressor. In addition, the NLRB is not required to meet the substantive and procedural standards imposed by the Norris-LaGuardia Act and its state counterparts, which restrict the employer's efforts to enjoin misconduct.[85]

It may be worthwhile to make a record at the NLRB level of the violent activity in case there are subsequent proceedings before the agency. For example, when there is a long-standing pattern of union violence, the NLRB may revoke the union's certification.[86]

---

82. *See generally*, A. THIEBLOT & T. HAGGARD, UNION VIOLENCE: THE RECORD AND THE RESPONSE BY COURTS, LEGISLATURES, AND THE NLRB 443 (University of Pennsylvania, 1983).
83. *See* Note, *Strike Violence: The NLRB's Reluctance to Wield Its Broad Remedial Power*, 50 FORDHAM L. REV. 1371, 1388-92 (May 1982).
84. *See* Squillacote v. Meat Cutters, Local 248, 534 F.2d 735, 92 L.R.R.M. 2089 (7th Cir. 1976) (Regional Director may obtain injunction against strike misconduct).
85. *See* Muniz v. Hoffman, 422 U.S. 454, 89 L.R.R.M. 2625 (1975).
86. *See* Union Nacional de Trabajadores (Carborundum Co.), 219 N.L.R.B. 862, 90 L.R.R.M. 1023 (1975), *enforced in part*, 540 F.2d 1, 92 L.R.R.M. 3425 (1st Cir. 1976), *cert. denied*, 429 U.S. 1039 (1977).

6.5.2 Timing of the Unfair Labor Practice Charge

An employer who decides to file a section 8(b)(1)(A) charge must carefully consider the appropriate timing. As noted above, the pursuit of state injunctive relief raises delicate questions as to what is the appropriate jurisdiction. If the NLRB receives the section 8(b)(1)(A) charge before relief is sought at the state court level, the union may claim that the state court's jurisdiction is preempted by the NLRB's consideration of the charge. Some state courts have properly held that they do have jurisdiction to enjoin violent or abusive conduct, even if the NLRB has assumed jurisdiction over a charge relating to the same picketing.[87] Such a favorable outcome, however, is not assured. Because the injunction may be more important than the charge, an employer should take care not to let the charge interfere with a state court's consideration of injunctive relief.

---

87. State *ex rel.* Retail Store Employees, Local 655 v. Black, 603 S.W.2d 676, 108 L.R.R.M. 2650 (Mo. App. 1980).

Appendix 6-A

WITNESS CHECKLIST
FOR STRIKE MISCONDUCT

[NOTE: This document should be used to prepare potential witnesses before or after strike misconduct has occurred. It should be given to all supervisors who will be working during the strike and who may be in a position to observe misconduct by strikers. You should read it carefully and edit it to fit the circumstances. If counsel is involved in the editing process and provided with all information generated through the checklist's use, you may be able to assert the attorney-client privilege to protect the information from disclosure in the event of litigation.]

In the event our facility is picketed, there is the unfortunate possibility that pickets may engage in disruptive or violent conduct and that [Employer] may wish to take appropriate legal action. In that event, you or other key personnel may have to provide statements and testimony in support of [Employer].

This Witness Checklist is provided to help you be an effective witness for your employer. Whenever you take notes on any picketing activity, always try to describe events in detail, listing background information, date, time, location, reason, other witnesses, etc.

A. <u>Document.</u> Whenever picketing occurs, immediately document the situation. Write down everything as soon

Responding to Strikes

as possible, including the nature of the picketing, parties to the picketing, places, times, etc. Be sure you are truthful, specific, and accurate.

B. Collect Evidence. If possible, have an automatic camera or videotape equipment ready and use it to photograph or film any misconduct or mass picketing that impedes people trying to enter or exit the premises. Do not, however, photograph pickets not engaged in abusive or violent conduct or mass picketing.

C. Keep Your Cool. Do not antagonize strikers, especially if they are showing violent tendencies. Do not respond to abuse by abusing or attacking strikers. It is very important that the employer have "clean hands" when it asks law enforcement agencies or the courts for assistance in responding to picket line misconduct.

D. Identify. Always try to identify participants in misconduct. If you do not know the names of the individuals involved, at least attempt to determine their union affiliation, if any. This may be obvious from language on picket signs or hand bills, or from union insignia worn by picketers. Do not simply assume that all persons on the picket line are affiliated with the striking union.

E. Record Your Observations. Be sure to highlight the following areas, asking questions if necessary. In taking notes on these subjects, pay particular attention to dates, times, locations, individuals involved, other witnesses, and similar details.

1. Pickets. How many pickets were present at each entrance to the facility? How did these pickets behave? Were they standing still or milling about?

Strike Misconduct and Violence

2. <u>Access Problems.</u> Did any person have difficulty entering or exiting the premises? Did any person complain of difficulty in entering or exiting the premises? Who? When? What entrance were they using?

3. <u>Threats to Prevent Access.</u> Did any picketer, handbiller, or union representative indicate that pickets would prevent people from entering or exiting the premises? Who said what? To whom, when, and where was it said?

4. <u>Union Identification.</u> Did any participants in the picketing wear any union insignia? Did the insignia designate any particular local? Did any picket signs identify a particular union? If so, which one?

5. <u>Union Participation.</u> Did any union officer or representative walk the picket line? If so, who was it and what is his/her office? When, where, and in what manner did the officer or representative participate?

6. <u>Threats of Violence.</u> Did any picketer, handbiller, or union representative threaten violence against any person or property? If so, do you know the labor organization to which the person making the threat belonged? What was the precise nature of the threat? To whom, when, and where was it made?

7. <u>Verbal Abuse.</u> Has any person crossing the picket line been subjected to abusive or obscene language or behavior? When and where? Who was abusive or obscene? Does that person belong to any labor organization? If so, which one? How do you know?

8. <u>Surveillance.</u> Have picketers or other strikers placed persons crossing the picket line under surveillance, either by photographing them or following them after their departure? Who engaged in the surveillance? Who, when, and where was

surveillance conducted? Who was subjected to surveillance?

9. <u>Slanderous Remarks.</u> Have picketers, handbillers, or union representatives slandered the employer to persons attempting to cross the picket line? Who engaged in such slander and to what organization do they belong? What exactly was said? To whom, when, and where was it said? What was the reaction of the person to whom the employer was slandered?

10. <u>Physical Contact or Violence.</u> Has any picketer, handbiller, or union representative jostled, shoved, or engaged in any physical violence, no matter how slight, against any person seeking to enter or exit the premises? Who perpetrated the violence and to what organization, if any, do they belong? Who suffered the violence? Were they injured? When and where did that occur?

11. <u>Projectiles.</u> Did any picketer, handbiller, or union representative throw anything at any person or any company property? What was thrown and who threw it? When and where did that occur?

12. <u>Weapons.</u> Were any weapons seen or rumored to be present? Who had them or was rumored to have them?

13. <u>Property Damage.</u> Has any company property been damaged under suspicious circumstances during the strike? What was damaged? When, where, and how did the damage occur? Who perpetrated the damage? How do you know?

14. <u>Repairs of Damage.</u> What amounts have you expended to repair damage caused by pickets? If property has been destroyed, what was its value? How much will it cost to replace it?

15. <u>Physical Injuries.</u> Has anyone been hurt? How seriously? Who? How? When? Where? Where are they now? What is their condition?

Strike Misconduct and Violence

16. <u>Effect on Customers.</u> Has any customer withdrawn or threatened to withdraw business? When? Why? What did the customer say about the pickets? What is the customer's address and telephone number?

17. <u>Loss of Business.</u> If picketing was at first peaceably conducted, was there a significant downturn in business after it became violent? Do your records verify this? How much business do you believe was lost? How do you know?

18. <u>Contract Schedules.</u> Have you been unable to meet contract schedules because of violence or the threat of violence? Why? How much has this cost you?

19. <u>Loss of New Business.</u> Has the violence prevented you from obtaining new business? How do you know this business was available? How do you know you could have obtained this business? How much was this business worth?

20. <u>Security Costs.</u> Have you been required to hire any extra security guards to cope with strike misconduct? How much has this cost?

21. <u>Security Threats.</u> Have security guards been subjected to any verbal or physical abuse or threats? If so, describe the circumstances in detail and request any written reports given by the security guards to their superiors.

This is not an all-inclusive checklist. It raises only major questions. If any other incidents do occur, be certain to document them and verify *exactly* what occurred. Should you have any questions or comments, please do not hesitate to contact _____ (_____), who will consult our counsel for legal advice as necessary.

Appendix 6-B

SAMPLE PRELIMINARY INJUNCTION

[NOTE: This document is for illustrative purposes only. It must be carefully modified to reflect the employer's particular fact situation. It must also be tailored to the legal requirements applicable in the jurisdiction in which the employer brings its action.]

(Employer),	)
	)
Plaintiff	)
	)
v.	) PRELIMINARY
	) INJUNCTION
(Union), affiliated with _____	)
_____ _____,	)
all of its members, and the following officers and/or agents of that labor organization, individually and in their official capacities: Its President, _____; Its Vice-President, _____; Its Secretary-Treasurer, _____ _____; Its Picketing or Demonstration Coordinators or Organizers (whose names are presently unknown); Its Agents or Employees who were or are involved in labor disputes, picketing or demonstrations involving Plaintiff (whose names are pres-	)

Strike Misconduct and Violence

ently unknown); and all other)
persons associated with or acting)
by or through or under or in con-)
cert or in connection with the)
above-named defendants or any)
of them,)
                    Defendants.)

THIS MATTER came on for hearing on _____, 19 ___, after due notice, before the undersigned Judge of the above-entitled Court upon Plaintiff's motion for entry of a Preliminary Injunction as prayed for in the verified Complaint on file in this action. The Plaintiff was represented by its attorneys, _____ and _____; the Defendants were represented by their attorneys, _____ and _____.

The Court has considered the verified Complaint, the Motion and other pleadings herein, the Affidavits filed in support of Plaintiff's Motion for a Preliminary Injunction, and the arguments of the parties, both oral and written. It appears to the Court that, unless a Preliminary Injunction is entered pending trial in this action, Plaintiff will suffer not only damage to its property and economic loss from an inability to carry on its business, but also irreparable harm, including loss of employees, loss of goodwill, physical harm to its employees, and loss of their ability to carry on their activities freely and without unlawful and violent interference. If further appears that Defendants have engaged in the following conduct, although Defendants deny such conduct has occurred:

1. Stationing pickets in large numbers at and adjacent to Plaintiff's _____ facility at

(See Exhibits __ and __ attached hereto), who have attempted to block and have blocked ingress to and egress from these facilities by massing at such entrance ways

Responding to Strikes

and from time to time parking vehicles in such manner and in such close proximity that the entrance ways have been blocked in whole or in part or passage through them has been made difficult;

2. Stationing pickets so close to vehicles entering and leaving the _____ facility that drivers have been unable safely to drive such vehicles in and out of these facilities;

3. Blocking windows and mirrors of Plaintiff's vehicles to prevent the drivers from being able to see where they are going;

4. Gathering around Plaintiff's vehicles while they are being moved to make it unsafe for the drivers to proceed;

5. Approaching vehicles while they are entering and leaving the _____ facility and the _____ facility and attempting to unfasten mechanical devices in order to keep Plaintiff's vehicles from operating;

6. Yelling obscenities, spitting, and throwing objects at Plaintiff's drivers when they pass through the picket line at the _____ facility and the _____ facility;

7. Throwing rocks, glass and railway spikes at Plaintiff's vehicles and in their path at the _____ facility and the _____ facility;

8. Slashing tires of Plaintiff's vehicles parked at the _____ facility and breaking headlights and windows on such vehicles;

9. Inflicting property damage to automobiles owned and driven by certain of Plaintiff's nonstriking employees;

10. Throwing firecrackers and shooting bottle rockets into Plaintiff's _____ facility;

11. Committing assaults and batteries on Plaintiff's nonstriking employees with the sole purpose of intimidating and coercing such employees; and

12. Following Plaintiff's nonstriking employees in lawful pursuit of their business and threatening and harass-

ing such nonstriking employees by intentionally operating motor vehicles illegally on the public streets and highways with disregard to public safety.

In view of these facts, and the Court being otherwise fully advised, NOW, THEREFORE, IT IS HEREBY

ORDERED that during the pendency of this action or until further order of the Court, all persons, including but not limited to the above-named Defendants, are restrained and enjoined from engaging in any of the following activities:

(a) From physically obstructing or interfering with or attempting to obstruct or interfere with the free use, occupancy and enjoyment of Plaintiff's premises by Plaintiff, its agents, employees, customers, guests or invitees;

(b) From physically obstructing in any manner any entrance or exit to or from Plaintiff's premises;

(c) From physically obstructing, harassing or interfering with the movement of any vehicle or person entering or leaving, or attempting to enter or leave, or approaching or attempting to approach, or departing or attempting to depart from Plaintiff's premises;

(d) From threatening or coercing Plaintiff or Plaintiff's agents, employees, subcontractors, customers, guests, invitees, or any other person having business with Plaintiff;

(e) From assaulting, jostling or causing or threatening to cause physical injury to any of Plaintiff's employees, subcontractors, customers, guests or invitees;

(f) From threatening or causing damage to the property of Plaintiff, or the property of its employees, subcontractors, guests, invitees, or any person having business with Plaintiff;

(g) From harassing Plaintiff's employees, subcontractors, customers, agents, invitees, and guests by the use of racial slurs or abusive, profane, or threatening language;

(h) From trespassing on Plaintiff's premises;

(i) From maintaining, stationing, or placing more than one picket, demonstrator or other person at any one time every _____ yards along the public roadway, otherwise known as _____, adjacent to the _____ facility;

(j) From maintaining, stationing or placing more than one picket, demonstrator or other person at any one time at each of the __ entrances to the _____ facility, which entrances are located at the places specified on Exhibit __.

(k) From harassing Plaintiff's employees by the operation of motor vehicles in an unsafe or illegal manner; and

(l) From directing, encouraging or suggesting expressly or by implication that any other individual or entity do or cause to be done any of the above-described acts.

IT IS FURTHER ORDERED that Plaintiff and its sureties shall remain liable upon the original written undertaking in the sum of _____ Dollars ($_____) previously filed and approved by this Court for the payment of such costs and damages as Defendants may incur or suffer if they are found to have been wrongfully enjoined or restrained by the issuance of this Preliminary Injunction.

IT IS FURTHER ORDERED that a copy of this Order shall be served forthwith upon the named labor organization.

DONE IN OPEN COURT this __ day of _____, 19__.

JUDGE

7
Responding to Secondary Activity

The National Labor Relations Act attempts to balance the economic weapons available to employers and unions. In striking this balance, Congress prohibited union efforts to enmesh uninvolved parties in labor disputes, outlawing pressure against an employer through coercion of those who do business with the employer. Such pressures, described in section 8(b)(4) of the Act,[1] have come to be known as "secondary activity." If a union engages in secondary activity, an affected employer may file an unfair labor practice charge with the NLRB, which may then seek an injunction against the union. The employer may also sue the union to recover damages caused by the secondary action. Because these are powerful remedies, an employer should pay close attention to union activities that may violate the statute.

Section 8(b)(4) makes it an unfair labor practice for unions or their agents to apply pressure designed to accomplish secondary objectives. The most important of section 8(b)(4)'s proscriptions prohibits union coercion designed to force one person to "cease doing business" with another.[2] This provision covers those situations in which a union applies pressure, or encourages others to

---

1. 29 U.S.C. § 158(b)(4).
2. § 8(b)(4)(B); 29 U.S.C. § 158(b)(4)(B), provides:

> It shall be an unfair labor practice for a labor organization or its agents—...
> (4)(i) to engage in, or to induce or encourage any individual employed by any person engaged in commerce or in an industry affecting commerce to engage in, a strike or a refusal in the

219

apply pressure, against an employer with whom it has no dispute (the secondary or neutral employer) in an effort to persuade that employer to stop doing business with the employer with whom the union does have a dispute (the primary employer). The union's goal is to force the primary employer to accede to labor's demands so that normal business relationships with secondary employers can resume.

The Act's prohibition of secondary activity is limited. Primary strikes or picketing, even if they have secondary effects, are expressly permitted by section 8(b)(4). Furthermore, section 8(b)(4) does not preclude a person from refusing to enter the premises of an employer whose workers are engaged in a strike authorized by their bargaining representative. Nor does it prohibit publicity "other than picketing" designed to "truthfully" advise the public that a secondary employer is distributing products produced by a primary employer. *Picketing* of a secondary employer is also permitted if it is narrowly focused on a primary employer's *product*, without urging persons to cease doing business altogether with the secondary employer.

This complex interaction of prohibitions and protections leaves little doubt that Congress perceived a conflict between limitations on secondary activity and labor's freedom to wield economic power against primary employers. As the Supreme Court

---

course of his employment to use, manufacture, process, transport, or otherwise handle or work on any goods, articles, materials, or commodities or to perform any services; or (ii) to threaten, coerce, or restrain any person engaged in commerce or in an industry affecting commerce, where in either case an object thereof is—. . .

(B) forcing or requiring any person to cease using, selling, handling, transporting, or otherwise dealing in the products of any other producer, processor, or manufacturer, or to cease doing business with any other person . . . *Provided*, That nothing contained in this clause (B) shall be construed to make unlawful, where not otherwise unlawful, any primary strike or primary picketing . . . .

observed in *N.L.R.B. v. Denver Building and Construction Trades Council*, section 8(b)(4) reflects

> dual congressional objectives of preserving the right of a labor organization to bring pressure to bear on offending employers in primary labor disputes and of shielding unoffending employers and others from pressures and controversies not their own.[3]

Unions, of course, prefer to tip the balance in their favor. Consequently, strike activities will frequently be accompanied by attempts to embroil secondary employers as an additional measure of pressure. Unions are most likely to engage in such efforts when the primary employer's business depends upon continued trade with neutral employers and other union tactics have failed. Secondary pressures should be of particular concern to employers in highly competitive industries. The disruption engendered by such unlawful activities may cause a loss of business lasting beyond the strike's end.

The subject of secondary pressures should be approached with care and respect for its complexity. However, employers need to know how to identify secondary action so that unlawful activity can be reported promptly to the NLRB, which alone has the power to seek an injunction for violations of section 8(b)(4). The strategy for responding to activity violating section 8(b)(4) should be developed well before a strike begins, in close consultation with labor counsel.

7.1 Identifying Secondary Activity

Union action that violates section 8(b)(4) has two essential characteristics. First, the union must apply *pressure* against a *neutral* person or employer, either by a strike, refusal to perform

---

3. NLRB v. Denver Bldg. & Constr. Trades Council, 341 U.S. 675, 692, 28 L.R.R.M. 2108 (1951).

Responding to Strikes

work or refusal to handle goods (or an inducement or encouragement of others to strike or refuse to perform work), or by threats, coercion, or restraint. Second, the union activity must have as an object one of the *unlawful goals*, such as causing a neutral employer to stop doing business with a struck employer.[4]

7.1.1 The Existence of Union Pressure against Neutral Employers

In the typical case, union pressure is readily observed. Strikes, picketing, refusals to work at a secondary employer's premises, and refusals to handle or work on particular goods do not go unnoticed. An employer may find it more difficult to determine if a union is encouraging such action, but either circumstantial or direct evidence of union encouragement is generally available.[5] Section 8(b)(4) clearly prohibits this kind of secondary pressure. The statute's prohibition of threats, restraint, or coercion is considerably more amorphous, encompassing virtually any form of economic pressure *other than* the filing of lawsuits.[6]

7.1.1.1 Threats and Coercion

A union lawfully may advise a neutral employer of its displeasure at the neutral's continued dealings with a primary employer.

---

4. *See* Teamsters, Local 812 v. NLRB, 657 F.2d 1252, 1261, 105 L.R.R.M. 2658 (D.C. Cir. 1980) (union's liability depends upon two factors: unlawful object and unlawful means).
5. *See, e.g.,* Virginia Elec. & Power Co. v. Boilermakers, 103 L.R.R.M. 3144, 3159 (D.W. Va. 1980) (union violated § 8(b)(4) by urging employees of secondary employer to honor picket lines, though they failed to do so).
6. *See* Commerce Tankers Corp. v. National Maritime Union, 553 F.2d 793, 802, 95 L.R.R.M. 2065, 2071 (2d Cir. 1977), *cert. denied*, 434 U.S. 923 (1977); Southern California Conference of Carpenters (D&E Corp.),

Secondary Activity

It may not, however, threaten to exert pressure, such as picketing, in the event those dealings continue.[7] It is often difficult to determine when a union has crossed the line separating lawful from unlawful activity. In one case, a union's statement that a neutral would face "serious problems" if its work continued to be performed by the primary employer did not rise to the level of a threat. The statement was considered ambiguous in the absence of economic action, such as a strike or picketing. However, the same union's unequivocal demand for payment in exchange for permitting the work to continue was found to be unlawful coercion.[8] Union publicity advocating a consumer boycott of an employer is also a form of coercion, although it will be authorized in some cases by the "publicity proviso" to section 8(b)(4).[9]

Nebulous union statements that do not threaten *specific* action are generally deemed noncoercive and lawful.[10] The NLRB has also held that a union's attempt merely to persuade an employer to make a particular business judgment, not dictated by threats of union action, is lawful.[11] Furthermore, a union pledge to engage in lawful picketing if nonunion contractors are awarded

---

243 N.L.R.B. 888, 890, 101 L.R.R.M. 1549, 1551 (1979); Sheet Metal Workers Int'l Ass'n (Young Plumbing & Supply), 209 N.L.R.B. 1177, 1179, 86 L.R.R.M. 1052 (1974).

7. *See, e.g.*, Building and Constr. Trades Council (Chatham Supermarkets, Inc.), 259 N.L.R.B. 970, 971, 109 L.R.R.M. 1061 (1982).

8. Electro-Coal Transfer Corp. v. Longshoremen, ILA, Local 1418, 591 F.2d 284, 100 L.R.R.M. 2009 (5th Cir. 1979). *See also* Laborers, Local 695 (Mautz & Oren, Inc.), 209 N.L.R.B. 410, 412, 85 L.R.R.M. 1610 (1974).

9. Service Employees, Local 399 (Delta Airlines, Inc.), 263 N.L.R.B. No. 153, 111 L.R.R.M. 1159, 1101 (1982). Section 7.1.7 discusses the publicity proviso in greater detail.

10. IBEW, Local 453 (Southern Sun Electric Corp.), 249 N.L.R.B. 384, 385, 104 L.R.R.M. 1156 (1980).

11. IBEW, Local 3 (L.M. Ericsson Telecommunications, Inc.), 257 N.L.R.B. 1358, 1369, 108 L.R.R.M. 1210 (1981). *But see* Texas Distributors, Inc. v. Plumbers, Local 100, 598 F.2d 393, 399, 101 L.R.R.M. 2758 (5th Cir. 1979) (questioning neutral employer's "business judgment" in doing business with primary may be "veiled threat").

work has been regarded as neither threatening nor coercive, regardless of the union's object.[12]

7.1.1.2 Inducement or Encouragement of Refusals to Work

The Supreme Court has commented that "the words 'induce or encourage' [in section 8(b)(4)] are broad enough to include in them every form of influence and persuasion."[13] The union, then, need not go so far as to call specifically for secondary picketing to violate section 8(b)(4). The question is whether a refusal to work would be the "logical and foreseeable consequence" of the union's action.[14] Thus, a union officer's statement to workers that "trade union principles" require a refusal to work on goods supplied by a particular employer falls within the statute's proscription,[15] as does distribution of a "Know Your Rights" pamphlet telling union members that they have a right to refuse to work alongside nonunion employees.[16] A union's implicit authorization of a refusal to work, combined with its representation that it will not discipline members who refuse to work, is also

---

12. IBEW, Local 278 (Kelinske Electric Co.), 232 N.L.R.B. 1044, 1045, 96 L.R.R.M. 1479 (1977).
13. Electrical Workers, Local 501 v. NLRB, 341 U.S. 694, 701, 28 L.R.R.M. 2115 (1951). A classic example of union encouragement occurred in 1980, when the International Longshoremen's Association "ordered immediate suspension in handling all Russian ships and Russian cargoes." See ILA, Local 1414 (Occidental Chemical Co.), 261 N.L.R.B. 1, 110 L.R.R.M. 1001 (1982), enforced, 112 L.R.R.M. 3088 (D.C. Cir. 1983).
14. Longshoremen, ILWU, Local 19 (West Coast Container Service, Inc.), 266 N.L.R.B. No. 38, 112 L.R.R.M. 1293, 1295 (1983).
15. NLRB v. IBEW, Local 3, 477 F.2d 260, 264-65, 82 L.R.R.M. 3190 (2d Cir. 1973); see also NLRB v. Painters, Local 48, 340 F.2d 107, 58 L.R.R.M. 2165 (9th Cir.), cert. denied, 381 U.S. 914 (1965) (struck employer's materials "unfair"); Truck Drivers & Helpers, Local 728 v. NLRB, 332 F.2d 693, 56 L.R.R.M. 2395 (5th Cir.), cert. denied, 379 U.S. 913 (1964) ("you don't have to handle no scab freight").
16. IBEW, Local 684 (Walsh & Maddox), 246 N.L.R.B. 549, 102 L.R.R.M. 1599 (1979).

Secondary Activity

unlawful inducement or encouragement.[17] Conversely, a union cannot take disciplinary action to induce members to withhold services from neutral employers with the purpose of forcing the neutrals to alter relations with the primary employer.[18] An employer therefore should pay close attention to and carefully document tacit union signals that fall short of explicit encouragement.[19]

7.1.2 Unlawful Objectives

In most cases, the union will not argue about whether it exerted pressure. Rather, the crucial question under section 8(b)(4) "is always to determine the object of labor activity."[20] The statute does not prohibit all secondary *effects*, for section 8(b)(4) expressly permits primary strikes or picketing "even though some neutral or secondary employers might be affected."[21] The inquiry is directed instead to the union's *objectives*. Effects are relevant, but only because they may shed light on whether the union's object is to embroil neutral employers.

---

17. NLRB v. IBEW, Local 3 (Northern Telecom, Inc.), 730 F.2d 870, 115 L.R.R.M. 3436 (2d Cir. 1984); IBEW, Local 3 (L.M. Ericsson Telecommunications, Inc.), 257 N.L.R.B. 1358, 1370, 108 L.R.R.M. 1210 (1981).
18. District Council of Carpenters (Commercial Industrial Contractors, Inc.), 259 N.L.R.B. 541, 545, 108 L.R.R.M. 1392 (1981); District Council of Carpenters (J.A. Stewart Constr. Co.,), 242 N.L.R.B. 585, 587, 101 L.R.R.M. 1173 (1979), *enforced*, 108 L.R.R.M. 2103 (9th Cir. 1980); District Council of Carpenters (Pace Constr. Co.), 222 N.L.R.B. 613, 91 L.R.R.M. 1205 (1976), *enforced*, 560 F.2d 1015, 96 L.R.R.M. 2001 (10th Cir. 1977); NLRB v. Glaziers & Glassworkers, Local 1621, 632 F.2d 89, 105 L.R.R.M. 2905 (9th Cir. 1980).
19. Statements that would reasonably be understood as a signal to neutral employees to stop work have generally been held unlawful. Sheet Metal Workers, Local 80 (Ciamello Heating & Cooling, Inc.), 268 N.L.R.B. No. 2, 114 L.R.R.M. 1232 (1983).
20. NLRB v. Northern California District Council of Hod Carriers, 389 F.2d 721, 725, 67 L.R.R.M. 2502 (9th Cir. 1968).
21. *Id.*

Determining the object of union pressure is a question of fact for the NLRB and the courts to resolve, based on the circumstances of each case.[22] Few hard and fast rules guide this determination. The statute prohibits strikes, refusals to work, threats, or coercion when "*an* object thereof" is the application of secondary pressure. To be lawful, then, a union's objectives must be entirely primary.[23] A union cannot justify its conduct by pointing to one lawful purpose among several unlawful ones. *All* of its purposes must be lawful. Bearing this principle in mind, some courts have found a secondary objective when the union has not taken all steps necessary to minimize the secondary impact of its action.[24]

Union picketing of a secondary employer's premises is the most obvious example of pressure having a secondary objective.[25] In such a situation, the union hopes the secondary employer's work force will honor the picket lines, forcing the secondary employer to shut down until it yields to the union's demands; the union will agree to remove the pickets only if the secondary employer stops doing business with the primary employer. Similarly, the union's objectives will be clear if it tells a neutral employer's employees to refuse to work on any products that have as compo-

---

22. Bean & Son v. Graphic Arts Local 96B, 76 F.R.D. 602, 96 L.R.R.M. 3311, 3312 (D. Ga. 1977).
23. NLRB v. Enterprise Ass'n of Pipefitters, Local 638, 429 U.S. 507, 530 n.17, 94 L.R.R.M. 2628 (1977); George E. Hoffman & Sons v. Teamsters, Local 627, 617 F.2d 1234, 103 L.R.R.M. 2605, 2610 (7th Cir. 1980), *cert. denied*, 449 U.S. 937 (1981); Texas Distributors, Inc. v. Plumbers, Local 100, 598 F.2d 393, 101 L.R.R.M. 2758 (5th Cir. 1979).
24. Allied Concrete v. NLRB, 607 F.2d 827, 830, 102 L.R.R.M. 2508 (9th Cir. 1979); Texas Distributors, Inc. v. Plumbers, Local 100, 598 F.2d 393, 400, 101 L.R.R.M. 2758 (5th Cir. 1979) ("the union has acted in a manner which it *knows* will have a secondary effect even though it could have acted otherwise"); Plumbers & Pipefitters, Local 98 v. NLRB, 497 F.2d 60, 65 (6th Cir. 1974). The NLRB has, however, generally refused to adopt this interpretation of the statute.
25. *See, e.g.,* Abreen Corp. v. Laborers, 709 F.2d 748, 756, 114 L.R.R.M. 2057 (1st Cir. 1983), *cert. denied*, 115 L.R.R.M. 2248 (1984).

Secondary Activity

nents goods or materials supplied by a primary employer. In each case, the union wants the secondary employer to cease doing business with the primary employer. Unfortunately, a union's purposes are not always so obvious.

7.1.3 Pickets at Common Work Sites

If a union applies pressure at a facility or jobsite shared by several employers, including the primary employer, its objectives are inherently ambiguous. As a result, the NLRB in *Sailors Union of the Pacific (Moore Dry Dock)*[26] developed evidentiary aids to determine the object of union action at a multiemployer site. These standards focus attention upon the *time* and *place* of the picketing, as well as the extent to which the pickets disclose their objectives. Specifically, the NLRB in *Moore Dry Dock* held that picketing at a multiemployer site would be *presumed* to have a primary object if: (1) the picketing is limited to times when the labor dispute's situs[27] is the common premises; (2) "the primary employer is engaged in its normal business at the situs at the time of the picketing"; (3) the picketing takes place reasonably close to the location of the labor dispute; and (4) the picketing clearly discloses the primary employer with which the union has a dispute.

The NLRB and the courts regard these standards as mere evidentiary tools. If other circumstances indicate that the union's objective is secondary, its action will be found unlawful, even if

---

26. 92 N.L.R.B. 547, 549, 27 L.R.R.M. 1108 (1950).
27. The term "situs" is often used to describe the precise location of a labor dispute. In most cases, the primary employer's premises will be the situs of the dispute. When the primary employer is a shipping company, however, as in *Moore Dry Dock*, the vessel itself may be the situs of the dispute. Similarly, a trucking company's vehicles, whatever their location, may be the situs of any dispute with its unions. Teamsters, Local 807 (Schultz Refrigerated Service, Inc.), 87 N.L.R.B. 502, 25 L.R.R.M. 1122 (1949).

Responding to Strikes

it has fully complied with *Moore Dry Dock's* directives.[28] The NLRB will consider any evidence showing the union's intent to embroil neutrals.[29] For example, a union officer's statement to a neutral employer that pickets will be removed only if business with the primary employer stops,[30] or the union's imposition of fines on members working for a neutral employer during the picketing,[31] may establish the union's secondary objective even if it has complied with *Moore Dry Dock* guidelines. Similarly, a secondary objective may be inferred if the union claims a clearly pretextual lawful motive, as sometimes occurs when pickets protest an employer's failure to pay prevailing union wages without determining what wages the employer does pay.[32] On the other hand,

---

28. Sherman Oaks Medical Arts Center Ltd. v. Carpenters, Local 1936, 680 F.2d 594, 597, 110 L.R.R.M. 2971 (9th Cir. 1982).
29. Texas Distributors, Inc. v. Plumbers, Local 100, 598 F.2d 393, 399, 101 L.R.R.M. 2758 (5th Cir. 1979), identifies six indicia of improper motive that may overcome a presumption of legality arising from compliance with *Moore Dry Dock's* directives. These include picketing the primary employer only at locations where other unions are working, refusing to answer inquiries as to the purpose of the pickets, and warning other unions that picketing is about to commence.
30. IBEW, Local 369 (Garst-Receveur Constr. Co.), 229 N.L.R.B. 68, 95 L.R.R.M. 1001 (1977), *enforced*, 609 F.2d 266, 102 L.R.R.M. 2894 (6th Cir. 1979). *But see* IBEW, Local 453 (Southern Sun Electric Corp.), 237 N.L.R.B. 829, 830, 99 L.R.R.M. 1076 (1978), *aff'd sub nom.* Southern Sun Electric Corp. v. NLRB, 620 F.2d 170, 104 L.R.R.M. 2081 (8th Cir. 1980) (union's statement to neutral employer that picketing would end if primary employer were removed from site not sufficient evidence of illegal objective to rebut inference of legality arising from compliance with *Moore Drydock* standards).
31. District Council of Carpenters (Pace Construction), 222 N.L.R.B. 613, 91 L.R.R.M. 1205 (1976), *enforced*, 560 F.2d 1015, 96 L.R.R.M. 2001 (10th Cir. 1977).
32. Bexar Plumbing Co. v. NLRB, 536 F.2d 634, 637, 92 L.R.R.M. 3612 (5th Cir. 1976); IBEW, Local 480 v. NLRB, 413 F.2d 1085, 1088, 70 L.R.R.M. 3339 (D.C. Cir. 1969); *see* Bricklayers, Local 13 (Bjork Builders, Ltd.), 265 N.L.R.B. No. 57, 111 L.R.R.M. 1638, 1640 (1982).

Secondary Activity

when the union adheres to *Moore Dry Dock* rules, and the evidence fails to establish the union's intent to embroil neutral employees, the picketing will be held lawful.[33] *Moore Dry Dock* should be viewed as a minimum standard. Compliance with its rules will not necessarily insulate a union from unfair labor practice charges. A failure to comply, however, should be fatal to the union because violation of any one of the *Moore Dry Dock* criteria indicates a secondary objective. Although pickets' failure to identify the primary employer will often result in a finding of a section 8(b)(4) violation,[34] unions most frequently violate *Moore Dry Dock* by picketing (1) when the primary employer is not engaged in its regular business at the common site or (2) away from the situs of the dispute. An alert employer can take steps to prove a union's violation of these two guidelines.

7.1.4 Establishing a Special Schedule for the Primary Employer

Under *Moore Dry Dock's* second criterion, picketing will be considered secondary activity if it occurs when the primary employer is not engaged in normal business at the location of the picketing.[35] Employers on common job sites therefore may insu-

---

33. Monarchi-Velikoff, Inc. v. Building & Construction Trades Council, 113 L.R.R.M. 2755, 2760 (N.D. Ohio 1983); IBEW, Local 38 (Cleveland Electro Metals Co.), 221 N.L.R.B. 1073, 1074, 91 L.R.R.M. 1022 (1975).
34. Sheet Metal Workers, Local 55 (Andtora Corp.), 244 N.L.R.B. 799, 801, 102 L.R.R.M. 1192 (1979); Carpenters, Local 630 (American Modulars Corp.), 203 N.L.R.B. 1112, 83 L.R.R.M. 1379 (1973).
35. Sheet Metal Workers, Local 80 (Ciamillo Heating & Cooling, Inc.), 268 N.L.R.B. No. 2, 114 L.R.R.M. 1232 (1983); Building & Construction Trades Council (Roy C. Anderson, Jr., Inc.), 222 N.L.R.B. 649, 650, 91 L.R.R.M. 1215 (1976), *enforced*, 542 F.2d 573, 93 L.R.R.M. 2943 (5th Cir. 1976).

late neutral employers from union pressure by establishing separate, regular work times for the primary employer. If the union receives clear notice of the primary employer's schedule, picketing during the primary's absence will violate the statute.[36] (See Appendix 7-A, Sample Notice to Primary's Union of Primary Employer's Schedule.) To minimize problems in case picketing continues, neutral employers' unions should also be advised of the schedule and its legal effect. (See App. 7-B, Sample Notice to Other Unions of Primary Employer's Schedule.)

This tactic will not succeed, and a union may continue to picket, if other circumstances show that the primary employer is engaged in normal business at the site notwithstanding its employees' absence. This rule is designed to prevent the employer from playing a cat-and-mouse game, forcing the union to guess when it may lawfully picket.[37] A union thus may picket the site during temporary, unpredictable, intermittent, or sporadic absences of the primary employer[38] or when the primary's work is

---

36. IBEW, Local 595 (Hayward Electric Co.), 261 N.L.R.B. 707, 709, 110 L.R.R.M. 1126 (1982); Painters, Local 1236 (Associated General Contractors), 180 N.L.R.B. 241, 244, 73 L.R.R.M. 1159 (1969); Plumbers, Local 519 (H.L. Robertson & Associates, Inc.), 171 N.L.R.B. 251, 257, 68 L.R.R.M. 1070 (1968), enforced, 416 F.2d 1120, 70 L.R.R.M. 3300 (D.C. Cir. 1969). In *H.L. Robertson,* the primary continued work during evenings and weekends. In *Hayward Electric,* on the other hand, the primary was absent from the site entirely for several days. *Associated General Contractors* involved both methods of insulating neutrals.
37. Operating Engineers, Local 675 (Industrial Contracting, Inc.), 192 N.L.R.B. 1188, 1189, 78 L.R.R.M. 1337 (1971), enforced, 82 L.R.R.M. 2687 (D.C. Cir. 1972); see also Linbeck Constr. Corp. v. NLRB, 550 F.2d 311, 319, 94 L.R.R.M. 3230 (5th Cir. 1977) (employer cannot insulate itself from picketing by playing hide-and-seek).
38. Monarchi-Velikoff, Inc. v. Building & Construction Trades Council, 113 L.R.R.M. 2755, 2759 (N.D. Ohio 1983); IBEW, Local 3 (New Power Wire & Electric Corp.), 144 N.L.R.B. 1089, 54 L.R.R.M. 1178, 1181 (1963), enforced, 340 F.2d 71, 58 L.R.R.M. 2123 (2d Cir. 1965); IBEW, Local 861, IBEW (Plauche Electric, Inc.), 135 N.L.R.B. 250, 49 L.R.R.M. 1446, 1449 (1962) (picketing may continue while primary employees depart for coffee breaks and lunch).

Secondary Activity

not scheduled so as to afford the union notice of the primary's absence.[39] There must be well-defined work times set aside for the primary employer.

Even when the union has been given clear notice of the primary's scheduled absence for a defined period of time, it may picket the site if materials for the primary's use continue to be delivered.[40] Such deliveries, the courts and the NLRB agree, are part of the primary's normal business. The fact that the primary employer continues to maintain an office or store materials at the site also bears upon the normal business issue.[41] In the absence of other indicia of normal business activity, however, the mere presence of the primary's supplies at the site will not justify picketing during its absence.[42]

7.1.5 Establishing Reserved Gates

The "reserved gate doctrine" is a product of *Moore Dry Dock's* requirement that unions limit picketing to areas reasonably close to the location of the dispute. The doctrine permits the establishment of separate gates for the entry of neutral and primary employers onto a common work site. Once the gates are established, a union picketing at the gate reserved for the neutral employer reveals that at least one of its objects is unlawful secondary pressure.

---

39. Georgia Pacific Corp. v. Columbia River Chapter of P.L.S.A., 386 F. Supp. 1199, 1201, 88 L.R.R.M. 2927 (D. Or. 1974), *aff'd*, 511 F.2d 1226, 88 L.R.R.M. 2929 (9th Cir. 1975).
40. Linbeck Constr. Corp. v. NLRB, 550 F.2d 311, 319, 94 L.R.R.M. 3230 (5th Cir. 1977).
41. Operating Engineers, Local 675 (Industrial Contracting, Inc.), 192 N.L.R.B. 1188, 78 L.R.R.M. 1337 (1971), *enforced*, 82 L.R.R.M. 2687 (D.C. Cir. 1972) (office and records maintained by primary on site).
42. Painters, Local 1236 (Associated General Contractors), 180 N.L.R.B. 241, 244, 73 L.R.R.M. 1159 (1969); IBEW, Local 595 (Hayward Electric Co.), 261 N.L.R.B. 707, 709, 110 L.R.R.M. 1126 (1982).

7.1.5.1 The Industrial Plant Model

The use of reserved gates was approved by the United States Supreme Court in 1961. In *Local 761, Electrical Workers (General Electric) v. NLRB*,[43] the Court considered the legality of picketing by striking General Electric employees at a gate reserved for neutral employers that had contracted to perform work at GE's plant. It enunciated the following standard for judging the effectiveness of reserved gates in industrial settings:

> There must be a separate gate, marked and set apart from other gates; the work done by the men who use the gate must be unrelated to the normal operations of the employer, and the work must be of a kind that would not, if done when the plant were engaged in its regular operations, necessitate curtailing those operations.[44]

In allowing employers to erect reserved gates only when the neutral is performing work unrelated to the primary's normal business, the Court sought to preserve unions' traditional right to appeal to neutrals, such as suppliers and delivery persons, whose work is essential to the primary employer's day-to-day operations.[45] A similar rationale underlies the Court's requirement that the neutral's work be capable of being performed during normal operations. Otherwise, the primary employer could emasculate the strike by using it as a convenient occasion to have work performed that would require a shut-down in any event, such as a major equipment overhaul. Those neutral employers whose work on the site neither relates to the primary employer's normal operations nor necessitates a curtailment of operations can be

---

43. 366 U.S. 667, 48 L.R.R.M. 2210 (1961).
44. 366 U.S. at 681, *quoting* United Steelworkers v. NLRB, 289 F.2d 591, 595, 48 L.R.R.M. 2106 (2d Cir. 1961).
45. *See* Steelworkers (Carrier Corp.) v. NLRB, 376 U.S. 492, 55 L.R.R.M. 2698 (1964).

Secondary Activity

insulated from strike activity by means of reserved gates. This device is most frequently used to protect neutral construction contractors who build additions to a primary employer's facilities.[46]

7.1.5.2 The Construction Site Model

Common job sites are most frequently encountered in the construction industry. In *NLRB v. Denver Building & Construction Trades Council*,[47] the Supreme Court held that contractors on a construction site are separate and distinct entities for purposes of section 8(b)(4), entitled to remain neutral in one another's disputes. The NLRB and the courts have thus uniformly found it inappropriate to apply the unrelated work requirement to the establishment of reserved gates at multiemployer construction sites.[48] A reserved gate may therefore be erected on a construction project without regard to work-relatedness. The sole requirement is that the gates be properly maintained and established.

---

46. *See* Service Employees, Local 32B-32J (New York Ass'n for the Blind), 250 N.L.R.B. 240, 247, 104 L.R.R.M. 1531 (1980); Hotel & Restaurant Employees, Local 343 (Kutscher's Country Club Corp.), 198 N.L.R.B. 1172, 1174, 81 L.R.R.M. 1100 (1972). Repairs, however, are generally deemed to be "related work" under *General Electric*. *See* OCAW (Firestone Synthetic Rubber), 173 N.L.R.B. 1244, 69 L.R.R.M. 1569 (1968).
47. 341 U.S. 675, 692, 28 L.R.R.M. 2108 (1951).
48. Carpenters, Local 1622 (Specialty Building Co.), 262 N.L.R.B. 1244, 1246, 111 L.R.R.M. 1059 (1982); Carpenters, Local 470 (Mueller-Anderson, Inc.), 224 N.L.R.B. 315, 317, 92 L.R.R.M. 1225 (1976) (work relatedness considerations do not apply on construction project even when primary owns premises), *enforced*, 564 F.2d 1360, 97 L.R.R.M. 2281 (9th Cir. 1977); Building & Construction Trades Council (Markwell & Hartz Inc.), 155 N.L.R.B. 319, 60 L.R.R.M. 1296 (1965), *enforced*, 387 F.2d 79, 66 L.R.R.M. 2712 (5th Cir. 1967), *cert. denied*, 391 U.S. 914 (1968).

7.1.5.3 The Ambulatory Primary Situs

Some employers, such as delivery services, generally perform their work at other employers' premises rather than at an established site. When such mobile employers are struck, the location of the labor dispute moves with their work, becoming what is known as an "ambulatory" primary situs. During times when the primary situs is located at a neutral employer's premises, a temporary common situs exists. Under the principles applicable to common situs picketing, a reserved gate may be established to protect the neutral employer whose premises are visited by the primary employer.

It is not clear whether the reserved gate may be erected at a temporary common situs without regard to the related work test enunciated in the *General Electric* case.[49] The NLRB has twice found issues of related work irrelevant to a determination of the effectiveness of reserved gates located on neutral premises.[50] In at least one case, however, the NLRB has alluded to the absence of work relatedness in approving reserved gates established at a neutral employer's facility.[51]

In practice, whether the neutral's work must be unrelated to the primary's business should make little difference in evaluating the propriety of reserved gates located at the neutral's ordinary

---

49. General Electric's work relatedness concept was "developed for industrial plants where the struck employer is the owner of the plant." J.F. Hoff Electric Co. v. NLRB, 642 F.2d 1266, 1273, 105 L.R.R.M. 2345 (D.C. Cir. 1980), *cert. denied*, 451 U.S. 918 (1981); *see also* Service Employees, Local 32B-32J (New York Ass'n for the Blind), 250 N.L.R.B. 240, 247, 104 L.R.R.M. 1531 (1980) ("work relatedness" test pertains to reserved gates located "at the premises of the primary employer").
50. Service Employees, Local 32B-32J (The Dalton Schools), 248 N.L.R.B. 1067, 1069, 104 L.R.R.M. 1162 (1980); Plumbers, Local 60 (Circle Inc.), 202 N.L.R.B. 99, 104, 82 L.R.R.M. 1755 (1973), *enforced*, 486 F.2d 1401, 84 L.R.R.M. 3010 (5th Cir. 1973).
51. IBEW, Local 332 (Lockheed Missiles & Space Co.), 241 N.L.R.B. 674, 679 n.11, 100 L.R.R.M. 1585 (1979).

Secondary Activity

premises. The thrust of the related work test is to determine whether the work [of the neutral] is of a character which is necessary to the [primary] employer's operations . . . ."[52] It is difficult to conceive of a situation in which the tasks of a neutral occupant of picketed premises would be so integral to the work of an ambulatory primary as to meet this standard. A neutral employer that expects to be visited by a struck employer, then, should be able to reserve a gate for the primary's use without worrying about work-relatedness issues.

7.1.5.4 Establishing the Gates

Well before a strike occurs, the potential primary employer should notify other employers who might be affected by the strike of the possibility of establishing reserve gates. (See Appendix 7-C, Memorandum to Employers.) This notice should explain the function of a reserved gate, the rules concerning its use, and instructions for designating the gate and notifying the union of its existence. The primary employer should stress its willingness to help minimize the inconvenience and disruption that a strike could cause.

When establishing the reserved gate, the employer must assure that the union is still able to make a lawful primary appeal. The purpose of the reserved gate doctrine is to minimize secondary effects "without substantial impairment of the effectiveness of picketing in reaching the employees of the primary employer."[53] The NLRB has thus held that when the reserved gate is so far

---

52. Chemical Workers (Crest, Inc.), 170 N.L.R.B. 168, 174, 73 L.R.R.M. 1372 (1969).
53. Carpenters, Local 1622 (Robert Wood & Associates, Inc.), 262 N.L.R.B. 1211, 1217, 111 L.R.R.M. 1057 (1982); Building & Construction Trades Council (H.E. Collins Contracting Co.), 172 N.L.R.B. 1138, 1140, 68 L.R.R.M. 1397 (1968), *enforced*, 425 F.2d 385, 73 L.R.R.M. 2988 (6th Cir. 1970).

removed from the primary's actual work that picketing at the gate makes no appeal to the primary's employees, the union may picket at a closer gate.[54] Similarly, establishing a reserved gate far removed from a job site will not prevent the union from picketing adjacent to the area where the struck work is being performed.[55]

Once the locations have been selected, the employer must post a sign at the reserved gate where the primary employer must enter, as well as separate signs at the gates designated for neutral parties' use. (See Appendixes 7-D, 7-E, Sample Gate Signs.) The signs must be large, and the gate designations must be easily read by anyone approaching the gates.[56] Even when a reserved gate has been properly established, the union is allowed to direct its appeals to employees of the primary's suppliers.[57] As a consequence, the signs *must* direct suppliers, as well as employees, of the primary employer to use the gate set aside for the primary's use. Failure to limit entry of suppliers appropriately may negate

---

54. IBEW, Local 453 (Southern Sun Electric Corp.), 237 N.L.R.B. 829, 830, 99 L.R.R.M. 1076 (1978), aff'd, 620 F.2d 170, 104 L.R.R.M. 2081 (8th Cir. 1980); Laborers, Local 1290 (Walters Foundation, Inc.), 195 N.L.R.B. 370, 371, 79 L.R.R.M. 1325 (1972). Cf. Carpenters, Local 354 (Sharp & Tatro Development Co.), 268 N.L.R.B. No. 58, 115 L.R.R.M. 1023 (1983) (employer not required to establish reserved gate so as to maximize union's opportunity to reach general public).
55. J.F. Hoff Electric Co. v. NLRB, 642 F.2d 1266, 1276, 105 L.R.R.M. 2345 (D.C. Cir. 1980).
56. *See, e.g.*, Ironworkers, Local 433 (Robert E. McKee, Inc.), 233 N.L.R.B. 283, 287, 97 L.R.R.M. 1167 (1977) (noting size, legibility, visibility, and location of signs), *enforced in part*, 598 F.2d 1154, 101 L.R.R.M. 2440 (9th Cir. 1979); *see also* Carpenters, Local 1622 (Robert Wood & Associates), 262 N.L.R.B. 1211, 1218-19, 111 L.R.R.M. 1057 (1982) (although gate not clearly reserved for neutrals, system effective where gate for primary clearly designated).
57. Steelworkers (Carrier Corp.) v. NLRB, 376 U.S. 492, 55 L.R.R.M. 2698 (1963).

Secondary Activity

the effectiveness of the reserved gate system, permitting the union to picket the gate intended to be insulated from pressure.[58] If it complies with *Moore Dry Dock*, a union usually does not violate section 8(b)(4) by picketing *all* gates at a common job site before it has notice that the employer has established a reserved gate.[59] At the time gates are established, then, the union must be notified of their existence. This should be done by telephone and immediately confirmed in writing (preferably by mailgram or telegram),[60] advising the union of the reserved gate and of the consequences of a failure to observe it. (See Appendix 7-F, Sample Notice to Primary Union.) All other unions working on the premises should also be notified. (See Appendix 7-G, Sample Notice to Other Unions.)

7.1.5.5 Maintaining the Gates

Even when a gate system is properly established, it will lose its legal effect unless it is scrupulously maintained.[61] Monitoring

---

58. Huber & Antilla Constr. Co. v. Carpenters, Local 470, 659 F.2d 1013, 1018, 108 L.R.R.M. 2951 (9th Cir. 1981), *cert. denied*, 456 U.S. 977 (1982); Plumbers, Local 398 (Robbins Plumbing & Heating Contractors, Inc.), 261 N.L.R.B. 482, 486, 110 L.R.R.M. 1093 (1982). *But see* Ironworkers, Local 433 (Robert E. McKee, Inc.), 233 N.L.R.B. 283, 287, 97 L.R.R.M. 1167 (1977), *enforced in pertinent part*, 598 F.2d 1154, 1159, 101 L.R.R.M. 2440 (9th Cir. 1979) (failure to make provision for suppliers in sign will not necessarily affect gate's integrity when union indicates belief that reserved gate validly established).
59. *See* Monarchi-Velikoff, Inc. v. Building & Construction Trades Council, 113 L.R.R.M. 2755 (N.D. Ohio 1983); Ironworkers, Local 433 (Robert E. McKee, Inc.). 233 N.L.R.B. 283, 287, 97 L.R.R.M. 1167 (1977), *enforced in part*, 598 F.2d 1154, 1158, 101 L.R.R.M 2440 (9th Cir. 1079).
60. NLRB v. IBEW, Local 58, 638 F.2d 36, 106 L.R.R.M. 2269 (6th Cir. 1981) (notice to union by mailgram is sufficient).
61. *See, e.g.*, Monarchi-Velikoff, Inc. v. Building & Construction Trades Council, 113 L.R.R.M. 2755 (N.D. Ohio 1983).

Responding to Strikes

suppliers' activity presents the most difficult problem. When suppliers of a struck employer use a gate set aside for neutral employers the gate may be picketed by the union.[62] This is commonly known as "mixed use" or "pollution" of the gate.

In deciding which gate a particular supplier should use, the employer must determine whether the supplies are to be used by a neutral or primary employer. Title to the goods is irrelevant. Supplies destined for use by the primary should not be delivered through a neutral gate even if a neutral employer holds title at the time of delivery.[63] On the other hand, the integrity of the gates will probably be preserved if a struck employer arranges and pays for supplies for a neutral that are delivered through a neutral gate.[64] The more cautious course is to instruct suppliers of goods ordered by the primary, even if ultimately used by a neutral, to enter the site through the gate reserved for the primary.

Although all violations of the reserved gate system should be avoided, minor and isolated mixed use of the gate reserved for neutral employers and suppliers may not be fatal, depending upon the extent of the mixed use, the relationship between the union's action and the gate's pollution, and the steps taken to assure the gate's future integrity.[65] Furthermore, mixed use of the

---

62. Huber & Antilla Constr. Co. v. Carpenters, Local 470, 659 F.2d 1013, 1018, 108 L.R.R.M. 2951 (9th Cir. 1981), *cert. denied*, 456 U.S. 977 (1982); Air Engineering Metal Trades Council (Pan Am World Services, Inc.), 265 N.L.R.B. No. 19, 111 L.R.R.M. 1457 (1982); Carpenters, Local 1622 (Robert Wood & Assocs., Inc.), 262 N.L.R.B. 1211, 1217, 111 L.R.R.M. 1057 (1982).
63. J.F. Hoff Elec. Co. v. NLRB, 642 F.2d 1266, 1274-75, 105 L.R.R.M. 2345 (D.C. Cir. 1980), *cert. denied*, 451 U.S. 918 (1981); Linbeck Constr. Corp. v. NLRB, 550 F.2d 311, 318, 94 L.R.R.M. 3230 (5th Cir. 1977).
64. *See* Carpenters, Local 1622 (Specialty Building Co.), 262 N.L.R.B. 1244, 1246, 111 L.R.R.M. 1059 (1982).
65. *See, e.g.*, Plumbers, Local 274 (Stokely-Van Camp, Inc.), 267 N.L.R.B. No. 183, 114 L.R.R.M. 1143 (1983); Pipefitters, Local 48 (Calvert General Contractors Inc.), 249 N.L.R.B. 1183, 1187, 104 L.R.R.M. 1317

Secondary Activity

gate reserved for the primary employer will not impermissibly pollute the system; what is important is that the *neutral* gate remain inviolate.[66]

7.1.5.6 Reserved Gate Rehabilitation

Should the reserved gate system break down, it can be rehabilitated. This requires that the system be revised, preferably by switching gate locations and replacing signs. Effective gate rehabilitation also necessitates renewed notice to the unions and an effort to prevent further violations.[67] (See Appendixes 7-H, 7-I, Sample Notices of Reestablishment of Gates.) If significant pollution of the gates has occurred, an employer should restructure the system. Stubborn insistence upon a tainted gate system offers no protection under section 8(b)(4).

7.1.5.7 Violation of Gates

A reserved gate system limits the situs of a labor dispute to the gate reserved for the primary employer.[68] Because *Moore Dry Dock* requires that picketing be confined to the location of the

---

(1980), *enforced*, 656 F.2d 901, 108 L.R.R.M. 2175 (D.C. Cir. 1981); Operating Engineers, Local 18 (Dodge-Ireland, Inc.), 236 N.L.R.B. 199, 203-04, 98 L.R.R.M. 1374 (1978).

66. Building & Construction Trades Council (Roy C. Anderson, Jr., Inc.), 222 N.L.R.B. 649, 650, 91 L.R.R.M. 1215 (1976), *enforced*, 542 F.2d 573, 93 L.R.R.M 2943 (5th Cir. 1976); Janesville Typographical Union No. 197 (Gazette Printing Co.), 173 N.L.R.B. 917, 921, 69 L.R.R.M. 1457 (1968).

67. *See* IBEW, Local 76 (Gaylord Broadcasting Co.), 268 N.L.R.B. No. 27, 114 L.R.R.M. 1246 (1983); Carpenters, Local 1622 (Specialty Building Co.), 262 N.L.R.B. 1244, 1246, 111 L.R.R.M. 1059 (1982).

68. Ironworkers, Local 433 v. NLRB, 598 F.2d 1154, 1157, 101 L.R.R.M. 2440 (9th Cir. 1979); Bricklayers, Local 2 v. NLRB, 562 F.2d 775, 785, 95 L.R.R.M. 3310 (D.C. Cir. 1977).

dispute, picketing at neutral gates evidences a secondary objective violating section 8(b)(4).[69] A union's zealous effort to comply with the law governing reserved gates may in some circumstances allow it to escape the consequences of improper picketing of the neutral gate.[70] To minimize the union's ability to claim confusion over the appropriate location for picketing, the employer should prepare a short description of the reserved gate system for distribution to picketers who fail to confine their activity to the proper gate. (See Appendix 7-J.)

Unions may attempt to subvert the reserved gate system by posting an observer at neutral gates, ostensibly to assure that their integrity is not violated. This does not necessarily indicate a secondary objective, as the union is entitled to determine whether employees or suppliers of the primary are using a neutral gate.[71] However, when the observer's role is to *signal* neutral employees not to enter a neutral gate, the NLRB and the courts will find a section 8(b)(4) violation.[72] Proving intent will be

---

69. Lane Crane Service, Inc. v. IBEW, Local 177, 704 F.2d 550, 553-54, 113 L.R.R.M. 2396 (11th Cir. 1983); NLRB v. Broadcast Employees, Local 31, 631 F.2d 944, 104 L.R.R.M. 3121, 3126 (D.C. Cir. 1980); Linbeck Constr. v. NLRB, 550 F.2d 311, 316, 94 L.R.R.M. 3230 (5th Cir. 1977); *see* IBEW, Local 323 (Renel Constr. Inc.), 264 NLRB No. 81, 111 L.R.R.M. 1309, 1311 (1982) (picketing 100 feet from neutral gate evidenced secondary objective).
70. Helgesen v. Iron Workers, Local 498, 548 F.2d 175, 183, 94 L.R.R.M. 2254 (7th Cir. 1977); Constar, Inc. v. Plumbers, Local 447, 568 F. Supp. 1440, 1453-54, 114 L.R.R.M. 2314 (E.D. Cal. 1983) (noting "Union's bumbling but earnest attempts to comply with the law").
71. NLRB v. Operating Engineers, Local 825, 659 F.2d 379, 387, 108 L.R.R.M. 2480 (3d Cir. 1981) (observers not identified as union members and spoke to no one entering the jobsite); Carpenters, Local 1245 (New Mexico Properties), 229 N.L.R.B. 236, 242, 96 L.R.R.M. 1509 (1977).
72. Plumbers, Local 274 (Stokely-Van Camp, Inc.), 267 N.L.R.B. No. 183, 114 L.R.R.M. 1143 (1983); Ironworkers, Local 433 (Robert E. McKee, Inc.), 233 N.L.R.B. 282, 287-88, 97 L.R.R.M. 1167 (1977), *enforced in part*, 598 F.2d 1154, 101 L.R.R.M. 2440 (9th Cir. 1979); *see also* Virginia Elec. Power Co. v. Boilermakers, 103 L.R.R.M. 3144, 3159 (N.D.

Secondary Activity

difficult. An employer should therefore carefully monitor the activity of gate observers, paying close attention to any contact they have with neutral employees, as well as any union buttons or badges they might wear.

Unions may also attempt to reach neutral employees by picketing public access roads leading to the site where the gates are established—roads that neutral employees must use. Unless the road is the closest the union can get to the primary situs,[73] the picketing is not properly limited and violates section 8(b)(4).[74] The NLRB has also rejected union efforts to appeal to neutrals by picketing at neutral gates to publicize the primary employer's alleged payment of substandard wages.[75]

There is some question whether the erection of reserved gates will protect a neutral employer from "between the headlights" picketing directed against an ambulatory primary employer. This activity occurs when striking workers picket in the immediate vicinity of the primary employer's vehicles while they are making deliveries at the neutral's business.[76] In *Teamsters, Local*

W. Va. 1980) (violation where strikers were "loitering in an ominous manner in front of the [reserved gate], stopping vehicles and interrogating the drivers").

73. Air Engineering Metal Trades Council (Pan Am World Services, Inc.), 265 N.L.R.B. No. 19, 111 L.R.R.M. 1457 (1982) (picketing of access roads lawful where state court injunction prohibited picketing at gates).

74. Laborers, Local 383 (Hensel Phelps Constr. Co.), 268 N.L.R.B. No. 13, 114 L.R.R.M. 1240 (1983); IBEW, Local 323 (Renel Constr. Inc.), 264 N.L.R.B. No. 81, 111 L.R.R.M. 1309, 1311 (1982); Plumbers, Local 388 (Barton Malow Co.), 262 N.L.R.B. 126, 129, 110 L.R.R.M. 1288 (1982), aff'd, 704 F.2d 1294, 113 L.R.R.M. 3528 (D.C. Cir. 1983); IBEW, Local 332 (Lockheed Missiles & Space Co., Inc.), 241 N.L.R.B. 647, 679-80, 100 L.R.R.M. 1585 (1979).

75. IBEW, Local 211 (Atlantic County Improvement Authority), 248 N.L.R.B. 168, 172, 103 L.R.R.M. 1453 (1980).

76. *See* Teamsters, Local 612 (AAA Motor Lines, Inc.), 211 N.L.R.B. 608, 610, 87 L.R.R.M. 1029 (1974). Indeed, employees striking an employer making deliveries to a neutral *must* picket "between the headlights" unless the property owner denies a request to allow such picketing. If that

Responding to Strikes

83 (*Allied Concrete*), the NLRB held that such picketing between the headlights was lawful even though the primary employer had established a reserved gate where the pickets could have made their appeal.[77] The NLRB's decision in *Allied Concrete* was, however, emphatically rejected by the Ninth Circuit Court of Appeals, which held that the union should have limited its activities to the gate reserved for the primary employer.[78]

7.1.6 Ally Problems

A union does not violate section 8(b)(4) when it pickets or exerts other pressure against a primary employer's ally. The ally is subject to the same union pressures as the primary employer. An ally is an employer whose neutrality has been compromised, generally because (1) it performs struck work that would ordinarily be performed by the striking workers, or (2) it and the primary are viewed as a single enterprise or joint employers because of common control. These tests are not rigidly applied. The NLRB and the courts will consider any facts indicating that the primary and the purported neutral "have such identity and community of interests as negative the claim" of neutrality.[79]

---

occurs, the strikers then may picket at the gates to the premises. *Id.* If reserved gates are established, such picketing at the gates presumably must be limited to the gate reserved for use of the primary employer.

77. Teamsters, Local 83 (Allied Concrete, Inc.), 231 N.L.R.B. 1097, 1098, 96 L.R.R.M. 1165 (1977).
78. Allied Concrete, Inc. v. NLRB, 607 F.2d 827, 831, 102 L.R.R.M. 2508 (9th Cir. 1979).
79. Teamsters, Local 560 (Curtin Matheson Scientific, Inc.), 248 N.L.R.B. 1212, 1213-14, 104 L.R.R.M. 1003 (1980), *quoting* Teamsters, Local 282 (Acme Concrete & Supply Corp.), 137 N.L.R.B. 1321, 1324, 50 L.R.R.M. 1374 (1962).

Secondary Activity

7.1.6.1 Performance of Struck Work

To be an ally under the struck work theory, the employer must perform work that would have been performed by the striking employees but for the strike.[80] The test is whether the purportedly neutral employer improves its position by performing work that ordinarily would be performed by strikers. The most obvious ally cases involve employers that begin doing the primary employer's work as the direct result of the strike.[81] An employer that increases its dealings with the primary as a consequence of the strike also compromises its neutrality.[82] However, an employer that simply continues a preexisting business relationship after the strike begins does not become an ally.[83] Nor is a company an ally simply because it takes work usually performed by *neutral* employers who have stopped doing business with the primary because of the strike.[84] Finally, a customer of a struck employer does not subject itself to picketing

---

80. NLRB v. Western States Regional Council No. 3, 319 F.2d 655, 53 L.R.R.M. 2609 (9th Cir. 1963) (even if neutral aids primary, it does not become ally unless struck work performed); Teamsters, Local 659 (Totem Ocean Trailer Express, Inc.), 266 N.L.R.B. No. 134, 113 L.R.R.M. 1047 (1983) (same).
81. *See, e.g.*, NLRB v. Business Machines Local 459 (Royal Typewriter), 228 F.2d 553, 558, 37 L.R.R.M. 2219 (2d Cir. 1955), *cert. denied*, 351 U.S. 962 (1956) (ally relationship found when struck repair work performed, despite absence of direct contract between primary and allies).
82. Douds v. Metropolitan Federation of Architects, Local 231 (Ebasco Services, Inc.), 75 F. Supp. 672, 21 L.R.R.M. 2250 (S.D.N.Y. 1948).
83. Laborers, Local 859 v. NLRB, 446 F.2d 1319, 1321, 77 L.R.R.M. 2577 (D.C. Cir. 1970) (customer does not become ally by continuing to purchase supplies from struck employer, even if it arranges for delivery of supplies by third parties); Metal Polishers, Local 171 (Climax Machinery Co.), 86 N.L.R.B. 1243, 25 L.R.R.M. 1052, 1053 (1949).
84. Teamsters, Local 656 (Totem Ocean Trailer Express, Inc.), 266 N.L.R.B. No. 134, 113 L.R.R.M. 1047 (1983).

Responding to Strikes

by performing work formerly handled by the primary, so long as it is merely "attending to its own needs as a neutral employer."[85] The NLRB has also held that ally status attaches only if it is the primary employer who initiates an arrangement for performance of struck work.[86]

Some employers attempt to avoid the ally doctrine's impact by entering into agreements *before* the strike, to obscure the fact that work is being farmed out because of the strike. If the NLRB determines that anticipation of the strike prompted the agreement, it will find the employers to be allies.[87] Nor can the "ally" label be avoided by providing for performance of the work for a fixed term, instead of the term of the strike. If the agreement has been motivated by imminent strike action, the NLRB will find an ally relationship.[88]

The struck work tests apply to all industries, including the construction business. Construction contractors are not allies just because they perform work on a common jobsite.[89] However, a

---

85. Service Employees, Local 32B-32J (The Dalton Schools), 248 N.L.R.B. 1067, 1069, 104 L.R.R.M. 1162 (1980); Operating Engineers, Local 675 (Industrial Contracting Co.), 192 N.L.R.B. 1188, 1200, 78 L.R.R.M. 1337 (1971), *aff'd*, 82 L.R.R.M. 2687 (D.C. Cir. 1972).
86. The courts, however, have not yet accepted the NLRB's position in this regard. *See* Laborers, Local 859 (Thomas S. Byrne, Inc.), 180 N.L.R.B. 502, 73 L.R.R.M. 1278 (1969), *modified*, 446 F.2d 1319, 1321, 77 L.R.R.M. 2577 (D.C. Cir. 1970); *see also* Graphic Arts, Local 277 (S & M Rotogravure Service, Inc.), 219 N.L.R.B. 1053, 1054, 90 L.R.R.M. 1081 (1975), *petition for review denied sub nom*. Kable Printing Co. v. NLRB, 540 F.2d 1304, 1309 n.6, 93 L.R.R.M. 2013 (7th Cir. 1976).
87. *See* Mine Workers (Lone Star Steel Co.), 231 N.L.R.B. 573, 584, 96 L.R.R.M. 1083 (1977), *enforced in part*, 639 F.2d 545, 104 L.R.R.M. 3144 (10th Cir. 1980), *cert. denied*, 450 U.S. 911 (1981).
88. Brewery Workers, Local 8 (Bert P. Williams, Inc.), 148 N.L.R.B. 728, 57 L.R.R.M. 1035, 1038 (1964).
89. NLRB v. Denver Bldg. & Constr. Trades Council, 341 U.S. 675, 28 L.R.R.M. 2108 (1951); Sacramento District Council of Carpenters (Malek Constr. Co.), 244 N.L.R.B. 890, 894, 102 L.R.R.M. 1234 (1979).

Secondary Activity

contractor performing struck work on a common jobsite is an ally and subject to lawful union pressure, even if its employees enter the jobsite through an otherwise neutral gate.[90] In a reserved gate situation, then, allies must avoid using the neutral gate. Otherwise the gate may be polluted, allowing the union to picket entrances reserved for neutrals.

When ally status exists by virtue of performance of farmed out struck work, the ally may regain its neutrality. To do this, the ally must relinquish the struck work and notify the union of its action.[91]

7.1.6.2 Common Ownership or Control

The test for ally status by reason of common ownership or control is not well defined. The courts and the NLRB generally consider four factors to determine whether two employers are allies because they are a single enterprise: "interrelation of operations, common management, centralized control of labor relations and common ownership."[92] Common ownership, by itself, does not create an ally relationship. There must also be *actual* common control or integration of operations so that the two employers should be considered a single enterprise.[93] When actual common control is lacking, even two divisions of the same company will not be considered allies.[94]

---

90. Bricklayers, Local 29 (J.E. Hoetger & Co.), 221 N.L.R.B. 1337, 1339, 91 L.R.R.M. 1157 (1976).
91. Laundry Workers, Local 259 (Morrison's of San Diego, Inc.), 164 N.L.R.B. 426, 65 L.R.R.M. 1091, 1093 (1967).
92. Broadcast Technicians, Local 1264 v. Broadcast Services of Mobile, Inc., 380 U.S. 225, 256, 58 L.R.R.M. 2545 (1965) (*per curiam*).
93. Printing Pressman, Local 46 (Knight Newspapers, Inc.), 138 N.L.R.B. 1346, 51 L.R.R.M. 1169, 1170 (1962), *enforced*, 322 F.2d 405, 409, 53 L.R.R.M. 2629 (D.C. Cir. 1963).
94. Teamsters, Local 391 (Vulcan Materials Co.) v. NLRB, 543 F.2d 1373, 1376, 92 L.R.R.M. 2987 (D.C. Cir. 1976) (*per curiam*), *cert. denied*, 430

Common control over labor relations policies is perhaps the most important indication of an ally relationship. The following types of involvement in employee relations have been sufficient to indicate ally status: a parent corporation's final authority over its subsidiary's labor negotiations, even when the subsidiary handles day-to-day matters,[95] participation in day-to-day administration of employee relations,[96] a contractual right to exercise substantial control over a primary employer's labor relations,[97] an "agreement on a common labor policy,"[98] and the primary's obligation to use the purported neutral's labor relations staff in bargaining.[99] To avoid ally status, employers should maintain completely independent labor relations programs.

Geographical location often plays an important role in ally cases.[100] Like the other factors, geographical proximity is not dispositive, though it may suggest interrelation of operations. Conversely, if the circumstances considered as a whole show that

---

U.S. 967 (1977); Los Angeles Newspaper Guild, Local 69 (Hearst Corp.), 185 N.L.R.B. 303, 304, 75 L.R.R.M. 1014 (1970), *enforced*, 443 F.2d 1173, 77 L.R.R.M. 2895 (9th Cir. 1971) (*per curiam*), *cert. denied*, 404 U.S. 1018 (1972).

95. *See* Royal Typewriter Co. v. NLRB, 533 F.2d 1030, 1043, 92 L.R.R.M. 2013 (8th Cir. 1976) (holding parent and subsidiary single employer for purpose of unfair labor practice charge, using tests for ally relationship).

96. Industrial Workers, Local 2356 (Duke City Lumber Co. Inc.), 253 N.L.R.B. 808, 815, 106 L.R.R.M. 1205 (1980).

97. Bricklayers, Local 29 (J.E. Hoetger), 221 N.L.R.B. 1337, 1339, 91 L.R.R.M. 1157 (1976); Teamsters, Local 363 (Roslyn Americana Corp.), 214 N.L.R.B. 868, 88 L.R.R.M. 1102 (1974).

98. Building Service Employees Int'l v. NLRB, 313 F.2d 880, 883, 52 L.R.R.M. 2254 (D.C. Cir. 1963).

99. *See* Teamsters, Local 391 v. NLRB, 543 F.2d 1373, 1375, 93 L.R.R.M. 2158 (D.C. Cir. 1976) (noting use of staff optional), *cert. denied*, 430 U.S. 967 (1977).

100. *See, e.g.,* Graphic Arts, Local 262 (London Press, Inc.), 208 N.L.R.B. 37, 39, 85 L.R.R.M. 1196 (1973); Lithographers, Local 235 (Henry Wurst, Inc.), 187 N.L.R.B. 490, 76 L.R.R.M. 1083 (1970) (commonly owned employers allied when all located in same building and performing related work).

Secondary Activity

an employer is not truly neutral, its mere geographical separation from the primary will not protect it from union action.[101]

7.1.7 Publicity and Consumer Picketing

One of a union's most powerful tools is the ability to persuade the general public to pressure struck employers. Section 8(b)(4) of the Act permits "*publicity, other than picketing*" designed to advise the public "truthfully" that a neutral employer is distributing a product produced by a primary employer. This authorizes union publicity designed to encourage consumer pressure on neutral employers distributing the primary employer's products. The activity contemplated by this publicity proviso cannot, however, induce employees of the neutral employer to refuse to perform any work at the neutral employer's premises. This type of union pressure is lawful only if it is designed to keep the public from buying, rather than to keep employees from working. Non-picketing publicity may, however, urge consumers to boycott a secondary employer's entire business, rather than directing its attention solely to the primary employer's products.[102]

The Supreme Court has also held that a union may engage in *consumer picketing* at the premises of a neutral employer who distributes the primary employer's products.[103] Unlike the non-picketing activity permitted by the publicity proviso, consumer picketing may urge only that consumers refrain from purchasing the primary's products.

---

101. Teamsters, Local 560 (Curtin Matheson Scientific, Inc.), 248 N.L.R.B. 1212, 104 L.R.R.M. 1003 (1980) (geographically separate warehouses of same employer found to be allies due to "cross shipping" between warehouses and veto power over collective bargaining).
102. Operating Engineers, Local 139 (Oak Constr., Inc.), 226 N.L.R.B. 759, 760, 93 L.R.R.M. 1385 (1976); *see also* NLRB v. Fruit & Vegetable Packers (Tree Fruits), 377 U.S. 58, 70-71, 55 L.R.R.M. 2961 (1964).
103. NLRB v. Fruit & Vegetable Packers (Tree Fruits), 377 U.S. 58, 55 L.R.R.M. 2961 (1964).

Responding to Strikes

7.1.7.1 Products "Produced" by the Primary

To be subject to lawful nonpicketing publicity, a neutral employer must distribute products produced by the primary. The term "produced" is given a broad meaning; anyone who adds "capital, enterprise and service" to a product is a producer.[104] In *NLRB v. Servette, Inc.*,[105] for example, the Supreme Court held that a wholesale distributor of candy was a producer, even though it did not manufacture anything. As a consequence, a union having a dispute with the wholesaler was allowed to handbill at a grocery store, urging consumers not to purchase products that the store bought from the wholesaler.

Relying on *Servette*, one court has held that a television station was a producer of the goods and services it advertised.[106] Merchants distributing products advertised on the station, then, could be subject to consumer publicity. Construction contractors have also been held to produce products as that term is used in section 8(b)(4), entitling a union to publicize labor disputes at the premises of employers who have hired struck or nonunion contractors.[107] But the mere fact that a company is a subsidiary of another does not make it a producer of the products manufactured by its parent or related entities.[108]

---

104. Teamsters, Local 537 (Lohman Sales Co.), 132 N.L.R.B. 901, 48 L.R.R.M. 1429, 1432 (1961).
105. 377 U.S. 46, 55 L.R.R.M. 2957 (1964).
106. Great Western Broadcasting Corp. v. NLRB, 356 F.2d 434, 436, 61 L.R.R.M. 2364 (9th Cir.), *cert. denied*, 384 U.S. 1002 (1966).
107. See Building & Construction Trades Council (K-Mart Corp.), 257 N.L.R.B. 86, 107 L.R.R.M. 1464 (1981) (union may distribute handbills urging boycott of store chain using nonunion labor to build new store); IBEW, Local 712 (Golden Dawn Foods), 134 N.L.R.B. 812, 49 L.R.R.M. 1220, 1221 (1961).
108. Pet, Inc. v. NLRB, 641 F.2d 545, 549, 106 L.R.R.M. 2477 (8th Cir. 1981). If the subsidiary added capital, enterprise, or service to its parent's products, of course, it would "produce" those products, as that term is used in the proviso.

Secondary Activity

7.1.7.2 Products "Distributed" by the Neutral

More recent controversy has centered on whether the neutral employer distributes the primary's product. A neutral employer does not distribute the primary's product simply because it derives some benefit from the primary's efforts. There must be a business relationship between the primary and the neutral *or* the neutral must distribute "products whose chain of production can reasonably be said to include" the primary.[109] In *Edward J. DeBartolo Corp. v. NLRB*, the Supreme Court held that a union's publicity could not call for a boycott of an entire shopping mall when the dispute concerned a contractor working on only one store within the complex. The owners of the other stores clearly did not distribute the contractor's products. At the most, the Court found, the publicity proviso might protect calls for a boycott of the company whose store was being built by the primary.[110]

7.1.7.3 Permissible Scope of Nonpicketing Publicity

The proviso requires that publicity be truthful. This means that the union may not have an "intent to deceive," and its materials can contain no "substantial departure from fact."[111] The union's publicity must therefore clearly specify the employer that distributes the struck employer's products,[112] as well as iden-

---

109. Edward J. DeBartolo Corp. v. NLRB, 51 U.S.L.W. 4984, 113 L.R.R.M. 2953 (U.S. 1983).
110. *Id.*
111. Teamsters, Local 731 (Servair Maintenance, Inc.), 229 N.L.R.B. 392, 402, 96 L.R.R.M. 1128 (1977) ("substantial" misstatements on handbills); Teamsters, Local 537 (Lohman Sales Co.), 132 N.L.R.B. 901, 906, 48 L.R.R.M. 1429, 1431 (1961).
112. Honolulu Typographical Union, Local 37 (Hawaii Press Newspapers, Inc.), 167 N.L.R.B. 1030, 1032, 66 L.R.R.M. 1194 (1967), *enforced*, 401 F.2d 952, 68 L.R.R.M. 3004 (D.C. Cir. 1968).

Responding to Strikes

tify the struck employer.[113] Furthermore, because the proviso merely extends the range of pressure that may be applied against the primary employer, it does not protect publicity attacking the neutral.[114]

The proviso excludes picketing from its protection. Both the NLRB and the courts have therefore held otherwise legitimate publicity to be outside the Act's protection when it occurs in conjunction with and near picketing.[115] When handbilling explicitly refers to pickets at lawful locations nearby, for example, it has been deemed to extend the picketing to the site of the handbilling, rendering it unlawful.[116] Similarly, if other circumstances indicate that ostensibly lawful handbilling is a mere continuation of prior unlawful picketing, it will not be protected by the publicity proviso.[117]

7.1.7.4 Consumer Picketing and the Integrated and Dominant Product Doctrines

Despite the exclusion of picketing from the publicity proviso, the Supreme Court has held that a union may post consumer

---

113. Service Employees, Local 399 (Delta Air Lines, Inc.), 263 N.L.R.B. 996, 111 L.R.R.M. 1159, 1161 (1982).
114. *Id.*, 111 L.R.R.M. at 1161.
115. Kroger Co. v. NLRB, 477 F.2d 1104, 1108, 83 L.R.R.M. 2149 (6th Cir. 1973); Teamsters, Local 732 (Servair Maintenance, Inc.), 229 N.L.R.B. 392, 400, 96 L.R.R.M. 1128 (1977); Cement Masons, Local 337 (California Ass'n of Employers), 190 N.L.R.B. 377, 77 L.R.R.M. 1255 (1971), *supplemented by* 192 N.L.R.B. 377, 77 L.R.R.M. 1825 (1971), *aff'd sub nom.* Hoffman v. Cement Masons, Local 337, 468 F.2d 1187, 1191, 81 L.R.R.M. 2641 (9th Cir. 1972), *cert. denied*, 411 U.S. 986 (1973).
116. Broadcast Employees, Local 31 (CBS, Inc.), 237 N.L.R.B. 1370, 1376, 99 L.R.R.M. 1534 (1978), *enforced*, 631 F.2d 944, 951, 104 L.R.R.M. 3121 (D.C. Cir. 1980).
117. Lumber & Sawmill Workers, Local 2797 (Stoltze Land & Lumber Co.), 156 N.L.R.B. 388, 61 L.R.R.M. 1046, 1047 (1965). *But see* Operating Engineers, Local 139 (Oak Construction, Inc.), 226 N.L.R.B. 759, 93 L.R.R.M. 1385 (1976) (finding handbilling after cessation of illegal picketing to be protected).

Secondary Activity

pickets at neutral premises to persuade consumers not to purchase the struck employer's products.[118] The scope of permissible consumer picketing is much narrower than that of other forms of lawful union publicity. Consumer picketing must be "closely confined."[119] Although pickets may urge the consumer "to be selective among products once inside the secondary's premises," they cannot encourage a complete refusal to deal with the secondary.[120] Limiting the appeal to the primary's products also means refraining from encouraging neutral employees to stop work. The NLRB and the courts will find that pickets are unlawfully appealing to neutral employees, rather than consumers, when there is an

> absence of any effort to negate an appeal to employees of the various secondary employers, and the absence of any appeal for specific conduct on the part of consumers . . . .[121]

In these cases, the union has violated section 8(b)(4).

Sometimes the primary employer's product is distributed only as a constituent part of a neutral employer's product. A consumer cannot refrain from purchasing the primary's product in such circumstances without simultaneously refusing to purchase a neutral employer's product. Picketing that urges a consumer boycott of a struck product that is thus merged or integrated with other products cannot be properly limited to the primary em-

---

118. NLRB v. Fruit & Vegetable Packers, Local 760 (Tree Fruits), 377 U.S. 58, 55 L.R.R.M. 2961 (1964).
119. 377 U.S. at 72.
120. Hoffman v. Cement Masons, Local 337, 468 F.2d 1187, 1192, 81 L.R.R.M. 2641 (9th Cir. 1972), cert. denied, 411 U.S. 986 (1973).
121. NLRB v. Building Service Employees, Local 105, 367 F.2d 227, 229, 63 L.R.R.M. 2307 (10th Cir. 1966); NLRB v. Building Service Employees, Local 254, 359 F.2d 289, 292, 61 L.R.R.M. 2709 (1st Cir. 1966); Carpenters, Local 550 (Steiner Lumber Co.), 153 N.L.R.B. 1285, 59 L.R.R.M. 1622, 1623 (1965), enforced, 367 F.2d 953, 63 L.R.R.M. 2328 (9th Cir. 1966).

ployer's products and is unlawful. Under this doctrine, pickets have been held to violate section 8(b)(4) when they asked that restaurant patrons refrain from buying the primary employer's bread[122] or meat,[123] that customers of a newspaper's advertiser stop buying products advertised in the primary employer's newspaper,[124] that grocery store customers stop using the primary employer's grocery bags,[125] and that the public refuse to use or purchase structures on which the primary employer has performed some construction work[126] or in which its products have been installed.[127]

A similar situation arises when the neutral employer's business consists almost exclusively of selling the struck product. In such cases, consumer picketing is "reasonably calculated to induce customers not to patronize the neutrals at all."[128] The picketing

---

122. Teamsters, Local 327 (American Bread Co.), 170 N.L.R.B. 91, 93, 67 L.R.R.M. 1427 (1968), *enforced*, 411 F.2d 147, 71 L.R.R.M. 2243 (6th Cir. 1969).
123. Maxey v. Meat Cutters, Local 126 (King-O-Meat Co.), 627 F.2d 912, 915, 105 L.R.R.M. 2015 (9th Cir. 1980) (union's threat to picket restaurants serving primary's meat was threat of unlawful conduct under "integrated products" doctrine).
124. Honolulu Typographical Union v. NLRB, 401 F.2d 952, 955-56, 68 L.R.R.M. 3004 (D.C. Cir. 1968) (struck employer's advertising integrated in products distributed by advertisers who could not, therefore, be picketed).
125. Kroger Co. v. NLRB, 647 F.2d 634, 105 L.R.R.M. 2897 (6th Cir. 1980), *on remand*, 258 N.L.R.B. 67, 108 L.R.R.M. 1073 (1981), *reversing* Paperworkers, Local 832 (Duro Paper Bag Manufacturing Co.), 236 N.L.R.B. 1525, 98 L.R.R.M. 1430 (1978).
126. *See* Operating Engineers, Local 139 (Oak Construction, Inc.), 226 N.L.R.B. 759, 93 L.R.R.M. 1385 (1976); Plasterers, Local 337 (California Association of Employers), 190 N.L.R.B. 261, 77 L.R.R.M. 1255 (1971), *enforced*, 468 F.2d 1187, 81 L.R.R.M. 2641 (9th Cir. 1972), *cert. denied*, 411 U.S. 986 (1973).
127. NLRB v. Twin City District Council of Carpenters, 422 F.2d 309, 73 L.R.R.M. 2371 (8th Cir. 1970).
128. Retail Clerks, Local 1001 (Land Title Insurance Co.), 226 N.L.R.B. 754, 757, 93 L.R.R.M. 1338 (1976), *enforced*, 627 F.2d 1133, 101 L.R.R.M. 3084 (D.C. Cir. 1979), *rev'd*, 447 U.S. 607, 104 L.R.R.M. 2567 (1980).

Secondary Activity

would thus threaten the neutral "with ruin or substantial loss," rather than simply cut into sales of the primary's product.[129] The Supreme Court has therefore found it to be unlawful.[130]

Consumer picketing is permitted, then, only when the union's appeal can be and is limited to the struck product. The picket signs themselves must clearly show that the union objects only to the primary's products.[131] If the union violates this requirement, subsequent picket signs appropriately limited in appeal may merely continue the initial unlawful activity, especially if the wording on the signs changes only slightly. A hiatus may be necessary after the illegal picketing for subsequent picketing at the same premises to be lawful.[132] In some circumstances, however, the NLRB may find that picketing still has an unlawful object even if there is a brief interlude before appropriately limited pickets begin patrolling the premises.[133]

7.1.8 Union Pressure Relating to Hot Cargo Clauses

Section 8(e) of the Act prohibits labor contract provisions under which an employer agrees not to handle, use, sell, transport, or otherwise deal in another employer's products, or consents not to do business with any other person. These unlawful provisions are often called "hot cargo clauses," even though the phrase now

---

129. NLRB v. Retail Store Employees, Local 1001, 447 U.S. 607, 615, n.11 104 L.R.R.M. 2567 (1980).
130. *Id.*
131. *See* Teamsters, Local 812 (Monarch Long Beach Corp.), 243 N.L.R.B. 801, 809, 102 L.R.R.M. 1272 (1979), *enforced*, 657 F.2d 1252, 105 L.R.R.M. 2658 (D.C. Cir. 1980); Meat Cutters, Local 248 (Milwaukee Independent Meat Packers Ass'n), 230 N.L.R.B. 189, 202, 96 L.R.R.M. 1221 (1977).
132. Carpenters, Local 550 (Diamond Industries), 227 N.L.R.B. 196, 197, 94 L.R.R.M. 1426 (1976).
133. Butchers, Local 563 (Triple L Distributing Co.), 240 N.L.R.B. 427, 428, 100 L.R.R.M. 1218 (1979) (short hiatus insufficient to demonstrate that unlawful object had changed).

Responding to Strikes

refers to more than a simple agreement not to handle struck or nonunion (hot) cargo.

The Act prohibits hot cargo arrangements because they seek, by agreement rather than by union pressure, to entangle neutral employers in labor disputes not their own. In fact, Congress enacted section 8(e) to plug a loophole in section 8(b)(4), which had been construed to permit such agreements.[134] The section generally prohibits three types of contracts: (1) subcontracting clauses by which the employer agrees to subcontract only to union employers,[135] (2) agreements obliging the employer to refuse to handle a struck or nonunion employer's products,[136] and (3) clauses that prevent the employer from disciplining employees for refusing to cross *secondary* picket lines.[137] Two provisos exempt certain agreements dealing with the construction and garment industries from section 8(e)'s coverage.

An employer need not understand section 8(e)'s precise contours to engage in effective strike planning.[138] The following

---

134. *See* Carpenters, Local 1976 v. NLRB (Sand Door), 357 U.S. 93, 42 L.R.R.M. 2243 (1958).
135. Mine Workers, Local 1854 (Amax Coal Co.), 238 N.L.R.B. 1583, 1631, 99 L.R.R.M. 1670 (1978), *aff'd in pertinent part*, 614 F.2d 872, 103 L.R.R.M. 2482 (3d Cir. 1980), *rev'd on other grounds*, 453 U.S. 322, 107 L.R.R.M. 2769 (1981).
136. NLRB v. Joint Council of Teamsters, 338 F.2d 23, 31, 57 L.R.R.M. 2422 (9th Cir. 1964). A few courts have, however, found that clauses permitting employees to refuse to perform work that would otherwise be performed by a struck employer are lawful. Such a clause "embodies only the ally doctrine." NLRB v. Amalgamated Lithographers, 309 F.2d 31, 38, 51 L.R.R.M. 2093 (9th Cir. 1962), *cert. denied*, 372 U.S. 943 (1963).
137. *See, e.g.,* Bricklayers, Local 2 v. NLRB, 562 F.2d 775, 784-86, 95 L.R.R.M. 3310 (D.C. Cir. 1977); Teamsters, Local 467 (Mike Sullivan & Assoc., Inc.), 265 N.L.R.B. No. 214, 112 L.R.R.M. 1231 (1982).
138. The scope of section 8(e) has extremely significant implications under antitrust law. *See* Connell Constr. Co. v. Plumbers and Steamfitters, 421 U.S. 616, 89 L.R.R.M. 2401 (1975). To avoid running the risk of liability for treble damages under the antitrust statutes, employers should consult counsel before entering into any contract containing a clause resembling those prohibited by section 8(e).

discussion therefore provides only a simplified description of the statute's prohibitions. Because hot cargo clauses are an unusually intricate area of labor law, an employer must consult specialized counsel before entering into any restrictive agreement. For planning purposes, however, it is useful to know the statute's broad outlines, for a union commits an unfair labor practice if it engages in threats or coercion to secure a clause that violates section 8(e).[139] An employer may therefore file charges with the NLRB if a strike follows the employer's rejection of a union's demand for a hot cargo provision.

Like other types of secondary pressure, clauses ostensibly within section 8(e) must be evaluated with an eye toward their object. "Union standards" clauses, which permit subcontracting only to employers meeting prevailing union compensation standards, are lawful because they protect the union's primary interests by minimizing the economic benefits of subcontracting.[140] Similarly, when an agreement is designed solely to preserve work for the represented employees, rather than to exert pressure "calculated to satisfy union objectives elsewhere," it has a lawful primary objective.[141] This principle generally permits unions and employers to enter into "work preservation" agreements obliging the employer to keep within the bargaining unit all work traditionally performed by unit employees.

---

139. See § 8(b)(4)(A) of the Act, 29 U.S.C. § 158(b)(4)(A); see also Amax, Inc. v. NLRB, 614 F.2d 872, 885, 103 L.R.R.M. 2482 (3d Cir. 1980), rev'd on other grounds, 453 U.S. 322, 107 L.R.R.M. 2769 (1981); Feather v. UMW, District 2, Local 1600, 494 F. Supp. 701, 710, 104 L.R.R.M 2864 (W.D. Pa. 1980), aff'd in part, rev'd in part, 711 F.2d 530, 113 L.R.R.M. 3367 (3d Cir. 1983); Building & Construction Trades Council (Donald Schriver, Inc.), 239 N.L.R.B. 264, 271, 99 L.R.R.M. 1593 (1978), enforced, 635 F.2d 859, 105 L.R.R.M. 2818 (D.C. Cir. 1980), cert. denied, 451 U.S. 976 (1981).
140. Teamsters, Local 94 (California Dump Truck Owners Ass'n), 227 N.L.R.B. 269, 272, 94 L.R.R.M. 1210 (1976).
141. National Woodwork Manufacturers Ass'n v. NLRB, 386 U.S. 612, 644, 64 L.R.R.M. 2801 (1967).

Responding to Strikes

A union may use economic force to obtain a work preservation agreement or an agreement within section 8(e)'s construction and garment industry provisos.[142] But unions violate section 8(b)(4)(B), the basic secondary boycott provision, if they strike or exert pressure to *enforce* work preservation clauses when the employer does not control the work.[143] Similarly, clauses valid under the construction industry proviso may not be enforced by economic action.[144] Such clauses violate section 8(e) to the extent they purport to authorize enforcement through union self-help.[145]

7.2 Procedure upon Filing a Charge; Injunctive Relief

An employer initiates an unfair labor practice charge against a union by filling in a preprinted form designed for that purpose

---

142. Donald Schriver, Inc. v. NLRB, 635 F.2d 859, 869, 105 L.R.R.M. 2818 (D.C. Cir. 1980), *cert. denied*, 451 U.S. 976 (1981); Carpenters, Local 112 (Silver Bow Employers Ass'n), 200 N.L.R.B. 205, 210, 82 L.R.R.M. 1189 (1972). *But see* Los Angeles Bldg. & Constr. Trades Council (B & J Investment Co.), 214 N.L.R.B. 562, 87 L.R.R.M. 1424 (1974) (union may not exert pressure to secure clause valid under construction industry proviso if it has object of forcing employer to cease doing business with specific subcontractor).
143. NLRB v. Enterprise Ass'n of Pipefitters (Austin Co.), 429 U.S. 507, 94 L.R.R.M. 2628 (1977); Electro-Coal Transfer Corp. v. Longshoremen, ILA, Local 1418, 1419, 591 F.2d 284, 290, 100 L.R.R.M. 2999 (5th Cir. 1979); U.S. Chamber of Commerce v. NLRB, 574 F.2d 457, 462, 98 L.R.R.M. 2023 (9th Cir.), *cert. denied*, 439 U.S. 981 (1978); Painters, Local 829 (Theatre Techniques, Inc.), 267 N.L.R.B. No. 136, 114 L.R.R.M. 1105 (1983) (union violates § 8(b)(4) even if it does not know that the pressured employer does not control the work).
144. Woelke & Romero Framing, Inc. v. NLRB, 456 U.S. 645, 665, 110 L.R.R.M. 2377 (1982).
145. NLRB v. Associated General Contractors, 709 F.2d 532, 534, 113 L.R.R.M. 3271 (9th Cir. 1983); Building & Construction Trades Council (Stark Electric, Inc.), 262 N.L.R.B. 672, 674, 110 L.R.R.M. 1336 (1982).

Secondary Activity

and filing it with the regional office of the NLRB. (See Appendix 7-K, NLRB Charge Form.) Along with that form, the employer's counsel should submit a notice of appearance designating counsel as the employer's representative in the proceeding. (See Appendix 7-L, NLRB Notice of Appearance Form.) Prior to filing the charge, the employer and its counsel should prepare its witnesses to assist the NLRB in immediately investigating the charge. This task will be simplified if appropriate individuals have kept careful records of their observations of secondary activity. (See Appendix 7-M, Witness Checklist for Secondary Activity.)

The employer and its counsel should also review all photographs, maps, copies of notices to the union, and other documents pertinent to the charge. These should be organized in a coherent fashion for presentation to the NLRB's investigator. It is important that the employer effectively present its case at these early stages. If the NLRB is not persuaded to charge the union with violating section 8(b)(4), the employer's remedies will be sharply limited: only the NLRB has authority to seek injunctions against secondary activity.[146]

An employer's charges under sections 8(b)(4) and 8(e) have "priority over all other cases except cases of like character" pending with the NLRB. The initial investigation of the charge generally occurs within a few days of its filing. If the Regional Director concludes that a complaint should issue against the union, section 10(l) of the Act *requires* the region to seek "appropriate injunctive relief pending the final adjudication of the Board." Because the NLRB is responsible for seeking the injunction, its attorneys will take the lead in preparing material for presentation to the court.

The Norris-LaGuardia Act's limitations on injunctive relief do not apply to injunctions sought under section 10(l).[147] Conse-

---

146. See, e.g., Asbestos Workers, Local 5 v. Superior Court, 182 Cal. Rptr. 732, 114 L.R.R.M. 3693 (Cal. App. 1982).
147. Section 10(l), 29 U.S.C. § 160(l) ("the district court shall have jurisdiction to grant such injunctive relief or temporary restraining order . . . notwithstanding any other provision of law").

257

quently, courts may grant injunctions against secondary activity without an evidentiary hearing, though they will require detailed affidavits to provide the factual foundation for relief.[148] If the NLRB satisfies the court that the complaint is not frivolous, the injunction will usually issue,[149] even when the secondary activity has only been threatened.[150]

Courts have the power to prohibit the full range of practices violating section 8(b)(4). They may enjoin picketing of gates set aside for neutral employers,[151] as well as union discipline of a member who has honored a reserved gate system.[152] In appropriate circumstances, a court may go so far as to enjoin all picketing, even primary pressure, for a period necessary to cure picketing of any secondary taint.[153]

---

148. Squillacote v. Graphic Arts Int'l Union, 540 F.2d 853, 860, 93 L.R.R.M. 2257 (7th Cir. 1976).
149. Lewis v. Clerks and Checkers, ILA, Local 1497, 724 F.2d 1109, 115 L.R.R.M. 3143 (5th Cir. 1984); Squillacote v. Teamsters, Local 344, 561 F.2d 31, 34, 95 L.R.R.M. 2977 (7th Cir. 1977); Kennedy v. Los Angeles Typographical Union, 418 F.2d 6, 8, 72 L.R.R.M. 2506 (9th Cir. 1969). *But see* Danielson v. Garment Workers, 494 F.2d 1230, 1244, 85 L.R.R.M. 2902 (2d Cir. 1974) (injunction will not issue when sought on the basis of new and incorrect legal theory, even if "sufficiently 'thoughtful' to escape being branded as 'insubstantial *and* frivolous' ").
150. Hirsch v. Building & Construction Trades Council, 530 F.2d 298, 305-06, 91 L.R.R.M. 2438 (3d Cir. 1976).
151. Hirsch v. IBEW, System Council U-2, 541 F. Supp. 224, 111 L.R.R.M. 2467, 2471 (D.N.J. 1982); Johansen v. Utility Workers, Local 246, 98 L.R.R.M. 2841 (S.D. Cal. 1978); Price v. Operating Engineers, Local 953, 99 L.R.R.M. 2865 (D.N.M. 1978).
152. Johansen v. Carpenters, Local 2361, 100 L.R.R.M. 2168 (C.D. Cal. 1978).
153. Scott v. Ironworkers, Local 377, 103 L.R.R.M. 2752, 2754 (N.D. Cal. 1980); Johansen v. District Council of Carpenters, 110 L.R.R.M. 3063, 3067 (C.D. Cal 1980); *see also* Miller v. UFCW, Local 498, 708 F.2d 467, 471, 113 L.R.R.M. 3107 (9th Cir. 1983) (hiatus in lawful picketing may be ordered "only when presumptively legitimate picketing would perpetuate the effects of prior illegal activity"). *But see* Potter v. Houston Gulf Coast Building Trades Council, 482 F.2d 837, 841, 83 L.R.R.M. 3042 (5th Cir. 1973) (vacating injunction against primary picketing); Allen v.

7.3 Discipline of Employees Engaging in Secondary Pressure

An employee honoring secondary picketing is engaged in unprotected activity. Indeed, contract clauses that purport to authorize refusals to cross secondary picket lines violate section 8(e).[154] Thus, an employer may discipline employees who refuse to cross illegal secondary picket lines.[155] Because of the complexity of issues arising under section 8(b)(4), the employer may expect the union to fiercely contest any such discipline.

7.4 Damage Suits Under Section 303

7.4.1 Persons Entitled to Sue

Section 303 of the Act entitles any person who has been "injured in his business or property by reason of any violation" of section 8(b)(4) to recover damages for that injury. Although section 303's clear intent was to give a remedy to neutral employers caught in the middle of a labor dispute, the primary employer with whom the union has a dispute may also sue for damages under section 303.[156] Even a third party (i.e., neither the primary nor the secondary employer) may sue under section 303, pro-

---

Carpenters, Local 1408, 111 L.R.R.M. 2353, 2355 (N.D. Cal. 1980) (denying motion for 60-day hiatus period).
154. See, e.g., Bricklayers, Local No. 2 v. NLRB, 562 F.2d 775, 784-86, 95 L.R.R.M. 3310 (D.C. Cir. 1077).
155. See Chevron U.S.A., Inc., 244 N.L.R.B. 1081, 1086, 102 L.R.R.M. 1311 (1979).
156. Jaden Electric v. IBEW, Local 334, 508 F. Supp. 983, 986, 112 L.R.R.M. 2492 (D.N.J. 1981); Brick & Clay Workers v. Deena Artware, Inc., 198 F.2d 637, 644, 30 L.R.R.M. 2485 (6th Cir.), cert. denied, 344 U.S. 897 (1952).

Responding to Strikes

vided it either suffers a direct property injury or has a close business relationship with the primary or secondary.[157] The owner of property affected by the secondary activity may therefore sue under section 303.[158] The courts have disagreed, however, on whether employees of injured employers may sue under section 303.[159]

7.4.2 Persons Liable

Damages may be assessed against the union only when it is responsible for the unlawful action under the laws of agency.[160] In lawsuits under section 303, the union's responsibility need be shown only by a preponderance of the evidence.[161] Union officers and individual union members, however, may not be sued under section 303.[162]

---

157. W.J. Milner & Co. v. IBEW, Local 349, 476 F.2d 8, 12, 82 L.R.R.M. 2977 (5th Cir. 1973); *see* Sapp v. Teamsters, Local 639, 542 F.2d 224, 93 L.R.R.M. 2605 (4th Cir. 1976) (*per curiam*) (independent contractor working for secondary employer could recover under § 303 when termination of his services was "one of the objects of the union's activities").
158. Abreen Corp. v. Laborers Int'l Union, 709 F.2d 748, 753-54, 114 L.R.R.M. 2057 (1st Cir. 1983), *cert. denied*, 115 L.R.R.M. 2248 (1984); Allentown Racquetball & Health Club, Inc. v. Building & Construction Trades Council, 525 F. Supp. 156 (E.D. Pa. 1981).
159. *Compare* Fulton v. Plumbers, Local 598, 695 F.2d 402, 407-08, 112 L.R.R.M. 2583 (9th Cir. 1982) ("employees of an injured employer" have no standing to sue under § 303), *cert. denied*, 114 L.R.R.M. 2776 (1983), *with* Wells v. Operating Engineers, Local 181, 303 F.2d 73, 75, 50 L.R.R.M. 2198 (6th Cir. 1962) (injured employees may sue under § 303).
160. Mine Workers v. Gibbs, 383 U.S. 715, 61 L.R.R.M. 2561 (1966). A union is liable under this standard if its agents, acting within the general scope of their agency, authorize, participate in, or ratify the activity. Carbon Fuel Co. v. Mine Workers, 444 U.S. 212, 216-17, 102 L.R.R.M. 3017 (1979).
161. Lane Crane Service, Inc. v. IBEW, Local 177, 704 F.2d 550, 554, 113 L.R.R.M. 2396 (11th Cir. 1983); C & K Coal Co. v. Mine Workers, 704 F.2d 690, 695, 113 L.R.R.M. 2117 (3d Cir. 1983).
162. Kerry Coal v. Mine Workers, 637 F.2d 957, 965, 106 L.R.R.M. 2225 (3d Cir.), *cert. denied*, 454 U.S 823 (1981); Park Electric Co. v. IBEW,

Because of the relative autonomy of local unions, it will generally be difficult to hold international organizations liable for damages arising from a section 8(b)(4) violation.[163] But if the prohibited activity is jointly undertaken by the international and the local, and the international makes no attempt to curb the secondary activity, the international may be jointly liable.[164]

7.4.3 Interaction between Sections 303 and 8(b)(4)

A union is liable under section 303 only when it engages in conduct prohibited by section 8(b)(4). The predicate for section 303 liability is, then, a violation of section 8(b)(4). A section 303 action may, however, be maintained even if a section 8(b)(4) charge has never been filed.[165] More frequently, the lawsuit follows on the heels of the NLRB's determination that the union violated section 8(b)(4). Most courts have held that, under the doctrine of collateral estoppel, such a ruling is conclusive in subsequent lawsuits, at least when the parties have had a full and fair opportunity to litigate before the NLRB.[166] Conversely, dismissal of the employer's complaint after hearing will probably

---

Local 701, 540 F. Supp. 779, 780 (N.D. Ill. 1982); Amoco Oil v. IBEW, Local 99, 536 F. Supp. 1203, 1211-12 (D.R.I. 1982); Universal Communications Corp. v. Burns, 449 F.2d 691, 78 L.R.R.M. 2480 (5th Cir. 1971) (*per curiam*); Bacino v. Musicians, Local 240, 407 F. Supp. 548, 552, 92 L.R.R.M. 2053 (N.D. Ill. 1976).

163. See Bacino v. Musicians, Local 240, 407 F. Supp. 548, 553, 92 L.R.R.M. 2053 (N.D. Ill. 1976).
164. Kerry Coal Co. v. Mineworkers, 637 F.2d 957, 963, 106 L.R.R.M. 2225 (3d Cir.), *cert. denied*, 454 U.S. 823 (1981) (international's "instigation, ratification and support" of activity sufficient to render it liable to employer); Noranda Aluminum, Inc. v. Carpenters, 528 F.2d 1304, 1308, 91 L.R.R.M. 2105 (8th Cir.), *cert. denied*, 429 U.S. 835 (1976).
165. Longshoremen & Warehousemen v. Juneau Spruce Corp., 342 U.S. 237, 244, 29 L.R.R.M. 2249 (1952).
166. Wickham Contracting Co. v. Board of Education, 715 F.2d 21, 26, 114 L.R.R.M. 2514 (2d Cir. 1983); Paramount Transport Systems v. Teamsters, Local 150, 436 F.2d 1064, 1065-66, 76 L.R.R.M. 2427 (9th Cir.

preclude the employer from relitigating the section 8(b)(4) violation in a later section 303 proceeding.[167] The NLRB's refusal to *issue* a complaint pursuant to an employer's section 8(b)(4) charge will have no collateral estoppel effect on later section 303 proceedings as it does not reflect a determination after hearing on the merits.[168]

The parties to the section 303 action may sometimes be different from those before the NLRB. Principles of collateral estoppel do not apply against a party who did not participate before the NLRB and thus had no opportunity to litigate the pertinent issue. Furthermore, even if a union has been named in the NLRB's complaint, it will not be collaterally estopped by an adverse ruling if it does not actually litigate the issues and have findings rendered against it.[169]

7.4.4 Damages in Section 303 Suits

Section 303 authorizes recovery of damages sustained by reason of the prohibited activity,[170] meaning that the employer can

---

1971) (collateral estoppel effect should be given with respect to determinations reached in proceedings comporting with due process); Allied Int'l, Inc. v. International Longshoremen's Ass'n, 554 F. Supp. 32, 34, 112 L.R.R.M. 2497 (D. Mass. 1982).

167. International Wire v. Electrical Workers, Local 38, 475 F.2d 1078, 1079, 82 L.R.R.M. 3064 (6th Cir.) (*per curiam*), *cert. denied*, 414 U.S. 867 (1973).

168. Clark Engineering & Constr. Co. v. Carpenters District Council, 510 F.2d 1075, 1082, 88 L.R.R.M. 2865 (6th Cir. 1975); Aircraft & Engine Maintenance Employees, Local 290 v. I. E. Schilling Co., 340 F.2d 286, 289, 58 L.R.R.M. 2169 (5th Cir. 1965), *cert. denied*, 382 U.S. 972 (1966); *see also* Edna H. Pagel, Inc. v. Teamsters, Local 595, 667 F.2d 1275, 1280 n.12, 109 L.R.R.M. 2663 (9th Cir. 1982) (discussing general effect of refusal to issue complaint).

169. Truck Transport, Inc. v. Allied Industrial Workers, 113 L.R.R.M. 2313, 2315-16 (N.D. Ill. 1982).

170. Teamsters, Local 20 v. Morton, 377 U.S. 252, 56 L.R.R.M. 2225 (1964).

Secondary Activity

recover only damages proximately caused by the illegal conduct.[171] Damages cannot be assessed for losses caused by lawful activity.[172] However, "the fact that certain losses may not have resulted directly from the specific acts that evidenced the union's unlawful intentions is irrelevant so long as the losses are traceable to actions forming part of the overall secondary activity."[173]

Courts have awarded a broad range of damages resulting from secondary activity, including lost sales (calculated by reference to the employer's projected growth rate), bonuses to managers, clerical salaries, and depreciation.[174] Fixed overhead, rental expenses, and start-up costs have also been recovered under section 303,[175] as well as extra interest expenses incurred because of the

---

171. Feather v. Mine Workers, 711 F.2d 530, 537, 113 L.R.R.M. 3367 (3d Cir. 1983); Pickens-Bond Constr. Co. v. Carpenters, Local 690, 586 F.2d 1234, 1242, 99 L.R.R.M. 3321 (8th Cir. 1978); Mead v. Retail Clerks, Local 839, 523 F.2d 1371, 1376, 90 L.R.R.M. 2769 (9th Cir. 1975).
172. See Riverside Coal v. United Mine Workers, 410 F.2d 267, 275, 70 L.R.R.M. 3214 (6th Cir.), cert. denied, 396 U.S. 846 (1969).
173. Abreen Corp. v. Laborers International Union, 709 F.2d 748, 759, 114 L.R.R.M. 2057 (1st Cir. 1983), cert. denied, 115 L.R.R.M. 2248 (1984); see also Feather v. United Mine Workers, 711 F.2d 530, 538, 113 L.R.R.M. 3367 (3d Cir. 1983); Mead v. Retail Clerks, Local 839, 523 F.2d 1371, 1379, 90 L.R.R.M. 2769 (9th Cir. 1975) (when strike has mixed primary and secondary objectives, recovery allowed only if "the unlawful motivation was a significant factor producing the union pressure"); Mine Workers v. Osborne Mining Co., 279 F.2d 716, 724, 46 L.R.R.M. 2380 (6th Cir.), cert. denied, 364 U.S. 881 (1960) (total damages from strike may be recovered when lawful and unlawful acts are intertwined).
174. Frito-Lay, Inc. v. Teamsters, Local 137, 623 F.2d 1354, 1364, 104 L.R.R.M. 2931 (9th Cir. 1980), cert. denied, 449 U.S. 1013, 1112 (1981).
175. Mason-Rust v. Laborers, Local 42, 435 F.2d 939, 947, 76 L.R.R.M. 2090 (8th Cir. 1970); Sheet Metal Workers, Local 223 v. Atlas Sheet Metal Co., 384 F.2d 101, 109, 65 L.R.R.M. 3115 (5th Cir. 1967) (start-up costs); Noranda Aluminum, Inc. v. Carpenters, Local 618, 382 F. Supp. 1258, 1263-64, 85 L.R.R.M. 2147 (E.D. Mo. 1973), aff'd, 528 F.2d 1304, 91 L.R.R.M. 2105 (8th Cir.), cert. denied, 429 U.S. 835 (1976); Virginia Electric & Power Co. v. Boilermakers, 103 L.R.R.M. 3144, 3165 (N.D.W. Va. 1980) (rental expense).

Responding to Strikes

activity.[176] An employer may recover lost profits on a contract terminated as a result of the section 8(b)(4) violation,[177] as well as "on an amount of work not bid that [the employer] would have done absent" the secondary activity.[178] The fact that a contract whose performance is impeded by the unlawful action is paid on a cost plus basis does not preclude recovery of damages, even if the employer would ultimately be required to turn over any recovery to the other contracting party.[179] An injured employer may also recover expenses it has incurred as a direct result of the unlawful secondary activity, such as the cost of security guards hired to deal with picketing,[180] travel, and long distance phone call expenditures resulting from efforts to end the union's activity,[181] and extra freight costs caused by secondary activity.[182]

Some damages are clearly not recoverable under section 303. A court may not award punitive damages.[183] Nor may the employer recover attorneys' fees incurred either in halting the illegal action or in pursuing the section 303 suit.[184] Attorneys' fees in-

---

176. Turnkey Contractors v. Cement Masons, Local 685, 580 F.2d 798, 800, 99 L.R.R.M. 2580 (5th Cir. 1978); Sillman v. Teamsters, Local 386, 535 F.2d 1172, 1174, 92 L.R.R.M. 2567 (9th Cir. 1976).
177. Refrigeration Contractors Inc. v. Plumbers, Local 211, 501 F.2d 668, 670, 87 L.R.R.M. 2475 (5th Cir. 1974).
178. George E. Hoffman & Sons, Inc. v. Teamsters, Local 627, 617 F.2d 1234, 1246, 103 L.R.R.M. 2605 (7th Cir.), *cert. denied*, 449 U.S. 937 (1980).
179. Mason-Rust v. Laborers, Local 42, 435 F.2d 939, 945, 76 L.R.R.M. 2090 (8th Cir. 1970).
180. Flame Coal Co. v. United Mine Workers, 303 F.2d 39, 46, 50 L.R.R.M. 2272 (6th Cir.), *cert. denied*, 371 U.S. 891 (1962); Virginia Electric & Power Co. v. Boilermakers, 103 L.R.R.M. 3144, 3165 (N.D.W. Va. 1980).
181. Abbot v. Plumbers, Local 142, 429 F.2d 786, 790, 74 L.R.R.M. 2879 (5th Cir. 1970).
182. Operating Engineers v. Dahlem Constr. Co., 193 F.2d 470, 472, 29 L.R.R.M. 2271 (6th Cir. 1951); Vulcan Materials Co. v. United Steel Workers, 316 F. Supp. 509, 515, 71 L.R.R.M. 2300 (N.D. Ala. 1969), *aff'd*, 430 F.2d 446 (5th Cir. 1970), *cert. denied*, 401 U.S. 963 (1971).
183. Teamsters, Local 20 v. Morton, 377 U.S. 252, 56 L.R.R.M. 2225 (1964).
184. Summit Valley Industries v. Carpenters, 456 U.S. 717, 727, 110 L.R.R.M. 2441 (1982).

curred in negotiating with a reluctant supplier against whom secondary pressure has been applied may, however, be a proper component of section 303 damages.[185]

7.4.5 Joinder of State Law Claims for Picket Line Misconduct

Because the statute permits actions "in any . . . court having jurisdiction of the parties," state courts may hear section 303 suits.[186] When an action is brought in state court, the employer frequently joins state law claims, such as a claim for damages resulting from picket line misconduct. Even when a suit is prosecuted in federal court, the employee may join state causes of action with the section 303 claim,[187] provided the state claim and the section 303 action arise from the same operative facts.[188] If joinder is appropriate, the employer should avail itself of state

---

185. Abreen Corp. v. Laborers Int'l Union, 709 F.2d 748, 760, 114 L.R.R.M. 2057 (1st Cir. 1983), cert. denied, 115 L.R.R.M. 2248 (1984).
186. Simpkins v. Southwestern Idaho Painters, District Council 57, 95 Idaho 165, 505 P.2d 313, 319, 82 L.R.R.M. 2870 (Idaho 1973); Collier v. Operating Engineers, Local 101, 228 Kan. 52, 612 P.2d 150, 156, 109 L.R.R.M. 2233 (Kan. 1980). Defendants in § 303 lawsuits filed in state courts are entitled to remove them to federal court. See 28 U.S.C. § 1441 (a), (b). As a practical matter, few such actions are heard by state courts.
187. See, e.g., Virginia Electric & Power Co. v. Boilermakers, 103 L.R.R.M. 3144, 3159 (N.D.W. Va. 1980) (claims for destruction of property and interference with contractual relations); see also Kerry Coal Co. v. Mine Workers, 637 F.2d 957, 965, 106 L.R.R.M. 2225 (3d Cir.) (state claims for interference with contractual relationships), cert. denied, 454 U.S. 823 (1981).
188. Ritchie v. Mine Workers, 410 F.2d 827, 831, 71 L.R.R.M. 2267 (6th Cir. 1969); Flame Coal v. Mine Workers, 303 F.2d 39, 42, 50 L.R.R.M. 2272 (6th Cir.), cert. denied, 371 U.S 891 (1962). But see Bean & Son, Inc. v. Graphic Arts, Local 96B, 76 F.R.D. 602, 607, 96 L.R.R.M. 3311 (D. Ga. 1977) (union state law claims based on violence and employer's § 303 claim did not share operative facts).

remedies that permit recovery of punitive damages, not otherwise available in a section 303 suit.[189]

7.4.6 Statutes of Limitation

The statute of limitations governing section 303 actions begins to run when the damages are ascertainable.[190] It is less clear just what the statute of limitation is. Most courts have applied state statutes of limitation pertaining to comparable actions.[191] In 1983, however, the Supreme Court decided that the six-month statute of limitations governing the filing of unfair labor practices also applies to employee breach of contract lawsuits arising under section 301.[192] The Court relied primarily on the fact that issues raised in employee section 301 actions have a "substantial overlap" with those litigated in unfair labor practice cases, as well as the "similarity of rights asserted" in the two proceedings. These same considerations might dictate a six-month statute of limitations for section 303 lawsuits. Until the issue is resolved, employers should file such actions within six months of the activity or before expiration of the analogous state limitations period, whichever is earlier.

---

189. See Mine Workers v. Meadow Creek Coal Co., 263 F.2d 52, 64, 43 L.R.R.M. 2445 (6th Cir.), cert. denied, 359 U.S. 1013 (1959).
190. Railing v. Mine Workers, 445 F.2d 353, 355, 77 L.R.R.M. 2887 (4th Cir. 1971).
191. Consolidated Express, Inc. v. New York Shipping Ass'n., 602 F.2d 494, 506, 100 L.R.R.M. 3170 (3d Cir. 1979), vacated on other grounds, 448 U.S. 901, 104 L.R.R.M. 2688 (1980); Operating Engineers v. Fischbach & Moore, Inc., 350 F.2d 936, 939, 60 L.R.R.M. 2141 (9th Cir. 1965), cert. denied, 384 U.S. 904 (1966); Mine Workers v. Meadow Creek Coal Co., 263 F.2d 52, 63, 43 L.R.R.M. 2445 (6th Cir.), cert. denied, 359 U.S. 1013 (1959). But see Carruthers Ready-Mix v. Cement Masons, 113 L.R.R.M. 2077 (D. Tenn. 1983) (holding 6-month statute of limitations for unfair labor practices under the Act applicable when no analogous state statute existed).
192. DelCostello v. Teamsters, 51 U.S.L.W. 4693, 113 L.R.R.M. 2737 (1983).

Appendix 7-A

TELEGRAM

TO: (Primary Union)
FROM: _____
SUBJECT: Work Schedule of (Primary Employer)

(Primary Employer) will have no employees performing work or supplies delivered at this company's _____ facility on any days between _____ and _____ [or on any days prior to _____ or on any days after _____ or between the hours of : .m. and : .m. each day]. (Primary Employer) will not maintain an office at the facility, nor will it store equipment or supplies on the premises during its absence. Your union will be notified if the work schedule for (Primary Employer) employees, agents, and suppliers changes.

    Picketing of this company's _____ facility during the absence of (Primary Employer) employees, agents, and suppliers would constitute unlawful secondary activity in violation of the National Labor Relations Act. Failure to limit picketing to periods when (Primary Employer) employees, agents, and suppliers are on the premises will result in immediate legal action being commenced against the (Primary Employer's) Union to enjoin the activity and recover any and all resulting damages.

Appendix 7-B

TELEGRAM

TO: (Other Unions)
FROM: _____
SUBJECT: Work Schedule of (Primary Employer)

(Primary Employer) will have no employees performing work or supplies delivered at this company's _____ facility on any days between _____ and _____ [or on any days prior to _____ or on any days after _____ or between the hours of : .m. and : .m. each day]. (Primary Employer) will neither maintain an office nor store supplies or equipment on the premises during its absence. Employees, agents, and representatives of other employers will continue to work during (Primary Employer's) absence. You will be notified if the work schedule for (Primary Employer) employees, agents, and suppliers changes.

Those of you who do not use our employees, but instead use our product (or services), should also consider some advance planning. You should be certain that your vehicles are stored in secure places and are protected. If at all possible, find out whether people that supply or move your goods are union or nonunion and make alternative plans to insure that there will be no problem with drivers crossing picket lines. Contact companies that supply or deliver for you to determine whether they have contracts with no strike clauses and the content of those clauses. Discuss their obligations to you.

Appendix 7-C

MEMORANDUM

PERSONAL AND CONFIDENTIAL

DATE: _____
TO: (Employers)
FROM: _____
SUBJECT: Strike Planning—Establishment of Reserved Gates

As you all know, we are bargaining for a new contract with the _____ ("Union"). The _____ and the Union are now well apart in their bargaining positions. It is possible, if not likely, that a strike will occur upon the expiration of the current Collective Bargaining Agreement. The strike date would be midnight _____, with a strike to start possibly at ____ a.m., _____. We hope that a strike will not occur. But because a strike is a very serious matter, we all should take steps to prepare for it. This memorandum, which is personal and confidential, should assist in strike preparation. Its release and distribution should be carefully regulated.

BASIC ACTION ITEMS

We recommend that those of you who use _____ employees by contract carefully review your security measures to guard against possible vandalism or sabotage. It would be useful to do this within the next week.

We also recommend the establishment of "Reserved Gates" for those of you who will be visited by our employees. If Reserved Gates are established properly, we should be able to minimize the negative effect any picketing might have on your operations. The proper way to establish Reserved Gates is discussed later in this memorandum.

Those of you who do not use our employees, but instead use our product (or services), should also consider some advance planning. You should be certain that your vehicles are stored in secure places and are protected. If at all possible, find out whether people that supply or move your goods are union or nonunion and make alternative plans to insure that there will be no problem with drivers crossing picket lines. Contact companies that supply or deliver for you to determine whether they have contracts with no strike clauses and the content of those clauses. Discuss their obligations to you.

RESERVED GATE

The Reserved Gate is a helpful tool when strike activity is directed against neutral secondary employers who are customers of the primary employer with which the union has a dispute. In our situation, the _____ is viewed as the primary employer. We believe that our current organization and relationship is such that each of you is an independent secondary employer. We are prepared to litigate this matter to the maximum extent necessary if the union contests that assumption.

Secondary Activity

If this assumption is correct, each of you can improve your chances of being protected from disruptive picketing activity by establishing a Reserved Gate. A Reserved Gate is "reserved" for the primary employer with which a union has its dispute, as well as the suppliers and agents of that primary employer. If the Reserved Gate is properly established and maintained, the union must limit its picketing to that gate. It will be precluded from applying pressure at other entrances to the facility.

A union must be notified in advance of the establishment of the Reserved Gate. The Reserved Gate must be prominently posted. A large sign must be painted and hung. Other gates must also have prominent signs announcing the existence of a Reserved Gate. A Reserved Gate should not be established in close proximity to other gates that are used by other employees and suppliers. It should, however, be located reasonably close to the area where _____employees will be working. The Reserved Gate must be scrupulously maintained (no other employees or suppliers may use it), as must "non-Reserved Gates." It is also recommended that there be materials available on site for explanation purposes in case some picketers do not understand that they should be located only at the Reserved Gate.

To assist you in preparing to set up your Reserved Gates, I am enclosing several documents. First is the text of a telegram that you should send to the Union when you establish your Reserved Gate. Second is the text of a telegram to send to all other affected unions. Third is the text of a sign that should be posted at the Reserved Gate. Fourth is the text of a sign that should be posted (a large sign, at least approximately three feet by two feet, is required) at all other gates. Fifth is the text of a brief notice or memorandum that should be available to be handed out to any picketers who do not picket at the Reserved Gate. Copies of all materials when used or issued should also be sent to me.

PREPARATION

Although this preparation may seem complex, this basic system is easy to follow if you prepare in advance. Consequently, I would strongly recommend that each of you have large signs made up for each of your non-Reserved Gates and that you designate a Reserved Gate now and prepare a sign for it as well. *Do not* post any signs yet. In addition, do not send any telegrams regarding this system yet. However, be sure that you have the telegrams and the signs and notices prepared in case you need them. If you have questions about where a Reserved Gate may be located, please contact _____, at _____, who has been working on this project. Our legal counsel is also available to discuss this matter in detail.

Appendix 7-D

RESERVED GATE SIGN

[*NOTE*: TO BE PAINTED ON LARGE PROMINENT SIGN (AT LEAST TWO FEET BY THREE FEET). THE SIGN MUST BE EASILY READ BY ALL PERSONS APPROACHING THE GATE.]

RESERVED   GATE

N O T I C E

This is a RESERVED GATE for the sole and exclusive use of the (PRIMARY EMPLOYER'S) employees, agents, and suppliers. All other parties must use our other entrances located at _____.

Appendix 7-E

NEUTRAL GATE SIGN

[*NOTE*: TO BE PAINTED ON LARGE PROMINENT SIGN (AT LEAST TWO FEET BY THREE FEET). THE SIGN MUST BE EASILY READ BY ALL PERSONS APPROACHING THE GATE.]

N O T I C E

This entrance is PROHIBITED for use by employees, agents, or suppliers of the (PRIMARY EMPLOYER), who are limited to use of the RESERVED GATE, located at _____.

Appendix 7-F

TELEGRAM

TO: (Primary Union)
FROM: _____
SUBJECT: Reserved Gate

Effective _____, this company, _____, is establishing a "Reserved Gate" at its _____ facility. The Reserved Gate is being established for the sole and exclusive use of the _____ ("Primary Employer") employees, agents, and suppliers. No one else is authorized to use the Reserved Gate. All other individuals, suppliers, employees, agents, or representatives of other employers are and will be specifically directed to our other entrances. The Reserved Gate is located at _____. Our other entrances remain at _____.

Picketing at any gates or entrances other than the Reserved Gate will constitute unlawful secondary activity in violation of the National Labor Relations Act. Failure to limit picketing to the Reserved Gate will result in immediate legal action being commenced against the (Primary Employer's) union to enjoin the activity and recover any and all damages.

Appendix 7-G

TELEGRAM

TO: (Other Unions)
FROM: _____
SUBJECT: Reserved Gate

    Effective _____, this company, _____, is establishing a "Reserved Gate" at its _____ facility. The Reserved Gate is established for the sole and exclusive use of the _____ ("Primary Employer") employees, agents, and suppliers. No one else is authorized to use the Reserved Gate. All other individuals, suppliers, employees, agents, or representatives of other employers are specifically directed to our other entrances. The Reserved Gate will be located at _____. Our other entrances remain at _____.

    Picketing at any gates or entrances other than the Reserved Gate will constitute unlawful secondary activity in violation of the National Labor Relations Act. Failure to limit picketing to the Reserved Gate will result in immediate legal action being commenced against the (Primary Employer's) union to enjoin the activity and recover any and all damages.

Appendix 7-H

TELEGRAM

TO: (Primary Union)
FROM: _____
SUBJECT: Reestablishment of Reserved Gate

Due to claims that (Primary Employer) employees, agents, and suppliers have failed to confine themselves to the gate reserved for their use, effective _____, this company, _____, is reestablishing a "Reserved Gate" at its _____ facility. In reestablishing the Reserved Gate, we do not concede that any employees, agents, or suppliers of (Primary Employer) have used any gate other than that set aside for their use. The Reserved Gate is being established for the sole and exclusive use of (Primary Employer) employees, agents, and suppliers. No one else is authorized to use the Reserved Gate. All other individuals, suppliers, employees, agents, or representatives of other employers are and will be specifically directed to our other entrances. The Reserved Gate is located at _____. Our other entrances remain at _____.

Picketing at any gates or entrances other than the Reserved Gate will constitute unlawful secondary activity in violation of the National Labor Relations Act. Failure to limit picketing to the Reserved Gate will result in immediate legal action being commenced against the (Primary Employer's) union to enjoin the activity and recover any and all damages.

Appendix 7-I

TELEGRAM

TO: (Other Unions)
FROM: _____
SUBJECT: Reestablishment of Reserved Gate

Due to claims that (Primary Employer) employees, agents, and suppliers have failed to confine themselves to the gate reserved for their use, effective _____, this company, _____, is reestablishing a "Reserved Gate" at its _____ facility. In reestablishing the Reserved Gate, this company does not concede that (Primary Employer) employees, agents, and suppliers have used gates other than the one reserved for their use. The Reserved Gate is being established for the sole and exclusive use of (Primary Employer) employees, agents, and suppliers. No one else is authorized to use the Reserved Gate. All other individuals, suppliers, employees, agents, or representatives of other employers are specifically directed to our other entrances. The Reserved Gate will be located at _____. Our other entrances remain at _____.

Picketing at any gates or entrances other than the Reserved Gate will constitute unlawful secondary activity in violation of the National Labor Relations Act. Failure to cross any such unlawful picket line and failure of your members to perform their duties will constitute a breach of the Collective Bargaining Agreement between this company and your union. If that occurs, legal action will immediately be commenced against your union and its members to enjoin the activity and recover any and all damages.

Appendix 7-J

N O T I C E

TO: (Picketers or Recalcitrant Employees, as Appropriate)
FROM: _____
SUBJECT: Improper Activity Related to Picketing

You are hereby advised that a RESERVED GATE for the sole and exclusive use of the (Primary Employer), its employees, agents, and suppliers, has been established. It is located at _____. No other employees are authorized to use the Reserved Gate, and only employees, agents, suppliers, and individuals connected with other employers are permitted to use the other entrances.

We believe that any picketing that occurs and/or continues at entrances other than the RESERVED GATE is unlawful secondary activity in violation of Federal law. Picketers are warned that continuation of such improper action on their part will lead this company to bring appropriate legal action for violation of labor law and recovery of damages suffered by reason of their actions.

Employees who do not work for (Primary Employer) or its suppliers are hereby directed to enter work through entrances other than the reserved gate, even if pickets are unlawfully posted at those entrances. Failure to cross any such unlawful picket line and failure to perform their duties will constitute a breach of the Collective Bargaining Agreement between their union and _____.

Appendix 7-K

FORM NLRB-508 (4-72)	UNITED STATES OF AMERICA NATIONAL LABOR RELATIONS BOARD **CHARGE AGAINST LABOR ORGANIZATION OR ITS AGENTS**	Form Approved O.M.B. No. 64-R0003
INSTRUCTIONS: File an original and 3 copies of this charge and an additional copy for each organization, each local and each individual named in item 1 with the NLRB regional director for the region in which the alleged unfair labor practice occurred or is occurring.	DO NOT WRITE IN THIS SPACE Case No. Date Filed	

1. LABOR ORGANIZATION OR ITS AGENTS AGAINST WHICH CHARGE IS BROUGHT

a. Name	b. Union Representative to Contact	c. Phone No.

d. Address (Street, city, State and ZIP code)

e. The above-named organization(s) or its agents has (have) engaged in and is (are) engaging in unfair labor practices within the meaning of section 8(b), subsection(s) _____ (List Subsections) _____ of the National Labor Relations Act, and these unfair labor practices are unfair labor practices affecting commerce within the meaning of the Act.

2. Basis of the Charge (Be specific as to facts, names, addresses, plants involved, dates, places, etc.)

3. Name of Employer	4. Phone No.
5. Location of Plant Involved (Street, city, State and ZIP code)	6. Employer Representative to Contact
7. Type of Establishment (Factory, mine, wholesaler, etc.)	8. Identify Principal Product or Service	9. No. of Workers Employed

10. Full Name of Party Filing Charge

11. Address of Party Filing Charge (Street, city, State and ZIP code)	12. Telephone No.

13. DECLARATION

I declare that I have read the above charge and that the statements therein are true to the best of my knowledge and belief.

By _____ _____
(Signature of representative or person making charge) (Title or office if any)

Address _____ _____ _____
(Telephone number) (Date)

WILLFULLY FALSE STATEMENTS ON THIS CHARGE CAN BE PUNISHED BY FINE AND IMPRISONMENT (U.S. CODE, TITLE 18, SECTION 1001)

NLRB Charges against Labor Organization or Agents

Appendix 7-L

Form NLRB-4701
(7-68)

National Labor Relations Board
NOTICE OF APPEARANCE

CASE NO.

TO: (Check one box only)1/

/ / Regional Director / / Executive Secretary / / General Counsel
National Labor   National Labor
Relations Board   Relations Board
Washington, D. C. 20570   Washington, D. C. 20570

The undersigned hereby enters his appearance as representative of _____

in the above-captioned matter.

Signature of representative (please sign in ink)	Representative's name, address, zip code (print or type)
Date	
	Area Code	Telephone Number

1/ If case is pending in Washington and Notice of Appearance is sent to the General Counsel or the Executive Secretary, a copy should be sent to the Regional Director of the Region in which the case was filed so that his records will reflect the appearance.

GPO 927-003

NLRB Notice of Appearance

Appendix 7-M

WITNESS CHECKLIST FOR SECONDARY ACTIVITY

[NOTE: This document is to be used to prepare potential witnesses before or after secondary activity has occurred. It is designed for distribution by the primary employer to neutral employers who might be affected by secondary action. It can, however, be easily adapted for a primary employer's use.

You should edit the checklist to fit the circumstances of your case. An employer using the checklist, whether the primary or a neutral, may wish to involve its counsel in this process and provide counsel with all information generated by the checklist's use. This may allow the employer to assert the attorney-client privilege to protect the information from disclosure in the event of litigation.]

In the event picketing or a related job action occurs at one or more of your locations, there is the unfortunate possibility that it might involve illegal secondary activity and that you or the (Primary Employer) may wish to take appropriate legal action. In that event, your key staff may have to serve as witnesses by providing statements and testimony.

If possible, try to have an experienced manager or supervisor available to serve as a witness if anything unusual occurs. This Witness Checklist is provided to help that person be an effective witness for you. When taking notes on the issues identified below, the witness

Secondary Activity

must always try to describe events in detail, listing background information, date, time, location, reason, other witnesses, etc. You should also instruct your potential witnesses as follows:

A. Document Picketing. Whenever picketing occurs, immediately document the situation. Write down everything as soon as possible, including the nature of the picketing, parties to the picketing, places, times, etc. Be sure you are truthful, specific, and accurate.

B. Record Language on Signs. If possible, have a camera ready and use it to photograph or film reserved gate signs and any picket signs. If a camera is not available, be certain to write down the exact wording on all picket signs you observe.

C. Establish and Observe the Reserved Gate System. Make sure your reserved gate is properly established. It is important that all gates be clearly designated, with one reserved solely for the use of the (Primary Employer), its agents, and suppliers. This reserved gate must be separate from your other entrances, but it must also be "reasonably close" to the area where the employees directly involved in the primary dispute perform work, so that they can be made aware of picket information. The instructions on the gates must be scrupulously followed.

D. Establish a Separate Schedule. If you have decided to continue to use (Primary Employer) employees, you may wish to schedule their work so that they will be absent from the work site for clearly defined and specific periods. Make sure that deliveries for (Primary Employer) do not continue during its absence.

Responding to Strikes

E. <u>Notify the Union</u>. If you establish a reserved gate, or clearly schedule absences of (<u>Primary Employer</u>) employees, you must notify the union of the reserved gate system or the schedule. You should keep a copy of all telegrams describing the reserved gate system or the scheduling and document any telephone conversations with union representatives or members relating to the gate or scheduling system.

F. <u>Obtain Union Literature</u>. Seek to obtain copies of any literature being distributed by pickets or handbillers. You cannot forcibly seize copies. However, if a copy is refused, seek an explanation and document the response.

G. <u>Find Out What the Union Wants</u>. Seek an explanation from picketers, handbillers, and/or union representatives as to why they are there. Also ask these individuals what it will take to get rid of the pickets or handbillers. Simply put, ask them what they want.

H. <u>Keep Maps</u>. If you have established reserved gates, be certain immediately to draw a map or a diagram of the locations of all parties, the reserved gate, other entrances, picket locations, streets, buildings, etc. Be sure to show distances on the map.

I. <u>Record Your Observations</u>. Be sure to highlight the following areas by asking relevant questions. In taking notes on these subjects, pay particular attention to dates, times, locations, individuals involved, other witnesses, and similar details.

1. <u>Purpose of Pickets</u>. Why are the pickets or handbillers there? Who said so? When?

2. <u>Reserved Gate Notices</u>. In establishing the reserved gate, did you notify all appropriate parties? Who? Do you have a copy of all

Secondary Activity

telegrams? Did you document any related telephone conversations?

3. Special Schedule Notices. If you decided to continue to use (Primary Employer) employees, did you set a specific and clear schedule in advance? Did you notify the union about the schedule? Do you have copies of telegrams? Did you document any related telephone conversations?

4. Reserved Gate Compliance. Are any employers or employees failing to obey the instructions on the reserved gate and other entrances? Are pickets and handbillers confining their activity to the reserved gate?

5. Integrity of Gates. Has the integrity of the reserved gate and neutral gates been maintained? Have no (Primary Employer) employees or suppliers used neutral gates? Can you verify this? How? Be specific. If there has been any "contamination," have you discussed this with the (Primary Employer) or legal counsel? Have you taken corrective action? What? When? Have you kept copies of telegrams and documented all relevant conversations?

6. Special Schedule Compliance. Are you adhering to any specific schedule set for (Primary Employer) employees? Is the union adhering to the schedule by picketing and handbilling only when (Primary Employer) employees are on the worksite?

7. Timing of Picketing. Exactly when were the pickets there? Exactly when were the (Primary Employer) employees there? What

happened at these times? Be specific, using as many names, times, and places as possible.

8. <u>Reason for Failure to Honor Reserved Gate</u>. If picketers are not staying by the reserved gate, why not? Who said so? When?

9. <u>Reason for Failure to Honor Special Schedule</u>. If picketers are not complying with the schedule regarding (<u>Primary Employer</u>) work, why not? According to whom? When?

10. <u>Wording of Pickets</u>. What do the picket signs or handbills say? Are they easily read (legible)? If not, why not? Is the object and reason for the picketing clear to a reader of the signs or handbills? Explain.

11. <u>Union Warnings</u>. Did union representatives or pickets tell you about the picketing beforehand? What did they say? Who? When?

12. <u>Willingness to Honor Reserve Gate</u>. Did union representatives tell you, or do you know from others, that employees will honor all picket lines regardless of reserved gates? Explain this, specifying the identity of all speakers and the time of any relevant conversations.

13. <u>Action Sought by Union</u>. What did the picketers or union representatives tell you would be necessary to stop picketing or handbilling? Explain, specifying the identity of all speakers and the time of relevant conversations.

14. <u>Picketing at Other Locations</u>. Did union representatives tell you where else the union

Secondary Activity

is picketing? Did they explain why? Specify who said what, when, and where it was said.

15. Selective Picketing. Is the union being selective in picketing only "unionized" work sites? Explain. What about other work sites that you have?

16. Offers to Stop Picketing. Did union representatives or picketers offer any agreement that picketing would stop if (Primary Employer) employees were no longer allowed to enter the work site? Specify who said what, when, and where it was said.

17. Picketers' Refusal to Talk. Are picketers refusing to talk with you? Explain.

18. Questioning Business Judgment. Have the picketers, handbillers, or union representatives ever questioned your "business judgment" in using the (Primary Employer) employees or continuing your operation on your own? Specify who said what, to whom it was said, and when and where it was said.

19. Union Responsibility. To whom have you been directed as spokesperson for the union? Has anyone linked control of different actions or the general outcome of the situation to the union, its representatives, or its attorneys? Explain in detail, specifying who said what, as well as to whom, where, and when it was said.

20. Union Threats. Has anyone connected with a union made any kind of threats to any

Responding to Strikes

employees and/or supervisors? What types of threats (physical, union fines, etc)? How did you find out about these threats?

21. Withdrawal of Business. Have any customers withdrawn or threatened to withdraw business? Who? What address and phone number? When? Why? What was attributed to the union? Other unions? Have you suffered any damages as a result? If so, describe in as much detail as possible.

22. Trespassing by Pickets. Have any picketers tried to come on company property at any time? How? What happened? When? Who?

23. Other Witnesses. Has anyone else in the community given you information about what to expect from the union, or anything else related to the dispute? Who? What address and phone number? When? What was said?

This is not an all-inclusive checklist. It raises only major questions. If any other incidents do occur, be certain to document them and verify *exactly* what occurred. Should you have any questions or comments, please do not hesitate to contact _____ (_____) of the (Primary Employer), who will contact the (Primary Employer) counsel for legal advice as necessary.

8
Responding to Jurisdictional Pressures

Section 8(b)(4)(D) of the Act prohibits a labor organization from inducing or encouraging employees to refuse to work, or from restraining or coercing "any person engaged in commerce" when an object of its action is to obtain a work assignment. This type of action is commonly called jurisdictional pressure because the union is asserting its members' jurisdiction over particular types of work. By placing this prohibition in section 8(b)(4), Congress classified jurisdictional pressures as secondary activity. Underlying this classification is the notion that the conflict in such cases is between whatever employee groups claim the work, rather than between a labor organization and an employer.

The construction industry, because of its traditional allocation of tasks to certain crafts and trades, is peculiarly susceptible to jurisdictional action. Other industries, however, must be aware of the potential for jurisdictional disputes, especially when new production methods create new tasks. The decision to assign new work to a particular craft or trade is always a sensitive undertaking, bearing the seeds for jurisdictional disputes.

New assignments may occur throughout the term of a collective bargaining agreement. Jurisdictional disputes and strikes are therefore not confined to the period when a new contract is being negotiated. Planning for jurisdictional strikes must be keyed to the event likely to cause the union's reaction. When a union's objections to a particular assignment remain unresolved at the time bargaining for a new contract commences, jurisdictional claims may be incorporated into the union's negotiating posture.

Responding to Strikes

If the union then strikes to enforce its jurisdictional claim, the employer may want to proceed under section 8(b)(4)(D) to resolve the work assignment issue.

8.1 Procedure upon Filing a Charge under Section 8(b)(4)(D)

An employer subjected to jurisdictional pressure may file a charge with the NLRB, following the same procedure as it would in filing a charge relating to other secondary pressures.[1] The Regional Director's response to a section 8(b)(4)(D) charge will differ from the approach taken to charges arising under the Act's other provisions. The Act's policy with respect to jurisdictional conflicts is to resolve the underlying dispute between the groups of employees claiming the work. Thus, after an employer charges that a union has unlawfully exerted pressure in support of a claim to work, the Regional Director will not issue a complaint against the offending organization. Instead, section 10(k) of the Act provides that, upon the filing of the charge, the NLRB must resolve the dispute by determining which employees should perform the work, unless the parties themselves agree upon a method of voluntary adjustment. If the NLRB should determine the issue under section 10(k), the Regional Director will promptly issue a notice of hearing to that effect.[2] Only after the NLRB awards the work will the Regional Director decide whether to issue an unfair labor practice complaint.[3]

---

1. *See* section 7.2, *supra*, for a description of the mechanics of filing a charge under section 8(b)(4).
2. 29 C.F.R. § 101.33. This regulation requires that the hearing be scheduled for no later than ten days after service on the union of the notice that an unfair labor practice charge has been filed. This short time limit is frequently extended by agreement of the parties.
3. 29 C.F.R. § 101.36.

Jurisdictional Pressures

8.2 Prerequisites to a Determination of the Dispute

The statutory requirement of a hearing to resolve the dispute is straightforward. However, certain conditions must exist before the NLRB will resolve the competing claims.

8.2.1 Reasonable Cause to Believe That Section 8(b)(4)(D) Has Been Violated

Before making a work assignment determination, the NLRB "must be satisfied that there is reasonable cause to believe that Section 8(b)(4)(D) has been violated."[4] The extent to which the union successfully coerces the employer is immaterial to this determination, and the union's threatened action need not be imminent.[5] Nor is it necessary that the threats be made by a union that has not been assigned the work. A labor organization violates the Act when it threatens an employer to force continuation of an existing assignment.[6]

8.2.1.1 The Objective of the Action

It is often hard to identify what is unlawful under section 8(b)(4)(D). An economic strike during contract negotiations that

---

4. *See, e.g.*, IBEW, Local 3 (Telecom Equipment Corp.), 266 N.L.R.B. No. 133, 113 L.R.R.M. 1009 (1983). This standard does not require the NLRB to resolve all conflicts in testimony before proceeding to resolve the dispute. Carpenters, Local 1026 (Intercounty Construction Corp.), 266 N.L.R.B No. 181, 113 L.R.R.M. 1090 (1983).
5. Steelworkers, Local 4454 (Continental Can Co.), 202 N.L.R.B. 652, 653-54, 82 L.R.R.M. 1728 (1973).
6. Lumber Workers, Local 2592 (Louisiana Pacific Corp.), 268 N.L.R.B. No. 10, 114 L.R.R.M. 1235 (1983); International Brotherhood of Painters (Delcon, Inc.), 267 N.L.R.B. No. 179, 114 L.R.R.M. 1167 (1983).

Responding to Strikes

seeks reassignment of work from replacements to striking workers does not violate section 8(b)(4)(D). To hold otherwise would permit employers to "make any strike unlawful by hiring replacements for the strikers."[7] On the other hand, when reassignment of work has been a union demand from the beginning of negotiations, a strike in support of that demand will violate section 8(b)(4)(D).[8]

The NLRB has held that a union does not violate section 8(b)(4)(D) if it pickets solely to obtain reinstatement of employees whom the employer has terminated to reassign their work to another group of employees. In such circumstances, the union has the lawful primary objective of preserving work performed under an existing collective bargaining agreement.[9] Union pressure designed to recover work that the employer has subcontracted to another location, allegedly in breach of a collective bargaining agreement, may also be lawful under section 8(b)(4)(D).[10] The NLRB has strictly limited application of the principles underlying these decisions to the peculiar facts involved in those cases.[11]

---

7. American Wire Weavers' Ass'n (Lindsay Wire Weaving Co.), 120 N.L.R.B. 977, 42 L.R.R.M. 1090, 1092 (1958).
8. UAW (General Motors Corp.), 239 N.L.R.B. 365, 366, 99 L.R.R.M. 1609 (1978); Longshoremen, ILWU, Local 8 (General Ore Co.), 124 N.L.R.B. 626, 44 L.R.R.M. 1445 (1959).
9. Longshoremen, ILA, Local 26 (American Plant Protection, Inc.), 210 N.L.R.B. 574, 86 L.R.R.M. 1151 (1974); Longshoremen, ILA, Local 8 (Waterway Terminals Co.), 185 N.L.R.B. 186, 75 L.R.R.M. 1042 (1970), vacated and remanded, 467 F.2d 1011, 81 L.R.R.M. 2449 (9th Cir. 1972), on remand, 203 N.L.R.B. 861, 83 L.R.R.M. 1232 (1973).
10. Chicago Web Printing Pressmen's Union, Local 7 (Metropolitan Printing Co.), 209 N.L.R.B. 320, 85 L.R.R.M. 1586 (1974).
11. See, e.g., Longshoremen, ILWU (California Cartage Co.), 208 N.L.R.B. 986, 85 L.R.R.M. 1289 (1974), enforced sub nom. Pacific Maritime Ass'n v. NLRB, 515 F.2d 1018, 90 L.R.R.M. 2844 (D.C. Cir. 1975), cert. denied, 424 U.S. 942 (1976); Lumber Workers, Local 2592 (Louisiana-Pacific Corp.), 268 N.L.R.B. No. 10, 114 L.R.R.M. 1235 (1983); Teamsters, Local 680 (Kraft, Inc.), 265 N.L.R.B. No. 117, 112 L.R.R.M. 1197 (1982); Redstone Workers Ass'n (Starks Construction Co.), 241 N.L.R.B. 945, 101 L.R.R.M. 1025 (1979).

The statute prohibits pressure where "*an object thereof is*" to secure a work assignment.[12] A union cannot, then, justify its conduct by pointing to one lawful purpose. It must instead show that it had no unlawful objective. For example, picketing purportedly relating to area wage standards will violate section 8(b)(4)(D) if it also seeks assignment of work.[13] Ostensibly recognitional picketing similarly violates the Act if it has as a companion goal the assignment of disputed work.[14] A work assignment objective violates the Act even if the employer's assignment breaches a collective bargaining agreement. In such a situation, the aggrieved union may lawfully seek arbitration or file a breach of contract suit against the employer.[15] If the union exerts economic pressure, however, the NLRB will resolve the dispute under section 10(k), even if a union grievance under the contract is pending.[16] The NLRB's subsequent deter-

---

12. § 8(b)(4)(D) (emphasis added), 29 U.S.C. § 158(b)(4)(D).
13. Operating Engineers, Local 487 (Epic One Corporation), 267 N.L.R.B. No. 105, 114 L.R.R.M. 1124 (1983); Plumbers, Local 80 (Stone & Webster Engineering Corp.), 267 N.L.R.B. No. 210, 114 L.R.R.M. 1213 (1983); Carpenters, Local 953 (T & P Iron Works), 266 N.L.R.B. No. 111, 113 L.R.R.M. 1004 (1983). *But see* Operating Engineers, Local 925 (Bradshaw Industrial Coatings), 264 N.L.R.B. No. 127, 111 L.R.R.M. 1378 (1982) (no violation of Section 8(b)(4)(D) where picketing related to area standards and did not seek work assignment).
14. Carpenters, Local 1026 (Intercounty Construction Corp.), 266 N.L.R.B. No. 181, 113 L.R.R.M. 1090 (1983). *But see* UFCW, Local 122 (FedMart Stores, Inc.), 262 N.L.R.B. 817, 818, 110 L.R.R.M. 1383 (1982) (demand for recognition as a bargaining representative for persons performing work does not create jurisdictional dispute).
15. Carey v. Westinghouse Electric Corp., 375 U.S. 261, 55 L.R.R.M. 2042 (1964); Operating Engineers, Local 139 v. Carl A. Morse, Inc., 387 F. Supp. 153, 160, 88 L.R.R.M. 2145 (E.D. Wis. 1974), *aff'd*, 529 F.2d 574, 91 L.R.R.M. 2415 (7th Cir. 1976); *see* Machinists, Local 850 v. T.I.M.E.—DC, Inc., 705 F.2d 1275, 113 L.R.R.M. 2677 (10th Cir. 1983) (ordering tripartite arbitration of union's work assignment claim).
16. *See* International Brotherhood of Painters (Delcon, Inc.), 267 N.L.R.B. No. 179, 114 L.R.R.M. 1167 (1983); Carpenters, Local 953 (T & P Iron Works), 266 N.L.R.B. No. 111, 113 L.R.R.M. 1004 (1983) (dispute heard by Board despite union's pursuit of grievance under the contract); *see also*

mination of the dispute will preempt any finding by an arbitrator construing the contract.[17]

8.2.1.2 The Employer Subject to Pressure

A union violates section 8(b)(4)(D) if it pressures an employer to secure work being performed by employees of another entity. Thus, the employer who has assigned the disputed work need not be subjected to direct pressure for a jurisdictional dispute to exist.[18] Such a situation arises if, for example, a union pressures an employer to obtain work that the employer has subcontracted to another business that employs members of another union. This type of pressure may also violate the Act's prohibition against secondary boycotts by coercing the pressured employer to cease doing business with the subcontractor.[19]

8.2.1.3 The Existence of Union Pressure

Most case law on the NLRB's "reasonable cause" requirement focuses on the union's objective. Sometimes, however, the very existence of union pressure is disputed. Although a labor organization's threats are often obvious, as when it threatens to picket

---

IATSE, Local 666 (Post-Newsweek Stations), 227 N.L.R.B. 810, 812, 95 L.R.R.M. 1023 (1977) (court-ordered tripartite arbitration will not preclude Board from conducting Section 10(k) hearing).

17. U.A.W. v. Rockwell International Corp., 619 F.2d 580, 104 L.R.R.M. 2050 (6th Cir. 1980).
18. Longshoremen, ILA (Rukert Terminals Corp.), 266 N.L.R.B. No. 152, 113 L.R.R.M. 1041 (1983); Redstone Workers Association (Starks Constr. Co.), 241 N.L.R.B. 945, 946, 101 L.R.R.M. 1025 (1979); *see also* Teamsters, Local 222 (Emery Mining Corp.), 262 N.L.R.B. 1064, 1067, 110 L.R.R.M. 1436 (1982).
19. NLRB v. Operating Engineers, Local 825 (Burns & Roe, Inc.), 400 U.S. 297, 76 L.R.R.M. 2129 (1971).

Jurisdictional Pressures

or to lead its employees off a job,[20] coercion of a more subtle nature also meets the threshold requirement of reasonable cause.[21] The NLRB has defined

the term "coercion" to mean "nonjudicial acts of a compelling or restraining nature, applied by way of concerted self-help consisting of a strike, picketing, or *other economic retaliation or pressure in a background of a labor dispute.*"[22]

A union's cancellation of a contract to pressure an employer to assign work has thus been deemed unlawful coercion,[23] as have bad faith grievances seeking money damages for an allegedly wrongful assignment[24] and concerted refusals to work overtime.[25]

8.2.2 The Existence of Competing Claims

The NLRB will not issue a determination if only one group of employees claims the work. In such cases, there is no dispute to be resolved under section 10(k).[26] Because only labor organiza-

---

20. *See, e.g.,* Cincinnati Mailers Union No. 17 (Rosenthal & Co.), 265 N.L.R.B. No. 125, 112 L.R.R.M. 1189 (1982).
21. *See* Plumbers District Council No. 16 (Tridair Industries, Inc.), 198 N.L.R.B. 1240, 1242, 81 L.R.R.M. 1120 (1972) (veiled threats to put a stop to contested assignment sufficient to give the NLRB reasonable cause).
22. Sheet Metal Workers International Association (Young Plumbing & Supply), 209 N.L.R.B. 1177, 1179, 86 L.R.R.M. 1052 (1974) (emphasis in original).
23. *Id.*
24. Teamsters, Local 85 (Pacific Maritime Association), 224 N.L.R.B. 801, 807, 93 L.R.R.M. 1405 (1976).
25. Hanford Atomic Metal Trades Council (Atlantic Richfield Hanford Co.), 227 N.L.R.B. 985, 987, 95 L.R.R.M. 1007 (1977).
26. Teamsters, Local 839 (Shurtleff & Andrews Constructors), 249 N.L.R.B. 176, 177, 104 L.R.R.M. 1103 (1980), *aff'd sub nom.* Foley-Wismer & Becker v. NLRB, 695 F.2d 424, 112 L.R.R.M. 2417 (9th Cir. 1982).

Responding to Strikes

tions or their agents can violate section 8(b)(4)(D), one set of claimants will always be union-represented. The other claimants to the work need not be represented by a union.[27] The "competing claim" requirement may also be satisfied by the demand of individual union members, even if their union acquiesces in other employees' claim.[28]

8.2.2.1 Union Disclaimers of the Work

To avoid a determination under section 10(k), unions sometimes deny the existence of a competing claim by disclaiming interest in the work. This tactic frequently causes dismissal of both the section 10(k) hearing and the underlying section 8(b)(4)(D) charge. The timing of the disclaimer is not necessarily determinative. The NLRB has terminated its proceedings when a disclaimer was made for the first time at the section 10(k) hearing,[29] or even after the hearing's close.[30]

8.2.2.2 Determinations Despite Disclaimers

In certain circumstances the NLRB will determine the dispute even when one union disclaims the work. If a union has exerted

---

27. Operating Engineers, Local 487 (Epic One Corporation), 267 N.L.R.B. No. 105, 114 L.R.R.M. 1124 (1983); Carpenters, Local 1026 (Intercounty Construction Corp.), 266 N.L.R.B. No. 181, 113 L.R.R.M. 1090 (1983).
28. Elevator Constructors, Local 1 (Elevator Industries Assn.), 229 N.L.R.B. 1200, 1202, 96 L.R.R.M. 1332 (1977); Bricklayers, Local 2 (Decora, Inc.), 152 N.L.R.B. 278, 59 L.R.R.M. 1065 (1965).
29. Service Employees, Local 372 (Pepper Construction Co.), 262 N.L.R.B. 815, 816, 110 L.R.R.M. 1362 (1982). *But see* Plumbers, Local 703 (Airco, Inc.), 261 N.L.R.B. 1122, 1124, 110 L.R.R.M. 1215 (1982) (discounting disclaimer made at close of hearing).
30. Plumbers, Local 262, Pipefitters (Dyad Construction, Inc.), 252 N.L.R.B. 48, 105 L.R.R.M. 1251 (1980). *But see* Carpenters, Local 102 (Frederick

Jurisdictional Pressures

pressure for the work assignment in the past, and there is a likelihood that disputes will recur, for example, the NLRB will proceed with the section 10(k) hearing despite a disclaimer.[31] Similarly, if the NLRB finds that the disclaimer is a subterfuge to avoid determination on the merits,[32] or the disclaiming union's members continue to claim the work,[33] or the union conditions the disclaimer upon the employer's continued assignment of the work to the disclaiming union,[34] the NLRB will proceed. However, the NLRB will sometimes honor disclaimers even if the union declines to abandon similar work at other job sites.[35] More frequently a union's refusal to disclaim its intention to seek the work in the future will convince the NLRB that the disclaimer is a ruse to avoid the section 10(k) determination.[36]

An employer who wants to resolve the dispute should not give up just because the union disclaims the work. This is especially true if there is evidence that the disclaimer is not genuine. Indeed, even after the NLRB quashes its section 10(k) hearing notice, it will determine the dispute if a disclaiming union subse-

---

Meiswinkel, Inc.), 260 N.L.R.B. 972, 975, 109 L.R.R.M. 1245 (1982) (discounting disclaimer made after close of hearing).

31. IBEW, Local 701 (Argonne National Laboratory), 255 N.L.R.B. 1157, 1160, 107 L.R.R.M. 1065 (1981); Laborers, Local 935 (Campbell Construction Co.), 194 N.L.R.B. 367, 368, 78 L.R.R.M. 1619 (1972).
32. Laborers, Local 100 (Jo Ba Construction Co.), 267 N.L.R.B. No. 192, 114 L.R.R.M. 1133 (1983); Plumbers, Local 703 (Airco, Inc.), 261 N.L.R.B. 1122, 1124, 110 L.R.R.M. 1215 (1982).
33. Boilermakers, Local 193 (Capital Boiler Works, Inc.), 263 N.L.R.B. 1084, 1085, 111 L.R.R.M. 1234 (1982). But see Teamsters, Local 85 (United California Express & Storage Co.), 236 N.L.R.B. 157, 158, 98 L.R.R.M. 1186 (1978).
34. Pulp & Paper Workers, Local 194 (Georgia-Pacific Corp.), 267 N.L.R.B. No. 13, 114 L.R.R.M. 1002 (1983).
35. Laborers, Local 66 (Georgia-Pacific Corp.), 209 N.L.R.B. 611, 612, 85 L.R.R.M. 1398 (1974).
36. See, e.g., Operating Engineers, Local 77 (C.J. Coakley Co.), 257 N.L.R.B. 436, 439, 107 L.R.R.M. 1559 (1981).

quently engages in conduct inconsistent with its representations.[37]

8.2.3 Absence of Agreed-upon Mechanism for Settlement

Section 10(k) of the Act provides that the NLRB's obligation to "hear and determine the dispute" is eliminated if

> within ten days after notice that such charge [under section 8(b)(4)(D)] has been filed, the parties to such dispute submit to the NLRB satisfactory evidence that they have adjusted, or agreed upon methods for the voluntary adjustment of, the dispute.

The NLRB thus will not resolve a dispute when all parties are bound by a private settlement mechanism. The ten-day limitation, however, has little practical effect. When one party believes that a voluntary means for resolving the dispute exists, it will move to quash the hearing notice.[38] The ruling on that motion may be reserved for the NLRB itself upon consideration of the section 10(k) hearing transcript. The section 10(k) hearing will then proceed pending disposition of the motion.

8.2.3.1 Parties to the Mechanism

To divest the NLRB of its authority to resolve the dispute, the employer and all claimants to the work must be bound to the

---

37. Operating Engineers, Local 825 (Cruz Contractors, Inc.), 239 N.L.R.B. 490, 491, 99 L.R.R.M. 1646 (1978).
38. If the NLRB quashes a notice of hearing, for whatever reason, most courts have held that the employer cannot appeal that decision. Shell Chemical Co. v. NLRB, 495 F.2d 1116, 86 L.R.R.M. 2708 (5th Cir. 1974), *cert. denied*, 421 U.S. 963 (1975); Trane Co. v. NLRB, 68 L.R.R.M. 3024 (6th Cir. 1968); Rafel & Co. v. IBEW, Local 9, 47 L.R.R.M. 2897 (7th Cir.), *cert. denied*, 366 U.S. 948 (1961); Manhattan Constr. Co. v. NLRB, 198

Jurisdictional Pressures

voluntary method for adjustment.[39] Moreover, the employer actually making the assignment must be bound. It is not enough if, for example, the general contractor on a construction site where the dispute arises is party to a voluntary mechanism if the affected employer is a subcontractor.[40]

8.2.3.2 Differing Dispute Procedures for Some Parties

The NLRB will determine the dispute unless all parties are bound to the *identical* voluntary procedure. This requirement is not met if the employer and two unions are, through two different contracts, bound to substantially the same procedures.[41] If one party withdraws from the voluntary mechanism before the dispute arises (and not simply because it anticipated the dispute), the NLRB will proceed with its determination.[42] When no party has withdrawn, however, the NLRB will defer to the private procedure even if a union cannot prevail because of its failure to comply with the dispute resolution body's regulations.[43]

F.2d 320, 30 L.R.R.M. 2464 (10th Cir. 1952). *But see* Foley-Wismer & Becker v. NLRB, 682 F.2d 770, 110 L.R.R.M. 3073 (9th Cir.), *supp. op.*, 695 F.2d 424, 112 L.R.R.M. 2417 (9th Cir. 1982).

39. NLRB v. Plasterers, Local 79, 404 U.S. 116, 78 L.R.R.M. 2897 (1971); NLRB v. Plumbers, Local 41 (Ashton Co.), 704 F.2d 1164, 1166, 113 L.R.R.M. 3120 (9th Cir. 1983). The NLRB will consider a party bound to a mechanism if it submits the dispute for voluntary resolution, even if no document formally requires the submission. Sheet Metal Workers, Local 292 (Gallagher-Kaiser Corp.), 264 N.L.R.B. No. 62, 111 L.R.R.M. 1503, 1508 (1982).
40. Iron Workers, Local 21 (Lueder Constr. Co.), 233 N.L.R.B. 1139, 1140, 97 L.R.R.M. 1042 (1977); Carpenters, Local 1622 (O. R. Carst), 139 N.L.R.B. 591, 51 L.R.R.M. 1379 (1962).
41. Iron Workers, Local 86 (Kulama Erectors), 264 N.L.R.B. No. 8, 111 L.R.R.M. 1398 (1982).
42. Carpenters, Local 1906 (Modern Erection Service, Inc.), 249 N.L.R.B. 234, 235-36, 104 L.R.R.M. 1110 (1980).
43. Carpenters District Council (Godwin Bevers Co.), 205 N.L.R.B. 155, 156, 83 L.R.R.M. 1600 (1973).

Responding to Strikes

8.2.3.3 Breakdown of the Voluntary Mechanism

If the voluntary settlement method contemplated by the parties no longer exists, as when an industry panel created to deal with jurisdictional disputes disbands, the NLRB will determine the dispute.[44] The NLRB has also resolved jurisdictional questions when the body designated by all parties flatly refuses to hear the dispute.[45] But the NLRB will not guess as to whether the private body will decline to consider the dispute. Thus, it will not conduct a section 10(k) hearing even if the work has been completed and the voluntary mechanism will treat the dispute as moot.[46] In such a situation, the parties must first submit the question to the voluntary procedure. If no resolution occurs because of mootness, the NLRB may then take jurisdiction and award the work.[47]

8.2.3.4 Procedure after NLRB Deferral to Voluntary Mechanism

When the NLRB defers to a voluntary adjustment mechanism, it will retain jurisdiction over the unfair labor practice charge. If the voluntary procedure fails to settle the dispute, the NLRB may dispose of the unfair labor practice charge without conducting a section 10(k) hearing.[48]

---

44. Ironworkers, Local 380 (Stobeck Masonry, Inc.), 267 N.L.R.B. No. 61, 114 L.R.R.M. 1038 (1983); Asbestos Workers, Local 66 (API, Inc.), 267 N.L.R.B. No. 16, 114 L.R.R.M. 1014 (1983).
45. Ironworkers, Local 383 (J. P. Cullen & Son Constr. Co.), 235 N.L.R.B. 463, 465, 97 L.R.R.M. 1547 (1978).
46. Operating Engineers, Local 17 (Sullivan and Humes), 254 N.L.R.B. 71, 73, 106 L.R.R.M. 1094 (1981).
47. Sheet Metal Workers, Local 418 (Young Plumbing and Supply), 224 N.L.R.B. 993, 996, 92 L.R.R.M. 1497 (1976). This is because the NLRB does not necessarily regard the case as moot simply because the tasks in question have been completed. See section 8.3.2, *infra*.
48. 29 C.F.R. § 102.93.

Jurisdictional Pressures

8.3 The NLRB's Determination of Jurisdictional Disputes

8.3.1 Standards Used to Resolve Jurisdictional Disputes

The Supreme Court has required the NLRB to determine jurisdictional disputes on their merits rather than rubber-stamp employer decisions.[49] The Court's mandate is premised on the notion that the real jurisdictional dispute is between the competing employee groups, with the employer as little more than an innocent bystander.[50] This conflicts with industrial realities, for an employer generally assigns work based upon cost considerations and a perception of the relative ability of the competing trades to perform the disputed functions efficiently. Because of this, the NLRB placed considerable emphasis on employer preference when it formulated its standards for resolving jurisdictional disputes:

> The Board will consider all relevant factors in determining who is entitled to the work in dispute, *e.g.*, the skills and work involved, certifications by the Board, company and industry practice, agreements between unions and between employers and unions, awards of arbitrators, joint boards and the AFL-CIO in the same or related cases, the assignment made by the employer, and the efficient operation of the employer's business. This list of factors is not meant to be exclusive, but is by way of illustration.[51]

---

49. NLRB v. Radio & Television Broadcast Engineers (Columbia Broadcasting System), 364 U.S. 573, 47 L.R.R.M. 2332 (1961).
50. 364 U.S. at 579.
51. International Ass'n of Machinists (J. A. Jones Constr. Co.), 135 N.L.R.B. 1402, 49 L.R.R.M. 1684, 1688 (1962).

Responding to Strikes

Although criticized,[52] these standards are still used by the NLRB. As a practical matter, their application generally results in affirmation of the employer's assignment. Indeed, the NLRB has found that, when all other factors are equal, the employer's preference will be determinative.[53]

The NLRB denies, of course, that it improperly defers to employer preferences.[54] To some degree, results bear out its claim of independent decision-making. The employer's assignment has not been honored when it contradicted its own past practice,[55] when the interested international unions agreed upon a different assignment,[56] or when a well-defined area practice contradicted the employer's choice.[57] An employer having a definite preference for work assignment should therefore vigorously advocate its case. Its failure to do so may prompt the NLRB to accord its wishes little weight.[58]

---

52. *See, e.g.,* NLRB v. Teamsters, Local 584, 535 F.2d 205, 207, 92 L.R.R.M. 2486 (2d Cir. 1976).
53. Laborers, Local 334 (Dynamic Constr. Co.), 236 N.L.R.B. 1131, 1134, 98 L.R.R.M. 1366 (1978).
54. Carpenters, Local 1026 (Intercounty Constr. Corp.), 266 N.L.R.B. No. 181, 113 L.R.R.M. 1090 (1983) (rejecting union argument that § 10(k) hearing procedure is a sham).
55. Longshoremen, ILWU, Local 50 (Brady-Hamilton Stevedore Co.), 223 N.L.R.B. 1034, 1036, 92 L.R.R.M. 1040 (1976); Plumbers, Local 412 (Zia Co.), 168 N.L.R.B. 494, 495, 66 L.R.R.M. 1326 (1967).
56. Lathers, Local 68 (Acoustics & Specialties, Inc.), 142 N.L.R.B. 1073, 53 L.R.R.M. 1181 (1963); *see also* Teamsters Local 150 (United Grocers, Ltd.), 225 N.L.R.B. 1183, 1186, 93 L.R.R.M. 1064 (1976).
57. Ironworkers, Local 380 (Stobeck Masonry Inc.), 267 N.L.R.B. No. 61, 114 L.R.R.M. 1038 (1983). *But see* Plasterers, Local 233 (Strescon Indus., Inc.), 267 N.L.R.B. No. 118, 114 L.R.R.M. 1096 (1983) (when area practice is contradicted by considerations of efficiency, preference, past practice, and collective bargaining agreements, it will not be determinative); Painters, Local 48 (Manganaro Corp.), 267 N.L.R.B. No. 191, 114 L.R.R.M. 1129 (1983) (area practice of diminished significance when employer comes from another jurisdiction and uses its own employees to perform disputed work).
58. Ironworkers, Local 380 (Stobeck Masonry, Inc.), 267 N.L.R.B. No. 61, 114 L.R.R.M. 1038, n.8 (1983) (employer left hearing early and filed no brief).

Jurisdictional Pressures

8.3.2 The Breadth of the NLRB's Determination

Because the NLRB generally will not issue its decision until several months after the section 10(k) hearing, disputed work is often completed prior to the determination. Even when the disputed tasks have been completed, however, the NLRB will award the work so long as "there is evidence of similar disputes between the parties in the past, or there is nothing to indicate that such disputes will not arise in the future."[59]

An NLRB award of the work typically applies only to the particular job or facility in question, even if work there has been completed. The NLRB will extend the determination's scope to other locations only if it finds that the charged union will likely exert unlawful pressure again.[60] If the contesting unions have disputed the work on a number of occasions, the NLRB will make a broad award.[61] Such an order will typically apply throughout the geographical jurisdiction of the union whose claim to the work has been rejected[62] or to the area where the competing unions' geographical jurisdictions overlap.[63]

Even if limited in scope, the NLRB's award has significant precedential value and lays the groundwork for future broad determinations in the event similar disputes arise. An employer is

---

59. IBEW, Local 3 (Northern Telecom, Inc.), 262 N.L.R.B. 1453, 1455, 110 L.R.R.M. 1484 (1982).
60. IBEW, Local 3 (Telecom Equipment Corp.), 266 N.L.R.B. No. 133, 113 L.R.R.M. 1009 (1983).
61. *See* Ironworkers, Local 426 (Associated Cement Contractors of Michigan), 267 N.L.R.B. No. 108, 114 L.R.R.M. 1045 (1983); IBEW, Local 3 (Madison Square Garden Center), 198 N.L.R.B. 380, 383, 80 L.R.R.M. 1659 (1972). *But see* Iron Workers, Local 3 (Spancrete Northeast, Inc.), 267 N.L.R.B. No. 152, 114 L.R.R.M. 1082 (1983) (denying broad order despite repeated disputes).
62. Ironworkers, Local 426 (Associated Cement Contractors of Michigan), 267 N.L.R.B. No. 108, 114 L.R.R.M. 1045 (1983).
63. Carpenters District Council (Northern California Drywall Ass'n), 265 N.L.R.B. No. 81, 112 L.R.R.M. 1298 (1982); IBEW, Local 3 (Northern Telecom, Inc.), 262 N.L.R.B. 1453, 1457, 110 L.R.R.M. 1484 (1982).

Responding to Strikes

therefore generally well-advised to pursue a section 10(k) hearing even if it is likely to complete the work before the NLRB issues its determination.

8.4 Procedure after Determination of the Dispute

The Regional Director will dismiss the unfair labor practice charge if the parties comply with the NLRB's determination.[64] Any evidence of a failure to comply, such as a union's refusal to give assurance of compliance to the Regional Director, will prompt the Regional Director to pursue the section 8(b)(4)(D) charge.[65] If the pressuring union prevails at the section 10(k) hearing (or in a private proceeding to which the NLRB has deferred), however, and the employer fails to respect the decision, the union may continue to pressure the employer without violating the Act.[66]

8.5 Other Relief for Violation of Section 8(b)(4)(D)

8.5.1 Injunctive Relief

The NLRB's Regional Director may seek a federal court injunction against coercive activity in support of a jurisdictional

---

64. Section 10(i) of the Act, 29 U.S.C. § 160(i); N.L.R.B. Rules & Regs., 29 C.F.R. § 102.91.
65. *See* Longshoremen, ILA, Locals 1413-1465 (Bridge Terminal, Inc.), 254 N.L.R.B. 903, 905, 106 L.R.R.M. 1206 (1981); Iron Workers, Local 595 (Bechtel Corp.), 112 N.L.R.B. 812, 36 L.R.R.M. 1105 (1955); N.L.R.B. Statements of Procedure, 29 C.F.R. § 101.36.
66. Brady-Hamilton Stevedore Co., 198 N.L.R.B. 147, 149, 80 L.R.R.M. 1611 (1972), *petition for review denied sub nom.* Operating Engineers v. NLRB, 504 F.2d 1222, 87 L.R.R.M. 2544 (9th Cir. 1974), *cert. denied*, 420 U.S. 973 (1975); *see also* 29 C.F.R. §§ 101.33, 101.36, 102.93.

Jurisdictional Pressures

claim.[67] The Regional Director has considerable discretion in determining whether to request an injunction. If the region does seek injunctive relief, the case has priority over all other cases in the region except cases involving claims of secondary activity.[68]

If an injunction is entered, it will prohibit the union from applying pressure in violation of section 8(b)(4)(D). A court cannot, however, order that a particular union's members be awarded the work pending the NLRB's section 10(k) adjudication.[69]

When a jurisdictional work stoppage violates a contract and the contract obliges the parties to arbitrate the dispute, the employer may be able to obtain injunctive relief on its own under *Boys Markets*, aside from pursuing its remedies under sections 8(b)(4)(D) and 10(k).[70] In such a situation, the court would likely order the parties to submit the jurisdictional dispute to an arbitrator for decision under the contract. This may result in a more rapid determination than the NLRB could provide. However, it is often difficult to bring all interested parties before the arbitrator, as the employer's contracts with the contesting unions may specify different methods of resolving the dispute. Construction employers may be able to negotiate project agreements that create a dispute resolution mechanism binding on all affected unions. When this is not possible, a resolution by the NLRB, which will bind all competing unions, may be preferable to piecemeal arbitration.

---

67. Section 10(l) of the Act, 29 U.S.C. § 100(1); Hendrix v. Operating Engineers, Local 571, 592 F.2d 437, 100 L.R.R.M. 2704 (8th Cir. 1979).
68. 29 C.F.R. § 101.32.
69. Kaynard v. Teamsters, Local 282, 576 F.2d 471, 479, 98 L.R.R.M. 2569 (2d Cir. 1978).
70. *See* William E. Arnold Co. v. Carpenters, 417 U.S. 12, 86 L.R.R.M. 2212 (1974); ACMAT Corp. v. Operating Engineers, Local 478, 442 F. Supp. 772, 774, n.2, 97 L.R.R.M. 2233 (D. Conn. 1977). *But see* Teamsters, Local 215 v. Industrial Contractors, Inc., 107 L.R.R.M. 2167, 2169 (S.D. Ind. 1979) (suggesting that NLRB has exclusive jurisdiction over jurisdic-

8.5.2 Ability to Recover Damages

Section 303 of the Labor-Management Relations Act permits an employer to recover damages caused by violations of section 8(b)(4) of the Act, including work stoppages in support of jurisdictional claims. The rules governing such suits, including the damages recoverable, are identical to those applicable to section 303 suits arising out of other subsections of section 8(b)(4).[71] The nature of jurisdictional disputes and the NLRB's method of resolving them, however, raise some unique issues.

Because the violation of section 8(b)(4) occurs upon application of the pressure prompting the section 10(k) determination, compliance with the NLRB's subsequent award of the work does not absolve a union of section 303 liability.[72] Nor will a disclaimer of the work by the union necessarily preclude the employer from seeking damages, even if the NLRB fails to issue a section 10(k) determination as a result.[73] But courts have held that a union's entitlement to the work for which it applied the pressure *is* a defense to a section 303 action.[74] The damage remedy under section 303 thus may depend upon the employer's success in having its assignment upheld.

---

tional disputes once strike action begins), *aff'd*, 636 F.2d 1223, 107 L.R.R.M. 2202 (7th Cir. 1980), *cert. denied*, 451 U.S. 970 (1981). Section 5.3.2, *supra*, discusses *Boys Markets* injunctions in greater detail.
71. Section 7.4, *supra*, discusses section 303 suits in greater detail.
72. Harnischfeger Corp. v. Sheet Metal Workers, 436 F.2d 351, 354, 76 L.R.R.M. 2268 (6th Cir. 1970).
73. SECO, Inc. v. Laborers, Local 135, 494 F. Supp. 168, 170 (E.D. Pa. 1980).
74. ACMAT Corp. v. Operating Engineers, Local 478, 442 F. Supp. 772, 781-2, 97 L.R.R.M. 2233, 2240 (D. Conn. 1977); Bechtel Corp. v. Laborers, Local 215, 405 F. Supp. 370, 379, 90 L.R.R.M. 3180 (M.D. Pa. 1975), *aff'd in part, rev'd in part*, 544 F.2d 1207, 93 L.R.R.M. 2860 (3d Cir. 1976).

Part III: Post-Strike Planning and Considerations

Introduction

As the end of a strike approaches, an employer should focus its attention on post-strike issues that may arise. Matters that employers often should consider include reinstatement of strikers, amnesty for strikers involved in misconduct, the fate of striker replacements, post-strike administration of employee benefits, and the post-strike relationship with the employees and the union.

Post-strike considerations are an integral but often overlooked part of the strike planning process. The NLRA restricts an employer's freedom to structure post-strike operations. For example, the employer has specific obligations regarding reinstatement of strikers. The Act's prohibition against discriminatory treatment of strikers also continues after the strike and reaches into many aspects of employment, including employee benefits, shift assignments, and discipline. Employers who know their post-strike rights, obligations, and alternatives can reduce the risk of committing unfair labor practices yet preserve flexibility and control over the post-strike transition. Issues such as striker reinstatement, amnesty, and benefits are sometimes resolved by means of a strike settlement agreement or a new collective bargaining agreement. A knowledgeable employer may improve its bargaining position in a settlement by thorough advance planning.

9
Striker Reinstatement

The most significant post-strike issue facing an employer is striker reinstatement. Over the course of a strike, the employer may have hired temporary or permanent replacements, eliminated or restructured particular positions, or subcontracted work to a third party. In some instances, there may be insufficient work to justify recalling all striking employees even if they have not been replaced. By the strike's end, an employer will have employees in some or all of the following categories: (1) employees who worked throughout the strike; (2) employees who initially struck but returned to work before the strike was over; (3) employees temporarily hired for the strike's duration; (4) employees hired during the strike on a permanent basis; (5) and employees who remained off the job for the entire period of the strike. The issues surrounding reinstatement affect all five groups.

The decisions by the NLRB and the federal courts involving reinstatement issues often focus on narrow legal issues and specific fact patterns. The approaches taken by both the courts and the NLRB can and do change over time. The NLRB, now dominated by Reagan appointees, may be particularly inclined to reverse prior Board decisions. Consequently, any employer confronting reinstatement issues should review recent NLRB decisions to detect new developments and analyses that may be contrary to those described here.

Post-Strike Planning

9.1 Strikers' Status as Employees

Strikers retain their status as employees throughout the strike and cannot be discharged for striking so long as their strike activity is protected by the NLRA (the Act).[1] An employer cannot lawfully discharge an employee solely for participating in either an economic or an unfair labor practice strike[2] unless the right to strike has clearly been waived in the collective bargaining agreement between the parties.[3] The discussion of reinstatement focuses on two types of strikes: unfair labor practice strikes and economic strikes. Although both types are generally considered protected concerted activity,[4] the employees' reinstatement rights vary according to the type of strike.

9.2 Right to Reinstatement

Unfair labor practice charges involving reinstatement issues generally fall under two statutory provisions: section 8(a)(1) and

---

1. 29 U.S.C. § 152(3). Section 3 provides:

    The term "employee" shall include any employee, and shall not be limited to the employees of a particular employer, unless this subchapter explicitly states otherwise, and shall include any individual whose work has ceased as a consequence of, or in connection with, any current labor dispute or because of any unfair labor practice, and who has not obtained any other regular and substantially equivalent employment . . . .

2. NLRB v. International Van Lines, 409 U.S. 48, 81 L.R.R.M. 2595 (1972); Mastro Plastics v. NLRB, 350 U.S. 270, 37 L.R.R.M. 2587 (1956). If sympathy strikers are engaged in protected activity, they have the same rights as economic strikers to reinstatement. See ch. 5, *supra*, for an extensive discussion of sympathy strikes.
3. See ch. 5, *supra*, for an extensive discussion of no-strike clauses.
4. See ch. 5 *supra*.

section 8(a)(3).[5] Among other things, section 8(a)(1) makes it an unfair labor practice for employers to stop employees from engaging in concerted activity such as strikes or interfere with the employees' right to strike. The relevant portions of section 8(a)(3) make it an unfair labor practice for an employer to discriminate in employment with the purpose of discouraging union membership. Unfair labor practice charges in reinstatement cases often allege violations of both provisions.

Because strikers continue to be employees during the strike, they ordinarily have a right to be reinstated and return to work once the strike has ended.[6] An employer's ignorance of its obligation to reinstate strikers is not a defense to an unfair labor practice charge.[7] The extent of the reinstatement right depends on whether the employees are unfair labor practice strikers or economic strikers. Therefore, the type of strike has significant poststrike implications for the employer.

---

5. Sections 8(a)(1) and 8(a)(3) provide in relevant part:

   (a) It shall be an unfair labor practice for an employer—

   (1) to interfere with, restrain, or coerce employees in the exercise of the rights guaranteed in section 157 of this title.

   . . . .

   (3) by discrimination in regard to hire or tenure of employment or any term or condition of employment to encourage or discourage membership in any labor organization . . .

   29 U.S.C. § 158(a)(1) and (3).
6. NLRB v. Fleetwood Trailer Co., Inc., 389 U.S. 375, 66 L.R.R.M. 2737 (1967). Strikers who have lost their employee status may, under some circumstances, be reinstated by the NLRB. Woodlawn Hospital v. NLRB, 596 F.2d 1330, 102 L.R.R.M. 1326 (7th Cir. 1979); NLRB v. Thayer Co., 213 F.2d 748, 34 L.R.R.M. 2250 (1st Cir.), *cert. denied*, 348 U.S. 883, 35 L.R.R.M. 2100 (1954).
7. Carbonex Coal Co., 262 N.L.R.B. 1306, 111 L.R.R.M. 1147 (1982).

9.2.1 Unfair Labor Practice and Economic Strikes Distinguished

A work stoppage is considered an unfair labor practice strike when employees have struck in protest of employer conduct that is an unfair labor practice or when a strike is prolonged or aggravated because of such conduct.[8] An economic strike is a strike in support of employee demands for better wages, hours, or working conditions, or for any reason other than to protest an unfair labor practice of the employer.[9] The classification of a strike as either economic or unfair labor practice is ultimately decided by the NLRB and the courts.

An economic strike can be converted into an unfair labor practice strike if the employer commits an unfair labor practice that prolongs or aggravates what is otherwise an economic strike.[10] Merely committing an unfair labor practice does not necessarily convert an economic strike into an unfair labor practice strike.[11] The unfair labor practice must also cause the strike to last longer than it otherwise would have lasted. It is not necessary, however, that the employer's unfair labor practice be the predominant reason for the employees continuing to strike. It is sufficient if the union's decision to continue the strike is made *in part* because of the employer's unfair labor practices.[12]

---

8. NLRB v. Mackay Radio & Telephone Co., 304 U.S. 333, 2 L.R.R.M. 610 (1938); Note, *The Unfair Labor Practice Strike: A Critique and Proposal for Change*, 46 N.Y.U. L. Rev. 988, 989 (1971).
9. C. Morris, The Developing Labor Law, 1007 (2d ed. 1983).
10. American Cyanamid Co. v. NLRB, 592 F.2d 356, 100 L.R.R.M. 2640 (7th Cir. 1979).
11. Road Sprinkler Fitters Local Union No. 669 v. NLRB (John Cuneo, Inc.), 681 F.2d 11, 110 L.R.R.M. 2845 (D.C. Cir. 1982), *cert. denied sub nom.*, John Cuneo, Inc. v. NLRB, 112 L.R.R.M. 2500 (1983).
12. Soule Glass & Glazing Co. v. NLRB, 652 F.2d 1055, 107 L.R.R.M. 2781 (1st Cir. 1981); NLRB v. Moore Business Forms, Inc., 574 F.2d 835, 98 L.R.R.M. 2773 (5th Cir. 1978).

Striker Reinstatement

Although the NLRB's General Counsel bears the burden of proving that the unfair labor practice did prolong the strike, the degree of proof required by the NLRB has varied. In some cases, the NLRB has examined all of the facts to ascertain whether the strike was actually prolonged as a result of the employer's unfair labor practice, instead of presuming that the employer's conduct lengthened the strike.[13] For example, the NLRB has held that if the strikers were unaware of the conduct,[14] if the union made it clear that the strike would continue until the economic demands were met,[15] or if no other direct link between the continuing strike and the employer's unfair labor practice was shown,[16] an economic strike has not converted into an unfair labor practice strike.

In other cases, the NLRB has decided that an economic strike was converted into an unfair labor practice strike once it found that the employer had committed an unfair labor practice.[17] The NLRB has applied this "conversion per se" doctrine most often in those cases where the employer has committed what the NLRB considers to be serious unfair labor practices, such as refusals to bargain[18] or encouraging formation of an employer-dominated union.[19]

---

13. Latrobe Steel Co. v. NLRB, 630 F.2d 171, 105 L.R.R.M. 2393 (3d Cir. 1980), *cert. denied*, 454 U.S. 821, 108 L.R.R.M. 2558 (1981); Burlington Homes, Inc., 246 N.L.R.B. 1029, 103 L.R.R.M. 1116 (1979); Anchor Rome Mills, Inc., 86 N.L.R.B. 1120, 25 L.R.R.M. 1027 (1949).
14. Burlington Homes, Inc., note 13 *supra*.
15. Anchor Rome Mills, Inc., note 13 *supra*.
16. Latrobe Steel Co. v. NLRB, note 13 *supra*.
17. Stewart, *Conversion of Strikes: Economic to Unfair Labor Practice*, 15 VA. L. REV. 1322 (1959).
18. NLRB v. Tom Joyce Floors, Inc., 353 F.2d 768, 60 L.R.R.M. 2334 (1965); Reliance Clay Product Co., 115 N.L.R.B. 1736, 38 L.R.R.M. 1155 (1956), *enforced*, 245 F.2d 599, 40 L.R.R.M. 2217 (5th Cir. 1957).
19. Crosby Chemicals, Inc., 85 N.L.R.B. 791, 24 L.R.R.M. 1481 (1949), *enforced in relevant part*, 188 F.2d 91, 27 L.R.R.M. 2541 (5th Cir. 1951).

9.2.2 Unfair Labor Practice Strikers

Unfair labor practice strikers are entitled to reinstatement to their former jobs or equivalent positions once they have made an unconditional offer to return to work.[20] An employer can rarely justify a failure to reinstate all unfair labor practice strikers.[21] Even if an employer has a substantial business reason for denying reinstatement, the employer is generally required to reinstate unfair labor practice strikers. Such strikers are entitled to reinstatement even if they have been permanently replaced during the strike[22] and even if permanent replacements would have to be discharged to make room for them.[23] But unfair labor practice strikers are ordinarily not entitled to reinstatement if they are guilty of serious strike misconduct.[24]

9.2.3 Economic Strikers

Economic strikers have a more limited right to reinstatement. Once they offer to return, economic strikers are entitled to reinstatement only if their former jobs or equivalent positions are available. They are not entitled to immediate reinstatement if they have been permanently replaced or if the employer has a

---

20. Mastro Plastics v. NLRB, note 2 *supra*; Pecheur Lozenge Co., 98 N.L.R.B. 496, 29 L.R.R.M. 1367 (1952), *enforced as modified*, 209 F.2d 393, 33 L.R.R.M. 2324 (2d Cir. 1953), *cert. denied*, 347 U.S. 953, 34 L.R.R.M. 2027 (1954).
21. Carruthers Ready Mix, Inc., 262 N.L.R.B. 739, 110 L.R.R.M. 1392 (1982).
22. NLRB v. Mackay Radio & Telephone, note 8 *supra*.
23. NLRB v. Efco Mfg., Inc., 227 F.2d 675, 37 L.R.R.M. 2192 (1st Cir. 1955), *cert. denied*, 350 U.S. 1007, 37 L.R.R.M. 2790 (1956). For a discussion of the employer's potential liability to the permanent replacements if they are discharged, *see* section 9.14.2 *infra*.
24. *See* ch. 6, *supra* and section 9.10.1 *infra*.

substantial business reason for not reinstating them.[25] They are entitled to reinstatement if their replacements are only temporary. Economic strikers who are not reinstated when the strike is over are entitled, however, to preferential recall as their former jobs or substantially equivalent positions become available.[26] The burden of proof is on the employer to show that replacements were hired as permanent employees and that no vacancy otherwise exists or that there is some other valid business reason for not returning the economic strikers to work.[27]

An employer must carefully distinguish between a discharge (termination) and a failure to reinstate an economic striker at the end of a strike. Economic strikers awaiting recall after a strike have not been discharged. They are still employees under the Act and are entitled to return to work as vacancies occur.[28] Their status is similar to that of workers on layoff. If an employer treats them as if they have been discharged or discharges them without cause, the employer has committed an unfair labor practice. Consequently, an employer should avoid using terms such as "discharged," "fired," or "terminated" when referring to unreinstated strikers,[29] except in those instances when an unreinstated

---

25. NLRB v. Mackay Radio & Telephone, note 8 *supra*. Serious strike misconduct and other specific circumstances may terminate reinstatement rights. *See* section 9.10 *infra*.
26. Laidlaw Corp., 171 N.L.R.B. 1366, 68 L.R.R.M. 1252 (1968), *enforced*, 414 F.2d 99, 71 L.R.R.M. 3054 (7th Cir. 1969), *cert. denied*, 397 U.S. 920, 73 L.R.R.M. 2537 (1970).
27. NLRB v. Fleetwood Trailer Co., Inc., note 6 *supra*; NLRB v. Great Dane Trailers, Inc., 388 U.S. 26, 65 L.R.R.M. 2465 (1967); NLRB v. Murray Products, Inc., 584 F.2d 934, 99 L.R.R.M. 3269 (9th Cir. 1978).
28. NLRB v. Fleetwood Trailer Co., Inc., note 6 *supra*; NLRB v. Great Dane Trailers, Inc., 388 U.S. 26, 65 L.R.R.M. 2465 (1967); NLRB v. Murray Products, Inc., 584 F.2d 934, 99 L.R.R.M. 3269 (9th Cir. 1978).
29. Although such references are not an unfair labor practice *per se*, Vulcan Hart Corp. (St. Louis Division) v. NLRB, 718 F.2d 269, 114 L.R.R.M. 2745 (8th Cir. 1983); Highland Plastics, Inc., 256 N.L.R.B. 316, 107 L.R.R.M. 1271 (1981), the employer's conduct will be closely scrutinized to determine whether the strikers were, in fact, terminated or treated as

Post-Strike Planning

economic striker is actually discharged for cause, such as serious strike misconduct.[30] An employer should also avoid any statements that might leave the impression that the strikers will never be returned to work. Unlawfully discharging or refusing to reinstate economic strikers (which is tantamount to a discharge) is sufficient to convert an economic strike into an unfair labor strike.[31] Upon conversion of the strike, the strikers become unfair labor practice strikers as of the date the strike converted and attain the reinstatement rights of unfair labor practice strikers.[32] If the strikers have not been permanently replaced by the date of the conversion, the strikers are entitled to immediate reinstatement once they unconditionally offer to return to work. If the strikers were permanently replaced prior to the conversion, the strikers are entitled to be placed on a preferential recall list once they offer to return.[33]

9.3 Employees Entitled to Reinstatement

Economic strikers are entitled to reinstatement unless they have been permanently replaced or no vacancies exist; unfair labor practice strikers are entitled to reinstatement without regard to replacements or vacancies. The application of these reinstatement principles to regular full-time or part-time employees

---

such. An employer who refrains from such references will save itself the time and expense of defending an unfair labor practice charge.
30. See ch. 6 and section 9.10.1, *infra*, for a discussion of discharge for strike misconduct.
31. NLRB v. Moore Business Forms, Inc., 574 F.2d 835, 98 L.R.R.M. 2773 (5th Cir. 1978).
32. Randle-Eastern Ambulance Service, Inc., 230 N.L.R.B. 542, 95 L.R.R.M. 1332 (1977), *enforced in relevant part*, 584 F.2d 720, 99 L.R.R.M. 3377 (5th Cir. 1978).
33. Charles D. Bonanno Linen Service, Inc., 268 N.L.R.B. No. 78, 115 L.R.R.M. 1084 (1984); Covington Furniture Mfg. Corp., 212 N.L.R.B. 214, 87 L.R.R.M. 1505 (1974), *enforced*, 514 F.2d 995, 89 L.R.R.M. 3024 (6th Cir. 1975).

is fairly straightforward. Questions do arise, however, over the reinstatement rights of other types of employees, such as temporary or probationary employees, employees on leave, former employees participating in the strike, and employees with marginal work records.

9.3.1 Temporary Employees

For purposes of reinstatement, temporary employees should be distinguished from temporary striker replacements. Temporary employees are those employees hired on a temporary basis for reasons unrelated to the strike. People hired to cover peak periods or perform interim jobs are temporary employees. People hired specifically to replace strikers for the term of the strike are temporary striker replacements. The rights of temporary striker replacements are discussed in section 9.14.1.

Temporary employees who go on strike may not be terminated during the strike if the jobs for which they were hired were not finished when the strike began. Such temporary employees have a right to reinstatement. They may, however, be discharged after the strike once their jobs are completed or the peak period has ended, if termination upon completion of a job is consistent with the employer's past practice.[34] An employer who usually transfers or reassigns a temporary employee to another position or department when the temporary work is completed (rather than discharging the employee) should continue to follow that practice after the strike unless there is a substantial business reason for not doing so.

9.3.2 Probationary Employees

An employer may not discharge probationary employees solely for participating in a strike or other protected activity. There

---

34. R.L. White Co., Inc., 262 N.L.R.B. 575, 111 L.R.R.M. 1078 (1982).

must be some reason independent of the strike that justifies discharge. The NLRB and the courts have disagreed on the proof that the employer must offer to justify discharging, rather than reinstating, probationary employees during or after the strike. Historically, the NLRB has closely scrutinized the employer's past practice and, under the Board's analysis, any disparity between the treatment of probationary employees before and after the strike would likely run afoul of the Act unless the employer had strong business reasons for its actions. The NLRB has previously held that if there is a fixed probationary period recognized by the employer and that period has not expired when the strike began, probationary employees are entitled to reinstatement at the end of the strike, regardless of job performance.[35] If it has been the employer's past practice to wait until the probationary period is over before making a discharge decision, the NLRB has ordered reinstatement, at least for the remainder of the employee's probationary period, even though the employee's job performance is unsatisfactory. The employer may then apply its usual standards in making a permanent employment decision at the end of the probationary period.[36]

Under some circumstances, however, the NLRB has approved a post-strike discharge of a probationary employee. An employer may discharge an unreinstated probationary employee after the strike if the employee had been warned about job performance problems prior to the strike and the discharge was delayed until the strike's end for a specific and valid business reason. In *Georgia Kraft Co.*,[37] for example, the employer had given three warn-

---

35. Mobile Home Estates, Inc., 259 NLRB 1384, 109 L.R.R.M. 1123 (1982); Waveline, Inc., 258 N.L.R.B. 652, 108 L.R.R.M. 1139 (1981). *See also* Orba Transshipment of Alabama, A Division of Orba Corp., 266 N.L.R.B. No. 167, 113 L.R.R.M. 1064 (1983).
36. G & H Products, Inc., 261 N.L.R.B. 298, 110 L.R.R.M. 1036 (1982).
37. Georgia Kraft Co., 258 N.L.R.B. 908, 108 L.R.R.M. 1223 (1981), *enforced*, Georgia Kraft Co., Woodkraft Division v. NLRB, 696 F.2d 931, 112 L.R.R.M. 2854, *rehearing denied*, 704 F.2d 1253 (11th Cir. 1983). The United States Supreme Court has vacated and remanded the case to the NLRB on an issue related to discharge for strike misconduct. 52 U.S.L.W. 3700 (U.S. March 27, 1984).

ings to a probationary employee before the strike began and delayed the discharge until strike's end solely because of its policy that employees not be discharged until they have talked with their supervisors. Once the strike was over and the employee had met with his supervisor, the NLRB held that the company acted properly in discharging rather than reinstating him.

The courts have recently held that if the probationary employees' work performances were poor, the employer need not reinstate them after the strike, even though there had been no warnings or reprimands prior to or during the strike.[38] Since the Supreme Court's approval of the *Wright Line*[39] analysis for dual motive cases,[40] several circuit courts have held that even if there was some anti-union motive behind the employees' discharges, the employer will not have violated the Act if it can show that the employees would have been fired even absent the strike.[41] Under this analysis, an employer who could prove that the probationary employee would ultimately have been discharged anyway need not make the futile gesture of reinstating probationary employees, only to fire them later.

9.3.3 Marginal Employees

Employees with marginal job performances are entitled to reinstatement after the strike unless the employer can clearly

---

38. G & H Products, Inc. v. NLRB, 714 F.2d 1397, 114 L.R.R.M. 2107 (7th Cir. 1983), *denying enforcement to*, 261 N.L.R.B. 298, 110 L.R.R.M. 1036 (1982); NLRB v. Mobile Home Estates, Inc. v. NLRB, 707 F.2d 264, 113 L.R.R.M. 2725 (6th Cir. 1983), *cert. denied*, 52 U.S.L.W. 3509, 115 L.R.R.M. 2248 (1984), *denying enforcement in relevant part to*, 259 N.L.R.B. 1384, 109 L.R.R.M. 1123 (1982).
39. Wright Line, Inc., 250 N.L.R.B. 1083, 105 L.R.R.M. 1169 (1980), *enforced*, 662 F.2d 899, 108 L.R.R.M. 2513 (1st Cir. 1981), *cert. denied*, 455 U.S. 989, 109 L.R.R.M. 2779 (1982).
40. NLRB v. Transportation Management Corp., 113 L.R.R.M. 2857 (1983).
41. *See, e.g.*, Airport Parking Management v. NLRB, 720 F.2d 610 (9th Cir. 1983); G & H Products, Inc. v. NLRB, note 38 *supra*.

show that there were sufficient pre-strike reprimands to warrant immediate dismissal.[42] Otherwise, the dismissal may be considered unlawful. Although the *Wright Line* dual motive analysis applied to probationary employees is also applicable to marginal nonprobationary employees, the employer's actions may be considered inherently more suspect. This is particularly true if the person discharged has been employed for a substantial period of time or was particularly active in union or strike activities. The employer should carefully check to see that any pre-strike performance problems and warnings have been well documented before attempting to discharge an unreinstated marginal employee during or after the strike.[43]

9.3.4 Employees on Leave

Employees who are on disability or sick leave during the strike and do not participate in or support the strike are entitled to return to work at leave's end, regardless of the date the strike ends. Employees who are on leave at the start of the strike but later participate in the strike to such an extent that they demonstrate they are no longer ill or disabled are entitled to reinstatement at strike's end just as the other strikers.[44] The burden of proof is on the employer to show that an employee's participation in the strike is sufficient to justify termination of sick or disability leave status.[45]

---

42. J. E. Steigerwald Co., Inc., 263 N.L.R.B. 483, 111 L.R.R.M. 1189 (1982); Carruthers Ready Mix, Inc., note 21 *supra*.
43. The issues surrounding post-strike discipline and reprimands are discussed in ch. 11 *infra*.
44. The payment of medical, disability, and other benefits during the period of the strike is discussed in ch. 11 *infra*.
45. Conoco, Inc., 265 NLRB 819, 112 L.R.R.M. 1001 (1983).

9.3.5 Other Employees

Even striker replacements may be entitled to reinstatement if they decide to join the strike.[46] Their reinstatement rights do not differ from those of the original striking employees. To the extent that the employer reinstates employees according to seniority, the replacements would be among the last recalled to work.

Employees who were lawfully discharged prior to the strike are not entitled to reinstatement when the strike is over, even if they have actively engaged in picketing or other strike activity.[47] Former employees cannot resurrect their jobs by joining the strike unless the employer specifically agrees to reinstate them along with the other strikers.

Sympathy strikers who refuse to cross a picket line on the premises of one of their employer's customers can be permanently replaced.[48] An additional requirement, however, is imposed on the employer to show there was a business need to replace the sympathy striker.[49] Sympathy strikers are otherwise entitled to reinstatement on the same basis as economic strikers.[50]

9.4 Unconditional Offers to Return to Work

There are two unconditional offers that must be made to effect reinstatement. First, the strikers (or the union on their behalf)

---

46. Cooperativa de Credito Y Ahorro Vegabajena, 261 N.L.R.B. 1098, 110 L.R.R.M. 1241 (1982).
47. NLRB v. Colonial Press, Inc., 509 F.2d 850, 88 L.R.R.M. 2337 (8th Cir.), cert. denied sub nom. Graphic Arts Int'l Union v. Colonial Press, Inc., 423 U.S. 833, 90 L.R.R.M. 2553 (1975).
48. NLRB v. Browning-Ferris Indus., Chemical Services, Inc., 700 F.2d 385, 112 L.R.R.M. 2882 (7th Cir. 1983). See ch. 5 supra.
49. See section 5.2.2.2 supra.
50. NLRB v. Browning-Ferris Indus., Chemical Services, Inc., note 48 supra.

must make an unconditional offer to return to work. Second, the employer must make an unconditional offer of reinstatement.

The offer to return to work must be made regardless of whether the strike is an economic or an unfair labor practice strike. The employer's obligation to reinstate strikers does not arise until the strikers make such an unconditional offer. Only unlawfully discharged strikers need not make an offer to return to work.[51] The offer to return to work may be either oral or written.[52] An offer to return remains valid even if the strikers continue to picket.[53]

In general, unfair labor practice strikers are entitled to immediate reinstatement in their former jobs with the same shifts, wages, and salaries they had before the strike. Consequently, their offers to return to work are still unconditional even if linked to a return to their previous shifts, salaries, and other working conditions.

The rulings on what constitutes an unconditional offer to return by economic strikers have been less straightforward. Because economic strikers can be permanently replaced, they have less freedom to condition their return to work. An offer requesting reinstatement of all economic strikers is conditional,[54] unless the strikers have conditioned their reinstatement on the good faith belief that they are unfair labor practice strikers.[55] An offer by economic strikers to return at specific salaries, however, may be unconditional.[56] An offer by economic strikers to return to

---

51. Abilities & Goodwill Co., 241 N.L.R.B. 27, 100 L.R.R.M. 1470 (1970), *enforcement denied on other grounds*, 612 F.2d 6, 103 L.R.R.M. 2029 (1st Cir. 1979).
52. Overhead Door Corp., 261 N.L.R.B. 657, 110 L.R.R.M. 1112 (1982).
53. NLRB v. W.C. McQuaide, Inc., 552 F.2d 519, 94 L.R.R.M. 2950 (3d Cir. 1977).
54. Soule Glass & Glazing Co. v. NLRB, 652 F.2d 1055, 107 L.R.R.M. 2781 (1st Cir. 1981).
55. H. & F. Binch Co. v. NLRB, 456 F.2d 357, 79 L.R.R.M. 2692 (2d Cir. 1972).
56. Decker Foundry Co., Inc., 237 N.L.R.B. 636, 99 L.R.R.M. 1047 (1978).

regularly assigned shifts or certain positions is not unconditional unless the strikers return willing to work other shifts and positions or otherwise indicate that they have dropped those conditions.[57] An offer by economic strikers to return is not unconditional if the return is contingent on the discharge of permanent replacements or the reinstatement of lawfully discharged employees.[58]

9.5 Unconditional Offers of Reinstatement

Upon its receipt of an unconditional offer to return to work by *unfair labor practice* strikers, the employer must reciprocate with an unconditional offer of reinstatement. A failure to reinstate at that point is an additional unfair labor practice, which will subject an employer to back pay liability. Upon receipt of an unconditional offer to return to work by *economic* strikers, the employer must make an unconditional offer of reinstatement to the extent that jobs have not been filled by permanent replacements. Otherwise, the employer commits an unfair labor practice that may convert an economic strike to an unfair labor practice strike. Employees who reject a valid reinstatement offer forfeit all reinstatement rights and all further claims for back pay.[59]

The employer must make the offer of reinstatement promptly after receiving the employees' offer to return to work, particularly for unfair labor practice strikers. The NLRB has held that

---

57. Georgia Kraft Co., note 37 *supra;* Continental Indus., 264 N.L.R.B. 120, 111 L.R.R.M. 1256 (1982).
58. Roberts Oldsmobile, Inc., 252 N.L.R.B. 192, 105 L.R.R.M. 1532 (1980). Neither unfair labor practice nor economic strikers may insist on reinstatement of lawfully discharged employees. If economic strikers are seeking reinstatement of unlawfully discharged employees, the strike would probably convert to an unfair labor practice strike and the strikers would become unfair labor practice strikers.
59. See section 9.9 *infra.*

more than a five-day lag between the unfair labor practice strikers' offer to return and the offer to reinstate is too long.[60] The effective date of a valid offer tolls any back-pay liability.[61] If the employer makes a bona fide reinstatement offer and the strikers elect not to return at that time, the employer is not liable for wages lost between the date the strikers were to report to work and the date they actually returned.

A valid offer must be a true and definite offer, not a request that the strikers express an interest in returning to work or a statement that there are possible vacancies.[62] For example, in *Charleston Nursing Center*, the employer sent a letter to all striking employees that stated:

> Are you still interested in employment at Charleston Nursing Center as an Aide?
>
> Please check on bottom of this letter and return to me. Also, please send current phone number.
>
> Enclosed is a self addressed and stamped envelope.
>
> ____ Yes, I am interested in employment
>
> ____ No, I am not interested in employment
>
> _____ Phone Number
>
> If we do not receive a reply, we will assume you are not interested.

---

60. Conair Corp., 261 N.L.R.B. 1189, 110 L.R.R.M. 1161 (1982), *enforced in relevant part*, 721 F.2d 1355, 114 L.R.R.M. 3169 (D.C. Cir. 1983). The NLRB applies a five-day rule in computing back-pay liability. Drug Package Co., 228 N.L.R.B. 108, 94 L.R.R.M. 1570 (1977), *enforcement denied in part on other grounds*, 570 F.2d 1340, 97 L.R.R.M. 2851 (8th Cir. 1978).
61. *See* section 9.9 *infra*.
62. Charleston Nursing Center, 257 N.L.R.B. 554, 107 L.R.R.M. 1533 (1981), *disapproved on other grounds*, Giddings & Lewis, Inc. v. NLRB, 675 F.2d 926, 110 L.R.R.M. 2121 (7th Cir. 1982). *See also* Pace Motor

The NLRB ruled that this letter was not a sufficient offer of reinstatement because it did not expressly offer the strikers any jobs. It was merely a solicitation of interest. Because it was not a valid offer, strikers' names could not be removed from the preferential recall list if they had not responded to the letter.

As with the strikers' offer to return to work, the employer's offer of reinstatement must be unconditional. The employer cannot condition reinstatement on acceptance of other terms in a strike settlement agreement,[63] on agreement to a preferential hiring list procedure even though the employer had not permanently replaced the strikers,[64] or on an agreement that a striker resign from union office and refrain from running for such office again.[65]

An employer should also be careful to review the terms of the employees' offer to return to work. If an employer does not intend to reinstate the strikers on the exact terms of their offer to return, it should explicitly state that fact in its reinstatement offer. For example, if an offer to return was made on behalf of all strikers and the employer does not intend to make a full reinstatement, it should specifically state in its reinstatement offer that it does not intend to reinstate all of the strikers. Otherwise, the employer may have tacitly agreed to reinstatement on the union's terms, *not* its own.[66]

Lines, Inc., 260 N.L.R.B. 1395, 110 L.R.R.M. 1153 (1982), *enforced*, 703 F.2d 28, 112 L.R.R.M. 3315 (2d Cir. 1983).

63. Cooperativa de Credito Y Ahorro Vegebajona, note 46 *supra*.
64. Presto Casting Co., 262 N.L.R.B. 346, 111 L.R.R.M. 1111 (1982), *enforced in relevant part*, 708 F.2d 495, 113 L.R.R.M. 3013 (9th Cir.), *cert. denied*, 114 L.R.R.M. 3392 (1983).
65. Vulcan-Hart Corp., 262 N.L.R.B. 167, 110 L.R.R.M. 1302 (1982), *enforced in relevant part*, 718 F.2d 269, 114 L.R.R.M. 2745 (8th Cir. 1983).
66. *See* Ingram Mfg. Co., 75 L.A. 113 (1980) (Caraway, Arb.); *see also* ch. 6, *supra*, for a discussion of condonation.

9.6 Availability of Work

9.6.1 Curtailment of Work

Unfair labor practice strikers are ordinarily entitled to reinstatement even if the employer claims a legitimate business reason for not reinstating them.[67] A curtailment of work is not sufficient to block reinstatement of unfair labor practice strikers if the NLRB perceives the curtailment to be voluntary or if the employer is not making sufficient efforts to regain lost business.[68] Because unfair labor practice strikers cannot be permanently replaced, the employer may not validly claim insufficient work if permanent replacements are working.

Economic strikers are entitled to reinstatement only to the extent there are vacancies for which they are or can be qualified. Economic strikers are not entitled to reinstatement if they have been permanently replaced or if there is a legitimate and substantial reason for not returning them to work.[69] The burden is on the employer to prove either that no vacancies exist or that there is a sufficient business reason for not reinstating the strikers.[70]

Elimination of particular positions during a strike is a sufficient basis for not reinstating economic strikers so long as the employer's action is not retaliatory, results in a financial savings, and was implemented during the strike, not after.[71] The claim must also be credible in light of the surrounding facts. For example, an employer cannot plausibly claim that some positions were

---

67. Lehigh Metal Fabricators, 267 N.L.R.B. No. 96, 114 L.R.R.M. 1064 (1983).
68. Mastro Plastics v. NLRB, note 2 *supra*; Pace Motor Lines, note 62 *supra*.
69. NLRB v. Mackay Radio & Telephone Co., note 8 *supra*; Laidlaw Corp., *supra* note 26.
70. Road Sprinkler Fitters Local Union No. 669 v. NLRB (John Cuneo, Inc.), note 11 *supra*.
71. Lincoln Hills Nursing Home, Inc., 257 N.L.R.B. 1145, 108 L.R.R.M. 1053 (1981).

eliminated due to a job restructuring if the strike only lasted two days.[72] Permanent subcontracting of work previously performed by economic strikers is not a valid business reason if the subcontracting was unilaterally implemented by the employer. Unless the employer has notified and offered to bargain with the union over permanent subcontracting, the strikers are entitled to reinstatement once they unconditionally offer to return.[73]

The employer does not have to offer reinstatement if the job in question is being performed on an occasional or temporary basis and the striker who previously held the job is only interested in full-time, permanent employment.[74] Temporary jobs are not considered vacancies. Temporary striker replacements can be recalled in lieu of unreinstated strikers to fill temporary jobs after the strike.[75]

9.6.2 Promotions, Transfers, and Rehires

An employer may not take post-strike personnel action that puts strikers at a disadvantage. To do so is an unfair labor practice. Consequently, an employer ordinarily violates the Act if it promotes or transfers another employee (whether permanent replacement, nonstriker, or early returning striker) to a position that has been or could be performed adequately by an unreinstated striker.[76] Transfers or promotions can be implemented, however, if they are necessary to correct production imbalances or prevent layoffs.[77]

---

72. Southern Florida Hotel & Motel Ass'n, 245 N.L.R.B. 561, 102 L.R.R.M. 1578 (1979); American Cyanamid Co., note 10 *supra*.
73. American Cyanamid Co., note 10 *supra*.
74. Overhead Door Corp., note 52 *supra*; Laidlaw Corp., note 26 *supra*.
75. Laidlaw Corp., note 26 *supra*.
76. Nolan Systems, Inc., 268 NLRB No. 202, 115 L.R.R.M. 1189 (1984); Overhead Door Corp., note 52 *supra*.
77. Lodges 743 & 1746, Int'l Ass'n of Machinists & Aerospace Workers v. United Aircraft Corp., 534 F.2d 422, 90 L.R.R.M. 2272 (2d Cir. 1975),

An employer may not rehire replacements instead of reinstating strikers. If replacements have voluntarily resigned from the employer's work force, they cannot be rehired until all qualified strikers have been reinstated.[78] Replacements who have been laid off or are on a bona fide leave of absence can be returned to work prior to unreinstated strikers.[79]

9.7 Reinstatement to Substantially Equivalent Positions

Unfair labor practice strikers must be reinstated to their former positions unless those jobs no longer exist.[80] If their jobs have been eliminated, they must be reinstated to substantially equivalent positions.[81] Unfair labor practice strikers may not be offered less desirable permanent positions than those they held prior to the strike.[82] To make such an offer is itself an unfair labor practice. Reinstatement to jobs on a different shift is not considered substantially equivalent employment for unfair labor practice strikers.[83]

---

cert. denied sub nom., International Ass'n of Machinists v. NLRB, 429 U.S. 825, 92 L.R.R.M. 2501 (1976).
78. Randall, Division of Textron, Inc. v. NLRB, 687 F.2d 1240, 111 L.R.R.M. 2437 (8th Cir. 1982), cert. denied, 113 L.R.R.M. 2192 (1983).
79. Id.; Giddings & Lewis Co., Inc. v. NLRB, 675 F.2d 926, 110 L.R.R.M. 2121 (7th Cir. 1982), denying enforcement to 225 N.L.R.B. 742, 106 L.R.R.M. 1391 (1981).
80. Atlas Metal Parts Co., Inc. v. NLRB, 660 F.2d 304, 108 L.R.R.M. 2474 (7th Cir. 1981); Mastro Plastics v. NLRB, note 2 supra; Pace Motor Lines, note 62 supra.
81. Atlas Metal Parts Co. v. NLRB, note 80 supra.
82. Conair Corp., note 60 supra. An employer may offer an unfair labor practice striker a temporary position in a less desirable job but acceptance of such a temporary position does not terminate that striker's right of reinstatement to his or her former job. Coca-Cola Bottling Co. of Memphis, 270 N.L.R.B. No. 160, 116 L.R.R.M. 1239 (1984).
83. Talbert Manufacturing, Inc., 258 N.L.R.B. 776, 108 L.R.R.M. 1282 (1981).

Striker Reinstatement

Economic strikers are also entitled to reinstatement in their former or substantially equivalent positions unless they have been permanently replaced. An economic striker who refuses reinstatement to an equivalent job terminates any further reinstatement rights. An offer of reinstatement to a night-shift position is not substantially equivalent to a day-shift position. [84] An employer is not necessarily precluded from offering nonequivalent positions to economic strikers but they do not lose their reinstatement rights if they refuse to return on that basis.[85]

9.8 Reinstatement Procedure

An employer should formulate its reinstatement procedure before the end of the strike. Because of its duty to reinstate promptly, an employer may have little time to plan once the strikers offer to return to work.

The NLRB has not made clear to what extent an employer must bargain with the union over the reinstatement procedure.[86] The NLRB has held that the "imposition of notification and registration requirements on former strikers" is a mandatory bargaining subject.[87] The language is quite broad. The cases themselves, however, have dealt with situations in which the em-

---

84. Harvey Engineering & Manufacturing Corp., 270 N.L.R.B. No. 186 (1984).
85. Atlas Metal Parts Co., Inc. v. NLRB, note 80 *supra*; Georgia Kraft Co., note 37 *supra*.
86. Whether there is any duty to bargain depends on the status of the union at the end of the strike. If there is a good-faith doubt regarding the union's majority status at strike's end, there may be no duty to bargain over reinstatement. See ch. 11 *infra*.
87. Atlantic Creosoting Co., Inc., 242 N.L.R.B. 192, 192, n.4, 101 L.R.R.M. 1144 (1979); Giddings & Lewis, Inc., 264 N.L.R.B. 561, 111 L.R.R.M. 1342 (1982); Food Service Co., 202 N.L.R.B. 790, 82 L.R.R.M. 1746 (1973), *enforcement denied on other grounds*, 710 F.2d 1280, 113 L.R.R.M. 3361 (7th Cir. 1983).

ployer had required strikers to fill out work applications within a certain period of time to be eligible for reinstatement. Whether the NLRB will expressly designate other aspects of the reinstatement procedure as mandatory bargaining subjects has yet to be determined. Any requirement that treats strikers as new employees may be an independent basis for an unfair labor practice, regardless of whether the employer consulted the union prior to imposing it.[88]

9.8.1 Basis for Determining Reinstatement Priority

Because unfair labor practice strikers are entitled to immediate reinstatement regardless of vacancies, issues of priority reinstatement generally arise only for economic strikers. An employer is free to adopt any method for determining the order of reinstatement so long as the chosen method does not discriminate against employees for having engaged in strike or union activity. Generally, an objective system such as seniority is adopted. Reinstatement of strikers in alphabetical order may be proper if the employer has a past practice of using such a system or if the employer has never adopted a seniority system.[89] An employer may use a more subjective system, such as merit selection, to determine priority if the employer has some reasonable basis for determining which strikers have the best skills.[90] As a practical matter, a subjective system may be viewed with greater suspicion and provoke greater dispute than would an objective system, such as seniority. Therefore, an employer who intends to implement a subjective system should have substantial reasons to justify its chosen method, particularly if that method departs from the employer's past practice. Use of a subjective system may be considered unlawfully discriminatory despite a valid business purpose if many union or strike leaders and organizers receive a

---

88. *See* section 9.11.1. *But see* Gem City Ready Mix Co., 270 N.L.R.B. No. 191, 116 L.R.R.M. 1266 (1984).
89. Carruthers Ready Mix, Inc., note 42 *supra*.
90. Soule Glass & Glazing Co. v. NLRB, note 54 *supra*.

lower priority under that system than they would have received under an objective system.

If an employer uses a seniority system, it can be applied on an area- or facility-wide basis, within a department or division,[91] or within a job classification.[92] Again, the employer should be careful to choose a seniority procedure that does not disproportionately discriminate against employees who were active in the strike or union activities.

Under a seniority system, an employer offers the jobs to the most senior qualified people within the particular category until all senior personnel are reinstated or all vacancies have been filled.[93] If vacancies still exist, the employer may offer the remaining positions to the most senior strikers who could reasonably qualify or be trained for the job.[94] Once all qualified strikers have been reinstated to their former or substantially equivalent positions, the employer may hire new employees as vacancies occur.[95]

The employer must provide the union with information on the chosen striker reinstatement procedure and any preferential recall lists if the union requests them.[96] The employer should request that the union notify it of any errors or discrepancies in the employer's reinstatement or recall list.[97] If the union fails to

---

91. Giddings & Lewis Inc., v. NLRB, note 79 *supra*.
92. Lincoln Hills Nursing Home, Inc., note 71 *supra*.
93. Giddings & Lewis, Inc. v. NLRB, note 79 *supra*.
94. *Id.*
95. It should be noted that although all strikers may have been reinstated, the issue regarding discriminatory treatment of strikers and promotion may still arise. *See* ch. 11 *infra*. Consequently, the employer should have substantial justification for any departures from past practice on promotions. Strike participation may not be weighed as a factor in making or 191, L.R.R.M. 1266(1987).
96. Florida Steel Corp., 242 N.L.R.B. 1333, 101 L.R.R.M. 1370 (1979), *enforced in relevant part*, 620 F.2d 79, 104 L.R.R.M. 2833 (5th Cir. 1980); Ohio Power Co., 216 N.L.R.B. 987, 88 L.R.R.M. 1646 (1975), *enforced*, 531 F.2d 1381, 92 L.R.R.M. 3049 (6th Cir. 1979).
97. Lincoln Hills Nursing Home, Inc., note 71 *supra*.

notify the employer of any errors, it is less likely to be found liable for any defects or omissions in the list.

9.8.2 Notice

It is the employer's duty to notify the strikers of the return date and other terms of the reinstatement offer. If the employer and the union have so agreed, the employer may give notice of the reinstatement offer to the union and the union then becomes responsible for communicating the details of the offer to its members.[98] Written notice such as a letter or telegram may be preferable to prove that notice was given. The employer may notify strikers by telephone, particularly if an emergency requires their immediate return to work.[99]

If strikers are placed on a recall list, the employer must recall those people in the order shown on the list.[100] An employer may be waiving any possible objection to reinstatement if it places a striker's name on the preferential recall list. It should be careful to exclude from the list any striker that it intends to discharge for serious strike misconduct or other sufficient cause. The employer should also verify that it intends to reinstate the strikers in the order that they appear on the list before submitting the list to the union.

The notice of reinstatement may include a request that those strikers on the preferential recall list submit updated addresses and telephone numbers at specified intervals (such as every six or twelve months). The NLRB has held, however, that strikers cannot be removed from the recall list for failing to submit updated information unless the union had previously agreed that

---

98. Birmingham Ornamental Iron Co., 251 N.L.R.B. 814, 105 L.R.R.M. 1251 (1980); Stauffer Chemical Co., 242 N.L.R.B. 98, 101 L.R.R.M. 1123 (1979).
99. Lincoln Hills Nursing Home, Inc., note 71 *supra*.
100. *Id.*

such responses would be mandatory.[101] The courts have been somewhat more sympathetic, allowing the employer to require periodic updates once the reinstatement process has extended over several years and the employer shows that many of the unreinstated strikers on the original recall list are rejecting reinstatement offers.[102] Even if an employer cannot remove such a striker from the list, it will not be liable for failing to reinstate if the striker could not be found at his or her last known address and the employer made a good faith attempt to locate the striker before reinstating the next striker on the list.[103]

9.8.3 Deadline for Return to Work

Although the employer has an obligation to extend an offer of reinstatement promptly after the strikers offer to return to work, the mandatory deadline by which strikers must be back at work cannot be unreasonably short. Requiring that the strikers return the following day[104] or within one to four days[105] to avoid loss of reinstatement rights may not necessarily be reasonable. An offer to reinstate the following day is not necessarily invalid if it is

---

101. NLRB v. Vitronic Division of Penn Corp., 630 F.2d 561, 102 L.R.R.M. 2753 (8th Cir. 1979); Giddings & Lewis, Inc., 264 N.L.R.B. 561, 111 L.R.R.M. 1342 (1982), *enforcement denied*, 710 F.2d 1280, 113 L.R.R.M. 3361 (7th Cir. 1983).
102. Giddings & Lewis, Inc. v. NLRB, note 79 *supra*.
103. Carruthers Ready Mix, Inc., note 21 *supra*. Locating unreinstated strikers can become particularly troublesome because the NLRB has declined to place time limits on reinstatement unless there is a strike settlement agreement specifying a definite reinstatement eligibility period. See section 9.10.2 *infra*. Consequently, an employer might be attempting to locate unreinstated strikers with information that is several years old.
104. Consolidated Dress Carriers, Inc., 259 N.L.R.B. 627, 109 L.R.R.M. 1015 (1981), *enforcement denied on other grounds*, 693 F.2d 277, 111 L.R.R.M. 3130 (2d Cir. 1982).
105. Conair Corp., note 60 *supra*.

made in a way that makes such a return voluntary and the employer does in fact reinstate strikers who return later.[106] The appropriate time period depends on the specific circumstances of the strike and is influenced by several factors, including the length of the strike. Prolonged strikes may merit longer call-back periods than brief ones. If the deadline is unreasonable, the employer cannot remove "no-shows" from the reinstatement or recall list.

9.9 Employer's Liability for Back Pay

Generally, strikers are not entitled to back pay for the period they choose to remain on strike.[107] Strikers must unconditionally offer to return to work before they have any back-pay claim.[108] Unfair labor practice strikers are entitled to prompt reinstatement regardless of whether they have been replaced. Consequently, the NLRB has adopted a rule that back pay and interest for unfair labor practice strikers accrues starting on the fifth day after they offer to return to work and continues until they are actually reinstated.[109] To prevent back-pay liability, the em-

---

106. NLRB v. Consolidated Dress Carriers, Inc., 693 F.2d 277, 111 L.R.R.M. 3130 (2d Cir. 1982).
107. F.W. Woolworth Co., 90 N.L.R.B. No. 41, 26 L.R.R.M. 1185 (1950).
108. Discriminatorily discharged strikers are entitled to back pay from the date of discharge until the date of reinstatement. They need not offer to return to work. Abilities & Goodwill Co., note 51 *supra*. If the unlawful discharge occurs during the strike, back pay begins to accrue on the discharge date (rather than the date the strike ends) unless the employer can prove that the striker was unwilling to return to work. Garrett Railroad Car & Equipment, Inc. v. NLRB, 683 F.2d 731, 110 L.R.R.M. 2919 (3d Cir. 1982); Abilities & Goodwill, Inc., note 51 *supra*.
109. Drug Package Co., 228 N.L.R.B. 108, 94 L.R.R.M. 1570 (1977). If the employer ignores, rejects, or attaches an unlawful condition to the unfair labor practice strikers' offer to return, the NLRB does not use the five-day rule. Back pay begins to accrue on the date of the offer to return.

Striker Reinstatement

ployer must make its reinstatement offer quickly so that the strikers have sufficient time to consider the offer (generally more than one day) and still be able to return the strikers to work within the five days.

Economic strikers are entitled to reinstatement only if they have not been permanently replaced and vacancies still exist. Back pay accrues only if the economic strikers offer to return unconditionally and the employer fails to reinstate them despite vacancies.[110] Although the NLRB has not applied the five-day rule to economic strikers, the employer is obligated to reinstate eligible economic strikers within a reasonable time after they offer to return to work.[111] If an employer fails to do so, it may be liable for back pay plus interest from the date it should have reinstated the strikers until the date the strikers actually return to work. If an economic strike converts to an unfair labor practice strike, the strikers are treated as unfair labor practice strikers for back-pay purposes.[112] A striker's rejection of a valid reinstatement offer terminates any back-pay liability.[113]

Money that strikers earn from other sources is deducted from the accrued back pay.[114] The NLRB does not, however, subtract

---

Teamsters Local Union No. 574, 259 N.L.R.B. No. 37, 108 L.R.R.M. 1378 (1981).

The applicable interest rate is the "adjusted prime interest rate" set by the Internal Revenue Service. Florida Steel Corp., note 96 *supra*.

110. Automatic Plastic Molding Co., 234 N.L.R.B. 681, 97 L.R.R.M. 1326 (1978), *enforced without opinion*, 106 L.R.R.M. 2869 (9th Cir. 1979).
111. Road Sprinkler Fitters Local Union No. 669 v. NLRB (John Cuneo, Inc.), note 11 *supra*.
112. See NLRB v. Acme Fire Works, Inc., 582 F.2d 153, 98 L.R.R.M. 3163 (2d Cir. 1978); National Car Rental System, Inc., 237 N.L.R.B. 172, 99 L.R.R.M. 1027 (1978), *enforcement denied on other grounds*, 594 F.2d 1203, 100 L.R.R.M. 2824 (8th Cir. 1979).
113. F.W. Woolworth Co., note 107 *supra*.
114. Strike benefits are not considered outside earnings unless the strikers have participated in strike activity that prevented them from seeking interim employment. Madison Courier, Inc., 202 N.L.R.B. 808, 82 L.R.R.M. 1667 (1972).

the total amount of outside earnings from the total accrued back pay. Instead, it deducts the earnings in a given quarter (the quarters begin on the first day of January, April, July, and October) from the back pay accruing during that quarter.[115] If the outside earnings are greater than the back pay in a given quarter, the NLRB will *not* offset the excess against the back-pay liability from another quarter.[116]

9.10 Termination of Reinstatement Rights

Although unfair labor practice strikers have a right to immediate reinstatement, that right is forfeited by participation in serious strike misconduct. Similarly, the reinstatement or preferential recall rights of economic strikers terminates if a striker participates in serious strike misconduct. An economic striker's reinstatement rights also terminate if the striker accepts equivalent employment elsewhere, or fails to return to work when scheduled.

9.10.1 Strike Misconduct

One of the most troublesome areas for employers is the handling of strikers involved in misconduct. Because strike misconduct is not protected by the Act, strikers who participate in serious misconduct may be discharged.[117] A valid discharge terminates any reinstatement rights the striker would have otherwise had. Strikers may also be disciplined for engaging in strike misconduct but any discipline short of discharge would have no effect on their reinstatement rights.

---

115. F.W. Woolworth, note 107 *supra*.
116. *Id.*
117. NLRB v. Fansteel Metallurgical Corp., 306 U.S. 240, 4 L.R.R.M. 515 (1939). *See* ch. 6 *infra*, for an extensive discussion of striker misconduct.

Striker Reinstatement

An employer may be asked to give amnesty to strikers who have participated in misconduct and should consider whether it is willing to do so. Some of the factors to be considered include: the seriousness of the misconduct (and the likelihood the discharge will withstand an unfair labor practice charge); the concessions the union would be willing to make in exchange for amnesty (such as forfeiting any disciplinary actions against nonstrikers); the effect that returning those strikers would have on employee morale or on customers; and the particular strikers' job performance.

An employer may be required to furnish the union with the names of any strikers the employer contends have forfeited their reinstatement rights through strike misconduct.[118] Regardless of whether the NLRB requires that such information be furnished, it may be in the employer's best interest to make its position clear if it does not intend to reinstate strikers involved in misconduct. If the errant strikers' names are included in the reinstatement list[119] or the employer explicitly acknowledges the possibility of their reinstatement during settlement negotiations,[120] the NLRB has sometimes ordered that the employer reinstate the strikers despite their misconduct. Similarly, the employer should not delay in discharging the striker once it has been made aware and had the opportunity to investigate the alleged misconduct.[121] The NLRB has sometimes interpreted delay as condonation of the strikers' conduct although the courts have been more reluctant than the NLRB to apply the condonation doctrine.[122]

---

118. *See* C. MORRIS, THE DEVELOPING LABOR LAW, 627-28 (2d ed. 1983) (*citing* Food Service Co., note 87 *supra*).
119. Lincoln Hills Nursing Home, Inc., note 71 *supra*.
120. Woodlawn Hospital, 233 N.L.R.B. 782, 97 L.R.R.M. 1386 (1977), *enforcement denied*, 596 F.2d 1330, 102 L.R.R.M. 1326 (7th Cir. 1979).
121. Iowa Beef Processors, Inc., 255 N.L.R.B. 1328, 107 L.R.R.M. 1124 (1981), *enforced*, 675 F.2d 1004, 110 L.R.R.M. 2232 (8th Cir. 1982).
122. *See, e.g.*, Woodlawn Hospital v. NLRB, note 120 *supra*.

9.10.2 Passage of Time

The NLRB has declined to limit the amount of time for which an economic striker retains a right of reinstatement and preferential recall.[123] Therefore, the right to reinstatement is generally unaffected by the passage of time. The Court of Appeals for the Seventh Circuit has stated that the reinstatement period should be equal to the length of pre-strike employment but has not as yet received support for this position from the other circuits or the NLRB.[124] Reasonable time limits may be placed on reinstatement by means of a strike settlement agreement, which is one of the chief advantages of pursuing such an agreement.[125]

9.10.3 Other Employment

Absent strike misconduct or cause for discharge, unreinstated economic strikers are generally entitled to reinstatement until they have found regular and substantially equivalent employment elsewhere.[126] Once they have found such employment, they may be removed from the preferential recall list unless they express a desire to return to work despite the new job.[127]

The NLRB has previously taken the position that a striker who accepts other regular and substantially equivalent employment, but is discharged or laid off from that job before receiving a

---

123. Nelson Filter Division, Nelson Industries, 255 N.L.R.B. 1080, 107 L.R.R.M. 1090 (1981); Brooks Research & Manufacturing, 202 N.L.R.B. 634, 82 L.R.R.M. 1599 (1973).
124. Giddings & Lewis, Inc. v. NLRB, note 79 *supra*.
125. *See* ch. 10 *infra*.
126. 29 U.S.C. § 152 (3); NLRB v. Fleetwood Trailer Co., Inc., note 6 *supra*; Laidlaw Corp., note 26 *supra*.
127. Little Rock Airmotive, Inc., 182 N.L.R.B. 666, 74 L.R.R.M. 1198 (1970), *enforced in relevant part*, 455 F.2d 163, 79 L.R.R.M. 2544 (8th Cir. 1972); Waveline, Inc., note 35 *supra*.

reinstatement offer from the struck employer, remains entitled to reinstatement.[128]

Although the determination of substantially equivalent employment is an ad hoc comparison of particular jobs, the factors given greatest weight by the NLRB include: wages or salaries; fringe benefits, such as retirement or health insurance; seniority for vacation, retention and promotion; location and distance from home; difference in working conditions and job responsibilities; and ability to perform the work.[129] Temporary employment during the strike does not terminate the right to reinstatement.[130] If the striker has kept in contact with the employer, renewed a reinstatement request, or submitted updated information, the NLRB is likely to find that the new position held by the striker is not regular and substantially equivalent employment regardless of the outcome of a wage or benefit comparison.[131] Consequently, the striker would retain full reinstatement rights.

9.10.4 Failure to Return or Voluntary Resignation

If the employer gives a reasonable deadline by which reinstated strikers are to report for work, on economic striker's failure to report or notify the employer of an intended absence is sufficient to terminate that striker's reinstatement rights.[132] If unfair labor practice strikers fail to return to work when scheduled, their reinstatement rights are not terminated[133] but the employer

---

128. Waveline, Inc., note 35 *supra*.
129. Little Rock Airmotive, Inc., note 127 *supra*
130. Waveline Inc., note 35 *supra*.
131. *Id.*
132. Beverly Enterprises, 263 N.L.R.B. 428, 111 L.R.R.M. 1054 (1982).
133. Teamsters Local No. 115 v. NLRB (Haddon House Food Products, Inc.), 640 F.2d 392, 106 L.R.R.M. 2462 (D.C. Cir.), *cert. denied*, 454 U.S. 827, 108 L.R.R.M. 2558 (1981).

has no obligation to reinstate them unless or until there are vacancies.[134]

A voluntary resignation terminates reinstatement rights. If an unreinstated striker expresses a preference not to return to work and makes reference to having other employment, the striker can be presumed to have voluntarily resigned.[135] Making reference to another job is probably not a voluntary resignation if the unreinstated striker indicates an interest in returning to work at his previous job or to another position with the struck employer.[136] Casual conversation or an accidental meeting during which a striker indicates disinterest is not sufficient to terminate reinstatement rights, particularly if the circumstances suggest that the striker's remarks were not taken seriously.[137]

9.10.5 Discharge

Strike participation does not completely insulate an employee from discharge and forfeiture of reinstatement rights. Although an employer cannot discharge an employee merely for participating in a protected strike or use strike participation as a factor in a decision to terminate an employee, an employer does retain the right to discharge a striker on other valid grounds. If an employer has independent reasons sufficient to justify discharging a striker, that striker can be discharged and is no longer entitled to reinstatement.[138] For example, employee theft or job-related violence are adequate reasons for discharging a striker if the discharge is consistent with the employer's past practice and any

---

134. Birmingham Ornamental Iron Co., note 98 *supra*.
135. Lincoln Hills Nursing Home, Inc., note 71 *supra*.
136. *See* section 9.10.3 *supra*.
137. Carruthers Ready Mix, Inc., note 21 *supra*.
138. Pullman, Inc., Trailmobile Div'n, 168 N.L.R.B. 230, 66 L.R.R.M. 1307, *enforced sub nom.*, Trailmobile Div'n, Pullman, Inc. v. NLRB, 407 F.2d 1006, 70 L.R.R.M. 2849 (5th Cir.), *affirmed en banc*, 415 F.2d 1007, 72 L.R.R.M. 2576 (5th Cir. 1969).

customary disciplinary procedure has been followed.[139] The fact that the discharged employee had participated in the strike would neither insulate him from discharge for cause nor entitle him to reinstatement.

9.11 Status of Reinstated Strikers

9.11.1 Prohibition against Treatment as New Employee

Strikers are employees and when reinstated, they regain their previous rights and seniority status. They may not be treated as new employees. For example, an employer cannot require returning strikers to fill out new job application forms[140] or participate in individual job interviews.[141] The employer also cannot routinely require reinstated strikers to fill out new insurance forms[142] or take new physical examinations unless required under the terms of its insurance policy.[143] Any other actions generally reserved for new employees, such as probationary periods, would be similarly prohibited.

---

139. Kansas City Power & Light Co. v. NLRB, 641 F.2d 553, 106 L.R.R.M. 2525 (8th Cir. 1981), *enforcing* 244 N.L.R.B. 620, 102 L.R.R.M. 1177 (1979); Chassen Brothers, Inc., 259 N.L.R.B. 1151, 109 L.R.R.M. 1127 (1982).
140. Shelly & Anderson Furniture Mfg. Co., Inc. v. NLRB, 497 F.2d 1200, 86 L.R.R.M. 2619 (9th Cir. 1976); Conair Corp., note 60 *supra*; Denzil S. Alkire, 259 N.L.R.B. 1323, 109 L.R.R.M. 1107 (1982), *enforcement denied on other grounds*, 716 F.2d 1014, 114 L.R.R.M. 2180 (4th Cir. 1983).
141. Soule Glass & Glazing Co. v. NLRB, note 54 *supra*.
142. Conair Corp., note 60 *supra*. The question of a strike's impact on insurance benefits is discussed more extensively in ch. 11 *infra*.
143. Leon W. Craw, Jr., Vernon E. Craw, and Daniel G. Leonard, d/b/a Craw & Son, 244 N.L.R.B. 241, 102 L.R.R.M. 1116 (1979), *enforced without opinion*, 622 F.2d 579 (3d Cir. 1980). An employer would probably be able to request that a returning striker submit to a physical examination if the employer has some reason to question whether the

9.11.2 Seniority

An employer cannot change the hire dates on personnel records[144] or otherwise extinguish strikers' previous service. To the extent that seniority governs shift or job assignments, vacation preference, promotions, or order of layoff and recall, the employer may not advance the original hire date to adjust for the time spent out on strike.[145] For example, if a striker had been hired on January 1, 1980, the employer could not change the hire date to March 1, 1980 if the employee had participated in a two-month strike. The original hire date would still be the date used for calculating the employee's seniority. Otherwise, the employer is violating section 8(a)(1) of the Act by restraining employees from engaging in protected activity and section 8(a)(3) by discriminating against strikers.

The employer may adjust service dates for benefits that are directly related to time worked, rather than to seniority. If the employer has a net service credit that determines length of vacation, entitlement to pension or sick leave benefits, termination pay, or other similar fringe benefits, and it has a policy of adjusting the credited time to reflect unpaid absences, the employer may deduct the time spent on strike from the strikers' length of actual service.[146] In essence, vacation, pension, and other benefits would stop accruing during the period of the strike

---

striker is physically capable of performing the job once the striker returns to work. For example, if the employer learned that a striker had suffered a debilitating back injury during the strike, the employer could probably request that the striker's fitness for work be verified by a doctor. The employer could not request that all strikers reporting for work routinely submit to such a physical examination.

144. Conair Corp., note 60 *supra*.
145. System Council T-4 v. NLRB, 446 F.2d 815 (7th Cir. 1971), *enforcing*, Illinois Bell Telephone Co., 179 N.L.R.B. 681, 76 L.R.R.M. 1023 (1969), *cert. denied*, 404 U.S. 1059, 79 L.R.R.M. 2314 (1972).
146. *Id.*; General Electric Co., 80 N.L.R.B. 510, 23 L.R.R.M. 1094 (1948).

so long as it was consistent with the employer's past practice or previous collective bargaining agreements.[147]

9.12 Status of Unreinstated Economic Strikers

Unreinstated economic strikers generally retain employee status even though they have not returned to work after the strike.[148] This does not mean that they are necessarily entitled to all employee benefits, such as employer-paid insurance benefits, but only that they may not be discharged and must be recalled before nonemployees can be hired to fill job vacancies that occur. Some state laws require that an employer permit an employee to continue insurance coverage at that employee's expense. Any applicable state statutes should be reviewed before terminating benefits.

Although unreinstated strikers have a right to preferential recall, this recall right does not take precedence over the rights of reinstated strikers, non-strikers, or permanent replacements who have been laid off. One federal court in disagreeing with the NLRB has upheld an employer's right to recall such employees on layoff status before recalling any unreinstated strikers, regardless of seniority.[149]

Unreinstated economic strikers whose jobs have been permanently eliminated for valid economic reasons *unrelated* to the strike are no longer employees, are not eligible for reinstatement, and are not part of the bargaining unit. Such strikers are ineligible to vote in union elections.[150] If their jobs were eliminated due to the economic impact of the strike or other strike-related rea-

---

147. See ch. 11 *infra*.
148. Laidlaw Corp., note 26 *supra*.
149. Giddings & Lewis, Inc. v. NLRB, note 79 *supra*.
150. K & W Trucking Co., Inc., 267 N.L.R.B. No. 21, 113 L.R.R.M. 1134 (1983); Kable Printing Co., 238 N.L.R.B. 1092, 99 L.R.R.M. 1384 (1978).

sons, the unreinstated strikers are still eligible to vote. Unreinstated strikers who have been permanently replaced, but whose jobs were not eliminated, retain their eligibility to vote in any election held within twelve months of the date the strike started.[151] Replacing a worker is not considered to be a permament elimination of his job. Strikers who have *not* been replaced (but have not been reinstated because of a work shortage) also retain their voting eligibility for twelve months (measured from the date the strike commenced). Unreinstated strikers lose their voting eligibility if they take employment elsewhere, are discharged for cause, or their jobs are permanently eliminated.[152]

9.13 Status of Nonstriking Employees

Employees who do not strike or who return to work prior to the strike's end also retain their employee status. They cannot, however, be given more favorable treatment than reinstated strikers. If shift or job assignments are normally determined by seniority, an employer cannot give preference to less junior employees who worked through the strike or returned early. The employer is not required, however, to discharge such employees to make room for more senior economic strikers. Junior employees who worked through the strike or returned early may continue their employment even if it results in senior economic strikers remaining unreinstated at the end of the strike. Although the employer is not required to discharge these more junior employees, it may not promote or transfer them to positions that could be adequately performed by an unreinstated striker.[153]

If nonstrikers or early returning strikers are subsequently laid off, an employer can recall those employees before they recall

---

151. 29 U.S.C. § 159(3); BioScience Laboratories v. NLRB, 542 F.2d 505, 93 L.R.R.M. 2154 (9th Cir. 1976).
152. W. Wilton Wood, Inc., 127 N.L.R.B. 1675, 46 L.R.R.M. 1240 (1960).
153. *See* section 9.6.2 *supra*.

strikers who have not yet been reinstated, regardless of seniority.[154] This preferential recall after a layoff applies only to preference over *un*reinstated strikers. It does not give nonstrikers or early returning strikers preference over strikers who were reinstated but subsequently laid off. Any such preference would favor nonstrikers over strikers and such discrimination is unlawful. Priority among nonstriking employees and reinstated strikers would have to be based on some neutral ground, such as seniority.

9.14 Status of Striker Replacements

The status of replacements as temporary or permanent determines their rights to continued employment after the strike.[155]

9.14.1 Distinguishing Temporary Replacements

Whether a replacement is considered temporary or permanent depends on the terms of the written or oral employment offer made to the replacements and the terms of the replacements' acceptance. An employer's intent that the replacements be permanent is not enough; an offer of permanent employment must be explicitly communicated to the replacements and accepted as such.[156] If an employer intends that replacements hired on a temporary basis be made permanent, the employer must notify the replacements and give them an opportunity to respond.[157]

---

154. Giddings & Lewis, Inc. v. NLRB, note 79 *supra*. *See* text accompanying note 149 *supra*.
155. NLRB v. Mackay Radio & Telephone Co., note 8 *supra*.
156. NLRB v. Murray Products, Inc., 584 F.2d 934, 99 L.R.R.M. 3269 (9th Cir. 1978).
157. Associated Grocers, 253 N.L.R.B. 31, 105 L.R.R.M. 1633 (1980), *enforced without opinion sub nom.*, Transport & Local Delivery Drivers, Local 104 v. NLRB, 672 F.2d 897, 109 L.R.R.M. 2360 (D.C. Cir. 1981),

Only replacements who accept an offer of permanent employment or acknowledge their conversion from temporary to permanent status are considered permanent replacements.[158] In addition, allegedly permanent replacements will be considered temporary by the NLRB if they are clearly inadequate or unqualified for the jobs they are performing, particularly if it is shown that there is anti-union feeling on the employer's part.[159]

9.14.2 Permanent Replacements

Unfair labor practice strikers are entitled to reinstatement regardless of whether they have been permanently replaced.[160] The right of permanent replacements to continued employment after the strike, however, does not depend on the type of strikers they replaced. Permanent replacements have an expectation of continued employment without regard to the length of the strike or the status of the strikers. An employer who discharges permanent replacements to make room for returning strikers (whether economic or unfair labor practice) may face breach of contract lawsuits brought by the replacement workers. In *Belknap, Inc. v. Hale*, the Supreme Court ruled that permanent replacements who are discharged to make room for returning strikers may sue the employer without regard to the reason for their displacement.[161] Even if the NLRB has ordered reinstatement or the employer and the union agreed to reinstatement, an employer may not discharge or lay off permanent replacements without potentially subjecting itself to liability. Under *Belknap*, federal labor law does not prevent such discharged or laid-off permanent

---

cert. denied sub nom., Associated Grocers v. NLRB, 459 U.S. 825, 111 L.R.R.M. 2472 (1982).
158. Id.
159. J.E. Steigerwald Co., Inc., note 42 *supra*.
160. NLRB v. Mackay Radio & Telephone Co., note 8 *supra*.
161. Belknap, Inc. v. Hale, 113 L.R.R.M. 3057 (1983).

replacements from bringing suit in state court to recover monetary damages.

Because of *Belknap*, employers may face a dilemma if they have hired permanent replacements during an economic strike and the strike later converts to an unfair labor practice strike. Upon conversion, the economic strikers become unfair labor practice strikers entitled to immediate reinstatement once they unconditionally offer to return, even if they have been permanently replaced. The employer is then confronted with the choice of (1) refusing to reinstate the strikers (an unfair labor practice); (2) discharging the permanent replacements and facing possible breach of contract lawsuits; or (3) carrying too many employees on its payroll.

An employer may be able to prevent the dilemma by making any permanent replacement offers subject to a reinstatement order or a settlement between the employer and the union. For example, the offer of employment could be couched in the following language:

> This offer is for continued employment, not temporary striker replacement, but it is subject to any order of the National Labor Relations Board or the courts, or any settlement agreement reached with the union, requiring reinstatement of striking employees for any reason.

It should be noted that although such an offer may eliminate liability to laid-off or discharged permanent replacements, it is not clear that it would be considered an offer of permanent employment sufficient to preclude reinstatement of economic strikers at the strike's end.[102] The NLRB has yet to rule on whether replacements accepting such a conditional offer would be considered permanent. It may determine that a permanent replacement who can be made impermanent by an NLRB order or settlement between the employer and the union cannot dis-

---

162. *Id.* at 3062 n.8, 3067 n.2 (Blackmun, J., concurring), 3077-78 (Brennan, J., dissenting).

place an economic striker who offers to return. In that event, the employer would be obligated to reinstate economic strikers immediately even though it had intended to replace them permanently.

9.14.3 Seniority

An employer may not discriminate against employees who participate in a protected strike or otherwise engage in conduct that is inherently destructive of certain employee rights, such as the right to strike.[163] Granting preferential treatment to nonstrikers is generally considered to be inherently destructive,[164] and granting superseniority to striker replacements has specifically been deemed unlawful.[165] Replacements begin accruing seniority only from their date of hire; they cannot be given additional service credit beyond the time actually worked. In *NLRB v. Erie Resistor Corp.*,[166] the employer had given each striker replacement twenty years service credit so that the replacements, rather than the returning strikers, would receive the benefits of seniority. The United States Supreme Court held that the employer's action granting such superseniority violated the NLRA. Under *Erie Resistor*, to the extent that seniority is used to determine priority for job assignments, vacations, or other benefits, the original hire dates of all employees (whether reinstated striker, striker replacement, or nonstriker) must be used to calculate the employees' term of service. The NLRB has upheld the termination of strikers' seniority when the employer has reached agreement with the union on that issue and the waiver of the strikers' seniority rights is clear and unequivocal.[167] It is clear, however, that under *Erie Resistor* an employer could not take such action unilaterally.

---

163. NLRB v. Erie Resistor Corp., 373 U.S. 221 (1963).
164. *See generally* ch. 11 *infra*.
165. NLRB v. Erie Resistor Corp., note 163 *supra*.
166. 373 U.S. 221, 53 L.R.R.M. 2121 (1963).
167. Gem City Ready Mix Co., note 88 *supra*.

10
Strike Settlement Agreements

An employer may choose to resolve some post-strike issues by negotiating a strike settlement agreement with the union. Many strike settlement agreements are negotiated by the employer and the union independently of the NLRB. When strike activity has generated unfair labor practice charges against the employer, however, a settlement must be approved by the NLRB Regional Director to resolve pending charges.

Strike settlement agreements are as varied and individually tailored as collective bargaining agreements. Such agreements commonly deal with reinstatement priorities, procedures, and amnesty but could include other strike-related topics, such as employee benefits and back pay, as well. When deciding whether to enter into a strike settlement agreement, the employer should be aware that these agreements can be a mixed blessing. On the one hand, they can establish a uniform understanding on key questions and hasten a return to normal pre-strike operations. On the other hand, the employer may be required to make significant concessions in exchange for settling the strike only to find that the agreement does not necessarily foreclose challenges by either disgruntled employees or the NLRB.

10.1 General Considerations

Neither the NLRB nor the courts have explored the limits of strike settlement agreements in detail. Therefore, an employer should be cautious in negotiating such agreements. Even though the employer and the union may agree to a particular settlement of a strike and unfair labor practice charges, the NLRB has been willing to strike down any settlement provisions that it believes unreasonably restrict strikers' statutory rights and then substitute its own remedy.[1] The NLRB has also inferred a discriminatory intent or objective as the motive for entering into a settlement if the employer has negotiated a particularly advantageous agreement.[2]

The NLRB has had a practice of rejecting settlements when the award or remedy agreed to by the parties is less than what would have been received through litigation of claims or charges.[3] Unions may also become increasingly reluctant to offer significant concessions for fear of provoking claims by their members that the unions have breached their duty of fair representation. The NLRB has also reevaluated and rejected previously approved settlements when subsequent unfair labor practices have occurred or the agreement has been breached.[4] Consequently, a strike settlement agreement has not necessarily been the final resolution of strike-related disputes. The NLRB retains jurisdiction and at its discretion may reject a particular agreement as being contrary to the policies of the National Labor

---

1. *See, e.g.*, Airport Parking Management, 264 N.L.R.B. No. 2, 112 L.R.R.M. 1013 (1982); Wooster Division of Borg-Warner Corp., 121 N.L.R.B. 1492, 43 L.R.R.M. 1006 (1958).
2. Nelson Filter Division, Nelson Industries, 225 N.L.R.B. 1080, 107 L.R.R.M. 1090 (1981).
3. Hotel Holiday Inn de Isla Verde v. NLRB, 723 F.2d 169, 115 L.R.R.M. 2188 (1st Cir. 1983); *see, e.g.*, American Cyanamid Co., 239 N.L.R.B. 440, 100 L.R.R.M. 1082 (1978), *enforced*, 592 F.2d 356, 100 L.R.R.M. 2640 (7th Cir. 1979).
4. *See* Wallace Corp. v. NLRB, 323 U.S. 248, 15 L.R.R.M. 697 (1944).

Strike Settlement Agreements

Relations Act.[5] The NLRB has been chastised for its reluctance to defer to private settlements.[6] As the composition of the NLRB has changed since that time, the Board's approach may also vary. Future NLRB decisions may show a greater willingness to defer to private settlements.

The general purpose of a settlement agreement is to encourage an employer and a union to resolve the strike and return the strikers to work.[7] Strike settlement agreements do give the employer and the union the opportunity to establish mutually agreeable reinstatement procedures and priorities before reinstatement actually begins. If the union has agreed to the procedure adopted by the employer, reinstatement may proceed more smoothly and quickly than if disputes arise while the employer is in the midst of the reinstatement process. By having the union agree in advance to the employer's particular reinstatement procedure, unfair labor practice charges and grievances may also be avoided.

10.2 Contractual Restrictions on Reinstatement Period and Seniority

A major benefit of using agreements to settle economic strikes is that reinstatement rights may be limited in ways that may have otherwise been unavailable to the employer. There are, how-

---

5. Corhart Refractories Co., 267 N.L.R.B. No. 197, 114 L.R.R.M. 1154 (1983); Airport Parking Management, note 1 *supra;* Wooster Division of Borg-Warner Corp., note 1 *supra.* The NLRB has stated:

    > In any event, we would not in our discretion honor a private settlement which purported to deny to employees the rights guaranteed them by the Act.

    Erie Resistor Corp., 132 N.L.R.B. 621, 631, 48 L.R.R.M. 1379, *enforced on remand*, 328 F.2d 723, 55 L.R.R.M. 2659 (3d Cir. 1964).
6. Hotel Holiday Inn de Isla Verde v. NLRB, note 3 *supra.*
7. Retail Clerks v. Lion Dry Goods, Inc., 369 U.S. 17, 49 L.R.R.M. 2670 (1962).

ever, some limitations. A private agreement can place reinstatement limitations only on economic strikers and any such settlement must conform to the general policies of the Act.[8] The union cannot bargain away the rights of unfair labor practice strikers to immediate, unconditional reinstatement or completely waive economic strikers' rights to reinstatement.[9]

The NLRB has declined to establish a specific time limit on the preferential recall period for economic strikers.[10] If a strike settlement agreement is used, however, the parties can negotiate a fixed deadline on the preferential recall period so long as that deadline is not unreasonably short and the agreement was reached through good faith bargaining.[11] An employer may also, by means of a strike settlement agreement, establish a specific time limit for reinstatement of strikers employed elsewhere at strike's end.[12] Strikers who fail to return to work by the end of that period may then be removed from the recall list. This is permitted only if the reinstatement period is of a reasonable length, such as several years.[13] The NLRB has recently upheld a strike settlement agreement, drafted by a union business representative, that waived all prestrike seniority of the returning strikers.[14] The NLRB found that the strikers fully understood nonstriking employees and striker replacements would have seniority over them and that the strikers were willing to waive their seniority rights as a means of ending the strike. The NLRB held that, under the circumstances, the strikers' waiver of their statutory rights was clear and unequivocal.

---

8. Airport Parking Management, note 1 *supra*.
9. *Id*.
10. Brooks Research & Manufacturing, Inc., 202 N.L.R.B. 634, 82 L.R.R.M. 1599 (1973).
11. Lodges 743 & 1746, Int'l Ass'n of Machinists & Aerospace Workers v. United Aircraft Corp., 534 F.2d 422, 90 L.R.R.M. 2272 (2d Cir. 1975), *cert. den*., 429 U.S. 825, 92 L.R.R.M. 2501 (1976); Nelson Filter Division, Nelson Industries, note 2 *supra*.
12. Nelson Filter Division, note 2 *supra*.
13. Corhart Refractories Co., note 5 *supra*.
14. Gem City Ready Mix Co., 270 N.L.R.B. No. 191, 116 L.R.R.M. 1266 (1984).

10.3 Other Restrictions on Reinstatement Rights

An employer may be able to use a strike settlement agreement to place other limitations on the reinstatement and recall procedure. The courts have upheld an agreement that allowed the employer to use a striker's last known address when sending out offers of reinstatement and required a response within three days to prevent removal of the strikers' names from the preferential recall list.[15] A strike settlement agreement may also provide an employer flexibility in reassigning strikers to specific positions. For example, an employer may wish to negotiate an agreement that allows reinstatement of economic strikers to any available positions if their pre-strike positions are not available at the time of reinstatement.[16]

Even if the NLRB refuses to enforce the exact terms of a settlement, the employer may still be in a better position for having entered into the agreement. In *Stauffer Chemical Co.*,[17] the employer and the union had agreed to impose an application deadline on economic strikers. If the strikers missed the deadline, their names were to be removed from the preferential recall list. The NLRB ordered the employer to reinstate the strikers who had missed the application deadline but suggested that the employer could treat them as new employees for seniority purposes.

If the employer is able to negotiate a waiver or restriction of reinstatement rights, it should ensure that the language of the waiver of rights is clear and unmistakable. An employer can propose that all unfair labor practice charges (and presumably grievances or lawsuits) be dropped as part of a settlement agreement so long as the employer does not insist on this to impasse.[18]

---

15. NLRB v. Vitronic Division of Penn Corp., 630 F.2d 561, 102 L.R.R.M. 2753 (8th Cir. 1979).
16. Lodges 743 & 1746, Int'l Ass'n of Machinists & Aerospace Workers v. United Aircraft Corp., note 11 *supra*.
17. Stauffer Chemical Co., 242 N.L.R.B. 98, 101 L.R.R.M. 1123 (1979).
18. Roberts Oldsmobile, Inc., 252 N.L.R.B. 192, 105 L.R.R.M. 1532 (1980).

Post-Strike Planning

10.4 Scope of the Settlement

A major advantage of a strike settlement agreement is the opportunity it presents to the employer and the union to resolve key issues prior to actual reinstatement. A corresponding disadvantage, however, is that a strike settlement agreement might instead crystallize issues that lead to impasse and a longer strike. Consequently, an employer should weigh the benefits of a comprehensive and formal agreement against the possibility that such an agreement might intensify or expand the areas of dispute and possibly lengthen the strike. Attempting to formalize agreement on reinstatement or other post-strike issues may solidify each party's position and intensify disputes. A second possible drawback is the desire to have the agreement cover all potential issues that could arise, multiplying the likelihood of disagreement between the employer and the union. The employer may want to consider limiting a settlement agreement to the most fundamental and important issues.

10.5 Enforceability of the Agreement

A strike settlement agreement does offer the union an additional forum to challenge the employer if it believes the employer is not honoring the terms of the settlement. The Supreme Court has ruled that strike settlement agreements are enforceable under section 301 of the N.L.R.A.[19] If the union believes that a strike settlement agreement has been breached or unfairly manipulated by the employer, the union may sue in federal or state court to enforce its terms.[20] Therefore, the union has additional avenues

---

19. Retail Clerks v. Lion Dry Goods, note 7 *supra*.
20. Retail Clerks v. Lion Dry Goods, note 7 *supra*; General Teamsters, Local 162 v. Mitchell Brothers Truck Lines, 682 F.2d 763, 110 L.R.R.M. 2474 (9th Cir. 1982). *See also* Soule Glass & Glazing Co. v. NLRB, 652 F.2d 1055, 107 L.R.R.M. 2781 (1st Cir. 1981) (NLRB authority to revoke settlement agreement approval when employer failed to comply.)

Strike Settlement Agreements

in which to pursue a dispute, and this may be more expensive and time consuming for the employer than either a grievance or unfair labor practice proceeding. Because strike settlement agreements are specifically enforceable, just as standard collective bargaining contracts are, the employer should approach the negotiation of such an agreement as it would collective bargaining and be willing to implement the terms to which it has agreed.

10.6 Waiver and Leverage in Settlement Negotiations and Agreements

An employer should be careful to state any limitations on reinstatement that it intends to pursue. For example, if a strike settlement agreement names the particular strikers to be reinstated, the employer has probably waived its right to discharge any named striker for strike misconduct or to litigate that question.[21] An employer should therefore be careful to exclude strikers that it intends to discharge for strike misconduct or other good cause. Unless other actions clearly show that the employer has not condoned misconduct or otherwise waived a right to discharge strikers, a failure to put a discharge or strike misconduct clause in the strike settlement agreement may waive the right to discharge those strikers.[22]

Reinstatement may not be used directly as a lever to force other union concessions. Even though the employer and the union are negotiating a strike settlement agreement, the employer cannot condition reinstatement of economic strikers on the acceptance of other conditions that the employer wishes to include.[23] Economic strikers have a right to reinstatement if vacan-

---

21. Kodiak Oil Field Haulers, Inc. v. Teamsters Union Local No. 959, 611 F.2d 1286, 103 L.R.R.M. 2288 (9th Cir. 1980).
22. Southern Florida Hotel & Motel Ass'n, 245 N.L.R.B. 561, 102 L.R.R.M. 1578 (1979). See ch. 6 *supra*.
23. Cooperativa de Credito Y Ahorro Vegabajena, 261 N.L.R.B. 1098, 110 L.R.R.M. 1241 (1982).

cies exist. Although a settlement can place some limitations on that right, an employer cannot refuse to reinstate economic strikers to force agreement on other issues.

10.7 Duration of a Strike Settlement Agreement

A union can negotiate a settlement agreement even though it is not the exclusive employee representative at that time.[24] Similarly, the agreement can outlive the union's status as exclusive representative. The enforceability of a strike settlement agreement is not affected by a subsequent decertification of the union.[25] Consequently, an employer that negotiates a strike settlement agreement remains bound by that agreement for its duration, regardless of the union's status either at the time of signing or later.

10.8 Amnesty

Finally, an employer should consider an amnesty agreement when settling a strike. A mutual amnesty clause protects nonstrikers and replacements against discrimination or discipline by the union and protects strikers against such actions by an employer.[26] Both the union and employer may gain by including such a clause in the settlement agreement. An amnesty policy may help defuse a potentially troublesome post-strike atmosphere

---

24. Retail Clerks v. Lion Dry Goods, note 7 *supra*.
25. Nelson Filter Division, Nelson Industries, note 2 *supra*.
26. *See* Office & Professional Employees Int'l Union, AFL-CIO, 267 N.L.R.B. No. 165, 114 L.R.R.M. 1144 (1983) (amnesty provision prohibiting reprisals covers internal union charges). *See also* Hospital & Institutional Workers Union, Local 250, SEIU, 254 N.L.R.B. 834, 106 L.R.R.M. 1284 (1984); Stationary Engineers Local 39, Int'l Union of Operating Engineers (San Jose Hospital & Health Center), 240 N.L.R.B. 1122, 100 L.R.R.M. 1388 (1979).

Strike Settlement Agreements

in the workplace. Factors that should be considered when contemplating an amnesty clause include the extent and severity of striker misconduct, the likelihood of union discipline, fines or penalties against nonstrikers or replacements, and the concessions that the union is willing to make in exchange for amnesty.

One possible amnesty clause is:

> The [Employer] and the [Union] agree that neither party shall in any manner discriminate against, punish, or discipline any persons for their decision to participate or not participate in the strike that ended [date], so long as such persons engaged in lawful and protected activity.

Such an amnesty clause would not shield strikers who had engaged in strike misconduct that was sufficiently serious in nature to lose protected status.[27]

Employers could alternatively consider a total amnesty clause that would prohibit discipline or discrimination against all strikers, regardless of their participation in either minor or serious misconduct. In deciding whether to agree to total amnesty, an employer should consider the effect that either partial or total amnesty would have on ending the strike and bringing people back to work, on striker behavior in possible future strikes, and on the morale of employees who may have been victims or targets of the strikers' activities.

---

27. It is questionable whether the employer would be giving up any of its rights to discipline or discharge strikers by agreeing to such a clause. Employers may not discipline or discharge strikers for participating in protected activity. See ch. 6 *supra*. So long as the misconduct is minor and thus retains its status as protected activity, the employer would be committing an unfair labor practice if it were to discipline or terminate such strikers, even without an amnesty clause.

11
Post-Strike Relationship with the Employees and the Union

After the strike has ended and strikers return to work, an employer must guard against conduct that discriminates against strikers and favors replacements or nonstrikers. Discrimination against employees for engaging in strike activity is considered inherently destructive of employee rights and thus a violation of section 8(a)(3). Conduct by the employer seen as coercive or a restraint against strike activity is a violation of section 8(a)(1).[1] The prohibition against post-strike discrimination extends into areas such as vacation, disability, accident and sickness benefits, bonuses, job and shift assignments, and discipline.

The outcome of the strike may also affect the union's majority status. If the union loses majority support, the employer's rela-

---

1. NLRB v. Great Dane Trailers, Inc., 388 U.S. 26, 65 L.R.R.M. 2465 (1967). Sections 8(a)(1) and (3) provide in relevant part:

> (a) It shall be an unfair labor practice for an employer—
> (1) to interfere with, restrain, or coerce employees in the exercise of the rights guaranteed in Section 57 of this title;
> . . . .
> (3) by discrimination in regard to hire or tenure of employment or any terms or condition of employment to encourage or discourage membership in any labor organization
> . . .

29 U.S.C. § 158(a)(1), (3).

tionship with that union may change, up to and including a possible withdrawal of recognition.

11.1 Administration of Employee Benefits

The analytical framework for evaluating charges of discriminatory benefit payments was established in *NLRB v. Great Dane Trailers, Inc.*[2] In *Great Dane*, the United States Supreme Court held that if the employer's benefits policy has an adverse effect on strikers, the NLRB must then evaluate the validity of the employer's business justification, if any, and the degree to which the conduct affects employees rights. If the employer does not offer a legitimate business purpose or if the conduct is considered inherently destructive of employee's rights, the employer is guilty of an unfair labor practice without regard to its motive in setting the policy. If the employer offers a valid business reason and the impact on employees' rights is comparatively slight, the union must prove that the employer had an anti-union motive underlying its actions.

Since the *Great Dane* decision, the NLRB has generally looked at five factors when deciding whether an employer has discriminated against strikers in administering employee benefits. First, the NLRB examines whether strikers and nonstrikers were treated differently. Even if an employer applies a uniform policy to both strikers and nonstrikers, however, the NLRB may find it discriminatory if it effectively puts strikers at a disadvantage. Second, the NLRB determines whether any business reason offered by the employer justifies its actions. Third, the NLRB examines the impact of the benefits policy on strikers. Fourth, the NLRB interprets the language of any document, such as a contract or insurance policy, that governs administration of the disputed benefit. Fifth, the NLRB examines whether the post-strike policy departs from the employer's past practice.

---

2. NLRB v. Great Dane Trailers, Inc., note 1 *supra*.

11.1.1 Vacation Benefits

One of the most frequently disputed areas of benefits administration is vacation benefits. Issues arise as to whether strikers are eligible for or can receive vacation pay during the strike,[3] whether the period of the strike can be deducted from the length of service or classified as an unexcused absence,[4] and whether the employer can reschedule vacations as a result of the strike.[5] For all three types of disputes, the NLRB and the courts have looked to vacation provisions in any collective bargaining agreement (whether new or expired) or any company policy to determine whether vacation benefits have accrued at the time of the strike and the effect, if any, of the strike on accrual or payment of such benefits.[6]

---

3. NLRB v. Great Dane Trailers, Inc., note 1 *supra;* NLRB v. Westinghouse Electric Corp., 603 F.2d 610, 101 L.R.R.M. 2870 (7th Cir. 1979); NLRB v. Knuth Bros., Inc., 584 F.2d 813, 99 L.R.R.M. 2784 (7th Cir. 1978); NLRB v. Duncan Foundry & Mach. Works, Inc., 435 F.2d 612, 75 L.R.R.M. 2781 (7th Cir. 1970); Laredo Coca Cola Bottling Co., 258 N.L.R.B. 491, 108 L.R.R.M. 1271 (1981); Georgia Kraft Co., 258 N.L.R.B. 908, 108 L.R.R.M. 1223 (1981), *enforced,* Georgia Kraft Co., Woodkraft Division v. NLRB, 696 F.2d 931, 112 L.R.R.M. 2854 (11th Cir.), *vacated and remanded as to other issue,* 52 U.S.L.W. 3700 (U.S. March 27, 1984); Gulf Envelope Co., 256 N.L.R.B. 320, 107 L.R.R.M. 1435 (1981); Metro St. Louis Bargaining Ass'n, 79 L.A. 1294 (Nitka, Arb.) (1982).
4. NLRB v. Westinghouse Electric Corp., note 3 *supra;* Laredo Coca Cola Bottling Co., note 3 *supra;* Ace Beverage Co., 253 N.L.R.B. 951, 106 L.R.R.M. 1052 (1980); Glomac Plastics, Inc., 194 N.L.R.B. 406, 78 L.R.R.M. 1662 (1971); Roegelein Provision Co., 181 N.L.R.B. 578, 73 L.R.R.M. 1396 (1970).
5. Stokely-Van Camp, Inc. v. NLRB, 722 F.2d 1324, 114 L.R.R.M. 3560 (7th Cir. 1983), NLRB v. General Time Corp., 650 F.2d 872, 107 L.R.R.M. 2868 (7th Cir. 1981).
6. NLRB v. Westinghouse Electric Corp., note 3 *supra* (existing collective bargaining agreement); NLRB v. Duncan Foundry & Machine Works, Inc., note 3 *supra* (expired collective bargaining agreement); Laredo Coca Cola Bottling Co., note 3 *supra* (expired collective bargaining agreement); Ace Beverage Co., note 4 *supra* (existing collective bargaining agreement).

11.1.1.1 Vacation Eligibility

The legal decisions on vacation eligibility depend so heavily on the specific contract or company policy involved that it is difficult to offer more than general principles. First, the employer must give strikers vacation benefits upon request if they have clearly met all contractual prerequisites.[7] Strikers may also be entitled to vacation benefits under some circumstances even if they have not met all contractual requirements. Many of the cases turn on whether vacation benefits have been accrued by the strikers at the time of the strike. If the strikers have not worked the minimum amount of time necessary to be eligible for vacation, the vacation benefits have not accrued and a denial of vacation has been held proper by the NLRB and the courts. For example, if the collective bargaining agreement requires that the employees work at least forty-two weeks in a calendar year,[8] or a full twelve months,[9] and the strikers have not done so because of the strike, the NLRB has held that an employer does not commit an unfair labor practice in refusing to pay vacation benefits to strikers.

If the employer has paid vacation benefits to nonstrikers, early returning strikers, or striker replacements who have not met the contract's eligibility requirements, the employer may not rely on the contract to deny strikers those benefits. Unequal treatment of strikers and nonstrikers is always considered overt discrimination and a violation of sections 8(a)(1) and 8(a)(3).[10] But evenhanded application of vacation eligibility requirements to strikers and nonstrikers alike does not necessarily ensure that the employer may safely deny vacation benefits. A neutral vacation policy that adversely affects strikers may also run afoul of the Act. If vaca-

---

7. NLRB v. Great Dane Trailers, Inc., note 1 *supra;* Georgia Kraft Co., note 3 *supra.*
8. Ace Beverage Co., note 4 *supra.*
9. Glomac Plastics, Inc., note 4 *supra. See also* Stokely-Van Camp, Inc. v. NLRB, note 5 *supra.*
10. NLRB v. Westinghouse Electric Corp., note 3 *supra.*

tion benefits have accrued, an employer's reliance on other technical eligibility requirements has rarely been successful to support denial of vacation benefits, unless the employer has offered a compelling business reason for the technicality.[11] The employer must explicitly state any business purpose on which it is relying; it will not be inferred.[12]

In *NLRB v. Westinghouse Electric*,[13] the contract required employees to have one full year of service. Strikers had met this condition. The Westinghouse contract also required that the employees be on the active employee roll and have thirty days' continuous service by the last business day preceding the vacation period. Because of the strike, the strikers were not on the active payroll and had not worked the thirty days preceding Westinghouse's annual one-week mandatory vacation and plant shutdown that occurred during the strike. Because the employees had accrued vacation benefits and because the employer had not uniformly applied the eligibility rules to nonstrikers, the NLRB and the federal court that approved the NLRB's order held that the employer's denial of vacation benefits to the strikers was an unfair labor practice.

In *NLRB v. Knuth Brothers*,[14] the contract required that an employee meet a length of service requirement and be on the active payroll as of March 1 of the calendar year in which the vacation would be taken. The strikers who had been denied vacation benefits would have been eligible except for the fact that, due to the strike, they were not on the active payroll March 1. Because the vacation benefits had accrued and the employer did not provide a sufficient business purpose for the March 1 eligibility requirement, the NLRB and the federal court held that the employer had committed an unfair labor practice.

The most common exceptions to the general rule that technical eligibility requirements are an inadequate reason for denying

---

11. NLRB v. Great Dane Trailers, Inc., note 1 *supra*.
12. NLRB v. Duncan Foundry & Machine Works, Inc., note 3 *supra*.
13. NLRB v. Westinghouse Electric Corp., note 3 *supra*.
14. NLRB v. Knuth Bros., Inc., note 3 *supra*.

vacation benefits are those instances in which application of the contract language to strikers is clear or the bargaining history clearly demonstrates that a strike's effect on vacation was bargained over, agreed to, or acquiesced in by the union.[15] If the strike's impact on benefits is clearly understood, the employer may strictly apply the eligibility requirements.

If confronted with a request to pay vacation benefits to strikers during the strike, an employer should review the provisions of any collective bargaining agreement (either expired or existing, depending on which agreement governs the accrual of vacation during the period in question) to determine whether vacation benefits have accrued and other requirements have been met. If benefits have accrued, the employer must be prepared to provide a business justification for any requirements not met by the strikers. The NLRB and the courts will closely scrutinize any proffered reason. An employer who waives technical requirements and pays nonstrikers or replacements for vacation time should be prepared to make similar payments to strikers.

11.1.1.2 Deduction of Strike Time

Another related vacation benefits issue is whether the strike period can be deducted as an unauthorized or unexcused absence from the employment period used to calculate vacation eligibility. Again, the NLRB relies heavily on contractual language in determining the strike's effect on vacation benefits. In *Laredo Coca Cola Bottling Co.*,[16] the expired collective bargaining agreement provided that, if an employee was gone for more than 180 hours during the year for reasons other than vacation or holidays, no vacation benefits accrued. Because the strike lasted more than 180 working hours, the NLRB found that the employer did not violate the Act when it refused to grant vacations.

---

15. *See, e.g.*, Deister Concentrator Co., Inc., 253 N.L.R.B. 358, 106 L.R.R.M. 1053 (1980).
16. Laredo Coca Cola Bottling Co., note 3 *supra*.

Past practice is a major factor in determining whether vacation benefits have accrued. For example, in *Lincoln Hills Nursing Home, Inc.*,[17] the company's vacation policy provided that an employee was eligible for a vacation if he had been with the company for one full year. After a strike, the employer required the strikers to make up a period equal to the term of the strike before becoming eligible for vacation. The NLRB approved the employer's action, primarily because it was consistent with the employer's past practice. Arbitrators facing the issue have also decided that strike time can be deducted from a vacation allotment if it conforms to past practice.[18] If a strike-time deduction is made, the deduction should be the same for all strikers. For example, the deduction should not be based on the number of years worked or based on a percentage of accrued vacation as such treatment would affect senior strikers more severely than others.[19]

11.1.1.3 Rescheduling of Vacations

A federal court of appeals has ruled that a struck employer can refuse to grant vacation time or pay to any nonstriking or striking employees during the strike, so long as the employer allows the workers to reschedule vacations once the strike has ended.[20] The court found that the company applied the policy evenhandedly to both nonstrikers and strikers so that there was no inducement for strikers to break ranks and return to work. Consequently, the employer's conduct was not inherently destructive of employee rights but fell into the comparatively-slight classification. Be-

---

17. Lincoln Hills Nursing Home, Inc., 257 N.L.R.B. 1145, 108 L.R.R.M. 1053 (1981).
18. Metro St. Louis Bargaining Ass'n, note 3 *supra;* Continental Oil Co., 70 L.A. 636 (Gottlieb, Arb.) (1978).
19. Continental Oil Co., note 18 *supra.*
20. Stokely-Van Camp, Inc. v. NLRB, note 5 *supra.*

cause the impact was slight and the court found no significant evidence of an anti-union motive behind the rescheduling, the denial of vacation pay during the strike was not an unfair labor practice.[21]

11.1.2 Disability, Accident, and Sickness Benefits

Two issues arise over disability, accident, or sickness benefits. The first is what impact the strike has on a striker's eligibility for these benefits once the strike is over. The second, more common issue is whether the employer must continue disability, accident, or sickness payments during the term of the strike.

Any contractual disability, accident, or sick leave provisions are relevant to determining the impact of the strike on employee eligibility after the strike is over. The analysis is similar to that adopted in vacation benefits cases. For example, in *Lincoln Hills Nursing Home, Inc.*,[22] the requirement that the employee have one full year of service applied to both vacations and to sick leave. The employer required strikers to make up the strike time before they could again become eligible for sick leave benefits. Because the employer's action was consistent with its past practice, the NLRB held that the employer's actions were not an unfair labor practice.

The more common issue is whether the employer may terminate payment of benefits to sick or disabled workers during the strike. Normally, an employer must continue to pay benefits to employees who were on disability or sick leave when the strike began, so long as they remain disabled or ill or until the contractual benefits period has expired.[23] If the disabled or sick em-

---

21. See section 11.1.1 *supra*.
22. Lincoln Hills Nursing Home, Inc., note 17 *supra*.
23. E.L. Wiegand Div., Emerson Electric Co. v. NLRB, 650 F.2d 463, 107 L.R.R.M. 2112 (3d Cir. 1981), *cert. denied*, 455 U.S. 939, 109 L.R.R.M. 2778 (1982); Conoco, Inc., 265 N.L.R.B. 819, 112 L.R.R.M. 1001 (1982); American Totalisator Co., 264 N.L.R.B. 1100, 111 L.R.R.M. 1293 (1982);

ployee participates in the strike and shows he or she is no longer sick or disabled, the employer may terminate the disability, accident, or sickness benefit.[24] The employee must have demonstrated that he or she was no longer disabled or sick and shown support for the strike.[25] Merely visiting the picket line is not sufficient[26] unless the employee actively engages in picketing and the picketing is sufficiently strenuous to indicate the employee is no longer ill or disabled.[27] The fact that previous strikes had 100 percent employee support or that the employee in question supported past strikes is not sufficient to show support of a current strike.[28] If disabled or ill workers participate in the strike, the employer should determine whether their strike efforts were as strenuous as their job duties. If the strike activity is as strenuous or more strenuous than the job, the employer may terminate the disability or sick leave benefits.[29] Any employee on sick or disability leave who participates in the strike and whose benefits are terminated has the same reinstatement rights as any other striker.[30]

One federal court has recently held that an employer who terminated disability benefits at the start of the strike did not violate section 8(a)(3) of the Act.[31] The strike caused a complete shutdown of the employer's plant, benefits had been terminated for both strikers and nonstrikers, and the employer's actions were consistent with its past practice. Under those circumstances, the

---

Texaco, Inc., 260 N.L.R.B. 1192, 109 L.L.R.M. 1373 (1982); *enforced*, 700 F.2d 1039, 112 L.R.R.M. 3206 (5th Cir. 1983); Texaco Oil Co., 259 N.L.R.B. 408, 108 L.R.R.M. 1370 (1981).
24. E.L. Wiegand Div., Emerson Electric Co. v. NLRB, note 23 *supra*.
25. Conoco, Inc., note 23 *supra*.
26. Texaco Oil Co., note 23 *supra*.
27. Texaco, Inc. v. NLRB, 700 F.2d 1039, 112 L.R.R.M. 3206 (5th Cir. 1983).
28. Texaco Oil Co., note 23 *supra*.
29. E.L. Wiegand Div., Emerson Electric Co. v. NLRB, note 23 *supra*.
30. *Id.*
31. NLRB v. Sherwin-Williams, 714 F.2d 1095, 114 L.R.R.M. 2506 (11th Cir. 1983).

court held that there was no anti-union motivation behind the employer's actions. Whether the NLRB or other federal courts would reach a similar conclusion has yet to be seen.

11.1.3 Insurance Benefits

An employer may not treat returning strikers as it would new employees. This prohibition normally extends to insurance benefits and coverage, unless the terms of the employer's insurance policy require different treatment and are outside the employer's control. For example, an employer can require a waiting period on insurance coverage for returning strikers only if the employer's insurance policy explicitly requires that strikers be subject to a new waiting period[32] or if the insurance policy does not except a strike from the categories considered to be a cessation of work.[33] If the employer's insurance policy dictates a particular treatment of strikers, the employer has a legitimate business reason for treating strikers differently.

Although the cases deal specifically with the insurance coverage waiting period, the same analysis may carry over to other issues involving insurance coverage or eligibility. Employers should review the requirements of insurance policies before acting on post-strike insurance issues. Employers should also be aware that state law may grant strikers additional rights regarding insurance and should review applicable state law before acting.

11.1.4 Bonuses and Other Benefits

After the strike is over, an employer cannot discriminate against strikers by paying nonstrikers or strike replacements a

---

32. Randall, Division of Textron, Inc. v. NLRB, 687 F.2d 1240, 111 L.R.R.M 2437 (8th Cir. 1982), *cert. denied*, 113 L.R.R.M. 2192 (1983).
33. NLRB v. Moore Business Forms, Inc., 574 F.2d 835, 98 L.R.R.M. 2773 (5th Cir. 1978).

Post-Strike Relationship

higher wage or salary than a striker performing identical or similar work.[34] The statutory prohibition on discrimination against strikers extends, in general, to the payment of bonuses. The NLRB has even ruled that annual bonuses should be given to unreinstated strikers on the preferential rehire list.[35] Although the NLRB examines whether payment of bonuses has a discriminatory impact on strikers, the scrutiny may be less severe than in other types of benefit cases. In *Crown Zellerbach Corp.*,[36] the NLRB held that the employer did not violate the NLRA when it entered into an agreement with the union that bonus payments made to employees would be based on the number of hours worked the previous year. Because of the strike, some strikers received smaller bonuses than nonstrikers, and other strikers received nothing. The agreement with the union was a significant factor in the NLRB's finding that no unfair labor practice had been committed. This case may be another example of union acquiescence preventing the employer's actions from being considered motivated by anti-union feelings. The NLRB also noted that the unreinstated strikers would have been ineligible for bonuses under the terms of the collective bargaining agreement because only those employees working at the time of the agreement's ratification were eligible for bonuses. Consequently, the unreinstated strikers would not have received bonuses even if they had been given credit for the period during which they were on strike.

Similarly, a federal court has held that conditioning payment of a bonus on the employee being listed on the active payroll for both the last day of the fiscal year and the date the bonus was to be paid did not violate the Act.[37] The court found past practice to be relevant, noting that the employer had not generally given

---

34. Soule Glass & Glazing Co. v. NLRB, 652 F.2d 1055, 107 L.R.R.M. 2781 (1st Cir. 1981).
35. Deister Concentrator Co., Inc., note 15 *supra*.
36. Crown Zellerbach Corp., 266 N.L.R.B. No. 207, 113 L.R.R.M. 1121 (1983).
37. NLRB v. Electro Vector, 539 F.2d 35, 93 L.R.R.M. 2021 (9th Cir. 1976).

bonuses. The bonus was thus considered a gift rather than compensation or anticipated remuneration. The strikers therefore had no expectation or entitlement to the bonus.

Granting a bonus in the form of an extra day's vacation to nonstriking employees or early returning strikers is an unfair labor practice even if the employer's act was claimed to be compensation for added responsibility during the strike.[38]

11.2 Prohibition against Discriminatory Treatment of Strikers

The prohibition on discrimination against strikers extends beyond employee benefits. Employer policies regarding job and shift assignments, discipline, and other on-the-job matters are also covered. As with the employee benefits cases, the NLRB looks to both contractual provisions and the employer's past practice in determining whether unlawful discrimination has taken place.

11.2.1 Job and Shift Assignments

If an employer intends to change assignment procedures after the strike, it should be sure either that the change does not place strikers at a disadvantage or that there is a strong business justification for the change. The issue of discriminatory job and shift assignments arises primarily when such assignments have traditionally been made by seniority. If senior workers have priority to transfer to particular shifts or positions, the employer cannot discontinue the seniority shift or position preference if the discontinuation will favor striker replacements or nonstrikers and is not

---

38. NLRB v. Swedish Hospital Medical Center, 619 F.2d 33, 104 L.R.R.M. 2751 (9th Cir. 1980).

justified by a substantial business reason.[39] For example, if a prior contract or practice allowed senior employees to bump junior employees from desirable shifts or positions, the employer probably cannot discontinue the seniority preference system once the strike is over. If the employer has assigned replacements or nonstrikers to favorable shifts or positions during the strike, the employer will probably have to allow senior reinstated strikers to exercise bumping rights and displace the employees working the more desirable assignments. Otherwise, the senior strikers have lost the benefits of their seniority by going out on strike.

Similarly, an employer who has regularly rotated shift assignments probably cannot discontinue that practice after the strike without committing an unfair labor practice.[40] For example, if an employer switched to a single shift during the strike and put all nonstrikers and replacements on that first shift, many returning strikers would be placed on the second (and perhaps less desirable) shift. If the employer then discontinued a policy of regular shift rotation, the strikers would be permanently assigned to the undesirable shift. They would be in a lesser position by virtue of their participation in the strike. Under these circumstances, discontinuing the rotation would violate the Act.

An employer is also prohibited from giving early returning strikers more favorable treatment than that given to strikers who return once the strike ends.[41] For example, an employer cannot give early returning strikers their previous jobs back without regard to production needs and place the other strikers in the lower paying and less desirable jobs that remain.[42] Giving early returning strikers preferential treatment would be seen as an

---

39. Randall, Division of Textron, Inc., note 32 *supra*; NLRB v. Moore Business Forms, Inc., note 33 *supra*.
40. NLRB v. Moore Business Forms, Inc., note 33 *supra*.
41. American Olean Tile Co., Inc., 265 N.L.R.B. 206, 112 L.R.R.M. 1080 (1982).
42. George Banta Co., Inc. v. NLRB, 606 F.2d 10, 110 L.R.R.M. 3351 (D.C. Cir.), *amended*, 111 L.R.R.M. 2591 (1982), *cert. denied*, 113 L.R.R.M. 2112 (1983).

inducement for the strikers to break ranks and return to work. Such an inducement is considered inherently destructive of employee rights under the Act.

The prohibition against discriminatory job and shift assignments does not completely tie the employer's hands in making needed personnel changes. An employer can cross-train strikers if it has a past practice of doing so and if the new positions for which the strikers are being trained are at least as desirable as their previous positions.[43] Similarly, the employer can reclassify strikers if their jobs were phased out for valid financial reasons.[44]

11.2.2 Post-Strike Discipline and Other Conditions of Employment

The prohibitions against discriminatory discipline fall into two main categories: (1) the discriminatory application of existing disciplinary rules and procedures; and (2) the enactment of new disciplinary rules and procedures as punishment for any employees who engaged in strike activity. For example, an employer cannot impose new rules regarding tardiness immediately after a strike, unless it can demonstrate a need for making that change at that time.[45] Nor can the employer subject only strikers to either new or existing tardiness rules even though the rules and procedures may, themselves, be reasonable.[46] An employer cannot require that only strikers submit to a polygraph test even though the employer claims it is investigating allegations of strike misconduct.[47] Similarly, an employer cannot reimburse strike

---

43. R.L. White Co., Inc., 262 N.L.R.B. 575, 111 L.R.R.M. 1078 (1982).
44. Atlas Metal Parts Co., Inc. v. NLRB, 660 F.2d 304, 108 L.R.R.M. 2474 (7th Cir. 1981).
45. Road Sprinkler Fitters Local Union No. 669 v. NLRB (John Cuneo, Inc.), 681 F.2d 11, 110 L.R.R.M. 2845 (D.C. Cir. 1982), *cert. denied sub nom.*, John Cuneo, Inc. v. NLRB, 112 L.R.R.M. 2500 (1983).
46. *Id.*
47. Associated Grocers, 253 N.L.R.B. 31, 105 L.R.R.M. 1633 (1980), *enforced without opinion*, Transport & Local Delivery Drivers, Local 104 v.

replacements or early returning strikers for strike-related property damage and not reimburse the strikers, unless the employer can give a valid business reason for making such a distinction.[48]

Just as the employer cannot impose unequal discipline, an employer cannot discriminate against strikers in discharge decisions. The employer may not discharge a striker for having participated in the strike nor discharge a striker for a lesser offense than it would discharge either a nonstriker, a striker replacement, or an early returning striker. Again, the employer should apply a uniform standard to both strikers and nonstrikers when administering discipline or contemplating discharge. As always, the reasons for the employer's actions should be well documented and substantiated.

11.3 Post-Strike Treatment of the Union

If an employer has made a substantial number of permanent striker replacements during an economic strike or the strike has ended without a new collective bargaining agreement being reached, the employer's relationship with, and treatment of, the union could possibly change. Altered relationships are, of course, less likely in the case of an unfair labor practice strike when all strikers will be returning to work at the strike's conclusion and a collective bargaining agreement may still be in effect.

11.3.1 Majority Status

A union is irrebuttably presumed to have majority support for a period of one year after it is certified as the exclusive bargaining

---

NLRB, 672 F.2d 897, 109 L.R R.M. 2360 (D.C. Cir. 1981), cert. denied sub nom., Associated Grocers v. NLRB, 459 U.S. 825, 111 L.R.R.M. 2472 (1982).

48. Litton Microwave Cooking Products, 75 L.A. 724 (O'Connell, Arb.) (1980).

representative.[49] The NLRB has also held that an employer is prohibited by the contract-bar rule from withdrawing recognition of the union during the term of any collective bargaining agreement.[50] Obligations to bargain with a union that are created by NLRB-approved settlements of unfair labor practice charges extend for one year[51] or some other reasonable period.[52] Once the certification bar or contract bar has ended, however, the employer may withdraw recognition of the union if the employer can prove that the union does not have majority support or if the employer has a good faith doubt regarding continued majority support and that doubt is based on objective factors. To justify withdrawal of recognition, the lack of union support cannot have been caused or aided by employer unfair labor practices.[53]

If an employer has hired a large number of permanent replacements, the union representing the employees may not have majority status. Although there is some disagreement over what presumptions of union support may be applied, several principles have been clearly announced by the NLRB and the courts. First, the employer must include replaced or unreinstated strikers in any count taken.[54] Consequently, there must be a greater number of nonstriking employees and permanent replacements than strikers to even consider a possible withdrawal of recognition.

---

49. Brooks v. NLRB, 348 U.S. 96, 35 L.R.R.M. 2158 (1954).
50. Precision Striping, Inc., 245 N.L.R.B. 169, 102 L.R.R.M. 1264 (1979), *enforcement denied*, 642 F.2d 1144, 107 L.R.R.M. 2009 (9th Cir. 1981).
51. Straus Communications, Inc., 246 N.L.R.B. 846, 102 L.R.R.M. 1679 (1979), *enforced*, 625 F.2d 458, 104 L.R.R.M. 3061 (2d Cir. 1980).
52. Soule Glass & Glazing Co. v. NLRB, note 34 *supra*.
53. *Id.*
54. Vulcan-Hart Corp., St. Louis Div. v. NLRB, 718 F.2d 269, 114 L.R.R.M. 2745 (8th Cir. 1983); Soule Glass & Glazing Co. v. NLRB, note 34 *supra*; IT Services, 263 N.L.R.B. 1183, 114 L.R.R.M. 1229 (1982). At least one federal court has indicated that a one-year time limit is appropriate for including replaced strikers in the count. C.H. Guenther & Sons v. NLRB, 427 F.2d 983, 74 L.R.R.M. 2343 (5th Cir.), *cert. denied*, 400 U.S. 942, 75 L.R.R.M. 2752 (1970).

Second, only permanent replacements may be counted.[55] Temporary replacements may not be included in evaluating the strength of union support.

The major controversy is whether nonstriking employees and permanent striker replacements may be presumed to either favor or disfavor the union. The NLRB has often stated that new employees should be presumed to support the union in the same ratio as the workers they replace.[56] Although several federal courts have agreed that the NLRB's presumption should be applied when there is normal employee turnover, they have found the presumption to be less realistic in the striker replacement context.[57] Both the NLRB and the courts agree that replacements will not be presumed to support the union if the replacements have frequently crossed picket lines during the course of a lengthy and violent strike.[58] A similar analysis is applied to nonstriking employees. If the nonstriking employees or the replacements have not been crossing picket lines and the strike has been relatively nonviolent, the employer will need other objective evidence of nonsupport of the union. No one factor is dispositive; the NLRB and the courts look to all of the circumstances of the particular situation. If permanent replacements[59] or nonstriking employees[60] have told management they do not want union representation, if replacements know that the union is seeking their termination,[61] or if there is other corroborated evidence of disaf-

---

55. Soule Glass & Glazing Co. v. NLRB, note 34 *supra*.
56. *See, e.g.*, Libbie Convalescent Center a/k/a Libbie Rehabilitation Center, Inc., 251 N.L.R.B. 877, 105 L.R.R.M. 1389 (1980); Windham Community Memorial Hospital, 230 N.L.R.B. 1070, 95 L.R.R.M. 1565 (1977).
57. Vulcan-Hart Corp., St. Louis Div. v NLRB, note 54 *supra;* Garrett Railroad Car & Equipment, Inc. v. NLRB, 683 F.2d 731, 110 L.R.R.M. 2919 (3d Cir. 1982); National Car Rental System v. NLRB, 594 F.2d 1203, 100 L.R.R.M. 2824 (8th Cir. 1979).
58. National Car Rental System v. NLRB, *supra*, note 57; Stormor, Inc. Div. of Fuqua Industries, Inc., 268 N.L.R.B. No. 134, 115 L.R.R.M. 112 (1984); IT Services, note 54 *supra*.
59. IT Services, note 54 *supra*.
60. Stormor, Inc. Div. of Fuqua Industries, Inc., note 58 *supra*.
61. IT Services, note 54 *supra*.

fection for the union, the employer has a stronger basis for a good-faith doubt of majority status. The employer cannot use the percentage of negative votes from past union elections and apply that ratio to nonstriking employees to determine the presence or absence of union support.[62] The employer may want to consider petitioning for a representation election to determine conclusively whether the union has majority support.[63]

11.3.2 Withdrawal of Recognition

If the employer has a good-faith doubt regarding the union's majority status, the employer may withdraw recognition of the union.[64] Once there has been a valid withdrawal of recognition, the employer is no longer compelled to bargain or negotiate with the union. An employer should be wary of withdrawing recognition if there is *any possibility* that replacements are only temporary or that an economic strike may convert to an unfair labor practice strike. An employer who prematurely or mistakenly withdraws recognition and refuses to bargain runs the risk of committing an unfair labor practice if it is determined that the employer lacked a sufficient basis for its actions. Any employer contemplating withdrawal of recognition should have the factual and legal aspects of its situation carefully reviewed by counsel.

---

62. Windham Community Memorial Hospital, note 56 *supra*.
63. *See, e.g.*, National Car Rental System v. NLRB, note 57 *supra*.
64. Straus Communications, Inc., note 51 *supra*.

Tables

Cases

(References are to pages and footnotes)

Abbot v. Plumbers 264n.181
Abilities & Goodwill
 Co. 324n.51, 336n.108
Abreen Corp. v.
 Laborers . 226n.25, 260n.158,
  263n.173, 265n.185
Ace Beverage
 Co. 363nn.4, 6, 364 n.8
Ace Tank & Heater
 Co. 50n.24
ACF Indus., Inc. v.
 NLRB 154n.28, 155n.30,
  179n.119
ACMAT Corp. v. Operating
 Engineers 305n.70,
  306n.74
Acme Fire Works, Inc, v.
 NLRB 337n.112
Adamaczewski v.
 Machinists 116n.26
A. Duie Pyle, Inc., NLRB
 v. 205n.75
Advance Indus. v.
 NLRB 205n.75
Airco Speer Carbon-Graphite v.
 Electrical, Radio & Mach.
 Workers 168n.76,
  169n.82, 174nn.100, 101
Air Engineering Metal Trades
 Council (Pan Am World Serv.,
 Inc.) 238n.62, 241n.73

Aircraft & Engineering
 Maintenance Employees v.
 I.E. Schilling Co. ... 262n.168
Airline Pilots v. CAB Airport
 Parking Management 58n.43,
  60n.48
Airport Parking
 Management 352n.1, 353n.5,
  354nn.8, 9
Airport Parking Management v.
 NLRB 321n.41
A.J. Librera Disposal Serv.,
 Inc. 150n.13
Alabama Power Co. v.
 Laborers 174n.99
Alexander, NLRB v. 66n.78
Allelvia Cushion Co. 148n.4
Allen v. Carpenters 258n.153
Allen Bradley Local v. Wisconsin
 Employment Relations
 Board 189n.4
Allen Trucking Co. v. Mine
 Workers 200n.53
Allentown Racquetball & Health
 Club, Inc. v. Building &
 Constr. Trades
 Council 260n.158
Allied Concrete v. NLRB . 189n.4
Allied Int'l Inc. v.
 Longshoremen 262n.166

379

Tables

Allis-Chalmers Mfg. Co., NLRB v. 110n.5
Altemose Constr. Co. v. Building Constr. Trades Council 198n.39
Aluminum Workers v. Consolidated Aluminum Corp. 160n.45
Amax Coal Co. v. NLRB . 16n.11, 255n.139
American Book-Stratford Press, Inc. 24n.34
American Broadcasting Co. v. Writers Guild ... 25nn.38, 39
American Compress Warehouse, NLRB v. 71n.103
American Cyanamid Co. .. 352n.3
American Cyanamid Co. v. NLRB 310n.10, 229nn.73, 74
American Freight System v. NLRB 153n.25
American Health Enterprise, Inc. (Colonial Manor Nursing Home) 20n.26
American Medical Serv., NLRB v. 22n.31
American Nat'l Ins. Co., NLRB v. 69n.91
American Olean Tile Co. 373n.41
American Screw Co. 28n.49
American Ship Building Co. v. NLRB 62n.58, 63n.65
American Steel & Pump Corp. 118n.34
American Steel Works ... 150n.15
American Tel. & Tel. Co. 180n.122
American Totalisator Co. . 368n.23
American Welding & Industrial Sales, Inc. 118n.34
American Wire Weavers Ass'n (Lindsay Wire Weaving Co.) 292n.7
Amoco Oil v. IBEW 261n.162

AMPAC (Kane-Miller Corp.) 205n.76
Anchor Rome Mills, Inc. 315nn.13, 15
Anheuser-Busch v. Teamsters 27n.45
Apex Hosiery Co. v. Leader 60n.46
Arlan's Dep't Store 153n.23
Arlington Asphalt Co. ... 71n.104
Arrow Indus., Inc. 204n.69
Artesia v. Steelworkers ... 202n.63
A.S. Abell Co., NLRB v. ... 55n.35
Asbestos Workers (API, Inc.) 200n.44
Asbestos Workers v. Superior Ct. 257n.146
Ashtabula Forge, Div. of ABS Co. 180n.124
Associated Gen. Contractors 60n.54
Associated Gen. Contractors v. California St. Council of Carpenters 60n.47
Associated Gen. Contractors, NLRB v. 256n.145
Associated Grocers 347n.157, 348nn.161, 162, 370n.47
Associated Grocers v. NLRB (U.S.) 375n.47
Associated Grocers v. NLRB (1st Cir.) 203n.68, 204n.70
Atkinson v. Sinclair Ref. Co. 158n.35, 166n.70
Atlantic Creosoting Co. .. 231n.87
Atlantic Printing Specialties & Paper Prod. Union (the Mead Corp.) 27n.46
Atlas Metal Parts Co. v. NLRB 330nn.80, 81, 331n.85, 374n.44
Audobon Health Care Center 149n.10

380

Cases

Automatic Plastic Molding
   Co. 337n.110
Automobile, Aerospace &
   Agriculture Implement
   Workers v. National Right to
   Work Legal Defense & Educ.
   Foundation 116n.26
Automobile Transp., Inc. v.
   Ferndance 172n.91
Automobile Workers v.
   NLRB 203n.66
Auto Workers v. Hoosier Cardinal
   Corp. 165n.65

Bacino v. Musicians 261n.163
Baney Wilkerson Constr.
   Co. 112n.21
Baton Rouge Coca Cola Bottling
   Co. v. Truck Drivers 192n.21
Beacon Moving & Storage v.
   Teamsters 191n.17
Bean & Son v. Graphic Arts
   Local 226n.22, 265n.188
Bechtel Corp. v.
   Laborers 306n.74
Beck Co. 19n.22
Bedford Cut Stone Co. ... 62n.58
Belknap, Inc. v. Hale ... 350, 345
Bell Aerospace Co., NLRB
   v. 23n.32
Benson Produce Co. 69n.92
Bethlehem Steel Co.
   (Shipbuilding Div.) ... 13n.4
Bettendorf-Stamford Bakery
   Equip. Co. v. UAW . 195n.32
Beverly Enterprises 23n.31,
                           341n.132
Bexar Plumbing Co. v.
   NLRB 228n.32
Bio Science Laboratories v.
   NLRB 346n.151
Birmingham Ornamental Iron
   Co. 334n.98, 342n.134

B.N. Beard Co. 49n.19
Boilermakers (Capital Boiler
   Works, Inc.) 297n.33
Bonnano Linen Serv. v.
   McCarthy . 199n.47, 200n.52,
                           202n.61
Bookbinders v. NLRB 67n.85
Boston Buffalo Express v.
   Teamsters 197n.36
Bottoms v. B & M Coal
   Corp. 189n.9
Boyd v. Deena Artware,
   Inc. 190n.11
Boys Market v. Retail Clerks . 159,
   160-61, 162-63, 164, 305,
                       306n.70
Brady-Hamilton Stevedore
   Co. 304n.66
Braniff Master Exec. Council v.
   CAB 58n.42
Braswell Motor Freight Lines,
   Inc. 71n.107
Brennan v. Western Union Tel.
   Co. (Western Union I) . 48-49
Brewery Workers (Bert P.
   Williams, Inc.) 244n.88
Brick & Clay Workers v. Deena
   Artware, Inc. 259n.156
Bricklayers 25n.39
Bricklayers (Bjork Blars,
   Ltd) 228n.32
Bricklayers (Decora,
   Inc.) 296n.28
Bricklayers (J.E. Hoetger &
   Co.) 245n.90, 245n.97
Bricklayers (Lake Shore
   Hosp.) 20n.25
Bricklayers v. NLRB 239n.68,
             254n.137, 259n.154
Broadcast Employees (CBS,
   Inc.) 250n.116
Broadcast Employees, NLRB
   v. 240n.69

Tables

Broadcast Employees & Technicians (Skateboard Productions, Inc.) 108n.9
Broadcast Technicians v. Broadcast Serv., Inc. 245n.92
Brooks v. NLRB 376n.49
Brooks Research & Mfg. Co. 340n.123, 354n.10
Brown & Sharp Mfg. Co., NLRB v. 22n.3
Brown Food Stores, NLRB v. 63-64, 66n.80, 67n.84
Browning-Ferris Indus., NLRB v. 178n.111, 181n.127, 182nn.130, 132, 323nn.48, 50
Brunswick Corp. 171n.89
Buffalo Bituminous, Inc. v. NLRB 118n.32
Buffalo Forge Co. v. Steelworkers 161, 162, 170n.90, 184
Building & Constr. Trades Council (Chatham Supermarkets, Inc.) 223n.7
Building & Constr. Trades Council (Donald Schriver Inc.) 255n.139
Building & Constr. Trades Council (H.E. Collins Contracting Co.) 235n.53
Building & Constr. Trades Council (K-Mart Corp.) 248n.107
Building & Constr. Trades Council (Markwell & Hartz, Inc.) 233n.48
Building & Constr. Trades Council (Rog C. Anderson, Jr., Inc.) 229n.35, 239n.66
Building & Constr. Trades Council (Stark Elec. Co.) ... 256n.145
Building & Constr. Trades Council v. Brown & Roof, Inc. 189n.8, 190n.10

Building Serv. Employees v. NLRB 246n.98
Building Serv. Employees, NLRB v. 251n.121
Burlington Homes, Inc. 315nn.13, 14
Bush, People v. 194n.29
Business Machines (Royal Typewriter), NLRB v. 243n.81
Butchers (Triple L. Distrib. Co.) 253n.133
Butterworth-Manning-Ashmore Mortuary 181n.125

Cagle's, Inc. 115n.25
California Cotton Coop. Ass'n. 170n.87
California Trucking Ass'n v. Teamsters (9th Cir.) 167n.74, 168n.77, 173n.94, 183n.138
California Trucking Ass'n v. Teamsters (N.D. Cal.) 166n.71, 173n.170, 260n.160
Cameron Iron Works, Inc. 27n.46
Capital Parcel Delivery Co. v. Teamsters 190n.14
Carbon Fuel Co. v. Mine Workers . 166n.71, 173n.170, 260n.160
Carbonex Coal Co. 313n.7
Carey v. Westinghouse Elec. Corp. 293n.15
Carpenter Sprinkler Corp. v. NLRB 49n.20, 68n.89, 70n.99, 71n.102
Carpenters (Commercial Indus. Contractors, Inc.) ... 225n.18
Carpenters (Diamond Indus.) 253n.132

Cases

Carpenters (Frederick Meiswinkel, Inc.) 296n.30
Carpenters (J.A. Stewart Constr. Co.) 225n.18
Carpenters (Intercounty Constr. Corp.) 291n.14, 293n.14
Carpenters (Malek Constr. Corp.) 244n.89
Carpenters (Modern Erection Serv., Inc.) 299n.42
Carpenters (Mueller-Anderson, Inc.) 233n.48
Carpenters (New Mexico Properties) 240n.71
Carpenters (O.R. Carst) . 299n.40
Carpenters (Pace Constr. Co.) 225n.18, 228n.31
Carpenters (Robert Wood & Assoc., Inc.) 235n.53, 236n.56, 238n.62
Carpenters (Sharp & Tatro Dev. Co.) 238n.54
Carpenters (Silver Bow Employers Ass'n) 256n.142
Carpenters (Specialty Bldg. Co.) 233n.48, 238n.64, 239n.67
Carpenters (Steiner Lumber Co.) 251n.121
Carpenters (T & P Iron Works) 293nn.13, 16
Carpenters Council (Campbell Indus.) 27n.45
Carpenters Dist. Council (Godwin Bevers Co.) 299n.43
Carpenters Dist. Council (Northern Cal. Drywall Ass'n) . 303n.63
Carpenters v. NLRB (Sand Door) 254n.134
Carpenters, NLRB v. ... 252n.127
Carruthers Ready Mix .. 322n.42, 332n.89, 335n.103, 342n.137

Carruthers Ready Mix v. Cement Masons 266n.191
Caterpillar Tractor Co. v. NLRB 153n.23
Cedar Coal Co. v. Mine Workers 184n.142
Celanese Corp. 118n.33
Celotex Corp. v. OCAW . 160n.46
Cement Masons (California Ass'n of Employers) 250n.115
Certified Corp. v. Teamsters 166n.69
Charge Card Ass'n v. NLRB 150n.14
Charles D. Bonnano Linen Serv., Inc. 318n.33
Charleston Nursing Center ... 326
Chassen Bros., Inc. 343n.139
Chattanooga Mailers v. Chattanooga News Free Press 16n.13
Chemical Workers (American Cyanamid Co.) 228n.43
Chemical Workers (Crest, Inc.) 235n.52
Cheney Cal. Lumber Co. .. 15n.7
Chevron U.S.A., Inc. .. 179n.117, 180n.123, 259n.155
C.H. Guenther & Sons v. NLRB 276n.54
Chicago & N.W. R.R. v. United Transp. Union 69n.91
Chicago Web Printing Pressmen's Union (Metropolitan Printing Co.) 292n.10
Cincinnati Mailers (Rosenthal & Co.) 295n.20
City Disposal Systems, Inc., NLRB v. 148n.3
C & K Coal Co. v. Mine Workers 260n.161
C.K. Smith Co. 182n.133
C.K. Smith Co., NLRB v. 183n.134

383

Tables

Clark Engineering & Constr. Co. v. Carpenters 262n.168
Clarklift, Inc. 149n.9
Classic Prod. Corp. 149n.8
Clear Pine Moldings, Inc. 203n.67, 204n.71
Clune v. Publishers Ass'n .. 61n.48
Coast Valleys Typographical Union (Daily Breeze Div.) .. 108n.9
Cobra, LTD. 22n.31
Coca Cola Bottling Co. v. Memphis 330n.82
Cohart Retractories Co. ... 353n.5, 354n.13
Collier v. Operating Engineers 265n.186
Colonial Haven Nursing Home, Inc., NLRB v. 195n.31
Colonial Press, Inc. 323n.47
Colonie Fibre Co. v. NLRB 26n.43
Colony Furniture Co. ... 118n.32
Columbia ITU Union (Washington Post Co.) 25n.30
Commerce Tankers Corp. v. Maritime Union 222n.6
Commercial Management, Inc. 115n.25
Communication Workers v. Southwestern Bell Tel. Co. 16n.10
Complete Auto Transit v. Reis .. 166n.70, 172n.90, 175
Conair Corp. 326n.60, 330n.82, 335n.105, 343nn.140, 142, 344n.149
Connell Constr. Co. v. Plumbers & Steamfitters 254n.138
Conoco, Inc. ... 52n.28, 322n.45, 370n.23, 369n.25
Consolidated Dress Carriers, Inc. 335n.104

Consolidated Dress Carriers, Inc. v. NLRB 336n.106
Consolidated Express, Inc. v. New York Shipping Ass'n 266n.191
Consolidation Coal Co. v. Mine Workers (4th Cir. 1983) 175nn.103, 109
Consolidation Coal Co. v. Mine Workers (4th Cir. 1982) 163nn.57, 59
Consolidation Coal Co. v. UMW (10th Cir.) 175n.105
Consolidation Coal Co. v. UMW (D. Utah) 174nn.99
Constar, Inc. v. Plumbers 240n.70
Construction Workers v. Laburnum Constr. Corp. 199n.46
Continental Indus. 225n.57
Continental Oil Co. . 367nn.18, 19
Cooks Market, Inc. 115n.25
Cooper Thermometer ... 177n.110
Coopertira de Credito y Ahorro Vegebajona 323n.46, 327n.63, 357n.23
Coopersville Cooperative Elec. 24n.34
Coronet Casuals 103n.66
Corsicana Cotton Mills, NLRB v. 71n.105
Covington Furniture Mfg. Corp. 318n.33
Craw & Son 343n.143
Crosby Chemicals, Inc. .. 315n.19
Cross Co. v. Auto Workers 198n.43
Crown Zellerback Corp. . 50n.23, 367
Cunningham, United States v. 160n.46, 163n.58
Curreri v. Teamsters 189n.8, 200n.48, 201nn.55, 58, 202n.61

Cases

Dalmo Victor I 109n.13, 110
Dalmo Victor II ... 109, 110n.14, 112
Daniels Constr. Co. 148n.2
Danielson v. Garment Workers 258n.149
Darlington Veneer Co., NLRB v. 71n.105
Davison, NLRB v. 71n.104
Dean Foods Co. 112n.21, 116n.28
Decker Foundry, Inc. ... 324n.56
DeCostello v. Teamsters 266n.192
Deister Concentrating Co. 366n.15, 371n.35
Delaware Coca Cola Bottling Co. v. Teamsters 154n.29, 168n.78, 169n.83, 179n.126
Delhi-Taylor Ref. Div. ... 63n.59
Denver Bldg. & Constr. Trades Council, NLRB v. ... 221n.3, 244n.89
Denzil S. Alkire 343n.140
Desire Fashions, Inc. v. Garment Workers 201n.54
Distillery Workers (Capitol Husting Co.) 28n.46, 113n.22
Donald Schriver, Inc. v. NLRB 256n.142
Donovan v. Lone Star Motel 40n.4
Douds v. Architects 243n.82
Dow Chemical Co. v. NLRB 153n.23, 156n.31, 159n.35
Drake Bakeries, Inc. v. Bakery & Confection Workers 164n.63
Dresser Indus. v. Steel Workers 172n.92
Drug Package Co. 326n.60, 336n.109

Duncan Foundry & Mach. Works, NLRB v. 363nn.3, 6, 375 n.12
Dunn Bros., Inc. v. Retail Clerks 190n.14
Duro Fittings Co. 69n.94

East Chicago Rehabilitation Center v. NLRB ... 19n.24, 169n.85
Eastex, Inc. v. NLRB ... 178n.111
Eazor Express, Inc. v. Teamsters . 167n.73, 168n.80
Edna H. Pagel, Inc. v. Teamsters 262n.168
Edward G. Budd Co., NLRB v. 24n.35
Edward J. Alexander 66n.78
Edward J. De Bartolo Corp. v. NLRB 249nn.109, 110
Electrical Workers (General Elec.) v. NLRB 232, 232nn.43, 44, 234
Electrical Workers (IBEW) (Bergelectric Corp.) .. 26n.40
Electrical Workers (IBEW) (Hoffman Co.) 19n.22
Electrical Workers v. Illinois Bell Tel. Co. 116n.27
Electrical Workers v. NLRB 188n.3, 224n.13
Electrical Workers, NLRB v. 18n.17
Electrical, Radio & Mach. Workers (General Elec. Co.) . 113n.23
Electrical, Radio & Mach. Workers v. NLRB 158n.35
Electro Coal Transfer Corp. v. Longshoremen 223n.8, 256n.143
Electro Vector, NLRB v. . 371n.37
Elevator Constructors (Elevator Indus., Ass'n) 296n.28

385

Tables

Elevator Mfr's Ass'n v. Elevator Constructors 152n.20
Elk Lumber Co. 149n.8
E.L. Weigand Div. 52n.27
E.L. Weigand Div. v. NLRB ... 368n.23, 369nn.24, 29, 30
Emporium Capwell Co. v. Western Addition Community Organization 149n.6
Engineers & Scientific Guild (Lockheed) 109n.12
Erie Resistor Corp. .. 350, 353n.5
Erie Resistor Corp., NLRB v. 50n.23
Etco Mfg., Inc. NLRB v. 316n.23
Evening News Ass'n 59n.44

Fansteel Metalurgical Corp., NLRB v. 150n.11, 338n.117
Farmers Cooperative Congress 115n.25
Feather v. Mine Workers (3d Cir.) 263nn.171, 173
Feather v. UMW (W.D.PA) 255n.139
Federal Prescription Serv. Inc. v. Meat Cutters 202n.63
Fiberboard Paper Prod. Corp. v. Machinists 200n.50
Fiberboard Paper Prod. Corp. v. NLRB 54n.34
Firestone Tire & Rubber Co. v. NLRB 205n.73
First Nat'l Maintenance Corp. v. NLRB 54n.34
Fisher Foods, Inc. 157n.34
Flame Coal Co. v. Mine Workers . 199n.47, 264n.180, 265n.188

Fleetwood Trailer Co., NLRB v. 213n.6, 317nn.27, 28, 340n.126
Florida Power & Lt. Co. v. Building Traders Council 191n.17
Florida Power & Lt. Co. v. Electrical Workers ... 25n.38
Florida Steel Corp. 233n.96, 337n.109
Flowers Baking Co. 73n.111
Foley-Wismer & Becker v. NLRB 295n.26, 299n.38
Food & Commercial Workers (Alpha Beta Co.) 111nn.18, 20
Food Serv. Co. 331n.87, 339n.118
Frito-Lay v. Meatcutters .. 27n.45
Frito-Lay v. Teamsters . 263n.174
Fruit & Vegetable Packers (Tree Fruits), NLRB v. . 247nn.102, 103, 251nn.118, 119
Fulton v. Plumbers 260n.159
Furniture Workers (Brooklyn Spring Corp.) 206n.79
Furniture Workers (Fort Smith Chain Co.) v. NLRB . 18n.17
F.W. Woolworth Co. .. 236n.107, 337n.113, 340nn.115, 116

Garrett R.R. Car & Equip., Inc. 204n.69, 205n.74
Garrett R.R. Car & Equip., Inc. v. NLRB 336n.108, 377n.57
Gary-Hobart Water Corp. 154n.26, 155n.30
Gary-Hobart Water Corp. v. NLRB 153n.22, 177n.110
Gateway Coal v. Mine Workers 151n.17, 153n.25, 172n.90

Cases

Gem City Ready Mix
    Co. 33n.88, 350n.88, 354n.14
General Elec. Co. 50n.24, 344n.146
General Elec. Co. v. Electrical
    Workers 197n.36
General Elec. Co.,
    NLRB v. 117n.29
General Motors Corp. 26n.43
General Motors Corp. v.
    NLRB 111nn.17, 18
General Time Corp.,
    NLRB v. 363n.5
General Tire & Rubber
    Co. 178n.112
George Banta Co. v.
    NLRB 373n.42
George E. Hoffman & Sons v.
    Teamsters 226n.23, 264n.178
Georgia Kraft Co. 320
Georgia Kraft Co. v.
    NLRB 204n.71, 320n.37, 325n.57, 331n.85, 363n.3, 364n.7
Georgia Pac. Corp. v.
    PLSA 231n.39
G & H Prod., Inc. v.
    NLRB 321nn.38, 48
G & H Prod., Inc. 320n.36
Giant Food Markets, Inc. 193n.27
Giddings & Lewis,
    Inc. 331n.87, 335n.101
Giddings & Lewis, Inc v.
    NLRB 326n.62, 330n.79, 333nn.91, 93, 94, 335n.102, 340n.124, 345n.149, 347n.154
Girard, State *ex rel.* v.
    Percich 190n.13
Gissell Packing Co., NLRB
    v. 106n.2

Glomac Plastics, Inc. 363n.4, 364n.9
Gould, NLRB v. 154n.29, 179n.120
Goya Foods, Inc. 152n.21
G & P Trucking v.
    NLRB 180n.124
Granny Goose Foods v.
    Teamsters 159n.44
Graphic Arts (London Press,
    Inc.) 246n.100
Graphic Arts (S & M Rotogravure
    Serv., Inc.) 244n.86
Gray Line, Inc. 71n.107
Great Atl. & Pac. Tea
    Co. 114n.24
Great Dane Trailers, Inc., NLRB
    v. 50n.23, 317n.27, 323n.47, 361n.1, 362, 363n.3, 364n.7, 365n.11
Great Western Broadcasting Corp.
    v. NLRB 248n.106
Griffin Inc. 71n.106
Gulf Envelope Co. 363n.3
Gulf-Wandes Corp. v.
    NLRB 114n.24

Hanford Atomic Metal Trades
    Council (Atlantic Richfield
    Hanford Corp.) 294n.25
Harnischfeger Corp. v. Sheet Metal
    Workers 306n.72
Harris v. Plasterers & Cement
    Masons 110n.26
Harris-Teeter Supermarkets,
    Inc. 118n.35
Harvey Engineering & Mfg.
    Corp. 331n.84
Hawaii Tel. Co. v. Hawaii Dep't
    of Labor 55n.36
Helgesen v. Iron Workers . 240n.70

Tables

Hendricks County Rural Elec. Membership Corp. v. NLRB 21n.28, 23n.33
Hershey Foods Corp. 111n.18
Hendrix v. Operating Engineers 305n.67
Hess Oil & Chemical Co. v. NLRB 63n.59
H & F Binch Co. v. NLRB 324n.55
Highland Plastics, Inc. ... 317n.29
Hi-Grade Materials Co. ... 49n.19
Hirsch v. IBEW 255n.151
H.K. Porter 28n.48
Hobbs, Wall & Co. 63n.62
Hod Carriers, NLRB v. 225nn.20, 21
Hoffman v. Cement Masons 250n.115, 251n.120
Hoffman Beverage Co. .. 169n.85
Honolulu Typographical Union v. NLRB 252n.124
Hooker Chemical & Plastics Corp. 16n.11
Hospital & Institutional Workers 358n.26
Hospital Employees v. Lafayette Square Nursing Center, Inc. 192n.20
Hotel Holiday Inn de Isla Verde v. NLRB 352n.3, 353n.6
Hotel & Restaurant Employees 182n.133
Hotel & Restaurant Employees (Kutschers Country Club Corp.) 233n.46
Huber & Antilla Constr. Co. v. Carpenters 237n.58, 238n.62
Huck Mfg. Co. v. NLRB 50n.22, 70n.97, 71n.102, 73n.113, 106n.3
Hudgens v. NLRB 193n.26

IAM 26n.40
IATSE (Post-Newsweek Stations) 294n.16
IBEW (Argonne Nat'l Laboratories) 297n.31
IBEW (Atlantic County Imp. Anth.) 241n.75
IBEW (Cleveland Electro Metals Co.) 229n.33
IBEW (Garst-Receveur Constr. Co.) 228n.30
IBEW (Gaylord Broadcasting Co.) 239n.67
IBEW (Golden Dawn Foods) 248n.107
IBEW (Hayward Elec. Co.) 230n.36, 231n.42
IBEW (Kelinski Elec. Co.) 224n.12
IBEW (L.M. Ericsson Telecommunications, Inc.) 223n.11, 225n.17
IBEW (Lockheed Missles & Space Co.) 234n.51, 241n.74
IBEW (Madison Square Garden Center) 303n.61
IBEW (New Power Wire & Elec. Corp.) 230n.38
IBEW (Northern Telecom, Inc.) 303nn.59, 60, 63
IBEW (Planche Elec., Inc.) 230n.38
IBEW (Renel Constr. Co.) 240n.69, 241n.74
IBEW (Southern Elec. Corp.) (N.L.R.B. 1978) ... 228n.30, 236n.54
IBEW (Southern Sun Elec. Corp.) (NLRB 1980) 223n.10
IBEW (Telecom Equip. Corp.) 291n.4
IBEW (Welsh & Maddox) 224n.16
IBEW v. NLRB 228n.32

388

Cases

IBEW, NLRB v. 224n.15
ILA (Occidental Chemical
   Co.) 224n.13
Illinois Bell Tel. Co. ... 344nn.145,
    146
Imperial Outdoor Adv. ... 50n.21
Industrial Towel & Uniform Serv.
   Co. 114n.24
Industrial Workers (Duke City
   Lumber Co.) 246n.95
Ingram Mfg. Co. 327n.66
Inland Steel Co. 71n.108
Inland Steel Co. v.
   NLRB 157n.33
Inland Trucking Co. v.
   NLRB 67n.86
Interboro Contractors,
   Inc. 148n.3
Inter-Collegiate Press v.
   NLRB 67n.85
International Shoe Co. 63n.63
International Van Lines,
   NLRB v. 312n.2
International Wire v. Electrical
   Workers 262n.167
Iowa Beef Processors,
   Inc. 339n.121
Iowa Beef Processors v. Meat
   Cutters 183n.137
Iron Molders v. Allis-Chalmers
   Co. 62nn.55, 57
Ironworkers (Associated Cement
   Contractors) ... 303nn.61, 62
Iron Workers (Bechtel
   Corp.) 304n.65
Iron Workers (J.P. Cullen & Son
   Constr. Co.) 300n.45
Iron Workers (Kulama
   Erectors) 299n.41
Iron Workers (Lueder Constr.
   Co.) 299n.40
Ironworkers (Robert E. McKee,
   Inc.) 236n.56,
    237nn.58, 59, 240n.72

Iron Workers (Spancrete Northeast,
   Inc.) 303n.61
Ironworkers (Stobeck Masonry,
   Inc.) .. 300n.44, 302nn.57, 58
Ironworkers v. NLRB 239n.68
Irvin H. Whitehouse & Sons v.
   NLRB 153n.25
Isthmian SS. Co. v. Marine
   Engineers 192n.18
IT Services 376n.54,
    377nn.59, 61

Jacksonville Bulk Terminals v.
   Longshoremen 162n.52,
    164n.61
Jacksonville Maritime Ass'n v.
   Longshoremen 160n.45,
    161n.48
Jacobs Mfg. Co., NLRB v. . 15n.7
Jaden Elec. v. IBEW ... 259n.156
Janesville Typographical Union
   (Gazette Printing
   Co.) 239n.66
Jay Kay Metal Specialties v.
   Doe 198n.39
Jeffrey-De Witt Insulator Co. v.
   NLRB 62n.57
Jessop Steel Co. v. United
   Steelworkers 152n.18
J.E. Steigerwald Co. 322n.42,
    348n.159
J.F. Hott Elec. Co. v.
   NLRB 234n.49,
    230n.55, 238n.63
J.I. Case Co. v. NLRB .. 73n.111
Jim Walter Resources, Inc. v. Mine
   Workers 163nn.56, 59
Johansen v. Carpenters
   .... 258nn.152,
    153
Johansen v. Utility
   Workers 258n.151

389

John Cuneo, Inc. v.
  NLRB ... 314n.11, 374nn.45, 46
Johns Manville Prod.
  Corp. 67n.85
Joint Council of Teamsters,
  NLRB v. 254n.136
Jones & McKnight, Inc. v.
  NLRB 158n.36

Kable Printing Co. 345n.150
Kable Printing Co. v.
  NLRB 244n.86
Kansas City Power & Lt. Co. v.
  NLRB 338n.139
Kansas Milling Co. v.
  NLRB 118n.33
Katz, NLRB v. 73nn.112, 113
Kaufman & Broad Home Systems
  v. Firemen 165n.65
Kaynard v. Teamsters ... 305n.69
K-D Mfg. Co. 73n.111
Keebler Co. v. Bakery Workers
  (E.D.Pa.) 172n.93
Keebler Co. v. Bakery Workers
  (N.D.Ga.) 184n.142
Keller-Crescent Co. 178n.116
Keller-Crescent Co.,
  NLRB v. 183n.135
Kelly-Goodwin Hardware
  Co. 67n.87
Kennedy v. Typographical
  Union 258n.149
Kerry Coal Co. v. Mine
  Workers 202n.64,
    300n.162, 301n.164, 265n.187
Keyway, a Div. of Phase,
  Inc. 148n.5
Kodiak Oil Field Haulers, Inc. v.
  Teamsters 357n.21
Kohler Co. v. UAW 203n.66

Kolodziej v. Electrical
  Workers 202n.59
Krispy Kreme Doughnut Corp. v.
  NLRB 148n.4
Kroger Co. v. NLRB .. 250n.115, 252n.125
Kunth Bros., Inc.,
  NLRB v. 363n.3, 365
K & W Trucking Co. ... 345n.150

Laborers (Campbell Constr.
  Co.) 297n.31
Laborers (Dynamic Constr.
  Co.) 302n.53
Laborers (Georgia-Pac.
  Corp.) 297n.35
Laborers (Hensel Phelps Constr.
  Co.) 241n.74
Laborers (Jo Ba Constr.
  Co.) 297n.32
Laborers (Mautz & Oren,
  Inc.) 223n.8
Laborers (Mercy Hosp.) ... 19n.22
Laborers (Thomas S. Byrne,
  Inc.) 240n.86
Laborers (Walters Foundation,
  Inc.) 236n.54
Laborers v. NLRB 243n.83
Laclede Gas Co. 63n.59
Laidlaw Corp. 317n.26,
    328n.69, 329nn.74, 75, 340n.126, 345n.148
Lane Crane Serv., Inc. v.
  IBEW 240n.69, 260n.161
Laredo Coca Cola Bottling
  Co. 363nn.3, 4, 6, 366
Lathers (Acoustic & Specialties,
  Inc.) 302n.56
Latrobe Steel Corp. v.
  NLRB 315nn.13, 16
Laundry Workers (Morrison's
  Inc.) 245n.91

Cases

Lee A. Consaul Co. v.
NLRB 169n.85
Leeds v. Northrup Co. ... 117n.27
Lehigh Metal Fabricators   328n.67
Leisure Lodge Nursing
  Home 19n.24
Leveld Wholesale, Inc. ... 50n.21
Lewis v. Clerks &
  Checkers 258n.149
Libbie Convalescent
  Center 377n.56
Linbeck Constr. Corp. v.
  NLRB 230n.37, 231n.4,
           238n.63, 240n.69
Lincoln Hills Nursing
  Home ... 328n.71, 333nn.91,
           97, 334nn.99, 100,
           339n.119, 342n.135, 363,
           364n.22
Link Belt Co. 63n.61
Linn v. United Plant Guard
  Workers 190n.14
Lion Oil Co., NLRB v. 15n.7
Lithographers (Henry Wurst,
  Inc.) 246n.100
Lithographers, NLRB v.   254n.136
Little Rock Airmotive,
  Inc. 340n.127, 341n.129
Litton Microwave Cooking
  Prod. 375n.48
Lockwoven Co. 118n.35
Locomotive Firemen (Phelps
  Dodge Corp.) v. NLRB   16n.9
Long Beach Youth Center, Inc.
  NLRB v. 19n.24
Longshoremen (American Plant
  Protection, Inc.) 292n.9
Longshoremen (Brady-Hamilton
  Stevedore Co.) 302n.55
Longshoremen (Bridge Terminal,
  Inc.) ...., ... 304n.65
Longshoremen (California Cartage
  Co.) 292n.8

Longshoremen (General Ore
  Co.) 292n.8
Longshoremen (Rukert Terminals
  Corp.) 294n.18
Longshoremen (Waterways
  Terminal Co.) 293n.9
Longshoremen (West Coast
  Container Serv.,
  Inc.) 224n.14
Longshoremen v. Allied Int'l,
  Inc. 162n.52, 188n.3
Longshoremen & Warehousemen
  v. Juneau Spruce
  Co. 261n.16
Loomis Courier Serv.,
  Inc. 67n.87
Los Angeles Bldg. & Constr.
  Council (B&J Investment
  Co.) 256n.142
Louisiana Pac. Corp. v. Lumber &
  Sawmill Workers ... 198n.43
Lucky Stores, Inc. 21n.28
Luke Constr. Co. 28n.49
Lumber & Sawmill Workers
  (Stoltze Land & Lumber
  Co.) 250n.117
Lumber Workers (Louisiana Pac.
  Corp.) 291n.6, 292n.11

McDaniel v. Textile
  Workers 201n.55
Machinists (Boeing Co.) ... 108n.6
Machinists (Dalmo Victor
  II) 109, 109n.13
Machinists (General Elec.
  Co.) 206n.80
Machinists (J.A Jones Constr.
  Co.) 301n.51, 114n.21
Machinists (Menasco,
  Inc.) 109n.10, 206n.78
Machinists (Newfeld
  Porsche-Audi) 110n.16

391

Tables

Machinists (O.K. Tool Co.) 108n.7
Machinists (Tacoma Boat Bldg. Co.) 25n.39
Machinists v. NLRB (U.S.) 330n.77
Machinists v. NLRB (9th Cir.) 110n.15
Machinists v. T.I.M.E.-DC, Inc. 293n.15
Machinists & Aerospace Workers v. United Aircraft Corp. 329n.77, 354n.11, 355n.16
Mackay Radio & Tel. Co., NLRB v. . 314n.8, 316n.22, 317n.25, 328n.69, 347n.159, 348n.160
McLean Trucking Co. ... 170n.87
Madison Carrier, Inc. .. 337n.114
Manhattan Constr. Co. v. NLRB 298n.38
Marlene Indus. Corp. v. NLRB 181n.125
Marshall v. Barlow's Inc. .. 40n.4
Marshall v. Western Union Tel. Co. 49, 49nn.17, 18
Martin A. Gleason, Inc., NLRB v. 67nn.81, 82, 83
Maryland Shipbuilding & Drydock Co., NLRB v. 153n.25
Mason-Rust v. Laborers 263n.175, 264n.179
Mastro Plastics Corp. v. NLRB (U.S.) 153n.23, 312n.2, 316n.20, 328n.68, 330n.80
Mastro Plastics Corp. v. NLRB (2d Cir.) 15n.6
Maxey v. Meat Cutters (King-O-Meat Co.) . 252n.123
Mead v. Retail Clerks . 263nn.171, 173
Meatcutters 25n.39
Meatcutters (Milwaukee Ind. Meat Packing Ass'n) 253n.13

Meatcutters v. Jewel Tea Co. 72n.110
Meat Cutters v. Wetterau Foods 61nn.50, 51
Megers Indus., Inc. 21n.29, 148n.4
Metal Polishers (Climax Mach. Co.) 343n.83,
Metropolitan Edison Co. v. NLRB 171n.88, 183n.136
Metropolitan Life Ins. Co., NLRB v. 22n.30
Metro St. Louis Bargaining Ass'n. 363n.3, 367n.18
Michigan State Chamber of Commerce v. State ... 53n.30
Mid-American Regional Bargaining Ass'n v. Will County Carpenters 61n.49
Midwest Solvents, Inc. ... 204n.69
Milano v. Hotel & Restaurant Employees 189n.9
Milk, Ice Cream Drivers & Dairy Employees (Cream Top Creamery) 16n.9
Milk Wagon Drivers v. Meadowmoor Dairies, Inc. 189n.6, 197n.39
Miller v. UFCW 258n.153
Milwaukee Spring Co. 54n.34
Mine Workers (Amax Coal Co.) 254n.135
Mine Workers (Lone Star Steel Co.) 244n.87
Mine Workers v. Gibbs . 167n.72, 202n.59, 260n.160
Mine Workers v. Meadow Creek Coal Co. ... 202n.64, 266nn. 189, 191
Mine Workers v. NLRB 15n.7
Mine Workers v. Osborne Mining Co. 263n.173
Mobile Home Estates, Inc. 320n.35

392

Cases

Mobile Home Estates, Inc. v.
NLRB 321n.38
Molders v. Superior Ct. ... 197n.37
Monarchi-Velikoff, Inc. v.
Building & Constr. Trades
Council ... 229n.33, 230n.38,
237nn.59, 61
Montana-Dakota Util. Co. v.
NLRB 183n.135
Montefiore Hosp. & Medical
Center v. NLRB 19n.24,
114n.24
Montgomery Ward & Co. v.
NLRB (10th Cir.) ... 204n.72
Montgomery Ward & Co., NLRB
v. (9th Cir.) 69n.92
Moore Business Forms, Inc., NLRB
v. 204n.70, 314n.12,
318n.31, 370n.33,
373nn.39, 40
Moore Drop Forging Co. ... 69n.94
Moore Dry Dock 227-29,
227nn.26, 27, 228-29, 229,
231, 237, 239
Morand Bros. Beverage Co. v.
NLRB 62n.55
Mosher Steel Co. 114n.24
M P Indus., Inc. 204n.69
Municipality of Metropolitan
Seattle v. Department of
Labor & Industry ... 79n.116
Muniz v. Hoffman 207n.85
Murray Prod., Inc., NLRB
v. ... 317nn.27, 28, 347n.156
Murtha v. Pet Dairy Prod.
Co. 27n.45

NABET v. NLRB 108n.9
Nahas v. Retail Clerks ... 190n.13
Nash-Finch Co.,
NLRB v. 198n.41
National Car Rental System,
Inc. 337n.112

National Car Rental System, Inc.
v. NLRB 377nn.57, 58,
378n.63
National Fresh Fruit & Vegetable
Co. v. NLRB 70n.100
National League of Cities v.
Usery 12n.2
National Woodwork Mfr's Ass'n v.
NLRB 255n.141
Nelson Filter Div. 340n.123,
352n.2, 354nn.11, 12,
358n.25
Neufeld Porsche-Audi 110,
110n.16, 112
Newberry Energy 181n.126
New Orleans S.S. Ass'n v.
Longshoremen 164n.61
Newport News Shipbuilding Co. v.
NLRB 204n.71, 205n.75
Newspaper Guild (Hearst
Corp.) 246n.94
New York Newspaper Printing
Pressmen's Union 25n.39
New York Tel. Co. v. New York
State Dep't of Labor . 55n.36
NLRB v. Acme Fire Works,
Inc. 337n.112
NLRB v. A. Duie Pyle
Co. 205n.75
NLRB v. Alexander 66n.78
NLRB v. Allis Chalmers Mfg.
Co. 108n.5
NLRB v. Amalgamated
Lithographers 254n.136
NLRB v. American Compress
Warehouse 71n.103
NLRB v. American Medical
Serv 22n.31
NLRB v. American Nat'l Ins.
Co. 69n.91
NLRB v. A.S. Abell Co. .. 55n.35
NLRB v. Associated Gen.
Contractors 256n.145

Tables

NLRB v. Bell Aerospace
  Co. 23n.32
NLRB v. Broadcast
  Employees 240n.69
NLRB v. Brown Food
  Store 63n.58, 66n.80,
              67n.84
NLRB v. Brown & Sharp Mfg.
  Co. 22n.30
NLRB v. Browning-Ferris
  Indus. 178n.111,
    181n.127, 182nn.130,
    132, 323n.48, 50
NLRB v. Building Serv. Employees
  (1st Cir.) 251n.121
NLRB v. Building Serv. Employees
  (10th Cir.) 251n.121
NLRB v. Business Machines (Royal
  Typewriter) 243n.81
NLRB v. Carpenters 252n.127
NLRB v. City Disposal Systems,
  Inc. 148n.3
NLRB v. C.K. Smith,
  Inc. 179n.118, 183n.134
NLRB v. Colonial Haven Nursing
  Home, Inc. 195n.31
NLRB v. Colonial Press,
  Inc. 323n.47
NLRB v. Consolidated Dress
  Carriers, Inc. 336n.106
NLRB v. Corsicana Cotton
  Mills 71n.105
NLRB v. Darlington Veneer
  Co. 71n.105
NLRB v. Davison 71n.104
NLRB v. Denver Bldg. & Constr.
  Trades Council 221n.3,
                243, 244n.89
NLRB v. Duncan Foundry &
  Mach. Works, Inc. . 363nn.3,
                6, 365n.12
NLRB v. Edward G. Budd.
  Co. 24n.35

NLRB v. Efco Mfg. Co. . 316n.23
NLRB v. Electrical
  Workers 18n.17
NLRB v. Electrical Workers
  (Hoffman Co.) 19n.22
NLRB v. Electro Vector . 371n.37
NLRB v. Erie Resistor
  Corp. ... 50n.23, 350nn.163,
                165, 350
NLRB v. Fansteel Metalurgical
  Corp. 150n.11, 339n.117
NLRB v. Fleetwood Trailer
  Co. 313n.6, 317nn.27, 28
NLRB v. Fruit & Vegetable
  Packers (Tree
  Fruits) 247nn.102, 103,
                251nn.118, 119
NLRB v. General Elec.
  Co. 117n.29
NLRB v. General Time
  Corp. 363n.5
NLRB v. Gissell Packing
  Co. 106n.2
NLRB v. Glaziers &
  Glassworkers 225n.18
NLRB v. Gould, Inc. ... 154n.29,
                179n.120
NLRB v. Granite State Joint
  Bd. 108n.7
NLRB v. Great Dane
  Trailers 50n.23, 315n.11,
    317n.27, 361n.1, 362,
    363n.3, 364n.7
NLRB v. Hod Carriers . 225nn.20,
                21
NLRB v. IBEW (2d Cir.) 224n.15
NLRB v. IBEW (6th
  Cir.) 237n.60
NLRB v. IBEW (Northern
  Telecom, Inc.) 312n.2
NLRB v. International Van
  Lines 312n.2
NLRB v. Jacobs Mfg. Co. ... 15n.7

394

Cases

NLRB v. Joint Council of
   Teamsters 254n.136
NLRB v. Katz 73nn.112, 113
NLRB v. Keller-Crescent
   Co. 183n.135
NLRB v. Kunth Bros. 363n.3, 365
NLRB v. Lion Oil Co. 15n.7
NLRB v. Long Beach Youth
   Center, Inc. 19n.24
NLRB v. MacKay Radio & Tel.
   Co. 314n.8, 316n.22,
            317n.25, 328n.69,
           347n.155, 348n.160
NLRB v. Martin A. Gleason,
   Inc. 67nn.81, 82, 83
NLRB v. Maryland Shipbuilding &
   Drydock Co. 153n.25
NLRB v. Metropolitan Life Ins.
   Co. 22n.3
NLRB v. Montgomery Ward &
   Co. 69n.92
NLRB v. Moore Business Forms,
   Inc. 204n.70, 314n.12,
         318n.31, 370n.33,
         373nn.39, 40
NLRB v. Murray Prod.,
   Inc. 317nn.27, 28,
          347n.156
NLRB v. Nash-Finch Co. 198n.41
NLRB v. Oil, Chemical & Atomic
   Workers 109nn.11, 12
NLRB v. Operating
   Engineers 240n.71
NLRB v. Operating Engineers
   (Burns & Roe, Inc.) . 294n.19
NLRB v. Painters 224n.15
NLRB v. Pipefitters (Austin
   Co.) ..., 220n.23, 256n.143
NLRB v. Plasterers 299n.39
NLRB v. Plasterers (Ashton
   Co.) 299n.39
NLRB v. Poultrymen's Serv.
   Corp. 24n.34

NLRB v. Radio & Television
   Broadcast Engineers
   (Columbia Broadcasting
   System) 301nn.49, 50
NLRB v. Retail Store
   Employees ... 253nn.129, 130
NLRB v. Rockaway News Supply
   Co. 178n.113
NLRB v. Rock Hill Convalescent
   Center 19n.24
NLRB v. Sands Mfg.
   Co. 157n.34, 170n.86
NLRB v. Servette, Inc. 253
NLRB v.
   Sherwin-Williams ... 52n.27,
          369n.31
NLRB v. Southern Cal.
   Edison 152n.21, 154n.29,
       155n.30, 179n.120, 181n.128
NLRB v. Southern Greyhound
   Lines (5th Cir.) 181n.126
NLRB v. Southern Greyhound
   Lines (NLRB) 181n.126
NLRB v. Superior Fire Proof Door
   & Sash Co. 108n.3
NLRB v. Swedish Hosp. Medical
   Center 372n.38
NLRB v. Teamsters
   (U.S.) 206n.78
NLRB v. Teamsters (2d
   Cir.) 302n.52
NLRB v. Tex-Tan, Inc. ... 106n.3
NLRB v. Thayer Co. 313n.6
NLRB v. Tomco Communications,
   Inc. .,. 69n.95
NLRB v. Tom Juyce Floors,
   Inc. ...., ... 315n.18
NLRB v. Transportation
   Management Corp. . 321n.40
NLRB v. Trumbull Asphalt
   Co. 204n.70
NLRB v. Union Carbide 180n.124

NLRB v. Union Nacional de
    Trabajadores 206n.79
NLRB v. Virginia Elec. & Power
    Co. 69n.93
NLRB v. Vitronic Div. . 335n.101,
                        355n.15
NLRB v. Washington Aluminum
    Co. 148n.2, 149n.7
NLRB v. W.C. McQuaide,
    Inc. 203n.68, 324n.53
NLRB v. Western States Regional
    Council 243n.80
NLRB v. Westinghouse Elec.
    Corp. 363nn.3, 4, 6,
                  364n.16, 365
NLRB v. William S. Carroll,
    Inc. 182n.129
NLRB v. Wire Prod. Mfg.
    Corp. 62n.58
NLRB v. Wooster . 71nn.100, 101
Nolan Systems, Inc. 329n.76
N-1 Canteen Serv., Inc. . 179n.117
Norando Aluminum, Inc. v.
    Carpenters 261n.164,
                       263n.175
North River Energy Corp. v. Mine
    Workers .. 166n.71, 173n.95,
                      175n.104
Norwood Manor, Inc. 23n.31

OCAW (Firestone Synthetic
    Rubber) 233n.46
Office & Professional
    Employees 358n.26
Ohio Power Co. 333n.96
Oil, Chemical & Atomic Workers
    v. Johns Manville Prod.
    Corp. 67n.85
Oil, Chemical & Atomic Workers,
    NLRB v. 109nn.11, 12
Operating Engineers (Bradshaw
    Industrial Coatings) . 293n.13

Operating Engineers (C.J. Coakley
    Co.) 297n.36
Operating Engineers (Cruz
    Contractors, Inc.) ... 298n.37
Operating Engineers (Davis-McKee
    Inc.) 154n.26, 178n.114
Operating Engineers
    (Dodge-Ireland,
    Inc.) 239n.65
Operating Engineers (Epic One
    Corp.) 293n.13, 296n.27
Operating Engineers (Industrial
    Contracting, Inc.) .. 230n.37,
    231n.41, 244n.85
Operating Engineers (Kaiser
    Foundation Hosp.) ... 19n.21
Operating Engineers (Oak Constr.,
    Inc.) ... 247n.102, 250n.117,
                       252n.126
Operating Engineers (Sullivan &
    Humes) 300n.46
Operating Engineers v. Carl A.
    Morse, Inc. 293n.15
Operating Engineers v. Dahlen
    Constr. Co. 16n.13, 264n.182
Operating Engineers v.
    Fischback 266n.191
Operating Engineers v. NLRB (3d
    Cir.) 206n.78
Operating Engineers v. NLRB (9th
    Cir.) 304n.66
Operating Engineers,
    NLRB v. 240n.71
Operating Engineers (Burns & Roe
    Co.), NLRB v. 294n.19
Orba Transshipment 320n.35
Ottawa Silica Co. 62n.56
Overhead Door Corp.
    (1982) 324n.52,
                   329nn.74, 76
Overhead Door Corp.
    (1975) 150n.12
Overnite Transportation 181n.128

Cases

Owens-Illinois, Inc, v. Glass Bottle
  Blowers 175n.103,
              183n.137

Pacemaker Yacht Co. 153n.24
Pacemaker Yacht Co. v.
  NLRB 154n.28
Pace Motor Lines, Inc. .. 326n.62,
              328n.68, 330n.80
Pacific Maritime Ass'n v.
  NLRB 292n.11
Pacific Tel. & Tel. Co. . 180n.122
Painters (Associated Gen.
  Contractors) 230n.36,
              231n.42
Painters (Delcon, Inc.) ... 293n.16
Painters (Manganaro
  Corp.) 302n.57
Painters (St. Joseph
  Hosp.) 19n.20, 20n.25
Painters (Theatre Techniques,
  Inc.) 256n.143
Painters, NLRB v. 224n.15
Painting & Decorating
  Contractors 16n.11
Paperworkers (Duro Paper Bag
  Mfg. Co.) 252n.125
Paramount Transport Systems v.
  Teamsters 261n.166
Park Elec. Co. v. IBEW 260n.162
Parker-Robb Chevrolet ... 24n.35
Pattern Makers League .. 110n.15
PBA, Inc. 204n.72
Pease & Co. v. Local
  1787 .... 195n.30
Peat Mfg. Co. ,........ 118n.31
Pechcur Lozenge Co. 316n.20
Peck, Inc. 150n.11
Pedigo v Celanese Corp. . 189n.7
People v. Bush 194n.29
People v. Spear 189n.7

Pepsi Cola of Lamberton,
  Inc. 204n.70
Pet, Inc., v. NLRB 248n.108
Pickens-Bond Constr. Co. v.
  Carpenters 263n.171
Pilot Freight Carriers ... 118n.33,
              179n.18
Pipefitters (Calvert Gen.
  Contractors, Inc.) ... 238n.65
Pipefitters, NLRB v. 238n.65
Pipefitters (Austin Co.),
  NLRB v. 226n.23
Plasterers (California Ass'n of
  Employers) 252n.125
Plasterers (Strescon Indus.,
  Inc.) 302n.57
Plasterers, NLRB v. 299n.39
Plasterers (Ashton Co.), NLRB
  v. 256n.143
Plumbers (Airco, Inc.) .. 296n.29,
              297n.32
Plumbers (Barton Malow
  Co.) 241n.74
Plumbers (Circle, Inc.) .. 234n.50
Plumbers (Dyad Constr.
  Co.) 296n.30
Plumbers (H.L. Robertson &
  Assoc., Inc.) 226n.36
Plumbers (Robbins Plumbing &
  Htg. Contractors) ... 237n.58
Plumbers (Stokely-Van Camp,
  Inc.) 238n.65, 240n.72
Plumbers (Stone & Webster
  Engineering Corp.) . 293n.13
Plumbers (Tridair Indus.,
  Inc.) 295n.21
Plumbers (Zia Co.) ...,. 206n.55
Plumbers & Pipefitters v.
  NLRB 226n.24
Potter v. Houston Gulf Coast Bldg.
  Trades Council 258n.153
Potters (Macomb Pottery
  Co.) 113n.22

397

Tables

Poultrymen's Serv. Corp.,
  NLRB v. 24n.34
Precision Stripping, Inc. . 376n.50
Premium Distrib. Co. v.
  Teamsters .. 190n.9, 200n.51
Presto Castings Co. 327n.64
Price v. Operating
  Engineers 258n.151
Printing Pressmen (Knight
  Newspapers, Inc.) ... 245n.93
PTA Sales, Inc. v. Retail
  Clerks 189n.7, 190n.12,
  193n.24
Public Employment Relations
  Comm'n v. City of
  Kennewick 12n.2
Pullman, Inc. 342n.138
Pullman Std. Div. 24n.34
Pulp Paper Workers (Georgia Pac.
  Corp.) 297n.34
Purex Corp. v.
  Teamsters 159n.43,
  162n.53

Racine Die Casting Co. .. 71n.103
Radio & Television Broadcast
  Engineers (Columbia
  Broadcasting System), NLRB
  v. 301nn.49, 50
Rafel & Co. v. IBEW ... 298n.38
Railing v. Mine Workers 266n.190
Railroad Trainmen v. Long Island
  R.R. 60n.48
Railway Clerks (NCR
  Corp.) 26n.43
Rainbow Tours, Inc. v.
  Teamsters 200n.49
Randall Div. 330nn.78, 79,
  370n.32, 373n.39
Randle-Eastern Ambulance Serv.,
  Inc. 318n.32
Rawleigh Co. 118n.35
R.C. White Co. 319n.34

Redstone Workers Ass'n (Starks
  Constr. Co.) 292n.11,
  294n.18
Redwing Carriers 181n.128
Refrigeration Contractors, Inc. v.
  Plumbers 264n.177
Reliance Clay Prod. Co. . 315n.18
Retail Clerks (Carroll House) v.
  NLRB 16n.1
Retail Clerks (Land Title Ins.
  Co.) 252n.128
Retail Clerks v. Lion Dry Goods,
  Inc. ... 353n.7, 356nn.19, 20,
  358n.24
Retail Store Employee's, NLRB
  v. 253nn.129, 130
Retail Store Employees, State ex
  rel. v. Black 193n.25,
  208n.87
Richardson Paint Co. v.
  NLRB 158n.36
Ritchie v. Mine
  Workers .. 202n.60, 265n.188
Riverside Coal v. Mine
  Workers 263n.172
R.L. White Co. 374n.43
Road Home Constr. Co. . 114n.24
Road Sprinkler Fitters v. NLRB
  (John Cuneo,
  Inc.) 314n.11, 328n.70,
  337n.111, 374nn.45, 46
Robert A. Barnes, Inc. 17n.15
Roberts Oldsmobile,
  Inc. 325n.58, 355n.18
Rochester Musicians
  Ass'n 112n.21
Rochester Tel. Corp. v.
  Communications
  Workers 192n.21
Rockaway News Supply Co.,
  NLRB v. 178n.113
Rock Hill Convalescent Center,
  NLRB v. 19n.24

398

Cases

Roegelein Provision Co. . . . 363n.4
Roofers (Associated Blders &
   Contractors, Inc.) . . . 206n.81
Royal Typewriter Co. v.
   NLRB 246n.95
RWDSU (Federal Hill Nursery
   Center) 19n.23, 20n.25
RWDSU (Greater Pennsylvania
   Ave. Nursing, Inc.) . . 19n.20
RWDSU (United
   Hospitals) 19n.20
RWDSU, District 1194 . . . 19n.23
Ryder Truck Lines v.
   Teamsters . 154n.28, 157n.32

Safeway Trails, Inc. v. United
   Transp. Union 197n.36
Sailors Union (Moore Dry
   Dock) 227-29, 227nn.26,
             27, 228-29, 229,
             231, 237, 239
St. Regis Paper Co. 154n.27,
         178n.115, 183n.135
San Diego Bldg. Trades Council v.
   Garmon 193n.23
San Diego Newspaper Guild
   (Union Tribune) v.
   NLRB 55n.35
Sands Mfg. Co., NLRB
   v. 157n.34, 170n.86
Sapp v. Teamsters 260n.157
Saunders House v.
   NLRB 70nn.96, 98
Schreiber Mfg, Inc v.
   NLRB 205n.74
Scofield (Wisconsin Motor Corp.)
   v. NLRB 108n.6
Scooba Mfg. v. NLRB 148n.4
Scott v. Ironworkers 258n.153
Scripto Mfg. Co. 71n.104
Sears, Roebuck & Co. v.
   Carpenter . 184n.24, 194n.29

Seattle v. Department of Labor &
   Industry 79n.116
Seattle-First Nat'l Bank . . 29n.51,
       68n.89, 70nn.98, 99
Seattle Times Co. v. Mailers
   Union 152n.19, 168n.80,
                  169n.84
SECO, Inc. v. Laborers . . 306n.73
SEIU (Leland Stanford Jr. Univ.)
   v. NLRB 111n.18
Servette, Inc., NLRB v. 248
Service Employees 20n.25
Service Employees (The Dalton
   School) 234n.50, 244n.85
Service Employees (Delta Airlines,
   Inc.) 250nn.113, 114
Service Employees (New York Ass'n
   for Blind) . . 233n.46, 234n.49
Service Employees (Pepper Constr.
   Co.) 234n.49
Sheet Metal Workers (Ciamello
   Htg. & Cooling,
   Inc.) 225n.19, 229n.35
Sheet Metal Workers
   (Gallagher-Kaiser
   Corp.) 299n.39
Sheet Metal Workers (Young
   Plumbing & Supply Co.)
   (1974) 223n.6,
                291nn.22, 23
Sheet Metal Workers (Young
   Plumbing & Supply Co.)
   (1976) 300n.47
Sheet Metal Workers v. Atlas Sheet
   Metal Co. 263n.175
Shell Chemical Co. v.
   NLRB 208n.38
Shelly & Anderson Furniture Mfg.
   Co. v. NLRB 63n.60,
                  343n.140
Sherman Oaks Medical Arts
   Center, Ltd. v.
   Carpenters 228n.28

Sherwin-Williams, NLRB v. 52n.27, 369n.31
Shirley v. Retail Store Employees 194n.29
Sillman v. Teamsters ... 264n.176
Simpkins v. Painters 265n.186
Simplex Wire & Cable Co. 50n.24
Six-Carrier Mutual Aid Pact 61n.48
Smith's Complete Market, Inc. 115n.25, 116n.27
Soule Glass & Glazing Co. v. NLRB 50n.22, 314n.12, 324n.54, 332n.90, 343n.141, 356n.20, 371n.34, 377n.53, 54, 55
Southern Cal. Conference of Carpenters (D & E Corp.) 222n.6
Southern Cal. Edison Co. v. NLRB . 152n.211, 154n.29, 155n.30, 179n.120, 181n.128
Southern Fla. Hotel & Motel Ass'n 329n.72
Southern Greyhound Lines 21n.28, 24n.34
Southern Greyhound Lines, NLRB v. 181n.126
Southern Hotel & Motel Ass'n 357n.22
Southern Ohio Coal Co. v. Mine Workers 184nn.141, 143
Spear, People v. 189n.7
Squillacote v. Graphic Arts Int'l Union 258n.148
Squillacote v. Meat Cutters 207n.84
Squillacote v. Teamsters 258n.149
Stackpole Components Co. 71n.106
Standard Plumbing & Htg. Co. 116n.27

Star Brush Mtg. Co. 24n.34
State *ex rel.* Girard v. Percich 190n.13
State *ex rel.* Retail Store Employees v. Black ... 193n.25, 208n.87
Stationary Engineers (St. Jose Hosp. & Health Center) 358n.26
Stauffer Chemical Co. .. 334n.98, 355
Stearns Mining Co. v. Mine Workers 199n.45
Steelworkers (Asarco, Inc.) 27n.45
Steelworkers (Carrier Group) v. NLRB ... 185n.144, 232n.45, 236n.57
Steelworkers (Continental Can Co.) 291n.5
Steelworkers v. Alabaster Lime Co. 190n.11, 195n.32, 197n.36
Steelworkers v. Lorain .. 173n.95, 174n.102
Steelworkers v. NLRB ... 232n.44
Stokely-Van Camp, Inc. v. NLRB 363n.5, 364n.9, 367n.26
Stormor, Inc. 377nn.58, 60
Straus Communications, Inc. 376n.511, 378n.64
Struksnes Constr. Co. 114n.24
Stryjewski v. Teamsters .. 200n.49
Summit Valley Indus. v. Carpenters 264n.184
Superior Fire Proof Door & Sash Co., NLRB v. 106n.3
Swarco, Inc. v. NLRB ... 106n.3, 117n.30
Swedish Hosp. Medical Center, NLRB v. 372n.38
System Council T-4 v. NLRB 344nn.145, 146

Cases

Taft Broadcasting Co. 70n.96
Talbert Mfg., Inc. 330n.83
Teamsters 337n.109
Teamsters (AAA Motor Lines, Inc.) 241n.76
Teamsters (Acme Concrete Supply Co.) 242n.79
Teamsters (Allied Concrete) ... 241-42, 242n.77
Teamsters (American Bread Co.) 252n.122
Teamsters (California Dump Truck Owners Ass'n) 255n.140
Teamsters (Curtin Matheson Scientific, Inc.) 242n.79, 247n.101
Teamsters (Emery Mining Corp.) 294n.18
Teamsters (Kraft Co.) ... 292n.11
Teamsters (Lohman Sales Co.) 248n.104, 249n.11
Teamsters (Loomis Courier Serv., Inc.) 109n.10
Teamsters (McLean Trucking Co.) 158n.35
Teamsters (Mike Sullivan & Assoc., Inc.) 254n.137
Teamsters (Monarch Long Beach Corp.) 253n.131
Teamsters (Pacific Maritime Ass'n) 295n.24
Teamsters (Roslyn Americana Corp.) 246n.97
Teamsters (Schultz Refrigerated Serv., Inc.) 227n.27
Teamsters (Servair Maintenance, Inc.) 249n.111, 250n.115
Teamsters (Shurtleff & Andrews Constructors) 295n.26
Teamsters (Strong Bldg. Materials) 109n.10

Teamsters (Tech Weld Corp.) 26n.43
Teamsters (Toten Ocean Trailer Express, Inc.) .. 243nn.80, 84
Teamsters (United Cal. Express & Storage Co.) 297n.33
Teamsters (United Grocers, Ltd. 302n.56
Teamsters v. Bowman Transp. 197n.39
Teamsters v. Industrial Contractors, Inc. ... 305n.70
Teamsters v. King 165n.65, 169n.83
Teamsters v. Lucas Flour 151n.16, 159n.42
Teamsters v. Mitchell Bros. Truck Lines 356n.20
Teamsters v. Morton 53n.30, 262n.170, 264n.183
Teamsters v. NLRB (D.C. Cir. 1966) 71n.107
Teamsters v. NLRB (D.C. Cir. 1976) 246n.99
Teamsters v. NLRB (D.C. Cir. 1980) 222n.4
Teamsters v. NLRB (6th Cir.) 59n.49
Teamsters v. NLRB (9th Cir.) 181n.126
Teamsters v. NLRB (Haddon House Food Prod., Inc.) 341n.133
Teamsters (Vulcan Materials Co.) v. NLRB 245n.94
Teamsters v. Vevoda 111n.10
Teamsters, NLRB v. (U.S.) 206n.78
Teamsters, NLRB v. (2d Cir.) 302n.52
Teamsters, NLRB v. (9th Cir.) 254n.136

Television & Radio Artists v. NLRB 70n.96
Television Wisconsin, Inc. 115n.25
Tenneco Chemicals, Inc. v. Teamsters 152n.20, 168nn.76, 79
Texas Distrib., Inc. v. Plumbers 223n.11, 226nn.23, 24, 228n.29
Texaco, Inc. v. NLRB (5th Cir.) 52n.27, 369n.27
Texaco, Inc. v. NLRB (9th Cir.) 24n.35
Texaco Oil Co. 369nn.23, 26, 28
Tex-Tan, Inc., NLRB v. ... 106n.3
Textile Workers v. Blackburn's Mfg. Co. 159n.43
Textile Workers, NLRB v. .. 108n.7
Thayer Co., NLRB v. ... 203n.66, 313n.6
Thomas v. Flavin 190n.14
Thornhill v. Alabama 188n.3
Thurston Motor Lines .. 182n.131
Tidewater Oil Co. 205n.76
Timken Roller Bearing Co. 72n.110
Titus v. Tacoma Smelters 201n.56
TKB Int'l Corp. . 108n.9, 113n.23
Tom Joyce Floors, Inc. NLRB v. 315n.18
Tomco Communications, Inc., NLRB v. 69n.95
Torrington Constr. Co. . 181n.127
Trading Post, Inc. 50n.24
Trailmobile Div. v. NLRB 342n.138
Trane Co. v. NLRB 298n.38
Transport & Local Delivery Drivers 347n.157, 348n.158, 374n.47

Transportation Management Corp. v. NLRB 321n.40
Trap Rock Co. v. Teamsters 167n.75
Tribune-Star Pub. Co. ... 204n.68
Trico Prod. Corp. 13n.4, 26n.43, 27n.45
Truck Drivers & Helpers v. NLRB 224n.15
Truck Transport, Inc. v. Allied Industrial Workers 262n.169
Turnkey Contractors v. Cement Masons 264n.176
Twin City Dist. Council of Carpenters, NLRB v. 252n.127
Typographical Union (Hammond Pub. Co.) 26n.40
Typographical Union (Hawaii Press Newspapers) 249n.112
Typographical Union (Plain Dealer Pub. Co.) 26n.43
Typographical Union (Register Pub. Co.) 109n.12

UAW (Ex-Cell-O Corp.) . 109n.10
UAW (General Motors Corp.) 292n.8
UAW v. American Metal Prod. Co. 200n.53, 201nn.53, 55, 57
UAW v. Rockwell Int'l Corp. 294n.17
UFCW (Fed Mart Stores, Inc.) 293n.14
UFW Organizing Comm. v. La Casita Farms, Inc. .. 198n.39
Union Carbide, NLRB v. 180n.124

Cases

Union Nacional de Trabajadores, NLRB v. 206n.79
Union Nacional de Trabjadores (Carborundum Co.) . 207n.86
Union Starch & Ref. Co. . 111n.19
United Aircraft Corp. v. Machinists 200n.53, 201n.56
United Merchants & Mfrs., Inc. v. NLRB 150n.12
United Parcel Serv., Inc. v. Teamsters (2nd Cir.) 160n.46, 161nn.48, 49, 163n.35, 164nn.61-63
United Parcel Serv., Inc. v. Teamsters (D.Mass.) .. 190n.12, 195n.30
United States v. Cunningham 160n.46, 163n.58
United States Steel Corp. v. Mine Workers (3d Cir. 1976) 161n.49, 163n.55
United States Steel Corp. v. Mine Workers (3d Cir. 1972) 161n.50
United States Steel Corp. v. Mine Workers (5th Cir.) . 175n.103
United States Steel Corp. v. NLRB .. 157n.183, 179n.119, 195n.31
Universal Communications Corp. v. Burns 261n.162
Upjohn v. United States 46n.7
U.S. Chamber of Commerce v. NLRB 256n.143
U.S. Gypsum Co. 28n.48, 33n.50

Valley Oil Co. 69n.94
Villa Care, Inc. 19n.24

Virginia Elec. & Power Co. 158n.36, 170n.87
Virginia Elec. & Power Co. v. Boilermakers 199n.47, 200nn.51, 52, 221n.5, 240n.72, 263n.175, 264n.180, 265n.187
Virginia Elec. & Power Co., NLRB v. 69n.93
Vitronic Div., NLRB v. 335n.101, 355n.15
Vulcan-Hart Corp. 327n.65
Vulcan-Hart Corp. v. NLRB 317n.29, 376n.54, 377n.57
Vulcan Materials Co. v. Steelworkers 264n.182

Walker Methodist Residence 19n.24
Wallace Corp. v. NLRB .. 352n.4
Wantagh Auto Sales, Inc. 106n.3, 118n.31
W.A. Schaffer Pen Co. .. 114n.24
Washington Aluminum Co., NLRB v. 148n.2, 149n.7
Washington Post Co. v. Printing & Graphic Communications Union 196n.35, 199n.44
Waveline, Inc. 320n.35, 340n.127, 341nn.128, 130, 131
W.C. McQuaide, Inc., NLRB v. 194n.68, 324n.53
Wells v. Operating Engineers 200n.159
Western States Regional Council v. NLRB 59n.44, 243n.80
Western Union I (Brennan v. Western Union Tel. Co.) .. 48-49, 48n.15, 49n.16

403

Tables

Westinghouse Broadcasting Co. v. Dukakis 191n.15
Westinghouse Elec. Corp. v. Electrical, Radio & Mach. Workers 189n.7
Westinghouse Elec. Corp., NLRB v. ... 363nn.3, 4, 6, 364n.10, 365
Weyerhauser Co. 59n.44
Weyerhauser Timber Co. v. Everett Dist. Council . 189n.7
WGN of Colorado, Inc. ... 63n.94
Wheeling Pac. Co. 69n.94
Whirlpool Corp. v. Marshall 153n.25
Wickham Contracting Co. v. Board of Educ. 261n.166
Wiggins & Co. v. Retail Clerks 194n.28
Wilhow Corp. 16n.11
William E. Arnold Co. v. Carpenters . 159n.41, 305n.70
William S. Carroll, Inc., NLRB v. 182n.129
Windham Community Mem. Hosp. 377n.56, 378n.62
Wire Prod. Mfg. Corp., NLRB v. 62n.58
W.J. Milner & Co. v. IBEW 260n.157
Woelke & Romero Framing, Inc. v. NLRB 256n.144

W-1 Canteen Serv., Inc. . 154n.27
W-1 Canteen Serv., Inc. v. NLRB 154n.28, 157n.33, 179n.119
Woodlawn Hosp. . 339nn.120, 122
Woodlawn Hosp. v. NLRB 313n.6
Wooster Div. 352n.1, 353n.5
Wooster Div., NLRB v. 70n.100, 71n.101
W.P. Kennedy v. Long Island R.R. 60n.46
Wright Lines, Inc. 321, 322
W.W. Cross Co. v. NLRB 72n.110
W. Wilton Wood, Inc. 346n.152

Yearbook House 69n.94
Yellow Cab Co. v. Production Workers 192n.18
Youngdahl v. Rainfair 189n.5
Youngstown Sheet & Tube Co. 117n.30
Yu v. Hotel Employees .. 198n.40

Ziegler Coal Co. v. Mine Workers 184n.141

404

Statutes and Administrative Material

(References are to pages and footnotes)

Fair Labor Standards Act

Section
213 47

Labor-Management Relations Act

Section
301 ...159, 166, 167n.72, 266, 356
301(e) 166n.71
302 ....28, 28n.49

Section
303 ....167n.72, 259-60, 260, 261,
 261-64, 264, 265, 265n.186,
 266, 306

National Labor Relations Act

Section
2(11) 22, 25
2(14) 18n.18
7 ...21, 24n.35, 111, 148, 149, 205
8(a) 18
8(a)(1) 21, 149, 158, 193, 312, 313,
 313n.5, 344, 361, 361n.1, 364
8(a)(3) .111, 313, 313n.5, 344, 361,
 361n.1, 364, 369
8(b)(1)(A) 205, 206, 207, 208
8(b)(2) 111
8(b)(4) ..219-21, 221-22, 223, 224,
 225, 229, 233, 237, 239, 240,
 241, 242, 248, 252, 254, 256,

Section
 257, 258, 261, 264, 289, 306
8(b)(4)(A) 255n.139, 293n.12
8(b)(4)(B) 219n.2
8(b)(4)(D) 289, 290, 291, 292, 293,
 294, 296, 297, 298, 304, 305
8(c) 106, 117
8(d) 12n.1, 13n.5, 16, 17, 66
8(e) 253, 254-56, 257
8(g) 18-20, 73
10(i) 304n.64
10(k) 290, 293, 295, 296, 297, 298,
 300, 303, 304, 305, 306
10(l) 257, 305n.67

United States Code

Title	Section		Title	Section	
5	7101(a)	............5n.3	29	1441(a)	..........165n.66
7	2015(d)(3)	.........55n.37	29	15(c)	............106n.2
18	1231	..............53n.31		101 et seq.	.......158n.37

405

Tables

Title	Section		Section	
29	104	147n.1	158(b)(4)(B)	219n.2
	106	202n.59	158(b)(4)(D)	293n.12
	107	147n.1, 161n.50, 167n.71, 191n.16, 195n.33, 196n.34	158(c)	117n.30
			158(d)	12n.1, 13n.5, 66n.77, 71n.107
	107-09	160n.47	159(3)	346n.151
	107(a)	192n.22, 198n.42	160(i)	257n.147, 304n.64
	151	5n.2	160(l)	305n.67
	151 et seq.	5n.1	185	159n.40
	152(3)	312n.1	185(a)	165n.64
	152(14)	18n.18	185(e)	166n.71
	152(63)	340n.126	186	28n.47, 112n.21
	157-58	5n.1	186(c)	28n.49
	158(a)	62n.58	207	47n.8
	158(a)(1),(3)	313n.5, 361	218	47n.9
	158(b)(4)	219n.1	1441(a)	265n.186
	158(b)(4)(A)	255n.139	1441(b)	265n.186

Code of Federal Regulations

Title	Section		Section	
20	652.9	53n.32	541.1	53n.11
29	101.32	305n.68	541.1(f)	48n.12
	101.33	290n.2, 304n.66	541.2	48n.11
	101.36	304nn.65, 66	541.2(c)	48n.13
	102.60(b)	25n.37	541.3	48n.11
	102.61(d)	25n.37	541.109	55n.37
	102.91	304n.64	541.109(a)	48n.14
	102.93	300n.48	1402, 1403	15n.8
	541.0-541.602	47n.10		

Alabama Code

Title	Section	
37	450(3)	80n.117

Alaska Statutes

Section	
23.40200(b)	80n.117

State Statutes

Indiana Code

SECTION
22-6-1-1 ....192n.19

SECTION
22-6-1-4 et seq. ...147n.1, 158n.38

Massachusetts General Laws

CHAPTER SECTION
214   6 .....147n.1, 158n.38, 192n.19

Missouri Statutes

SECTION
105.530 ....80n.117

Nevada Revised Statutes

SECTION
288.230(2) 80n.117

New York Civil Service Law

SECTION
209.3 ....12n.1

SECTION
209.4 ....12n.1

New York Labor Law

SECTION
807 .....147n.1, 158n.38, 192n.19

SECTION
808 ....147n.1, 158n.38

Utah Code

SECTION
34-19-1 ..147n.1, 158n.38, 192n.19

Washington Revised Code

SECTION
42.21.075 ....50n.25
48.24.025 ....50n.25

SECTION
48.44.250 ....50n.25
49.44.100 ....53n.31

Tables

Wisconsin Statutes

Section	Section
111.70(3)(d) 79n.115	111.77 ....12n.1

Index

(References are to pages)

Abusive threatening language . 190
Accident benefits 368-70
Ally doctrine
    common ownership or
        control 245-47
    performance of struck
        work 53-54, 243-45
    tests .242
Arbitration
    as waiver of right to
        strike 151-52
    Boys Market rule 159-61,
        161, 162, 163, 164
    dispute causing strike . 161-62
    non-arbitrable issue . . 163-65
Avoiding Strikes 6-7

Back pay, strikers 326-28
Bonuses 370-72
Boys Market doctrine 159-61,
    161, 162, 163, 164
Buffalo Forge rule 161, 162
Byrnes Act, importing strike
    breakers 53

Collective bargaining agreements
    arbitration clause, effect on
        right to strike 151-52
    evergreen clauses 13-14
    extension clauses 14
    final offers 68-73
    independent no-strike
        clause 156-57

no-strike clauses 13-14,
    152-154
    notice of termination . . 15-17
    termination 15-20
Common work site
    picketing 227-29
Communicating with
    employees 106-07, 107-13
Communication plan
    during strike 116-19
    employer's story 106-07
    eve of strike 113-14
    in general 104-06
    network 40-41
    picket line advice 119
    strike planning 37-38
Confidential employees 23-24
Construction site reserved
    gate 233
Consumer picketing
    in general 247
    integrated and dominant
        product doctrines . . 250-53
Contracts, *see* Collective
    bargaining
Coterminous doctrine 151-52

Dalmo-Victor rule . . . 109-10, 112
Damage actions
    defendants 166-67
    evergreen clauses 166
    items recoverable 167-69,
    200
    jurisdictional pressure . . . 306

Index

secondary activity 259-64
strike misconduct ... 199-202
sympathy strikes 183
union liability 201-02
violation of no-strike
   clauses 165
who may recover 201
wildcat strikes 173-75
Defamation 190
Disability of employees ... 368-70
Discipline of employees
   breach of no-strike
     clauses 157-58
   post-strike 374-75
   secondary activity 259
   strike misconduct 203-05
   sympathy strikes 183
   wildcat strikes 170-71
Discriminatory treatment of
   strikers 372-75
Dominant product
   doctrine 250-53
Dues check off, during
   strike 27-29

Economic strikes
   defined 314-15
   reinstatement of
     strikers 316-18
   unreinstated strikers .. 345-46
Employee benefits
   administration after
     strike 362-72
   bonuses and other
     benefits 370-72
   deducting strike time . 366-67
   disability 368-70
   insurance 370
   vacations 363-68
Employee reinstatement, *see*
   Reinstatement

Employees communications during
   strike 117-19
   paying union dues 116
Evergreen clauses 13-14, 166

Fair Labor Standards Act, strike
   planning considerations 47-48
Federal Mediation & Conciliation
   Serv., notice of
   dispute 15-16, 116, 118-20
Final offers, collective bargaining
   communicating to
     employees 72-73
   good faith requirement ... 69
   identifying impasse 70-71
   prerequisites 68
Financial core membership 110-12
Forms
   charge against labor
     organization or its agents
     (NLRB form) 280
   contingency planning
     manual 88-89
   incident reports 45
   letter of strike plan
     considerations 81-87
   memo on crossing picket
     lines 139
   memo on determining strike
     intentions of
     employees 135-37
   memo on establishing reserved
     gate 269-72
   memo on polling
     employees 134
   memo on strike
     activity 122-24
   memo on supervisors vacation
     benefits 100
   neutral gate sign 274

410

Index

notice of appearance (NLRB form) 281
notice of contract termination or modification 30
notice of improper acts relating to picketing reserved gate 279
notice of stoppage in violation of contract 186
preliminary injunction 214-18
product-service priority list 94-95
public relations advertisement-employers offer 96-97
public relations advertisement-facts about strike 98-99
questions and answers regarding strikes ... 129-33
reserved gate sign 273
strike impact chart ... 125-26
strike incident log 101
strike incident report 100
strike issue analysis 127-28
strike headquarters checklist 92-93
strike plan checklist ... 90-91
strike vote memorandum 120-21
telegram to other unions on establishing reserved gate 276, 278
telegram to primary union on establishing reserved gate 275, 277
telegram of specialized work schedule of primary employer 267, 268
transfer to financial core status 140
union membership resignation 139

witness checklist for strike misconduct 209-13
witness checklist on secondary activity 282-88
Food stamps 55-56

Health care institution strikes
admissions 75
chaplains 76
dietary service department 77
drug security 76
laboratory & radiology ... 77
licenses, registrations 75
notice of contract termination ... 18-20, 113, 117
patient amenities 77-78
physician support 74
professional attitude 75
public relations 74
subcontracting 77
sympathy strikes 79
visitors 78
volunteer help 76
Hot cargo clauses 253-54

Impasse 70-71
Inducing refusals to work . 224-25
Industrial plant reserved gate 232-33
Injunctions
arbitrability of dispute 161-62
breach of no-strike clause 158-61
jurisdictional pressures 304-05
non-arbitrable issue .. 163-65
persons restrained 198-99
procedures 191, 194-97
public sector employees ... 80
scope and effect 197-98

411

Index

scope and
    enforcement 162-63
    strike misconduct 191-99
    sympathy strikes 161, 184
    trespassing pickets 193-94
    wildcat strikes 172-73
Insurance 370
Integrated product
    doctrine 250-53

Job and shift assignments .. 372-74
Jurisdictional pressure
    damages 306
    dispute determination
        absence of settlement
            mechanism ... 298-300
        competing claims 295-96
        employer subject to
            pressure 294
        existence of union
            pressure 294-95
        objective of
            activity 291-94
        reasonable cause
            standard 291-95
        union disclaimer of
            work 296-98
    employer filing charge ... 290
    in general 289-90
    injunctive relief 304-05
    NLRB determinations
        breadth 303-04
        standards 301-02
    procedure after
        determination 304
    procedure for 8(6)(4)(0)
        charge 290

Labor contracts, *see* Collective
    bargaining agreements
Legal assistance to
    employees 115-16

Legal counsel
    function in planning ... 34-35
    outlining strike planning
        considerations 81-87
Lockouts
    business reasons 63
    motives 63-64
    permissibility 62-63
    use of replacements 66-67

Management team
    confidential employees . 23-24
    identification 21-24
    managers 23
    supervisors 22-23
Marginal employees,
    reinstatement 322
Mass picketing 189
Moore Dry Dock formula . 227-30
Mutual Aid Pacts 58-61

No-strike clauses
    damage actions 165-169
    evergreen clauses 13-14
    in general 152-54
    independence from arbitration
        clause 156-57
    negating explicit
        clause 154-56
    response to breach ... 157-69
    wildcat strikes 169-76
Non-striking employees ... 346-47
Non-union employees, pre-strike
    planning 20-21
Non-wage benefits 50-51
Notices
    contract termination .. 15-17,
                          18-19
    dispute to Federal Mediation
        & Conciliation
        Service 15-16, 17-18,
                        18-20
    reinstatement 334-35

Index

Other employees,
    reinstatement 323

Partial strikes 149
Picketing
    advice on 119
    common work sites ... 227-29
    consumer 250-53
    injunctions for
        trespassing 193-94
    publicity 247-50
Plant security, strike
    planning 42-44
Police departments,
    coordination 43-44
Pre-strike planning
    dues check off 27-29
    jurisdictional
        considerations 11-12
    management team 21-24
    non-union employees ...20-21
    production planning ... 38-40
    reviewing other contracts . 20
    supervisors 24-26
    termination or extension
        notices 17-18
    union security
        agreements 26-27
Probationary employees,
    reinstatement 319-21
Production planning,
    pre-strike 38-40
Property damage 189-90
Public relations 41-42, 74
Public sector employees
    essential services 79
    injunctions 80
    jurisdictional
        considerations 11-12
    legality of strikes 380
    political considerations ... 78
    security 78-79
    state laws 80
    supervisors 79

Publicity picketing
    general 247
    permissible scope 249-50
    primary products 248
    products distributed by
        neutral 249

Recognition of union,
    withdrawal 378
Reinstatement of employees
    availability of work .. 328-30
    contractual
        restrictions 353-54
    curtailment of work .. 328-29
    deadline to return 335-36
    determining priority .. 332-34
    discharges 342-43
    economic strikers 316-18
    employees entitled ... 318-23
    failure to return 341-42
    liability for back pay . 336-38
    marginal employees .. 321-22
    notice 334-35
    other employees 323
    other employment 340-41
    other restrictions 355
    permanent
        replacements 348-50
    probationary
        employees 319-21
    procedure 331-36
    promotions, transfers and
        rehires 329-30
    regaining rights 343-44
    replacements 347-50
    seniority 344, 350
    status after 343-45
    status of non-strikers .. 346-47
    strike misconduct 338-39
    strikers' right 312-18
    strikers' status 312
    substantially equivalent
        position requirement 330-31
    temporary employees 319

Index

temporary
    replacements 347-48
termination of right .. 338-43
time limit 340
unconditional offer to
    reinstate 325-27
unconditional offer to
    return 323-24
unfair labor practice
    strikers 316
unreinstated economic
    strikers 345-46
voluntary resignation . 341-42
Replacement employees
    distinguishing
        temporary 347-48
    during lockouts 66-67
    permanent 348-50
    sympathy strikes 180-82
Reserved gate doctrine
    ambulatory primary
        site 234-48
    basis 231
    construction site 233
    establishing gate 235-37
    industrial plant 232-33
    maintaining gate 237-39
    options 57
    rehabilitating gate 239
    violations of gate 239-42
Resignations from union . 107-110

Secondary activity
    against neutral
        employees 222-25
    ally doctrine 242-47
    damage actions
        eligible plaintiffs . 259-60
        joining state law
            claim 265-66
        liability 260-61
        measure of
            damages 262-65

    section 8(6)(4)
        violation 261-62
        statute of limitations 266
    disciplining employees ... 259
    filing unfair labor
        charge 256-58
    identifying ... 221-31, 247-56
    inducing refusals to
        work 224-25
    in general 219-21
    NLRA prohibitions 219-21
    picketing common work
        sites 227-29
    publicity or consumer
        picketing 247-53
    related to hot cargo
        clauses 253-63
    reserved gate doctrine 231-42
    special work schedules 229-31
    threats or coercion ... 222-23
    unlawful activities ... 225-27
Secondary boycotts, *see* Secondary
    activity
Security, strike planning ... 42-45
Seniority
    contractual
        restrictions 353-54
    offer reinstatement 344
    replacement workers 350
Sick leave 51-52
Sick-outs 150
Sickness benefits 368-70
Sit-downs 149-50
Sit-ins 149-50
Special work schedules, primary
    employees 229-31
State omnibus statutes 11-12
Strike committees 34
Strike headquarters 37
Strike insurance 44
Strike logs 44-46
Strike misconduct
    abusive or threatening
        language 190

Index

as unfair labor
    practice 205-08
damages 199-202
disciplining employees 203-05
effect on
    reinstatement 338-39
in general 187-88
injunctions 191-99
kinds subject to relief . 188-90
libel or slander 190
mass picketing 189
NLRB remedies 206-07
property damage 189-90
surveillance 190
violence 189
Strike planning
    advising management ... 104
    ally doctrine 53-54
    benefits 49-51
    Byrnes Act restriction 53
    commencing 33
    communications
        network 37-38, 40-41
    complete commitment 9
    confidentiality 38
    contingency plan 36
    cross-training 54-55
    establishing policy 35-36
    evidence development 46
    food stamps 55-56
    health care institutions . 73-78
    implementing final
        offer 68-73
    in general 5-6
    inventory of skills 54
    legal counsel 34-35
    lockouts 61-73
    mutual aid pacts 58-61
    obtaining union rules 56
    police coordination 43-45
    preventive effects 6-7
    process 33-58
    production plans 38-40
    public relations 41-42

    public sector employers 78-80
    reports and logs 44-46
    reserved gate options 57
    security 42-46
    sick leave 51-52
    strike committee 34
    strike headquarters 37
    strike insurance 44
    striker replacements ... 52-53
    subcontracting 53-54
    supervisors 40
    supplies, utilities 57-58
    supply schedules and
        routes 43
    to balance position 8-9
    transportation 57
    unemployment
        compensation 55-56
    vacations 51
    wage and hour
        requirements 47-49
    work priority 39
Strike polling 114-15
Strike reports 44-46
Strike settlement agreements
    amnesty 358-59
    contractual
        restrictions 353-54
    duration 358
    enforceability 356-57
    forcing union
        concessions 357-58
    in general 351-52
    other restrictions 355
    scope 356
    reinstatement limitations . 357
Strike violations, *see* Strike
    misconduct
Strike votes 103-04
Striker reinstatement, *see*
    Reinstatement of Employees
Striker replacements, *see*
    Replacement employees

Index

Strikes, *see also* Reinstatement of employees, Strike misconduct
    other conditions of employment 374-75
    post-strike discipline .. 374-75
    prohibition on discriminatory treatment 372-75
    protected activities ... 148-49
    right to reinstatement . 312-18
    status as employees 312
    unprotected activities . 149-50
Strikes without proper notice .. 16
Subcontracting work ... 53-54, 77
Supervisors
    generating loyalty 24
    identifying 22-23
    public sector employers ... 79
    union membership 25-26
Supply schedules 43
Surveillance 190
Sympathy strikes
    concerted activity 180
    damages 183
    discipline of strikers .. 183-84
    health care institutions ... 19
    in general 176-77
    injunctions 161, 184
    protected status 177-78
    reinstatement 180
    remedies 183-84
    replacement of strikers 180-82
    responses 184-85
    unprotected underlying strike 179-80
    waiver of rights 178-79

Temporary employees, reinstatement 319
Threats and coercion against neutral employees 222-24

Unemployment compensation 55-56
Unfair labor practices
    filing 256-58
    identifying 314
    refusal to cross picket line 314
    reinstatement 316
    status without proper notice 16
    strike misconduct 205-08
Union discipline 116
Union fines, payment by employer 116
Union liability, strike misconduct 201-02
Union membership
    damage action for wildcat strike 175
    discipline for violation of no-strike clause 157-58
    financial core membership 110-12
    procedure to change status 113
    resignation 109-12
Union officers, liability ... 173-75
Union rules, obtaining 56
Union security provision ... 26-27
Union standard clauses 255
Unions
    majority status after strike 375-78
    withdrawal of recognition 378

Vacations
    benefits 363-66
    rescheduling 51
    strike planning 367-68
Violence, strikes 189
Volunteer help, health care institutions 76

Index

Wage and hour standards .. 47-49

Waiver of right to strike .. 151-57, 178-79

Wildcat strikes
    damage actions 173-75
    disciplining union
        members 170
    disciplining union
        officers 171
    in general 169-70
    injunctions 172-73
    protecting against 176

Work preservation clauses 256

Worker reinstatement, *see* Reinstatement of employees

About the Authors

The authors are all associated with the firm of Davis, Wright, Todd, Riese & Jones, of Seattle, Washington; Bellevue, Washington; Anchorage, Alaska; and Washington, D.C. All are members of the Washington State Bar.

MARK A. HUTCHESON is a partner and is the Chairman of its Labor Law Department. He is a graduate of the University of Washington Law School, where he was Phi Delta Phi, Order of the Coif, and Recent Developments Editor of the *Washington Law Review*. Mr. Hutcheson did his undergraduate work at the University of Puget Sound. He is a member of the Labor and Employment Law Section, American Bar Association, as well as a member of the Ad Hoc Labor Advisory Committee of the American Hospital Association.

ROBERT SEBRIS, JR. is a partner with the firm and is also admitted to the bar in the District of Columbia. He received a Bachelor of Science in Industrial and Labor Relations from Cornell University and his law degree from the National Law Center, George Washington University. He is a member of the Labor and Employment Law Section of the American Bar Association, as well as its Committee on Individual Rights and Responsibilities in the Work Place. Prior to his law practice he served in labor relations positions with Onondaga County (Syracuse, New York), the U.S. Labor Department, and the U.S. Treasury Department.

STEPHEN M. RUMMAGE graduated Phi Beta Kappa from Stanford University and received his law degree from the University of California at Berkeley, where he was selected to Order of

About the Authors

the Coif. He is author of "Union Officers and Wildcat Strikes," 4 *Industrial Relations Law Journal* 258 (1981).

DONNA M. PECK-GAINES graduated cum laude from the University of Washington School of Business Administration. She received her law degree from the University of Southern California, where she was Phi Alpha Delta and Managing Editor of the *Southern California Law Review*.

MICHAEL J. KILLEEN is a former clerk to the Washington Court of Appeals. He received his undergraduate and law degrees from Gonzaga University. While in law school, he was a member of Order of the Barristers and Editor-in-Chief of the *Gonzaga Law Review*.